Get the eBook FREE!

(PDF, ePub, Kindle, and liveBook all included)

We believe that once you buy a book from us, you should be able to read it in any format we have available. To get electronic versions of this book at no additional cost to you, purchase and then register this book at the Manning website.

Go to https://www.manning.com/freebook and follow the instructions to complete your pBook registration.

That's it!
Thanks from Manning!

Learn Go with Pocket-Sized Projects

ALIÉNOR LATOUR
DONIA CHAIEHLOUDJ
PASCAL BERTRAND

MANNING
SHELTER ISLAND

For online information and ordering of this and other Manning books, please visit www.manning.com. The publisher offers discounts on this book when ordered in quantity.

For more information, please contact

    Special Sales Department
    Manning Publications Co.
    20 Baldwin Road
    PO Box 761
    Shelter Island, NY 11964
    Email: orders@manning.com

Manning Publications Co.
20 Baldwin Road
PO Box 761
Shelter Island, NY 11964

Development editor:	Doug Rudder
Technical editor:	Egon Elbre
Review editors:	Dunja Nikitović and Aleksandar Dragosavljević
Production editor:	Keri Hales
Copy editor:	Julie McNamee
Proofreader:	Katie Tennant
Technical proofreader:	Mike Haller
Typesetter:	Tamara Švelić Sabljić
Cover designer:	Marija Tudor

ISBN 9781633438804
Printed in the United States of America

To Pulsar, that brought us together, and tea time, that keeps us together
—Aliénor

To Didier, Lila, my mum, and all the gophers
—Donia

To my parents, who nurtured in me a love for books
—Pascal

brief contents

contents

foreword

Programming is for everyone. This dream of making computers available and easier to use has been one of the guiding principles for so many pioneers in this still evolving field. We are the inheritors of this fantastic legacy. And by we, of course, I mean you and I, the generations of people who have been able to follow some of the many paths to computer use that have already been prepared for us, in particular, that collection of tools for thought known as programming languages.

A few of those very smart yet practical people created the Go programming language. Go can be quite expressive, despite having a small number of keywords compared to many other popular programming languages. This makes it a lot easier to remember, but certainly doesn't always make it obvious how to make Go do what you want, at least not without some guidance.

The real trick is to make it easier for people to make some relatively quick progress toward whatever they want to achieve, while at the same time preparing them with the deeper knowledge they will need to go further. And one of the best ways to accomplish this is by way of a well-thought-out book, such as the one you're looking at right now.

Learn Go with Pocket-Sized Projects gives you practical projects that are neither too big to wrap your head around quickly, nor too small to actually show you something useful. Along the way, the book is seasoned with a number of important techniques that you'll surely need, shared with a wry humor that keeps you smiling.

Regardless if you're a student, hobbyist, or professional practitioner, there's something for you to grab ahold of and run with for a bit. And that is a great way to learn.

The book introduces you to some among the wide spectrum of possibilities that Go can be used for. From an elaborated `hello, world`, to making LEDs blink on an

Arduino, it contains a nice collection of different small applications to help you feel full but not overstuffed.

Most importantly, the book does so with a sense of fun and playfulness. Learning doesn't happen when you're bored out of your mind; it happens when you are fully engaged. Grasping this simple truth and using it to write a book about Go programming just seems like a good idea, and I'm glad to see that my friends have done exactly that.

—Ron Evans,
Open Source Contributor, TinyGo, and
Technologist for Hire, The Hybrid Group

preface

Everything started with a friend story, one about three software engineers who found themselves facing a new set of challenges. We're Aliénor Latour, Donia Chaiehloudj, and Pascal Bertrand—three best friends with different technical backgrounds who crossed paths while working at Airbus Defence and Space in southeastern France. Our journey with Go began there, as we discovered its unique strengths for building the kind of reliable and scalable systems that could meet our industry's rigorous demands.

At first, we were drawn to Go's simplicity, but the more we worked with it, the more we saw the true depth behind its minimalistic design. We found that Go was not only fast and efficient but also naturally structured to handle the concurrent, distributed systems that modern applications increasingly rely on. As we shared our enthusiasm with others in the community, we noticed that, while Go has an incredible toolset, it can be intimidating for those approaching it for the first time.

That's how *Learn Go with Pocket-Sized Projects* came about. We wanted to create a friendly, hands-on guide to ease new learners into Go while challenging them to think critically about design, architecture, and testing. Instead of starting with heavy theory, we've built each chapter around a small, practical project that incrementally introduces key concepts. Our aim is to help you build confidence with Go by completing manageable tasks and seeing tangible results at each step.

This book focuses on Go's essential tools and its unique capabilities, guiding you from simple command-line applications to microservices, and even embedded systems. By exploring these projects, you'll learn not only syntax but also how Go's tools and libraries enable modern software development. We chose Go because it's fast, reliable, and especially well suited for the kind of scalable, cloud-first applications that drive today's tech ecosystems.

We hope you'll enjoy working through the projects as much as we've enjoyed creating them. Whether you're new to Go or just looking to deepen your skills, we're excited to share this journey with you. We believe you'll come away not only with a strong foundation in Go but also with the confidence to apply it to real-world challenges. Happy coding!

acknowledgments

As a trio of writers, we'd like to thank the Manning team, especially Doug Rudder, our development editor, as well as the entire production staff who helped shepherd this book into its final format. Another special thank-you goes to our technical editor, Egon Elbre, a principal engineer at Storj Labs. Both Doug and Egon especially helped guide our journey while writing this book. We'd also like to extend our thanks to the Pulsar team, where it all began, and to Salvador Cavadini.

Thanks also go to the many reviewers whose suggestions helped make this a better book: Abhishek Shivanna, Alceu Rodrigues de Freitas Junior, Alessandro Buggin, Andreas Schroepfer, Ariel Marcus, Arpit Singh, Ashish Kumar Pani, Brad Lambert, Brendan O'Hara, Clifford Thurber, Dan Sheikh, Deepak Sharma, Diana Maftei, Fernando F. Rodrigues, Giorgio Galante, Gopal Venkatesan, James Watson, Jehad Nasser, Joel Holmes, John Guthrie, Leonardo Taccari, Maria Ana, Mattia A. Di Gangi, Mihaela Barbu, Muneeb Shaikh, Naveen Achyuta, Neil Croll, Pablo Acuna, Paul Broadwith, Prahathess Rengasamy, Richard Hilliar, Ruben Gonzalez-Rubio, Stephen Griese, Sumedh Sathaye, and William Whitehead.

Aliénor Latour: Many thanks to my mother, who always kindly pushed me for excellence, my husband, for his supportive cooking; and my daughter, for her patience and laughter. Thanks go to Ravan, Joselia, and Zuzana for their technical support while writing this book; to Céline and Marie with their myriad inspiring projects; to Pascaline and Anne-Laure, for the music; and to Juliette, for the knitting advice.

Donia Chaiehloudj: I want to thank my mum for giving me the opportunities that shaped who I am today, and I want to thank my husband for creating the space I needed to pursue and accomplish this project. To my dearest friends—Maëlle, Anaïde, Alicia, and Cyrielle—for always asking, "How's the book going?" and pushing me forward with your unwavering encouragement. To the amazing Gophers across the internet and at GopherCon, thank you for your enthusiasm and interest—it's been a constant source of inspiration. To the mentors and friends I've met along the way in the Go community, your guidance and camaraderie have been invaluable.

Finally, to Aliénor and Pascal—my friends, companions, and guiding lights—thank you for always lifting me up and making this journey so much more meaningful.

Pascal Bertrand: My deepest gratitude to Thomas, Pierre, and Frédéric, who regularly keep my mind open, and to Mme Callon, who instilled in me a deep appreciation for learning and understanding the intricacies of all sorts of languages. *Κοῦφον γὰρ χρῆμα ποίησίς ἐστιν καὶ πτηνὸν καὶ ἱερόν.*

To my family, my friends, my colleagues, and anyone who, by simply asking about our progress on this project, was unknowingly fueling motivation to resume its writing.

about this book

Learn Go with Pocket-Sized Projects is designed to help you master the Go programming language through a series of engaging, hands-on projects. Each project is carefully crafted to be concise, focusing on practical, real-world applications while gradually introducing Go's core concepts.

The book covers a wide range of topics, from Go's unique approach to implicit interfaces, which play a crucial role in designing robust and testable code, to building microservices using both REST and gRPC—demonstrating Go's strengths in cloud computing. You'll also dive into exciting areas such as embedded systems, where we explore TinyGo and WebAssembly to show how Go can be applied in constrained environments.

Testing is integrated throughout the book, not only as a way to verify code but also to illustrate best practices in design and architecture decisions. By the end of the book, you'll not only have completed a series of pocket-sized projects, but you'll also have a solid understanding of how to use Go from server-side applications to low-level systems programming.

Who should read this book

Learn Go with Pocket-Sized Projects is ideal for developers looking to get started with Go or deepen their understanding of the language's unique features. The projects are designed to be engaging and easy to follow, providing a hands-on approach to learning Go.

This book assumes some prior programming experience, although not necessarily in Go, and is not intended for absolute beginners. Instead, it aims to help developers enhance their skills, improve their software design and testing practices, and adopt Go as part of their toolkit for modern software development.

How this book is organized: A road map

The book has 12 chapters that broaden in scope, except the last one, which is more of a bonus:

- Chapter 1 introduces the Go language and helps you set up your development environment. It explains the key reasons why Go is a language worth learning.
- Chapter 2 kicks off the pocket-sized projects with a simple `hello, world` program. You'll focus on testing edge cases and handling input/output in command-line applications.
- Chapter 3 delves into Go's `slices`, `maps`, and other key types. It also covers JSON handling and sorting techniques.
- Chapter 4 explores the design of an API, focusing on what to expose and why. You'll learn about the importance of logging and how to implement it in Go.
- Chapter 5 walks you through building a word game that runs in a terminal. You'll learn about error propagation and file reading in Go.
- Chapter 6 introduces making HTTP calls from a CLI tool and parsing XML. We'll also cover how to mock HTTP calls for testing.
- Chapter 7 introduces Go's generics and when to use them in production. This chapter also covers goroutines and concurrency in Go.
- Chapter 8 builds on chapter 5 by turning the word game into a web service. You'll learn how to design a REST API and handle HTTP responses and parameters.
- Chapter 9 puts your knowledge of goroutines into action, focusing on inter-goroutine communication. It also introduces image manipulation and GIF creation.
- Chapter 10 teaches you how to build a gRPC service while introducing Go's `Context`. You'll also learn about integration testing.
- Chapter 11 uses the habits tracker from chapter 10 to display data on an HTML page using Go templates. This chapter focuses on connecting your gRPC client to web output.
- Chapter 12 closes the book with an exploration of WebAssembly and TinyGo. You'll build lightweight projects for edge and embedded environments.
- Finally, the appendixes include short tutorials on topics such as benchmarking, fuzz testing, and database connections.

We recommend following the chapters in order, as they are carefully sequenced to progressively build your knowledge. Many later chapters reuse code and concepts introduced earlier, so moving through the book sequentially will help you develop a solid understanding of Go.

As you progress, you'll encounter discussions on important topics such as design choices, architecture patterns, testing strategies, and best practices. These insights are woven into the projects to deepen your comprehension of Go's strengths and challenges. By working through each chapter and writing the code yourself, you'll be better prepared for the more advanced topics later in the book.

About the code

This book contains many examples of source code both in numbered listings and in line with normal text. In both cases, source code is formatted in a `fixed-width font like this` to separate it from ordinary text.

In many cases, the original source code has been reformatted; we've added line breaks and reworked indentation to accommodate the available page space in the book. In some cases, even this was not enough, and listings include line-continuation markers ( ). Additionally, comments in the source code have often been removed from the listings when the code is described in the text. Code annotations accompany many of the listings, highlighting important concepts.

You can get executable snippets of code from the liveBook (online) version of this book at https://livebook.manning.com/book/learn-go-with-pocket-sized-projects. The complete code for the examples in the book is available for download from the Manning website at www.manning.com/books/learn-go-with-pocket-sized-projects, and from GitHub at https://github.com/alienorlatour/tiny-go-projects.

liveBook discussion forum

Purchase of *Learn Go with Pocket-Sized Projects* includes free access to liveBook, Manning's online reading platform. Using liveBook's exclusive discussion features, you can attach comments to the book globally or to specific sections or paragraphs. It's a snap to make notes for yourself, ask and answer technical questions, and receive help from the author and other users. To access the forum, go to https://livebook.manning.com/book/learn-go-with-pocket-sized-projects/discussion. You can also learn more about Manning's forums and the rules of conduct at https://livebook.manning.com/discussion.

Manning's commitment to our readers is to provide a venue where a meaningful dialogue between individual readers and between readers and the authors can take place. It is not a commitment to any specific amount of participation on the part of the authors, whose contribution to the forum remains voluntary (and unpaid). We suggest you try asking the authors some challenging questions lest their interest stray! The forum and the archives of previous discussions will be accessible from the publisher's website as long as the book is in print.

Other online resources

If you need additional help or want to connect with fellow Go enthusiasts, you can join the Gopher's Slack community—a great space to ask questions, discuss topics, and stay updated on all things Go. For readers of this book, there's a dedicated channel, #learn-go-with-pocket-sized-projects-book (https://app.slack.com/client/T029RQSE6/C07P9088UPM), where you can share your progress, exchange ideas, and engage with other learners as you work through the projects.

about the authors

Aliénor, Donia, and Pascal are Go developers who met a few years ago during a former working experience.

ALIÉNOR LATOUR is the CTO of Skipr and has been a Go developer since 2017, with experience in various domains, from social media marketing to satellite imagery and e-commerce. Through the course of her career, she tried her skills as a frontend developer and as a project manager, and enjoyed her role as technical leader and software architect before her current managing position, all the while reaching for quality and simplicity in her software.

Aliénor is known for her refactoring and decoupling perseverance and pushes for clean and maintainable architecture in Go. She strives for more diversity in tech, in particular in backend roles, and likes to share her values by mentoring junior developers and speaking at international conferences.

Outside of work hours, she travels Europe from Burgundy for Scottish country dance events, knits, sews skirts with pockets, and reads about linguistics and sociology.

DONIA CHAIEHLOUDJ is a senior software engineer with expertise in Go, specializing in cloud-native distributed systems. With experience spanning industries such as aerospace, gaming, and open source contributions, she enjoys the challenge of building efficient, scalable solutions. Donia has focused her career primarily on Go, using the language's strengths in cloud computing and distributed architectures.

Currently contributing to open source projects such as Cilium at Isovalent at Cisco, Donia is also actively involved in community building. In 2022, she began her journey as a public speaker, inspiring others—particularly women—to explore IoT and software development. She regularly organizes tech events and advocates for diversity and inclusion in the industry.

When not coding, Donia can be found hiking, swing dancing, sewing her latest piece of wardrobe, or playing the clarinet.

PASCAL BERTRAND has been developing with Go since 2017 as a software engineer, in both big and small companies. He strives for clear code and quality test coverage, and he enjoys reviewing pull requests. Before choosing Go, he worked for 10 years with languages such as C++, PHP, and Java, which allowed him to have a broad overview of how to get the best from each language for every situation a developer will face—coding, testing, documenting, deploying, and maintaining.

After 10 years in the French Riviera in the aviation, defense, and then aerospace and photogrammetry industries, Pascal moved to London to join Blòkur where he uses his experience in migrating a codebase to a microservice architecture. He uses his knowledge and experience in Go to mentor newcomers and ensure high-quality code in his company.

Pascal can usually be found playing board games, learning—through books and visits—about history and linguistics, or enjoying a walk in the wilderness. He enjoys twisting his mind over math problems.

Meet Go

1

This chapter covers

- Go's key features for modern software development
- Go's history and simplicity-driven philosophy
- Go's built-in tools for testing, benchmarking, and debugging
- How hands-on projects help you master Go
- Go's versatility for backend and cloud applications

In this book, we aim to help you discover the strengths of Go by guiding you through real-world scenarios. From its efficient concurrency model to its built-in tools for testing and benchmarking, Go empowers developers to write clean, maintainable code without unnecessary complexity. We'll tackle projects of varying complexity to ensure you get a hands-on understanding of what makes Go unique.

This book also provides you with a set of fun projects to progressively explore the features of the Go language. Each pocket-sized project is written in a reasonable number of lines. Our goal is to provide various exercises so any developer who wants to get started with Go or explore the language can follow the steps described in each chapter.

We want to help you become a better software developer by using the Go language. We'll use our experience as software engineers to provide meaningful advice for newcomers and seasoned developers alike.

This book also contains tutorials for implementing APIs with microservices, demonstrating how the language is great for cloud computing. We'll wrap the book up with a project that uses TinyGo, the compiler for embedded systems.

> **NOTE** If you're a beginning programmer, we wholeheartedly suggest starting your Go experience with *Get Programming with Go* (Manning Publications, 2018; www.manning.com/books/get-programming-with-go), by Nathan Youngman and Roger Peppé.

1.1 What is Go?

Go is a programming language that was originally designed to solve various problems in large-scale software development in the real world, initially within Google and then for the rest of the business world. It addresses slow program construction, out-of-control dependency management, complex code, and difficult cross-language construction.

Each language tries to address these problems in a different way, either by restricting the user or by being as flexible as possible. Go's team chose to tackle these problems by targeting modern engineering: removing the constraint of dealing with memory and making it simple to run parallel pieces of code. That's why it comes with a rich toolchain.

The toolchain covers compilation and construction, code formatting, package dependency management, static code inspection, testing, document generation and viewing, performance analysis, language servers, runtime program tracking, and much more.

Go was built for concurrency and networked servers, which explains the fast adoption of the language in software companies of all sizes in the past few years. Additionally, Go is used by a large community of developers who share their source code on public platforms for others to use or be inspired by. As developers, we love to share and reuse what other clever people have written. Go was designed to improve productivity during a time when multicore networked machines and large codebases were becoming the norm.

> *Go started in September 2007 when Robert Griesemer, Ken Thompson, and I began discussing a new language to address the engineering challenges we and our colleagues at Google were facing in our daily work.*
>
> —Rob Pike, coauthor of Go

The design choices are driven primarily by *simplicity*, which makes learning the language a quick task. There are only 25 reserved keywords in the entire language (as of November 2024). The rest is simply the sense you want to give to it—and poetry.

Even more important to us, Go provides for the needs of the modern software industry. Dependency management, tools for unit testing, benchmarking and fuzzing, formatters, and all the usual tools of a developer are built in and standardized.

According to the 2024 Go Developer Survey (https://mng.bz/ga9l), the language is most widely used for API/remote procedure call (RPC) services. The close second usage is runnable programs with a command-line interface (CLI), followed by libraries and frameworks, web services that return HTML, automation, data processing, and then agents and daemons. Just 7% of Go developers use the language on embedded systems, 4% use it for games, and 4% use it for machine learning or artificial intelligence (AI; figure 1.1).

I write the following in Go:
(Select all that apply.)

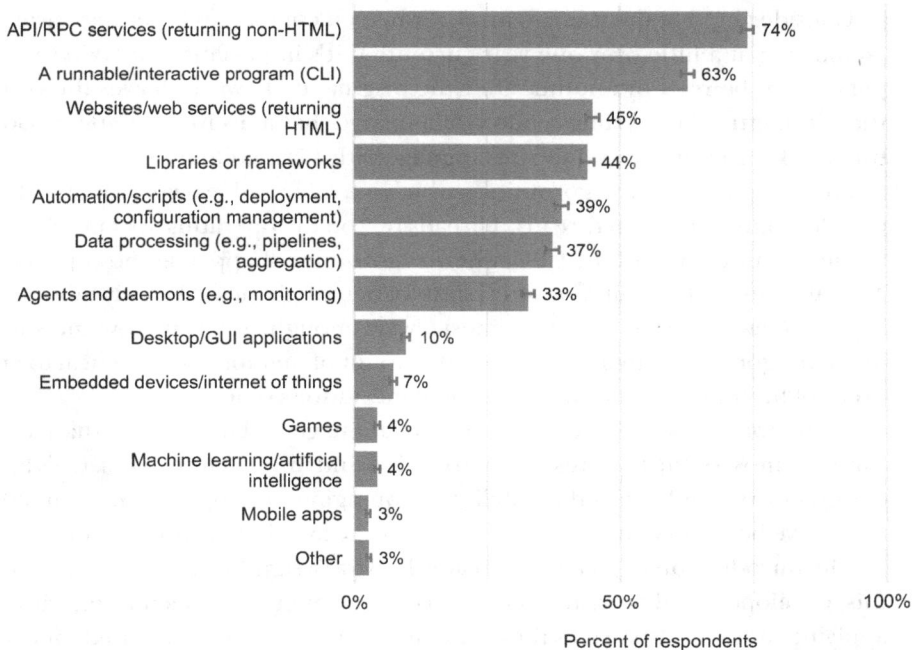

Category	Percent
API/RPC services (returning non-HTML)	74%
A runnable/interactive program (CLI)	63%
Websites/web services (returning HTML)	45%
Libraries or frameworks	44%
Automation/scripts (e.g., deployment, configuration management)	39%
Data processing (e.g., pipelines, aggregation)	37%
Agents and daemons (e.g., monitoring)	33%
Desktop/GUI applications	10%
Embedded devices/internet of things	7%
Games	4%
Machine learning/artificial intelligence	4%
Mobile apps	3%
Other	3%

Percent of respondents

n = 5,768

Figure 1.1 Extract from the Go Developer Survey 2024 H1 results

Although Go can't yet call on decades of libraries like Java-based languages, it benefits from a vast and welcoming community of bloggers, teachers, and open source contributors who create learning material in every form, including this book.

Go engineers are currently in high demand, so learning the language may be helpful for a big career jump forward. From the authors' personal experience, the recruiting fields include fintech, medtech, foodtech, gaming, music, all sorts of e-commerce platforms, aerospace research, and satellite imaging processing.

1.2 Why you should learn Go

Go was designed with simplicity and productivity in mind, making it a natural fit for backend services, APIs, and modern cloud computing needs. In this section, we'll explore practical examples of how Go's syntax, tools, and features come together to create maintainable and efficient applications. Let's see why Go is a great investment of your learning time as a developer.

1.2.1 How and where Go can help you

Go is a versatile language designed for maintainability and readability. It's optimal for backend software development and has great integration with modern cloud technologies.

Considering that the average turnover in tech companies is getting lower every year (stabilizing at a little over one year currently), it's important that code written by one person can be read by another after the original code writer leaves the company. It's therefore crucial companies choose a language that aims for readability. Go's key features make it a reliable and secure language with a fast build time.

Some applications use goroutines, which is a safer and less costly way of dealing with parallel computing than threads. Threads rely on the operating system, which is limited to the size and power of the CPU, whereas goroutines happen at the application's level. To make the stacks small, Go uses resizable, bounded stacks. A newly minted goroutine is given a few kilobytes, which is almost always enough, and can grow and shrink, allowing many goroutines to live in a modest amount of memory. It's practical to create hundreds of thousands of goroutines in the same address space.

Even though it's not an object-oriented language and has no inheritance system, Go supports most of the features via composition and implicit interfaces. Go's approach to design favors simplicity and flexibility, encouraging developers to use embedded types to achieve behaviors similar to inheritance while avoiding its complexities.

The introduction of *generics* in version 1.18 was a significant milestone for Go. Before this, developers had to write repetitive code for operations such as filtering `slices` or applying functions to `maps`, as these operations had to be implemented for each specific type. Generics now make it possible to write reusable, type-safe functions for such tasks, significantly reducing boilerplate code. As of now, the community continues to refine and expand the use cases for generics to ensure they enhance the language without compromising its core principles.

Go is a compiled language, meaning that all syntax errors will be found during compilation rather than at runtime. We all prefer to know about mistakes in the safety of our own computers rather than discovering them, say, in production.

It's easier to run applications at scale with Go than with many other languages. Google built Go to solve problems at a Google-size scale, so it's ideal for large concurrent applications, yet also handy for smaller uses.

Cloud platforms love Go and provide support for Go as a major language. For example, cloud functions and lambdas support Go in all the most-used providers. Major cloud tools, such as Kubernetes or Docker, are written in Go.

1.2.2 Where can Go cannot help you

Despite its high versatility, there are a few use cases that Go isn't made to cover. Go relies on a garbage collector to release the memory it uses. If your application requires full control over memory, pick a lower-level language like the C family can provide. Go can wrap libraries written in C/C++ with cgo, a translation layer created to ease the transition between the two languages. With this cgo twist, you can wrap dynamically linkable libraries (we won't use cgo in this book, however).

The Go toolchain mostly produces executables—generating a Go-compiled library is painfully achievable (not covered in this book). In most common cases, updating the version of a Go dependency implies rebuilding the binary with that new version, which also means you need to have access to its source code to use a Go library.

The Go compiler supports an interesting list of different platforms and operating systems, but we wouldn't recommend writing an operating system with Go, although many brave souls have done it. The main reason for this is how memory is handled in Go: the garbage collector regularly discards bits that are no longer used. As with all garbage collectors, it's adjustable, but it won't release memory exactly how or when you want it to.

Go binary files are known to be bigger than average. It's usually not a problem in a cloud environment, but if you require light binaries, consider using the TinyGo compiler (introduced in chapter 12).

Last, there's the difficulty in Googling for answers to questions about Go (seriously, who names their language with such a common word? Google, apparently). Here's a pro tip: When searching for an answer related to Go, use "golang" in your search, which isn't the real name but is what search engines will recognize. Sometimes, it's like trying to find documentation in C on strings—you don't get what you expect.

We can also mention the difficulty in hiring Go developers, which is actually good for us developers. As the use of the language rises, this is becoming less of an argument.

1.2.3 Comparison with commonly used languages

The main reason for using a language other than Go, up to 2021, was the absence of some features and the lack of maturity in the ecosystem. That was before version 1.18, which changed the game.

In table 1.1, we compile some of the most important features to developers when considering which language will best address their project's needs. In our experience, verboseness and garbage collection are important language criteria for a productive, modern workflow.

Table 1.1   Comparison of four programming languages

	C++	Python	Java	Go
Design philosophy	High-level object-oriented programming (OOP), procedural, multiparadigm	High-level OOP	High-level OOP	Procedural and data-oriented programming, supports most OOP features
Error management	Via exceptions	Via exceptions	Via exceptions	Errors are values.
Types	Statically typed language	Dynamically typed	Statically typed	Statically typed language
Compilation	Compiled	Compiled at runtime	Compiled Runs in a virtual machine	Compiled
Concurrency	Either memory-level or OS-level threads	OS-level threads	Either memory-level or OS-level threads	Goroutines and channels
Interfaces	Explicit	Implicit and explicit	Explicit	Implicit
Memory release	Full control	Garbage collector	Garbage collector	Garbage collector
Main use cases	High performance, low overhead	Excellent for data analysis	Well-suited for web applications	Adapted for web APIs and cloud computing
Testing tools	External frameworks	Built-in native tools for testing	External framework JUnit	Built-in native tools (test, bench, fuzz)

1.3   Why pocket-sized projects?

Toward the end of the 19th century, several scientists and philosophers began studying and developing theories about learning. In 1897, John Dewey wrote a long list of good reasons why *doing* is the best way to learn (see *My Pedagogic Creed*, https://mng .bz/6e5G). Since then, experience has proven his claims in many education systems and learning situations.

The projects that we propose here are timed for busy people. We made sure to keep them as small as possible while still making them rewarding. We admit that some of them aren't particularly fun, but these are the most useful in a real-world project.

1.3.1   What you'll know after reading the book (and writing the code)

Our first aim is to help you clearly understand the concepts and implementations presented in this book. We'll guide you through our journey of chapters by describing the implementation of the current code iteratively, as we consider it important to understand what's happening bit by bit.

Second, we focus on providing good and clear examples for writing industry-level Go code with recommendations that apply outside our examples and that will help you venture into the real world of development. All of our examples contain functions that are reusable in a professional codebase. Last, our goal is to help you realize that you can write excellent Go code by yourself once you've understood the basics.

We start at the `hello, world` level, discovering the syntax of the language. Then, we progress all the way to a service ready to be deployed in the cloud by walking you through all the architectural decisions.

GRAMMAR AND SYNTAX

The first chapters focus on the grammar specific to Go. For example, you'll learn how all loops start with the same keyword and breaks are implicit in switches, as well as how to expose or not expose some of your constants and methods (what Java calls public or private).

The Go code design calls for making its interfaces *implicit*. In most of the other big languages, to have one entity (or class) be considered as implementing an interface, it needs to explicitly state it in its definition. In Go, implementing the methods is enough. You can therefore unknowingly implement an interface that you don't know yet. This opens worlds of new possibilities in how we envision mocking and stubbing, dependency injection, and interoperability.

Even though goroutines are a great feature of Go, we won't dwell on them. In our experience, you can program efficiently in Go without them. Only one project uses them in this book.

Finally, as you'll learn throughout the book, Go doesn't use exceptions. It prefers to consider errors as values. This changes the way we deal with flows that don't follow the happy path, where nothing ever fails. Every program has to deal with errors at some point, and we'll cover this throughout the projects.

TESTING YOUR CODE

The first 11 chapters include unit testing (chapter 12 doesn't because it's more of an exploration chapter). No developer today would dream of delivering code in production that isn't covered by at least some tests, whatever their level. Tests are indispensable for any evolution the software grows through, so we include unit tests everywhere. After the first chapters, you'll be able to write most of them autonomously, and we only give tips where necessary at that point.

Go is also great at benchmarking different algorithms with a built-in bench command. It allows developers to compare versions, too, which means you can use it to check on every commit that your code-level performance doesn't deteriorate.

One last recent feature of the Go tooling test chain is fuzzing. *Fuzzing* is a way to test a system by throwing random values at it and seeing how it behaves. Fuzzing is a great help in checking for vulnerabilities.

CLEAN CODE BEST PRACTICES

Any code of your own that you haven't looked at for six or more months might as well have been written by someone else.

—Eagleson's Law

While the first few projects fit in one file, we'll quickly need to organize the code in a way that makes it easy to maintain. By maintain, we mean that it should allow a newcomer to find their way through your code to fix a bug or add a feature. This fictional newcomer could be you in a very short time.

We suggest and explain some code organization practices. Go is great for domain-driven design, so we organize our code accordingly. There is, of course, no single folder organization for a Go project, but we aim for what makes the most sense.

What to expose and what to keep for yourself has shaken humanity for millennia and software developers for decades. This question is covered as soon as we create something that goes beyond one package.

ARCHITECTURAL DECISIONS

As Go is mostly used for writing services deployed in cloud environments, we added two projects to help you pick your favorite protocol: one serves HTML over HTTP, and the other uses Protobuf over gRPC. You'll write fully functioning services that you can easily deploy to play around and see what you prefer and what best fits your needs.

Once they're running, you need to monitor what happens in your programs. One of the early and easy projects is a logger that goes beyond what the default standard library does. Another one, Gordle as a service, reads an API and acts as an anti-corruption layer to insert the data from that API into your domain. A third is a simple cache for your system's performance, which you can make more complex according to your needs.

YOUR GO TOOLBOX

Go doesn't come as just a compiler for your architecture. Instead, it's a complete suite of tools that are all integrated for linting and formatting, testing, benchmarking, building, and executing. In chapter 12, we'll venture into the world of other architectures, including microcontrollers, and see how we can even ship a Go program as WebAssembly in a web page.

Now, it's time to set up your development environment and prepare to start coding! Head over to appendix A for detailed instructions on installing Go and the essential tools you'll need before diving into your first project.

SIDE QUESTS

Throughout the book, we've included extended exercises we call *side quests*, which are designed to help you practice and think more deeply about Go. These optional tasks allow you to expand your skills by applying concepts in new and creative ways. While you're encouraged to solve them independently, you're welcome to review the provided code afterward for additional insights or to compare approaches. We encourage you to use these side quests to enhance your understanding while making the journey more interactive and rewarding.

Summary

- Go is a modern, industry-oriented, simple, and versatile language that is best for backend development, widely used for cloud-oriented tools, great for CLI, and even adapted to embedded systems.
- Its simplicity and design philosophy make Go easy to learn, enabling teams to quickly become productive while maintaining readable, maintainable codebases.
- Go's built-in tools for testing, benchmarking, and profiling streamline development and ensure high-quality software.
- With its lightweight concurrency model, powered by goroutines and channels, Go is an excellent choice for scalable and concurrent applications.
- The language's growing community and increasing adoption across industries make learning Go a valuable career investment.
- Pocket-sized projects provide a hands-on approach designed to teach Go's features step-by-step, from basic syntax to cloud-ready applications.

Hello, earth! Extend your hello, world

This chapter covers

- Writing to the standard output
- Testing writing to the standard output
- Writing table-driven tests
- Using a hash table to hold key-value pairs
- Using flags to read command-line parameters

As developers, our main task is to write valid programs. These programs are executed on a computer; they'll accept some inputs (e.g., keys pressed on a keyboard, a signal received from a microphone) and will produce outputs (e.g., emit a beep, send data over the network). The simplest program of all does nothing, and simply exits. That wouldn't be a very gratifying introduction to coding, would it? Instead, let's print a hearty welcoming message!

Since 1972, learning programmers have discovered their new language through variations of the same sentence: `hello, world`. A programmer's first autonomous step is, thus, usually to change this standard message and see what happens when the greeting message slightly changes. Type, compile, run, smile—this is what developing a `hello, world` is about.

Programmatic greeting history

The `hello, world` programmatic greeting was made popular by Brian Kernighan and Dennis Ritchie's *The C Programming Language*, published in 1978. The sentence originally came from another publication, also by Brian Kernighan, "A Tutorial Introduction to the Language B," published in 1972. This was, in all honesty, actually the second example of printing characters in this publication—the first one having the program print `hi`! The reason was that the B language limited the number of ASCII characters in a single variable to four characters. `Hello, world`, as a result, was achieved with several calls to the printing function. The original article (https://www.scribd.com/document/494619413/btut) printed `hell`; then `o, w`; then `orld`, and finally `!`; resulting in `hello, world`! This message was inspired by a bird hatching out of its egg, as shown in a comic strip.

The goal of this chapter is to go a bit beyond these simple steps. Good code should be both documented and tested, so we need to understand how to test a function whose purpose is to write to the standard output. On top of that, thanks to Go's native support of Unicode characters, this chapter will be our opportunity to greet people using languages other than English and writing systems other than the Latin alphabet.

If you don't have the Go compiler on your machine yet, install it by following the steps in appendix A. We'll assume that the setup of your development environment has been completed from here on.

To print our welcoming message, our project requires the following:

- Write a program that takes the human language of your choice and prints the associated greeting.
- Ensure this program is covered by unit tests.

2.1 Any travel begins at home

Our journey as developers starts where everyone's started: on a chair in front of a keyboard and a screen. To initiate this wonderful adventure, let's write a small program that will greet us every time we run it—the well-honed `hello, world`. As good programmers, we'll also want to ensure the code works as expected, so we'll test it properly.

As mentioned in appendix A, Go code runs inside modules. Start fresh by creating a new directory for your project—let's call it `hello`. Enter this directory, and initialize your module using `go mod init` followed by the name you choose for your package. This name is usually the path to your code repository, for example,

```
> go mod init example.com/your-repository
```

or

```
> go mod init learngo-pockets/hello
```

You should now see a new file called `go.mod`.

2.1.1   *Our first program: main.go*

How can we achieve getting a program to print a message to our screen? Let's get into it! We need to write the necessary code in a file named `main.go`. In the directory of your project, create a new file named `main.go`, and add the following code.

Listing 2.1   `main.go`

```
package main

import "fmt"

func main() {
    fmt.Println("Hello world")
}
```

Phew! That was a lot for a first mission. Before we take a step into these lines, you might fancy some satisfaction and run this first program. The Go command for this is as follows (run it in the same directory as the `main.go` file):

```
> go run main.go
Hello world
```

Yay! Hopefully, you're delighted to see the expected message appear on your screen!

> **What's in a name?**
>
> As programmers, when it comes to writing code, the biggest challenge we face on a daily basis is giving names to variables, constants, types, package aliases, functions, or files, as well as Git repositories, microservices, endpoints, namespaces, and so forth. The list is endless. Here are some tips that will help you name variables in future projects:
>
> - If the scope of the variable is limited to two to three lines, a one- or two-letter placeholder is perfectly valid. However, don't pick random letters. Use something that immediately reminds you of the purpose of this variable. We'll be using `l` for language and `tc` for test case later in this chapter.
> - Stay consistent between different functions: if the variable represents the same entity, use the same name.
> - Otherwise, use a name that explicitly refers to the current entity. There is no need for abbreviations unless they're used in some other place in the code— `url` and `id`, for example, will be clear enough and understandable by everyone. Think `row`, `column`, `book`, `address`, `order`, and so on.
> - When it comes to naming, Go's convention is to use camelCase for unexposed functions, types, variables, and constants—yes, constants too. For packages, try as much as you can to use a single word.
> - Go's variables don't need to describe their type. The Hungarian notation isn't in use in Go. Your IDE will be kind enough to let you know if a variable is a pointer or a value.

- Variable names can't start with a number, nor can functions, types, or constants.

Our next step is to understand what we just wrote. Our tasks as Go developers will scarcely be achievable with mere copies of what we can find in remote resources. The creative part in coding shouldn't be ignored. As for every craft, practice makes perfect, and pretty soon, we should have acquired enough knowledge to alter this first program to meet our aspirations. This book will guide you through the different steps that will eventually guarantee self-confidence through understanding. For starters, we'll focus on the first line of the program:

```
package main
```

Every Go file begins with the name of its package, in this case, `main`. Packages are Go's way of organizing code, similar to modules or libraries in other languages. For now, everything fits in the `main.go` file, which must reside in the `main` package. We'll see more on how to make and use packages in chapter 3.

The `main` package is a bit particular, for two reasons. First, it doesn't respect Go's convention of naming the package after its directory (or the other way around). Second, this is how the compiler knows the special function called `main()` will be found here. The `main()` function is what will be executed when the program is run.

After the package's name, next comes the list of required imports this file will use. Imported packages are composed of standard library packages and third-party libraries:

```
import "fmt"
```

Most Go programs rely on external dependencies. A single Go file, without the help of imported packages, can only handle a limited set of tools. For the sake of the language's unapologetic simplicity, these tools don't provide much, and writing to external devices isn't in that limited set.

To use features in such external dependencies, we need to import the package where they reside via the `import` keyword, which provides visibility of the functions and variables in a specific package somewhere else. External libraries are identified by the URL to their repository (more on this in section 7.2.4 of chapter 7). For the moment, it's important to remember that any import that doesn't look like a URL is from the standard library, meaning it comes with the compiler.

In our case, we use the `fmt` package, the standard library package for formatting and outputting any kind of data thanks to the `Println` function, which stands for "print with new line." This is a very useful function for cheap debugging!

Finally, we have the `main()` function itself. It doesn't take any argument and doesn't return anything—simple. Go is a simple language:

```
func main() {
    fmt.Println("Hello world")
}
```

From the `fmt` package, the `Println` function writes to the standard output. If you give the function an integer or a Boolean variable, it will display the human-readable version of that value. `Println` is a sibling of a vast family of functions in charge of formatting messages.

Note that indentation in Go is made with tabs. No need to start a debate, it's written in the documentation and everyone does it that way. If you don't indent, nobody will be able to read your code, but the compiler will understand. Don't do that, even if it works.

A capital question

You might wonder why `Println` starts with an uppercase letter. The whole story about scope and visibility is explained here:

- Any symbol starting with a capital letter is exposed to external users of the package.
- Anything else isn't accessible from outside the package. Common examples of unexposed names include those starting with a lowercase letter and those starting with an underscore.

This applies to variables, constants, functions, and types. And that's it—really.

The `Println` function starts with a capital letter so that we can use it from outside the package.

2.1.2   *Let's test with the Example function*

Now that we wrote the program, we can test it! As you'll see, this isn't the only way of developing—sometimes, we can start with writing the tests and then the code. What's important is that code and tests go hand in hand. Writing code with no tests is as dangerous as thinking your brand-new toaster will return perfectly crispy and still tender bread on its first use without checking any of its settings.

But what's in a test? By "test," we mean automated tests (or at least automatable), not relying on human evaluation. The test could be written in shell script, in Fortran, in Go, or in any language of your choice. It has to be able to tell the human user that everything went fine or that something didn't—in which case, some verboseness is always welcome. For this first project, we consider that running the code and "seeing" with human eyes that the output is `Hello world` isn't enough, at least not as the sole test of our code. What if that space character between the words were a nonbreakable space character, which we humans can't differentiate from a regular space character? The output string wouldn't be the same, but we wouldn't be able to tell.

And why should we test? After all, the code did execute as we wanted when we ran it, right? Although this is true, it's only been true once. And, in a larger project, where a piece of code isn't executed just once and is regularly tinkered with, tests are a great method of ensuring we didn't break previous behavior. Tests are an important block of any continuous integration pipeline—if not the most important.

EXAMPLE VS. TEST

A little technical foreword is needed here. While Go functions usually return values, very few write specifically to the standard output. The test strategy that we'll implement here is only necessary when checking the standard output, which means it won't be the default approach for the rest of the code. However, because this is our first function and we want to test it, this is the easy way. We'll see more about test functions shortly.

Examples are not only used for testing the standard output but also, as their name suggests, for giving the users and maintainers of your code a good starting point. They will appear in the documentation generated by go doc. Fortunately, they are also run by the test tool, so this is the solution we use when checking what happens on the standard output.

Go offers many tools to test the code, so let's use them! Here, our goal will be to test the main function—a task that is quite uncommon. The vast majority of Go code lies in other functions—if not other packages—and those are the functions that we heavily test. Most of the time, the main function will call these tested functions and will simply be in charge of printing a string or returning a status code. Apart from this occasion, the tests in this book won't be on the main function, but rather on the functions it calls.

First, we need a test file. We'll name the file main_internal_test.go, for the following reasons:

- main, because the file we test is named main.go.
- internal, because we want to access unexposed methods, a convention that we choose to follow in this book.
- test, because this is a test file. When it comes to building or executing the program, *_test.go files are ignored by the compiler. Only when running tests will *_test.go files be considered.

Internal and external testing

There are two approaches to testing. In *external testing*, we test from the user's point of view, so we can only test what is exposed. The test files should be in the {packagename}_test package and in the same folder.

In *internal testing*, on the other hand, we know everything that goes on inside and we want to test the unexposed functions. The test files should be in the same package as the source file.

These two approaches aren't exclusive; they are complementary.

RAISE THE STANDARD

How do we test our code? How can we make sure that something is sent to the standard output from within a function? Go provides a specific tool based on a test function's name, which can be used to test the standard output of that function. If a function's name in a test file matches the `Example<FunctionName>` pattern—in our case, `ExampleMain`—Go will identify it as eligible for standard output verifications. Even though `main` isn't exposed, the function is in PascalCase, requiring a capital M here. The testing function wraps a call to `main`, the tested function, at line 4 in the following code.

Listing 2.2 `main_internal_test.go`: **Testing the printed output**

```
package main

func ExampleMain() {        Calls main
    main()
    // Output:
    // Hello world          Defines the expected output
}
```

To assert that the expected output message `Hello world` has been sent to the standard output, we use Go's `Example` syntax, which allows us to write a commented line containing `Output:`. Any commented lines right after this one will be the expected value that Go's test utility uses to check the output generated by this `Example` function.

If an `Example` function doesn't include the `// Output:` comment, it will still be compiled, but it won't be executed during tests. However, such a function will still appear in the documentation generated by `go doc` or similar tools. This makes `Example` functions without `// Output:` particularly useful for illustrating usage without enforcing specific outputs.

LET'S RUN THE TEST

To run the test, we must call Go's `test` command. This will execute all tests in the current directory:

```
> go test
PASS
ok      learngo-pockets/hello      0.008s
```

The output lists the test files that Go processed, showing the module name followed by the path to the tested package. If the `main` package resides at the root of the module, only the module name will appear in the output, as there is no additional path to display.

> **NOTE** Always remember what Edsger Dijkstra said: "Testing can prove the presence of bugs, but not their absence!" A single test won't demonstrate a piece of code is error proof at all. The more tests we have, the more trustworthy the code is.

Writing tests comes with several benefits. First, we have an automatable process that will check that the code we have produces a deterministic output. Second, with this test, we can start altering the code—and every change, every tiniest bit of line we modify, can be validated with a run of the previous test. Finally, as mentioned previously, writing tests with `Example` plays an important part in Go's documentation.

2.1.3 *Calling the greet function*

The goal of this chapter isn't just to print a nice message to the user. We want some variations, some modularity. Taking a step back, the `main` function does two distinct things: (1) defines a specific message and (2) prints it. We've cobbled everything on a single line in the previous code, but that doesn't leave any space for adaptations.

Because we aim to enrich the message, we need some flexibility here. We'll begin by extracting the message generation into a dedicated `greet` function. This function returns a string that we can keep in a variable we call `greeting`. Following is the full code refactored with the extraction.

Listing 2.3 `main.go`: **Moving the** `Println` **call**

```
package main

import "fmt"

func main() {
    greeting := greet()          Extracts the string
        fmt.Println(greeting)    into a variable
}

// greet returns a greeting to the world.    Creates a new
func greet() string {                        function
    // return a simple greeting message
    return "Hello world"
}
```

Let's look closer. The new function is called `greet` because it will return the greeting message. For now, it takes no parameters and simply returns the message in the form of a string:

```
// greet returns a greeting to the world.
func greet() string {
    return "Hello world"
}
```

In the main function, we call the new `greet` function and store its output in the `greeting` string variable, which we print:

```
func main() {
    greeting := greet()
        fmt.Println(greeting)
}
```

We refactored. Does the test still pass? Congratulations, you've made your first refactoring in Go. It should pass, but it's not as unitary as it could be. We can write a test around greet with a lot more flexibility.

2.1.4   *Testing a specific function with the testing package*

Refactoring, as we just did, shouldn't change the code's behavior. We can still run our previous test, and it should still pass. But because we'll want to enrich the greet function, we should be covering it with dedicated tests, as meager as it is.

As part of Go's standard library packages, the package testing is available for your use. We'll be using it a lot throughout this book, trying to benefit from every aspect that the Go designers put into the language so that we don't have to write our own tools or spend time benchmarking independent testing libraries. As its name nicely suggests, the testing package is written for writing tests.

We've already seen the Example<FunctionName>() syntax, which is used for documentation and for testing standard output. Let's venture into a new set of test functions: those with the Test<FunctionName>(t *testing.T) signature. There's an important difference here with the previous category: these functions accept a parameter—a pointer to a testing.T structure. The reasons for using a pointer here are beyond the scope of this chapter, but we'll cover them in appendix E.

A TestXxx function runs one or more tests on a function, as defined by the developer. We'll start with one, and then grow from there. A test consists of calling the function and checking its returned value or the state of some variable against a wanted value or state. Should they match, the test is considered passing; otherwise, it's considered failing. Every test has four main steps:

- *Preparation phase*—This is where we set up everything we need to run the test—input values, expected outputs, environment variables, global variables, network connections, and so on.
- *Execution phase*—This is where we call the tested function. This step is usually a single line.
- *Decision phase*—This is where we check that the output we got corresponds to the output we want. This might include several comparisons, evaluations, and sometimes some processing, as well as the test failing or passing.
- *Teardown phase*—This is where we kindly clean back to whatever the state was prior to the test's execution. This step is made extremely simple thanks to Go's defer keyword: anything that was altered or created during preparation should be fixed or destroyed here.

Our TestGreet function will be written in the same main_internal_test.go file as earlier, mostly because the tested function, greet, is also in the same main.go file. Let's have a look at the additions we brought to the file. In Go, we like to use want for the expected value and got for the actual one, as shown in the following listing.

Listing 2.4 `main_internal_test.go:` Testing `greet`

```go
package main

import "testing"

func TestGreet(t *testing.T) {
    want := "Hello world"

    got := greet()

    if got != want {
        // mark this test as failed
        t.Errorf("expected: %q, got: %q", want, got)
    }
}
```

The first difference with the previous version of this file is at line 3: we now need to import the `testing` package because we use a parameter of type `*testing.T` in our `TestGreet` function. This is a line that will appear in every single test file we'll see as Go developers. Its absence should be a red flag when reviewing industry code:

```go
import "testing"
```

The second important change in this file is, of course, the new `TestGreet` function:

```go
func TestGreet(t *testing.T)
```

We've added comments in the body of this function so that it follows the previous list of steps. The preparation step, in our case, consists of defining the expected output of the `greet` function call. Because this doesn't alter the environment, there is nothing to rewind after the execution of the test, and we don't need to defer any closure steps. The execution phase simply consists of calling the tested `greet` function and, of course, capturing its output into a variable. The following is an annotated listing showing the purpose of each line.

Listing 2.5 `main_internal_test.go:` Body of the test

```
                                        Preparation phase: defines the
                                        expected returned value
want := "Hello world"    ◄─────┘
                                        Execution phase: calls the
                                        examined greet function
got := greet()           ◄─────┘

if got != want {                  ◄───────      Decision phase: checks
    // mark this test as failed                 the returned value
    t.Errorf("expected: %q, got: %q", want, got)
}
```

The decision phase here isn't too tricky. We need to compare two strings, and we'll accept no alteration, so the != comparison operator works fine for us here. We'll soon face cases where comparing two strings isn't enough, but let's not skip steps, as we still have a final line here that needs more explanation:

```
t.Errorf("expected: %q, got: %q", want, got)
```

So far, the need for the t parameter hasn't been obvious. As mentioned earlier, a test needs to be either PASSing or FAILing. Calling t.Errorf is one way of letting the go test tool know that this test was unsuccessful. Errorf has a similar signature as Printf; see appendix B for more about formatting strings. Once again, you can run the tests with the same go test command as earlier.

Before we move on to the next section, now's the time for playing a bit. Change the contents of the want, and rerun the tests. The reason for this early refactoring might not appear obvious right now. By the end of this chapter, however, as we implement new functionalities in our code, the file will grow in size. It's good practice in Go, as in many other development languages, to keep the scope of a function narrow. This serves several purposes:

- Making the code testable
- Making debugging the code easier
- Making the mission of a function explicit

Overall, the cognitive charge of a function should be minimal. No one wants to face a wall of text featuring multiple layers of indentations.

We've now written a program that greets the user with a lovely message. We know it works fine because we've written tests to cover the code, but there's a small catch. The program will only write English greetings. We can improve the program using languages in addition to English to reach more people. Imagine you're applying at a Canadian company, where employees speak both French and English. How nice would it be if they could use our program too and be greeted with a language of their choosing?

2.2   *Are you a polyglot?*

Our program is static—it will always run and print the same message, regardless of the user. Let's adapt our code to support several languages, and let the users decide which language they want. In this section, we'll do the following:

- Add support for a new language in the greet method
- Handle the user's language request
- Adapt the tests and ensure we didn't break the previous behavior

To display Hello world in a different language, we need to tell the program which language we want to use. This will be performed in two iterations: (1) supporting new languages and (2) opening our program to the user's choice of language.

2.2.1 *Parlez-vous français? The switch angle*

Our current `greet` function only returns a hardcoded message. Because it can only return one message, we want some logic in there to determine which greeting to output. There are several options for this in Go. The first one that comes to mind, the `if` approach, only works for one or two different languages. Add more languages, and the code becomes an unnecessarily long list of checks. Here, we'll explore the other two options. Because we need to support another language, let's pick French. The full code now looks like the following listing.

Listing 2.6 `main.go`: **Adding a new language**

```go
package main

import "fmt"

func main() {
    greeting := greet("en")
    fmt.Println(greeting)
}

// language represents the language's code
type language string                          // Declares a type

// greet says hello to the world in the specified language
func greet(l language) string {
    switch l {                                // Switches on the
    case "en":                                // language value
        return "Hello world"
    case "fr":
        return "Bonjour le monde"
    default:
        return ""
    }
}
```

CLARITY THROUGH TYPING

Using the proper type for variables is important. We need to know what we're talking about, and what we're talking about is having a language parameter that will be used to specify which greeting message should be returned by the `greet` function. This language parameter can be a string containing the language description, an integer referring to an index of existing languages, the URL to a dictionary, or many, many other things. For now, we'll keep it simple and use a string:

```go
type language string
```

The input language will be a `string` that represents a `language`. This type definition helps us and the users of our libraries understand what values are expected and makes mixing up parameters harder.

Now that we have an explicit type, we can pass it as a parameter to the `greet` function. The new signature becomes

```
func greet(l language) string
```

To call it, we changed the first line of our main function:

```
greeting := greet("en")
```

The compiler knows if this `"en"` is a `string` or a `language` by looking at the signature of the function. `greet` requires a `language`, so it types the constant as such.

For the first iteration, we can add a `switch` on the `language` and return the corresponding greeting, as shown in listing 2.7. The default value for the moment is just an empty string. We consider that `switch` is clearer when dealing with most types—the exceptions being `error`, pointers, and `bool`.

Listing 2.7 `main.go`: **Switching on language**

```
switch l {
    case "en":
        return "Hello world"
    case "fr":
        return "Bonjour le monde'
    default:
        return ""
}
```

Note that between each case, contrary to many other programming languages, we don't break. Breaking is implicit in Go because it's such a potential source of errors. Of course, as we return here in each case, the point is moot, but now you know.

In the `main` function, we need to pass the desired `language` to our upgraded `greet` function—for example, `"en"` for English—and print the output.

2.2.2   *Adapt the test with Test<FunctionName> functions*

Previously, the `greet` function accepted no parameter. It now takes one, which means we broke the contract we had with the users of our code. Well, for now, the only user is a test, so we can change it. We now want to test the `greet` function with various inputs.

We'll make a call to the `greet` function by passing the desired input language and storing the output in a variable, so we can verify it. The preparation phase now contains two variables: the desired language and the expected greeting message.

Let's use a new convention of the `testing` package: when testing a function with two (or more) different scenarios, we can write several functions, `Test<FunctionName>_{ScenarioName}`. The full test file now looks like the following listing.

Listing 2.8 `main_internal_test.go`: Split test cases

```go
package main

import "testing"

func ExampleMain() {
    ...
}

func TestGreet_English(t *testing.T) {
    lang := language("en")
    want := "Hello world"

    got := greet(lang)

    if got != want {
        // mark this test as failed
        t.Errorf("expected: %q, got: %q", want, got)
    }
}

func TestGreet_French(t *testing.T) {
    lang := language("fr")
    want := "Bonjour le monde"

    got := greet(lang)

    if got != want {
        // mark this test as failed
        t.Errorf("expected: %q, got: %q", want, got)
    }
}

func TestGreet_Akkadian(t *testing.T) {
    // Akkadian is not implemented yet!
    lang := language("akk")
    want := ""

    got := greet(lang)

    if got != want {
        // mark this test as failed
        t.Errorf("expected: %q, got: %q", want, got)
    }
}
```

Preparation phase: defines the expected returned value of type language

Execution phase: calls the examined greet function

Decision phase: checks the returned value

As you can see, the `TestGreet_English` function is in charge of testing the English greeting, while the `TestGreet_French` function tests the French message. While this approach is interesting and worth remembering, you probably noticed that, in our case, there's no real change between the English and the French scenarios. Only the preparation step differs—only slightly. The next section will improve on this. To run the tests, simply run your new favorite `go test` command.

As you've noticed, we've added another function to test a language unknown to the program. Testing isn't always about making sure the "good" inputs provide "good" results. Making sure the safety nets are in place is almost more valuable than making sure the code works as intended.

2.3   *Supporting more languages with a phrasebook*

Adding entries to a `switch` clause reduces the readability of the code: it increases the size of the function, sometimes beyond screen dimensions, when the only answer we need is "if this language is supported, give me its greeting." To trim down our function without losing any functionality, in our next iteration of coding, we decide to use a `map`, a very common and useful data structure in Go. A `map` is a hash table, a set of pairs of distinct keys and their associated values. In this section, we'll do the following:

- Scale the number of supported languages
- Introduce the use of `map`

2.3.1   *Introducing the Go map hash table*

Let's look at the implementation of the code using a `map` to store these pairs of `<language, greeting>`. The code is given in the following listing.

Listing 2.9   `main.go`: Using a `map`

```
package main

import (
    "fmt"
)

func main() {
    greeting := greet("en")
    fmt.Println(greeting)
}

// language represents the language's code
type language string

// phrasebook holds greeting for each supported language          Declares a global
var phrasebook = map[language]string{                             variable
    "el": "Χαίρετε Κόσμε",     // Greek
    "en": "Hello world",       // English
    "fr": "Bonjour le monde",  // French
    "he": "שלום עולם",          // Hebrew
    "ur": "ہیلو دنیا",          // Urdu
    "vi": "Xin chào Thế Giới", // Vietnamese
}

// greet says hello to the world in various languages
func greet(l language) string {
    greeting, ok := phrasebook[l]                                Uses the map
```

```
    if !ok {
        return fmt.Sprintf("unsupported language: %q", l)
    }

    return greeting
}
```

Our map, defined in listing 2.10, associates a greeting message with every language as a pair of {language, greeting} where the greeting is stored as a string. For this chapter, we use a global variable that holds the greetings. While relying on global variables is generally considered bad practice, it's acceptable for the purposes of this simple project.

Listing 2.10 `main.go:` map **definition**

```
// phrasebook holds greeting for each supported language
var phrasebook = map[language]string{
    "el": "Χαίρετε Κόσμε",      // Greek
    "en": "Hello world",        // English
    "fr": "Bonjour le monde",   // French
    "he": "שלום עולם",          // Hebrew
    "ur": "ہیلو دنیا",          // Urdu
    "vi": "Xin chào Thế Giới",  // Vietnamese
}
```

Our next step is to use this phrasebook instead of the `switch` in the `greet` function. The following listing shows the code for this step.

Listing 2.11 `main.go:` `greet` **method**

```
// greet says hello to the world in various languages
func greet(l language) string {
    greeting, ok := phrasebook[l]
    if !ok {
        return fmt.Sprintf("unsupported language: %q", l)
    }

    return greeting
}
```

Accessing an item in a Go `map` returns two pieces of valuable information: a value—in our case, the message associated with the key language `l`—and a Boolean (`ok` per convention) that tells us whether the key was found. The syntax of assigning both returned values to two different variables on a single line might be new to some programmers—it doesn't exist in Java or C. This is something we do a lot in Go:

```
greeting, ok := phrasebook[l]
if !ok {
    return fmt.Sprintf("unsupported language: %q", l)
}
```

It's necessary to check the second return value of the access to the map. If the language were unsupported, we'd receive the zero value of a string, which is the empty string, with no knowledge of whether the map had an entry for our language.

Note that in production-ready code, we would be returning an error because an empty string doesn't carry any meaning. We chose to keep it simple for now. Errors will be covered in later chapters.

MULTIPLE RETURN VALUES

We'll see many occurrences of multiple value assignment, mostly in four common cases:

- When we read the value associated with a key from a map, we also receive whether that key was found in the map, as we did in this piece of code.
- When we use the range keyword, which allows us to iterate through all the key-value pairs in a map or all the index-value elements of a slice or array (an example appears in the next version of the test file, as well as more information in section 3.1.4 of chapter 3).
- When we read from a channel with the <- operator, which returns a value and whether the channel is closed (examples can be found in the maze solver in chapter 9).
- When we retrieve multiple values returned by a single function, which is the most frequent case, mostly due to Go's handling of errors (see chapters 3, 5, and 7 for examples).

At this point, both tests for French and English should still pass because our refactoring didn't change them, but now the Akkadian is failing. Let's refactor the test before we fix it.

2.3.2   *Writing a table-driven test*

Our previous tests were linear—they tested every language in a sequential way. Taking a step back, we realize each test runs the same sequence: take an input language, call the greet function, and check the greeting to see if that language is the expected one. This can be summed up in the following snippet of code that was executed for languages "en", "fr", or "akk" in our previous example.

> **Listing 2.12   main_internal_test.go: Calling greet and checking**

```
got := greet(language(lang))
if got != want {
    t.Errorf("expected: %q, got: %q", want, got)
}
```

There's no point in duplicating this piece of code every time we want to check that we're properly supporting a new language. Isn't the test always going to be the same? Do we really need to add an extra 10 lines to our test file if only 2 of these lines change?

This isn't sustainable. That was our motivation to use maps in the body of the greet function, and this is also our motivation to use maps in our tests! We can make use of table-driven tests to enhance the reusability and clarity of our test file, and get the nice side effect of shrinking it a lot! Let's look at the new test in the following listing before we explain it.

Listing 2.13 `main_internal_test.go`: **Table-driven tests**

```go
func TestGreet(t *testing.T) {
    type testCase struct {
        lang language
        want string
    }

    var tests = map[string]testCase{        // Preparation phase: defines
        "English": {                         // the expected returned value
            lang: "en",
            want: "Hello world",
        },
        "French": {
            lang: "fr",
            want: "Bonjour le monde",
        },
        "Akkadian, not supported": {
            lang: "akk",
            want: `unsupported language: "akk"`,
        },
        "Greek": {
            lang: "el",
            want: "Χαίρετε Κόσμε",
        },
        ...
        "Empty": {
            lang: "",
            want: `unsupported language: ""`,
        },
    }

    // range over all the scenarios            // Execution phase: calls the
    for name, tc := range tests {              // examined greet function
        t.Run(name, func(t *testing.T) {
            got := greet(tc.lang)             // Decision phase: checks
                                              // the returned value
            if got != tc.want {
                t.Errorf("expected: %q, got: %q", tc.want, got)
            }
        })
    }
}
```

As we've seen previously, every test we want to run needs two values: the language of the desired message and the expected greeting message that will be returned by the greet function. For this, we introduce a new structure that contains the input language, and the expected greeting. Structures are Go's way of aggregating data types together in a meaningful entity. In our case, because the structure represents a test case, we'll name it testCase. Our structure needs only to be accessible in the TestGreet function (and nowhere else), so let's define it there:

```
type testCase struct {
    lang language
    want string
}
```

This will make writing a test over a pair of <language, greeting> even simpler. Now that we can easily write one test case, let's see how to write a lot of them. In Go, the common way of writing a list of test cases is to use a map structure that will refer to each test case with a specific description key. The description should be explicit about what this case tests. We now have everything we need to write a list of test cases, as shown in the following listing.

Listing 2.14 main_internal_test.go: Test cases definition

```
var tests = map[string]testCase{
    "English": {
        lang: "en",
        want: "Hello world",
    },
    "French": {
        lang: "fr",
        want: "Bonjour le monde".
    },
}
```

To test these scenarios, we can iterate over the tests map and run each test case sequentially, as shown in listing 2.15. As you'll see in more detail in the next chapter, this for + range syntax returns the key and the value of each element of the map. We then pass the name as the first parameter to Run, a method from the testing package that makes tests so much easier to use: if a test case fails, the tool will give you its name so that you can find it and fix it. Most code editors also let you run one single test case if you use this syntax. Remember, this map associates a description to a test case, hence the name of the variable, tc.

Listing 2.15 main_internal_test.go: Execution and assertion phases

```
for name, tc := range tests {
    t.Run(name, func(t *testing.T) {
        got := greet(tc.language)

        if got != tc.want {
```

Execution phase: calls the function

Decision phase: checks the result

```
            t.Errorf("expected: %q, got: %q", tc.want, got)
        }
    })
}
```

Because the call to the `greet` function is the same regardless of the input language, creating a new test case only has us adding an entry in the `tests` map. You can see this in the following listing.

Listing 2.16 `main_internal_test.go`: **Test cases**

```
var tests = map[string]testCase{
    "English": {...},
    "French": {...},
    "Akkadian, not supported": {
        lang: "akk",
        want: `unsupported language: "akk"`,
    },
}
```

◄── Add new described scenarios here.

Quotes in Go

You've probably noticed we used a different set of quotation marks in the expected greeting for Akkadian (`akk`). There are three types of quotation marks used in Go, each for a specific need:

- The double quotation mark (`"`) is used to create literal strings. Example: `s := "Hello world"`
- The backtick (`` ` ``) is also used to create raw literal strings. Example: `s := ` `` `Hello world` ``
- The single quote (`'`) is used to create runes. Example: `r := '學'`. A rune is a single Unicode code point.

You've probably noticed the first two options can be used to create literal strings. The difference between raw literal strings and non-raw literal strings is that, in a raw literal string, there's no escape sequence. Writing a `\n` in a raw literal string will result in a backslash character (`\`) followed by the letter `n` when the string is printed. Raw literal strings are a nice way of not having to deal with escaping double quotation marks, which is very handy when it comes to writing JSON payloads.

We now have a program that can return a greeting in whichever language the user wants, but the only way the user gets to change the language used, so far, is to change the code of the program—which isn't optimal! We want to get the input from the user without changing the code every time the request is sent. Because the user is running the program from the command line—by running `go run main.go` or by executing the compiled executable—that's most likely where they'll want to inform us of their choice of language.

2.4   *Using the flag package to read the user's language*

How can we use the input to get the user's desired language of greeting? Go provides support for parsing the command-line arguments in both the os and flag packages. The former is very close to C/C++'s handling of arguments—you get to access them by their position on the line, but whether they are of the form --key=value, -key value, or -option is left up to the developer to implement. That's a real pain if you have repeatable fields. Oh, and that's only for parsing them—then we have to convert them to their right type.

On the other hand, the flag package offers support for a variety of types—integers, float numbers, time durations, strings, and Booleans. Let's roll with this one:

1 Use the flag (https://pkg.go.dev/flag) standard package to read from command-line arguments.
2 Call flag.Parse to retrieve the values.
3 Play with the program argument flags, and check the output.

2.4.1   *Add a flag*

The first thing we need to do, when it comes to exposing a parameter on our command-line executable, is to give it a nice, short name. Here, we'll offer the user a choice of language, which makes lang a fairly obvious choice. Let's have a look at the updated code of the main.go file in the following listing.

Listing 2.17   `main.go`: Using flags

```
package main

import (
    "flag"
    "fmt"
)

func main() {
    var lang string
        flag.StringVar(&lang,
        "lang",
        "en",
        "The required language, e.g. en, ur...")
    flag.Parse()

    greeting := greet(language(lang))
    fmt.Println(greeting)
}

// language represents a language
type language string

// phrasebook holds greeting for each supported language
var phrasebook = map[language]string{
```

> Go understands that a line finishing with a comma continues on the next line.

```
    ...
}

// greet says hello to the world
func greet(l language) string {
    ...
}
```

The goal of this section is to read the flags from the command line, which means we need to import the `flag` package:

```
import (
    "flag"
    "fmt"
)
```

Now that we've imported this package, let's use it. We want to read, from the command line, the name of the language in which the user expects their greeting. In our code, the type for that entity is a `language`, for which the closest type is a `string`.

The `flag` package offers two very similar functions to read a string from the command line. The first requires a pointer to a variable that it will fill up:

```
var lang string
flag.StringVar(&lang, "lang", "en", "The required language, e.g. en, ur...")
```

The second creates the pointer and returns it:

```
lang := flag.String("lang", "en", "The required language, e.g. en, ur...")
```

For this example, we'll use the first one, mostly because it will let us introduce the `&` operator. On the first line, we declare a variable of the type `string`. That variable will hold the value provided by the user. Let's have a look at the syntax and different parameters of the `StringVar` call:

1 We pass the address of the string into which we'll store the provided value to the function. Pointers are covered in detail in appendix E and used in the following chapters.

2 We pass the name of the option as it will appear on the command line.

3 We give the default value for this variable. The default value is used if the user doesn't provide the flag when calling the program.

4 We provide a short description of what this flag represents and some example values.

During the execution of a program, variables are stored in memory at a specific address. We can retrieve the address of a variable with the address operator `&`. Similarly, when we have a pointer and want to access the value, we can retrieve it with the indirection operator `*` used on the pointer.

In Go, when we call a function, the arguments are passed by copy. This means that if we want to allow a function to alter one of our variables, the simplest way is to give that function a pointer to our variable.

Finally, Go offers no pointer arithmetic. If you have a pointer to the first element of an `array`, it can't be used to access the second element.

There's one important thing to remember when we use the `flags` package: `StringVar`, `IntVar`, and `UintVar` don't scan the command line and extract the value of the parameter. What does this trick of parsing the command line is the `flag.Parse` function. It scans the input parameters and fills every variable we've identified as a receiver. If you need a mnemotechnical sentence to remember it, try "Sunset `BoolVar` begins at the `Parse`-ific Ocean."

After the call to `Parse`, the variable `lang` will contain the value passed by the user, and the rest of the code isn't touched. Note that this conversion to the language type is acceptable in this context, but in production code, it's the perfect place to add validation of the value against a list of supported values or at least a validation of the format (in our case, a string of two ASCII characters).

2.4.2   *Test the command-line interface*

We've now completed the code, and it's time to run some end-user testing. For this, we'll simulate calls from the command line. We have several options to make sure this works as expected. The first on our list is to simply try it out! After all, we've spent a good many pages making sure this works as we want, so we deserve some peace of mind and some time to rest our neurons. We can pass the parameter on the command line with `go run main.go -lang=en`. Here is an example of running the `main` file in Greek:

```
> go run main.go -lang=el
Χαίρετε Κόσμε
```

2.5   *Side quests*

Here is a series of exercises you can do:

1 Launch the program with the Urdu language as the `flag` argument.
2 Launch the program with no language.
3 Remember to check all possible scenarios. The user could be asking for languages our program doesn't know. Launch the program with an unsupported language, for example, Akkadian, `akk`.
4 Add support for the language of your choice.

This concludes the first project. We hope you enjoyed it and have already gained some practical insights into using Go.

Summary

- `go run` allows you to quickly execute a Go program without creating a binary, making it useful during development.

- Writing tests alongside your code, rather than after it, ensures the mental model of expected inputs and outputs is fresh and accurate, leading to better test coverage.

- `go test` is used to execute tests written for your code, following Go's naming conventions for test files and functions.

- The `testing` package provides everything you need to write and run tests, including support for assertions and benchmarks.

- Table-driven tests are a Go best practice for testing functions across multiple inputs and outputs. By using `slices` of test cases, you can easily iterate through various scenarios in a structured way.

- `Example` functions are special tests used to check the output of a function by verifying what is written to the standard output. These are often used to demonstrate usage.

- Each test generally follows four phases: preparation, where you set up inputs; execution, where you run the code being tested; decision, where you compare the result with expected output; and teardown, where you clean up resources.

- The `flag` package allows for parsing command-line arguments, making your Go applications more flexible and interactive.

- In Go, `maps` are powerful data structures for storing key-value pairs. Accessing a `map` returns both the value and a Boolean indicating if the key was found.

- Define custom types when they provide meaningful context over built-in types. For example, a `UserID` type can be more descriptive than an `int`.

- Use `if` statements for simple binary conditions. For more complex cases, prefer `switch` statements or `maps` to handle multiple conditions more cleanly.

3

A bookworm's digest: Playing with loops and maps

This chapter covers

- Ranging over `slice` and `map`
- Using a `map` to store unique values
- Learning how to open and read a file
- Decoding JSON files
- Sorting a `slice` with custom comparators

Since the invention of writing, people have been using the tool to carve their thoughts through the centuries. Books were knowledge and became a hobby. We've been reading and collecting books on shelves for centuries. With technology, we're now able to share information more than ever and give our opinion on everything, including books. In this chapter, we'll join a group of bookworms who have been reading books faithfully. Fadi and Peggy have started registering the books they keep on their bookshelves, and they wonder if we can help them find books that they both have read and, maybe, suggest future reads.

In this chapter, we'll reinforce what we learned about command-line interfaces (CLIs) in chapter 2 by creating a book digest from the bookworms' book collections. Step by step, by using a list of books from each reader, we'll build a program that returns and prints the books that are located on more than one shelf. As a bonus, we'll practice with `map` and `slice`, Go's dynamic, flexible data structures similar to `arrays`, to create a tool that recommends new books for the bookworms to read. The input of our executable is a JSON file, and we can learn how to read a file in Go and parse a JSON file using the standard Go libraries. For simplicity, we'll assume that each book has only one author (which is a bit ironic given the book you're reading right now). This project requires the following:

- Write a CLI tool that takes a list of bookworms and their book collections in the form of a JSON file.
- Find the books the bookworms have in common on their shelves.
- Print the books they have in common to the standard output.
- As a bonus, recommend books for each bookworm based on their matching books with other bookworms.

The project is limited in the following ways:

- We assume each book has only one author.
- The input JSON file won't surpass a megabyte.

3.1 Loading the JSON data

We're in a new chapter, so that means a new project and a new folder. Let's launch the command to initialize the module we'll be working on and call it `bookworms`:

```
> go mod init learngo-pockets/bookworms
```

As a good practice and a standard first step, we recommend creating a new `main.go` file with a simple empty `main` function:

```
package main

func main() {
    // will be completed along the way
}
```

We'll fill in the rest of the `main.go` file throughout the chapter. In this section, we'll create the input JSON file and load the data it contains.

3.1.1 Defining a JSON example

Let's look at some examples of input data. Here, we have a list of people with their names and their books. Each book has one author and a title.

> **A few words about the JSON format**
>
> *JavaScript Object Notation* (JSON) is a file format that stores data using `"key":value` pairs. JSON keys are always strings, enclosed with straight double quotation marks, and JSON values can be any of the following:

(continued)

- *Decimal numbers (no enclosing character)*—`4`, `3.1415`, `1e12`
- *Strings (enclosed in double quotation marks)*—`"Hello"`, `"1789"`
- *Arrays (enclosed in square brackets)*—`[1,2.5,-10]`
- *Boolean values (no enclosing character)*—`true`, `false`
- *Objects (enclosed in curly braces)*—`{"name":"Nergüi"}`

The fields for JSON objects aren't specifically sorted; in listing 3.1, we could have the author appear before or after the title, and the payload would be the same. Arrays, on the other hand, are ordered; switching the first and the second element would change the payload.

We can now write a sample bookworm file. The following listing provides the code for the file.

Listing 3.1   `testdata/bookworms.json`: Example of input file

```
[
  {
    "name": "Fadi",
    "books": [
      {
        "author": "Margaret Atwocd",
        "title": "The Handmaid's Tale"
      },
      {
        "author": "Sylvia Plath",
        "title": "The Bell Jar"
      }
    ]
  },
  {
    "name": "Peggy",
    "books": [
      {
        "author": "Margaret Atwood",
        "title": "Oryx and Crake"
      },
      {
        "author": "Margaret Atwood",
        "title": "The Handmaid's Tale"
      },
      {
        "author": "Charlotte Brontë",
        "title": "Jane Eyre"
      }
    ]
  }
]
```

That's simple enough for now. There is a convention in Go by which any folder named testdata should contain—you guessed it—data for testing. To quote the go tool documentation, "the go tool will ignore a directory named "testdata", making it available to hold ancillary data needed by the tests." Linters and other static code analysis tools should also ignore it.

Create a file named bookworms.json within a testdata folder with some data like ours, and pick your favorite books. Alternatively, you can go to our repository and copy our version.

The first step for reading this data is to open the file and load its contents as a file. The second is to parse the JSON.

3.1.2 Opening a file

Because we don't like getting lost in overly long files, we chose to cut the logic of the project into two files: first, main.go knows that it runs in a terminal and can display text; second, bookworm.go has the business logic and could be copied and reused in a different setup. Don't overthink it yet. At this point, your file tree should look like this:

```
> tree
.
├── bookworm.go
├── go.mod
├── main.go
└── testdata
    └── bookworms.json
```

Loading the data will be the job of a new function, which we'll call loadBookworms. It takes the file path as a parameter filePath and returns the slice of Bookworms represented by the JSON document, as shown in listing 3.2. If something goes wrong (file not found, invalid JSON, etc.), it can also return an error. Don't forget to give it a docstring—in other words, a comment explaining what the function does.

Listing 3.2 bookworm.go: The loadBookworms signature

```
package main

// loadBookworms reads the file and returns the list of bookworms,
// and their beloved books, found therein.
func loadBookworms(filePath string) ([]Bookworm, error) {
    return nil, nil                          ◄─── Returns empty
}                                                 values for now
```

We talked about zero values previously in chapter 2, section 2.3.1, and you can refer to appendix C for specific information. In our case, the zero value of the slice of bookworms is nil, as is the zero value of the error interface. That's why loadBookworms returns nil and nil for the moment.

Go offers the platform-independent `os` package to operate system functionality. According to the documentation, "The design is Unix-like, although the error handling is Go-like; failing calls return values of type error rather than error numbers."

Inside the `os` package, there is an `os.File` type providing ways to open a file for reading or writing, changing rights of a file, creating a new file, and many other system operations you can perform on a file. The whole list can be retrieved with `go doc os.File`. The simplest function to open our file is `os.Open`. We'll give `os.Open` the path to our file as the `filePath` parameter, and it will return a pointer to a `File`, which is a file descriptor, or an error. The documentation is kind enough to let us know that the descriptor is in read-only mode and that the returned error is of type `*PathError`.

Differences between os.Create, os.Open, and os.OpenFile

As we can see in the documentation of the `os` package, several functions return a file descriptor, and each one has its best usage. Let's consider when `os.OpenFile` should be used to open a file instead of `os.Create` or `os.Open`:

- `Create` creates a file with both read and write (but not execute) rights for all users (0666). If the file already exists, `Create` truncates it, sending its contents to oblivion. When `Create` succeeds, the returned file descriptor can be used to write data to the file.
- `Open` opens the named file for reading only.
- `OpenFile` is a more generic approach that lets the user decide whether they want to open a file for writing or reading. Most of the time, you won't need it—a call to `Open` or `Create` should do the trick. However, there are two very specific cases in which it's useful. The first case is when you want to append data to a file, without discarding its contents. Using `Open` here wouldn't work (the `*File` would be in read-only), nor would `Create` (the file's contents would be erased). The second parameter of the `OpenFile` function is a flag controlling how we open the file. The full list can be found with `go doc os.O_APPEND`. These flags are constants and should be combined to your taste. When creating or appending, use `os.O_APPEND|os.O_CREATE|os.O_WRONLY`.

  The second case is when we want to create a file for which the rights aren't the `Create` default rights. `OpenFile` is the only one that enables you to set specific access rights to the file via its last parameter.

If there is an error for any of the three methods, it will be of type `*os.PathError`. Most of the time, we'll use `Open` and `Create`.

The constants in the `os` package are capitalized because they are part of the operating system standards. Otherwise, Go prefers constants to be defined in PascalCase, like everything else.

DEFER

When you've finished I/O operations with a `*File`, you *must* close it using the `Close()` method in your file. This way, system resources used by the file are released, and you don't create leaks with your program. If you don't close the descriptor, you may exhaust all available file handles of your system, and locking files has some complicated side effects on Windows, where you may end up blocking yourself from writing or deleting opened files. In theory, Go's garbage collector should close the file at some point (no later than when your program exits), but it's always better to know when and how the file descriptor is closed. In other words, be polite, and explicitly clean up after yourself.

How do we know when we're done with the operations? Usually, we're done by the end of the function, and that's where we would place the call to Close(). But imagine a case in which you have to refactor the function and remove a lot of the code. What if you accidentally remove the call to Close() or return before it's called? The best way to prevent the call to Close() from getting lost in the rest of the function is to keep it next to Open or Create.

In Go, the defer keyword postpones a statement's execution to the very end of the function, even if the defer appears at the beginning of it. The important point is that, whichever way a function returns, every defer the execution has been through will be executed. When a function returns, its deferred calls are executed in last-in, first-out order. Table 3.1 shows some simple examples.

Table 3.1 Program execution with and without defer

Examples	Code	Console output
| **Without defer** | ```go
package main

import "fmt"

func main() {
    fmt.Println("a bookworm")
    fmt.Println("you are")
}
``` | a bookworm<br>you are |
| **With defer** | ```go
package main

import "fmt"

func main() {
    defer fmt.Println("a bookworm")
    fmt.Println("you are")
}
``` | you are<br>a bookworm |
| **With two instances of defer** | ```go
package main

import "fmt"

func main() {
    defer fmt.Println("or not?")
    defer fmt.Println("a bookworm")
    fmt.Println("you are")
}
``` | you are<br>a bookworm<br>or not? |

In the case of os operations, the defer statement is located right after checking the error returned by Open. If you see a call to Open in the code, you must see the Close in the same code block; these two lines only make sense together.
```

The `defer` keyword is mostly used to close files, database connections, buffered readers, and so on. One of the Go libraries for the Kafka event manager uses `Close()` because the server needs a graceful disconnect to stop it from continuing to attempt to send messages to the connected clients. Sometimes, you'll find `defer` useful to compute the time spent inside a function.

Let's get back to our code. We want to open a file for reading. It may return an error that we have to deal with; in this case, we'll simply return it to the caller. Once this is done, we know that we have a valid file description, so we need to close the file. Let's update the `loadBookworms` function with the following code.

Listing 3.3   `bookworm.go`: **Opening a file**

```
f, err := os.Open(filePath)          ◄─── Opens the named file
if err != nil {                       ◄───
    return nil, err
}                                     Handles the error
defer f.Close()     ◄───
                    Defers the release
                    of resources
```

`io.Reader` and `io.Closer` are interfaces commonly used in Go packages, and `os.File` implements both of them. `io.Reader` enables reading a stream of data into a `slice` of bytes.

3.1.3   *Parse the JSON*

To parse some JSON data, we'll use the `encoding/json` package of Go. There's a good list of different encodings supported by Go's standard library's packages, including XML, CSV, and Base64. We'll discuss parsing in greater detail in chapter 6, when we start decoding responses from HTTP calls.

The structure of Go's standard library package doesn't represent a tree of dependencies but rather domains. Anything to do with the network will be in the `net` package or in a package nested in `net`. The `encoding` package is extremely lightweight—it only defines four interfaces—and we don't have to include it to make use of the contents of the `encoding/json` package.

DEFINING THE STRUCTURE ASSOCIATED WITH THE JSON FILE

The general idea is that the Go structure used for decoding must match the JSON structure. In our scenario, we have a list of people we call `Bookworms`, each with a `name` and a list of `Books`. To tell Go which JSON field corresponds to a field in our Go structures, we use tags, which are enclosed in backticks. Tags will contain the name of the standard followed by the name of the field there.

The type of the list of books here is called a `slice`, which we'll discuss very soon. For now, let's focus on the JSON first, as shown in the following listing.

Listing 3.4 `bookworm.go`: `Bookworm` **and** `Book` **structures**

```
// A Bookworm contains the list of books on a bookworm's shelf.
type Bookworm struct {
    Name  string `json:"name"`          ◀────────┐  Name of the person
    Books []Book `json:"books"`          ◀──────  │
}                                               └── List of books, as defined later

// Book describes a book on a bookworm's shelf.
type Book struct {
    Author  string `json:"author"`
    Title   string `json:"title"`
}
```

Look at the `json` tags. Each Go field is tagged with the name of the JSON field. Note that the name of the field doesn't have to match the name of the tag—it's simply a convention that makes it more readable. Here's another Go convention: fields that are `slices` should be named with a plural word.

Finally, one of the most important practices when using tags is to expose the field—the decoder we're about to code will need to write to the fields of our structure. For this, it needs to be able to "see" them, which means these fields must be exposed. Many an hour of debugging has been spent trying to understand why a field was always empty.

DECODING THE JSON FILE INTO A STRUCTURE

Once the file is opened and fully loaded, we can define a variable that will hold the information, as shown in listing 3.5. This variable must be a `slice` of `Bookworms` because this is what the `encoding/json` package is giving us. We then pass that variable's pointer to the decoder so that it can fill it up.

Remember, the alternative to passing a pointer is to pass a copy. The decoder would then fill up the copy and throw it away into the garbage collector, and we would be left empty handed.

Listing 3.5 `bookworm.go`: **JSON decoding in** `loadBookworms()`

```
var bookworms []Bookworm              ◀──────┐  Defines a slice of bookworms

// Decode the file and store the content in the value bookworms.
err = json.NewDecoder(f).              ◀──────┐  Creates a json decoder
    Decode(&bookworms)     ◀───────┐          │  around your data source
if err != nil {            ◀─────┐ │          
    return nil, err              │ │
}                                │ └── Decodes into the slice
                                 │
                                 └── If there is an error,
                                     simply returns it
```

Notice how we both created and used a decoder on a single line. We were able to do this thanks to `NewDecoder` returning only a `Decoder` (and no error). Because we don't use the decoder returned by `NewDecoder` anywhere else, it's common practice to avoid declaring a variable for it, unless something else dictates that we do (e.g., line length, meaning). Instead, we simply use NewDecoder by calling Decode.

There are a few more-refined ways of decoding big JSON inputs or files (e.g., via an explicit streaming mechanism that avoids loading the entire file's contents). You can look them up if you're curious in section 3.4.3, but for the project, we trust that your test file won't exceed a few megabytes.

After that, we just need to return the bookworms that were decoded. The finalized function should look something like the following listing.

Listing 3.6   bookworm.go: loadBookworms() parses the JSON file

```
// loadBookworms reads the file and returns the list of bookworms,
// and their beloved books, found therein.
func loadBookworms(filePath string) ([]Bookworm, error) {
    f, err := os.Open(filePath)          ◀── Opens the file for reading
    if err != nil {
        return nil, err
    }
    defer f.Close()                      ◀── Ensures we close the file

    // Initialize the type in which the file will be decoded.
    var bookworms []Bookworm

    // Decode the file and store the content in the variable bookworms.
    err = json.NewDecoder(f).Decode(&bookworms)   ◀── Decodes into an array
    if err != nil {                                    of bookworms
        return nil, err
    }

    return bookworms, nil
}
```

To make this whole file compile, you need to import the os and encoding/json packages. If you're using a clever enough editor, it may have done this for you.

Just before we write a test, as an early reward, we can manually check our example with a simple print. As shown in the following listing, call the loadBookworms function in your main function, give it the JSON file's path as a parameter, and print out the result.

Listing 3.7   main.go: Calling loadBookworms() in main()

```
package main

import (
    "fmt"
    "os"
)

func main() {
    bookworms, err := loadBookworms(
```

```
        "testdata/bookworms.json")
    if err != nil {
        _, _ = fmt.Fprintf(os.Stderr,
            "failed to load bookworms: %s\n", err)
        os.Exit(1)
    }

    fmt.Println(bookworms)
}
```

— **Passes the path to the JSON file**

— **Prints the error**

— **Exits with an error code**

— **Prints the output**

To run it, you can't use `go run main.go` anymore. Well, you can try, but you'll see Go is angry at you for calling an unknown function. This is because the `main` function makes a call to `loadBookworms`, a function that isn't declared in the `main.go` file nor in any of the packages that `main.go` imports. Indeed, `go run` won't look at files that weren't imported by the `main.go` file (why would it?). As a result, Go programs usually have a single file in the `main` package: `main.go`. Alternatively, it's possible to `go run` a package or a directory, rather than a single file. In this case, all files in that directory or package will be used for execution, and in our case, Go won't be angry at us anymore:

```
> go run .
```

The output is gibberish, but you can recognize the structure of the `slice` of `bookworms`:

```
[{Fadi [{Margaret Atwood The Handmaid's Tale} {Sylvia Plath The Bell Jar}]}
{Peggy [{Margaret Atwood Oryx and Crake} {Margaret Atwood The
Handmaid's Tale} {Charlotte Brontë Jane Eyre}]}]
```

This isn't the best UI, but it's enough for debugging.

3.1.4 Test It

How do we make sure this is going to work after future changes? One thing's for sure: executing a command and checking the results to see if the curly braces are in the correct position isn't sustainable.

Let's write a test for this function instead. The `testdata` folder is the perfect place to hold various JSON files with our different test cases. We're going to test an internal function that lies in the `bookworm.go` file, so we'll call our file `bookworms_internal_test.go` and write a test for `loadBookworms` named `TestLoadBookworms`.

The first step is to define the required parameters and returned values for our function. We'll need the path of a file in `testdata`, the expected result, which is a `slice` of `Bookworm`. Because we also test the unhappy path, we'll add whether we expect an error. For this chapter, we won't verify the exact type of the error but only the presence with a Boolean value.

Each test case can be the purpose of a different function, but this strategy is rarely extendable. Instead, we use a `map`, where the key is the name of the test for humans to understand what we want to test, and the value is a structure with all the values specific to our test case. We'll discuss `maps` further just after the test:

```
type testCase struct {
        bookwormsFile string
        want          []Bookworm
        wantErr       bool
}
tests := map[string]testCase{}
```

To keep the writing of the []Bookworm in test cases minimal, we can define books as global variables and reuse them over different tests. Global variables are usually not a good idea in code, but in tests, we want the handy solution, especially because files named *_test.go aren't accessible outside the package, even if you inadvertently name your variable with a capital letter:

```
var (
    handmaidsTale = Book {
        Author: "Margaret Atwood', Title: "The Handmaid's Tale",
    }
    oryxAndCrake = Book {
        Author: "Margaret Atwood", Title: "Oryx and Crake",
    }
)
```

Let's now write the test for the successful use case. We'll need a new JSON file, or we can reuse the existing one—whichever you prefer. Alternatively, you could steal those from our repository. We won't file a complaint.

We fill the expected result with the list of Bookworms, each bookworm's name, and the list of their books. Here's an example:

```
"file exists": {
    bookwormsFile: "testdata/bookworms.json",
    want: []Bookworm{
        {Name: "Fadi", Books: []Book{handmaidsTale, theBellJar}},
        {Name: "Peggy", Books: []Book{oryxAndCrake, handmaidsTale,
            janeEyre}},
    },
    wantErr: false,
}
```

We can identify at least two error cases: (1) if the indicated file doesn't exist, and (2) if the formatting of the file is invalid. Let's invent a file path that doesn't exist. You can probably fill in what the behavior of loadBookworms will be:

```
"file doesn't exist": {
    bookwormsFile: "testdata/no_file_here.json",
    want:          nil,
    wantErr:       true,
}
```

As you can see, the expected result is nil, as we expect an error because the opening of the file will fail early in the process, and we do want an error.

The second unhappy path that we can face is that if the file isn't valid, the format doesn't follow the JSON syntax rules (e.g., missing a bracket or a comma). In our test case, the file was truncated, so the file is missing its closing bracket (}). Again, we want to verify the presence of the returned error. Create a file in the `testdata` folder that has some invalid formatting, and write the corresponding test case:

```
"invalid JSON": {
    bookwormsFile: "testdata/invalid.json",
    want:          nil,
    wantErr:       true,
}
```

Easy, isn't it? We brushed over this in the previous chapter while writing table-driven tests, but to properly loop over the `map`, you'll need to know more about loops.

USING LOOPS IN GO

All loop syntaxes in Go use the keyword `for`—really, all of them—while other languages might use `while`, `foreach`, `for`, and so on. Let's consider a few examples.

First, we'll look at the classic `for`. There's nothing out of the ordinary here. We can count from a number to another number that we know:

```
for i := 0; i < 5; i++ {
for i := 0; i < arrayLength; i++ {
for i := firstIndex; i < limit; i++ {
```

As a side note, Go differs from some languages in its use of the postfix operators, `++` and `--`. In most languages, `i++` means "increment i by 1, and store that into i." The difference in Go as compared to other languages such as C++ or Java is that `i++` isn't an l-value. It isn't comparable to anything. We can't write `i++ < 5` or `fmt.Println(i++)` in Go. This also implies that Go doesn't have a prefix operator—we can't write `++i` to mean "increase the value of `i`, and return the increased value."

Let's look at the implementation in Go of the `while {Boolean}` syntax of other languages:

```
for iterator.Next() {
for line != lastLine {
for !gotResponse || response.invalid() {
```

Any Boolean expression is valid here; just make sure you don't end up in an infinite loop. If, on the other hand, you do need an infinite loop, there is a way to create one:

```
for {
```

This will go on and on—forever. Usually, these contain either a return, a break, or something that will exit the program entirely.

Finally, when we need to iterate over the items in an `array`, a `slice`, a `map`, or a channel, `for` can be paired with the keyword `range`. In the case of a `slice`—for example, the list of `Bookworms` we want to read from the file—`range` returns the index and a copy of the value at this index:

```
for i, bw := range bookworms {
```

At each iteration here, `i` will increase from 0 onward to `len(bookworms)-1`, and `bw` is the same as `bookworms[i]`. The main difference is that `bw` is a copy, so if you make changes to it, there will be no change to the contents of the `slice` itself, which can be a good or a bad thing, depending on what you expect. In the case of `maps`, like in our test, `range` simply returns a copy of the key and a copy of the value:

```
for name, testCase := range tests {
```

Before Go 1.20, the copies were made into the same variable, resulting in a few surprises when the variable was used in concurrent ways inside the loop. If you don't need one of the two parameters, you can ignore it in various ways. All of the following lines are valid; there's no difference between the second and third versions for the machine:

```
for _, bw := range bookworms
for i, _ := range bookworms
for i := range bookworms
```

Take the time to write the full test alone, and then compare your solution to the following listing.

Listing 3.8 `bookworms_internal_test.go:` Test `LoadBookworms()`

```
package main

import (
    "reflect"
    "testing"
)

var (
    handmaidsTale = Book{
        Author: "Margaret Atwood", Title: "The Handmaid's Tale",
    }
    oryxAndCrake = Book{Author: "Margaret Atwood", Title: "Oryx and Crake"}
    theBellJar   = Book{Author: "Sylvia Plath", Title: "The Bell Jar"}
    janeEyre     = Book{Author: "Charlotte Brontë", Title: "Jane Eyre"}
)

func TestLoadBookworms_Success(t *testing.T) {
    tests := map[string]struct {
        bookwormsFile string
        want          []Bookworm
        wantErr       bool
    }{
        "file exists": {
            bookwormsFile: "testdata/bookworms.json",
```

```
                want: []Bookworm{
                    {Name: "Fadi", Books: []Book{handmaidsTale, theBellJar}},
                    {Name: "Peggy", Books:
                        []Book{oryxAndCrake, handmaidsTale, janeEyre},
                    },
                },
                wantErr: false,
            },
            "file doesn't exist": {...},
            "invalid JSON": {...},
    }
    for name, testCase := range tests {
        t.Run(name, func(t *testing.T) {
            got, err := loadBookworms(testCase.bookwormsFile)
            if err != nil && !testCase.wantErr {
                t.Fatalf("expected an error %s, got none", err.Error())
            }

            if err == nil && testCase.wantErr {
                t.Fatalf("expected no error, got one %s", err.Error())
            }

            if !equalBookworms(got, testCase.want) {
                t.Fatalf("different result: got %v, expected %v",
                            got, testCase.want)
            }
        })
    }
}
```

Verifies the non-nil error value in a failure case

Verifies the nil error value in a successful case

Checks the obtained result against the desired one

What do we use to compare the expected Bookworms and the returned ones? The straightforward answer is to write an equal function to compare the content of two lists of Bookworms. We'll name the function equalBookworms. Let's see what it looks like in detail. First, the signature should be two lists of Bookworms; we'll name the one against which we want to check target. Because it's a utility function, we can specify to the compiler that it can be skipped and not to print line information by adding t.Helper() at the beginning of our helper function. To do so, we need to pass *testing.T as a parameter to equal, as shown in listing 3.9. We'll do the same for all the helpers in this chapter.

The content of the function consists of ranging over the bookworms and comparing each field: first the name, which is relatively straightforward, and then the books.

Listing 3.9 bookworms_internal_test.go: **Comparing** Bookworms

```
// equalBookworms is a helper to test the equality of two lists of Bookworms.
func equalBookworms(t *testing.T, bookworms, target []Bookworm) bool {
    t.Helper()

    if len(bookworms) != len(target) {
        return false
    }

    for i := range bookworms {
        if bookworms[i].Name != target[i].Name {
```

An early exit, as the numbers of the Bookworms are different

Verifies the name of the Bookworm

```
        return false
    }

    if !equalBooks(t,
        bookworms[i].Books, target[i].Books) {
        return false
    }
}

return true
}
```

Verifies the content of the collections of Books for each Bookworm

Everything is equal!

To compare the books, we can write a subfunction, `equalBooks`, encapsulating only the comparison of the books, which makes it easy to read and reuse (see listing 3.10). Regarding the implementation, don't forget that we can exit early by comparing the length of the two lists. Then, we can range over the books, compare the two lists, and return `false` if they are different.

Listing 3.10 `bookworms_internal_test.go`: A helper to compare `Books`

```
// equalBooks is a helper to test the equality of two lists of Books.
func equalBooks(t *testing.T, books, target []Book) bool {
    t.Helper()

    if len(books) != len(target) {
        return false
    }

    for i := range books {
        if books[i] != target[i] {
            return false
        }
    }

    return true
}
```

An early exit, as the numbers of Books are different

Verifies the content of the collections of Books for each Bookworm

Everything is equal!

Another way of doing this is using the standard package `reflect`, providing a simple but poorly performing function to compare interfaces: `reflect.DeepEqual`, which we'll explore later in the book. It's not recommended for production code because it's not designed for performance, but in our case, it will do the trick. Less code to write is always a good thing:

```
if !reflect.DeepEqual(got, testCase.want) {
    t.Fatalf("different result: got %v, expected %v", got, testCase.want)
}
```

We've now parsed an input JSON-structured file into a Go structure. This allows us to implement the second requirement—finding books that appear in more than one collection.

3.2 *Finding books that bookworms have in common*

Remember that the whole purpose of our tool is to find which books were read by both Fadi and Peggy or other bookworms. In this section, we'll go through all the bookworms' shelves, register books we find there, and then filter on those that appear more than once.

We'll write a function for that task called `findCommonBooks`. Let's write its signature first. As the following listing shows, it takes the data we have, which is a list of bookworms and their collections, and returns the books they have in common in the shape of a `slice` of `Book`.

Listing 3.11 `bookworm.go`: **The** `findCommonBooks()` **signature**

```
// findCommonBooks returns books that are on more than one bookworm's shelf.
func findCommonBooks(bookworms []Bookworm) []Book {
    return nil
}
```

How do we know that a book appears multiple times on shelves? Well, we need to count the number of occurrences of each book on all the bookworms' shelves, and when we find that a book has more than one occurrence, we know it's on multiple shelves.

But is that enough, really? What should we do if a single person has the same book more than once on their shelf? We, the authors, had a long conversation about that: Does it ever happen? Who has multiple copies of the same book? It turns out that one of us has the same novel series in three different languages. Another has different editions of the same book. The third was surprised.

Anyway, what do we do? Let's take for granted, for the time being, that each person's list only has one instance of each book to slightly simplify the algorithm.

3.2.1 *Count the books*

How do we count all the books? We have access to a `slice` of `Bookworms`, so we'll start there: looking at each bookworm's collection and "registering" each book we find there. To register a book, for now, we can use a counter representing the number of times that book has been seen on shelves so far.

> **NOTE** Go offers a limited number of built-in types: `arrays`, `slices`, `maps`, and, to a lesser extent, `channels`. These types are the core bricks that allow data collection. In Go, a `map` is an unordered associative `array` that contains pairs of keys and values. Each key is associated with a single value (but two keys could have the same value). `maps` are Go's idiomatic way of creating collections of unique keys, as we'll see in this chapter. The key of a `map` can be anything that is comparable. When in doubt, ask yourself this question: Can we write `key1 == key2`? Even though, at first sight, it might be easy to think everything is comparable in Go, the hard truth is that not everything is. `slices`, `maps`, and function types aren't, and this means any structure that contains a `slice`, `map`, or function type isn't. We'll face this soon enough.

WRITING TO A MAP

We have to store data inside our `map`. In Go, we associate the value `v` with the key `k` in the `map` with the following line:

```
myMap[k] = v
```

It's as simple as that.

READING FROM A MAP

Just like retrieving an item from a `slice` at index 3 is done with square brackets, retrieving an item from a `map` at key 3 looks exactly the same:

```
var mySlice []string
...
v := mySlice[3]

mapped := map[int]string{}
...
v := mapped[3]
```

The only difference is that a `map` will also return a Boolean, telling you whether it found the key. In the case of the `slice`, you know there is a value at index 3 as long as the length of the `slice` is at least 4 (yes, we still count from 0); otherwise, you're facing an error, leading to a `panic`. In the case of the `map`, if the key isn't found, the returned value is simply the zero value of its type—for `map[int]string`, this is the empty string `""` with the Boolean set to `false`:

```
v, ok := mapped[3]
if ok {...
```

Alternatively, you can write a more concise version by limiting the scope of the `v` variable to the scope of the `if` statement:

```
if v, ok := mapped[3]; ok {
    // do something with v
}
```

Now that we know how to access elements in a `map`, it's time to count the books. We'll do that next.

INIT COUNTER

The counter will be saved in a `map`, where the key is the book and the value is a `uint`, an unsigned integer. Although it can seem strange to have multiple copies of the same book (apparently), having fewer than zero copies is downright impossible.

The built-in `make` function creates a `map` (or `slice` or channel) by allocating memory for it. If we knew in advance the number of distinct books, say, 451, we could be explicit about the size of `map` we need. This would slightly optimize the execution:

```
count := make(map[Book]uint, 451)
```

These two lines have identical behaviors, and you can choose to be either explicit or concise:

```
count := make(map[Book]uint)
count := make(map[Book]uint, 0)
```

Now, let's fill up this counter. First, we need to iterate over our `Bookworms`. We'll use the `for` keyword that we described earlier. In this case, we'll make use of the value of the iterator, and we don't need the index. Let's give our iterator a bit more descriptive name than `bw`, though:

```
for _, bookworm := range bookworms {
}
```

Inside this loop, we can loop with the exact same syntax over the books this person has read:

```
for _, book := range bookworm.Books {
}
```

The key of our `map` is a `Book` structure. In Go, `maps` can have certain structures as their key. What matters here is that we need the structure to be hashable. Unlike in Java, Go's compiler doesn't need a `Hash` function—instead, it will know how to hash a structure to turn it into a valid key. Any type can be a `map` key as long as it's hashable. Types that aren't comparable also aren't hashable. A `slice`, for instance, isn't hashable, which means any structure that contains a `slice` can't be the key for a `map`. If you ever try to use a structure with a `slice` as a key, Go will let you know with the following compilation message: `invalid map key type`. Finally, we can increment the counter for this book:

```
count[book]++
```

But wait—we never set it to `0` in the first place. Should we set the counter to `1` if it's absent and only use `++` if it already exists? Well, no. We don't have to. Here comes the beauty of the zero value in Go.

You see, `count[book]` returns the value in the `map` at the index `book` or, if absent, the zero of the value type. Here, the value type is `uint`, so it means `0`.

As in most C-like languages, `a++` is just syntactic sugar for `a = a + 1`. If we replace `a` with `count[book]`, we first retrieve the value from the `map` or get `0` if it doesn't exist. Then, we add `1` and write back into the `map` in the same place.

This little counting logic is atomic enough that it would benefit from living in its own function. Let's call it `booksCount` and call it in `findCommonBooks()`. By now, it should look like the code in the following listing.

Listing 3.12   bookworm.go: **The** booksCount() **function**

```
// booksCount registers all the books and their occurrences
// from the bookworms shelves.
func booksCount(bookworms []Bookworm) map[Book]uint {
    count := make(map[Book]uint)          ◄─── Initializes the
                                               map counter
    for _, bookworm := range bookworms {   ◄─── Ranges over the
        for _, book := range bookworm.Books {   slice bookworms
            count[book]++                  ◄─── Increments the
        }                                       counter for each book
    }

    return count
}
```

Can we test this? It should be pretty straightforward.

TEST IT

Writing the test for this small function isn't particularly tricky. First, we can write a helper to compare the equality of two maps of books by verifying that the keys in the want map are present in what we got. Let's range over the want and call the key in got.

Listing 3.13   bookworms_internal_test.go: **Comparing** book **counts**

```
// equalBooksCount is a helper to test the equality of two maps of
// books count.
func equalBooksCount(t *testing.T, got, want map[Book]uint) bool {
    t.Helper()
                                               If the lengths are different,
    if len(got) != len(want) {        ◄─── the maps are different.
        return false
    }
                                                  Ranges over the map of
    for book, targetCount := range want {  ◄─── books count targeted
        count, ok := got[book]             ◄───
        if !ok || targetCount != count {   ◄───   Retrieves the count value
            return false        ◄───                 and the Boolean attesting
        }                  Exits early in the        the presence of the key
    }                      comparison
                                               Either Book is not found, or
    return true   ◄─── The two maps are equal.    the count values are different.
}
```

Note that, in this version, the nil and empty map are considered equal. Now that the helper is written, let's move to the longest part—think of all the test cases. The first test case is the nominal use case, and the second is having no bookworms at all, as shown in listing 3.14. There is also the case in which one bookworm has no books (probably not a real bookworm or at least a very unhappy person). Again, write the tests alone, and compare your solution.

Listing 3.14 `bookworms_internal_test.go`: **Testing** `booksCount`

```go
func TestBooksCount(t *testing.T) {
    tt := map[string]struct {
        input []Bookworm
        want  map[Book]uint
    }{
        "nominal use case": {
            input: []Bookworm{
                {Name: "Fadi", Books: []Book{
                    handmaidsTale, theBellJar,
                }},
                {Name: "Peggy", Books:
                    []Book{oryxAndCrake, handmaidsTale, janeEyre}},
            },
            want: map[Book]uint{
                handmaidsTale: 2,
                theBellJar: 1,
                oryxAndCrake: 1,
                janeEyre: 1},
        },
        "no bookworms": {
            input: []Bookworm{},
            want:  map[Book]uint{},
        },
        "bookworm without books": {...},
        "bookworm with twice the same book": {...},
    }

    for name, tc := range tt {
        t.Run(name, func(t *testing.T) {
            got := booksCount(tc.input)
            if !equalBooksCount(t, tc.want, got) {
                t.Fatalf(
                    "got a different list of books: %v, expected %v",
                    got, tc.want)
            }
        })
    }
}
```

Reuses the Books defined as a global variable earlier

An empty map is the same as when initialized.

Call to the helper equalsBooksCount()

Launch the tests. Everything is passing? Good, this means we can use the `booksCount` function.

We'll now add the call into a new function called `findCommonBooks`. Let's start with the bare bones of the code.

Listing 3.15 **bookworm.go:** `findCommonBooks()` **with** `booksCount()` **call**

```go
// findCommonBooks returns books that are on more than one bookworm's shelf.
func findCommonBooks(bookworms []Bookworm) []Book {
    booksOnShelves := booksCount(bookworms)

    return nil
}
```

Calls the counting function

Note that it shouldn't compile because we're not using the `booksOnShelves` variable for the moment. But it's time to use it!

3.2.2 *Keeping higher occurrences*

Now that we've counted the number of copies of each book on every bookshelf, the next step is to loop over all of them and keep those with more than one copy. Let's declare a `slice` that will contain all the books that were found multiple times in the collections of all bookworms:

```
var commonBooks []Book
```

```
return commonBooks
```

We could use the built-in `make` function again. But how?

WHAT IS A SLICE, AND WHAT IS AN ARRAY?

We keep using the word `slice` for a list of values of the same type. Many languages would simply call this an `array`, so what is the deal? Is it just a fancy new word? You already know how to range over a `slice`, but there is a bit of theory required at this point.

The type `[n]T` is an `array` of n values of type `T`. For example, `var a [5]string` declares a variable a as an `array` of five strings. The length of an `array` is part of its type, so `arrays` can't be resized, which is very limiting. In real life, we practically never use `arrays` directly.

A `slice` is a "dynamically sized, flexible view into the elements of an `array`," as described by the Go official website. The type `[]T` is a `slice` of elements of type `T`, built upon an `array`. As you can see, we don't specify its size.

`slices` have three fields that any developer needs to know about: the underlying `array`, stored as a pointer; the length of the `slice`; and the capacity of a `slice`. The length is the number of elements present in the `slice`, whereas the capacity is the number of elements that can be stored before a reallocation is necessary. You can get them via the `len` and `cap` built-in functions and set them when you initialize the `slice` with `make`. Note that maintaining the length as fields makes accessing this information an $O(1)$ operation.

The last very useful thing you can do to a `slice` is to append an item using the built-in append function. Let's look at some examples:

```
var books []Book
books = append(books, Book{...})
```

At first, the capacity and length are both `0`, the `slice` is `nil`, and the underlying `array` isn't initialized. After we append, the number of items in the `slice` is one, so `len(books)` is `1`. That's easy; the slice isn't `nil` anymore. But what's trickier is that the new `array` we point to has a capacity of one element.

Note that `append` returns a `slice`. We cover what happens internally in appendix E, but for now, the important message is that when appending to a `slice`, it's always safe to override the extended `slice` with `append`'s output.

Let's look at another example of a `slice` initialization, where we create a `slice` with a length of 5, a capacity of 5, and an underlying `array` of 5 zero-value `books`:

```
books := make([]Book, 5)
books[1].Author = "bell hooks"
```

All five books are created and zeroed, which means we can access them directly and write into them. In addition, if we `append` a `Book` to this `slice`, it will appear in sixth position, after the five zero-value `books` already there. Finally, if we know the final size of the `slice` but want to use `append`, we can specify both the initial length and the necessary capacity:

```
books := make([]Book, 0, 5)
```

Now that we know how to create `slices`, let's look at the code we've written so far. In section 3.1.3, we decoded the JSON message describing the bookshelves into a `slice` variable declared with the `var` syntax we just covered. We didn't perform a call to `make`, so we didn't cause any allocation. The trick was that we passed the address of the `slice` to the `Decode` function, which could then fill it with values. We explore the mysteries of passing a `slice` by address or by copy in appendix E.

RANGE OVER A MAP

To fill the `slice`, we need to loop over the `map` `booksOnShelves` returned by `booksCount()` and check the value of the counter for each book. Books with a counter larger than 1 were read by at least two bookworms—in our case, both Fadi and Peggy:

```
for book, count := range booksOnShelves {
    if count > 1 {
        commonBooks = append(commonBooks, book)
    }
}
```

The following listing shows the full code of the `findCommonBooks` function.

Listing 3.16 `bookworm.go`: **Implementing** `findCommonBooks()`

```
// findCommonBooks returns books that are on more than one bookworm's shelf.
func findCommonBooks(bookworms []Bookworm) []Book {
    booksOnShelves := booksCount(bookworms)        ◄──┐ Registers the count
                                                      │ of each book
    var commonBooks []Book

    for book, count := range booksOnShelves {      ◄──┘ Ranges over the books
        if count > 1 {                             ◄──┐ Keeps only if found
                                                      │ more than once
```

```
        commonBooks = append(commonBooks, book)
        }
    }

    return commonBooks
}
```

Testing this should be quite easy. Our input will be a list of bookworms, and our output should be a list of books. Some test cases are simple enough to write without our help:

- Everyone has read the same books.
- People have completely different lists.
- More than two bookworms have a book in common.
- One bookworm has no books (oh the sadness!).
- Nobody has any books (oh the agony!).

Listing 3.17 shows our version of the test. Run your test, and then run it again a few times. Do you notice something strange?

Listing 3.17 bookworms_internal_test.go: Testing findCommonBooks()

```
func TestFindCommonBooks(t *testing.T) {
    tt := map[string]struct {
        input []Bookworm
        want  []Book
    }{
        "no common book": {
            input: []Bookworm{
                {Name: "Fadi", Books: []Book{handmaidsTale, theBellJar}},
                {Name: "Peggy", Books: []Book{oryxAndCrake, janeEyre}},
            },
            want: nil,
        },
        "one common book": {...},
        "three bookworms have the same books on their shelves": {...},
    }

    for name, tc := range tt {
        t.Run(name, func(t *testing.T) {
            got := findCommonBooks(tc.input)
            if !equalBooks(t, tc.want, got) {        ◄──  Calling equalBooks(),
                t.Fatalf(                                  implemented earlier
                "got a different list of books: %v, expected %v",
                got, tc.want)
            }
        })
    }
}
```

3.2.3   *Determinism*

If you run your code a few times, you'll see that the order of the output keeps changing. The output might not always be in the expected order described in the `slice []` want.

When we loop over a `map`, Go doesn't guarantee the keys and values will be returned in a specific order. Depending on the situation, it can be better to be deterministic and always return the same result in the same order. It simplifies the testing, for one thing.

In this case, sorting the `slice` of `books` will make our lives easier. The `sort` package has a `Slice` function especially tailored for this situation: it takes a `slice` and a function. The function returns whether the item at the first of two indices must appear before the item at the second index. We can use an anonymous function defined at the level of this call because it's easier to evolve than to name it somewhere else. For now, we'll sort books by author and then title. If, at some later point, you want to sort by title first and then author, this is the place.

> **DEFINITION**   An *anonymous function* is defined without a name and is often used as an inline or temporary piece of code. In Go, anonymous functions are particularly useful when you need to pass a function as an argument or execute a small block of code immediately, without declaring it separately. For example, they are frequently used in sort functions or for defining short, task-specific logic in closures.

As the sorting logic isn't part of the algorithm to find common books, we prefer to put it in a different function. In the following listing, we put it in a function that wraps the call to `sort.Slice`.

Listing 3.18   `bookworm.go:` **Sorting the books**

```go
// sortBooks sorts the books by Author and then Title.
func sortBooks(books []Book) []Book {
    sort.Slice(books, func(i, j int) bool {        // The second parameter of sort.Slice is a function.
        if books[i].Author != books[j].Author {
            return books[i].Author < books[j].Author    // Compares strings with < for UTF order
        }
        return books[i].Title < books[j].Title
    })

    return books
}
```

Note that the original `slice` is modified, and the `sort.Slice` function doesn't create a sorted copy of the `array`. This can be good or bad, depending on the situation. This function's signature could be `sortBooks([]Book)` with no return value. We'll cover the details in appendix E.

NOTE   Because we mentioned runes in chapter 2, here is a disclaimer: using <
to compare strings will look at the UTF encoding of the titles. Therefore, Greek
titles, for example, will always appear after those written with Latin characters.

To use our sorting function, we just need to wrap the returning value of
`findCommonBooks`:

```
return sortBooks(commonBooks)
```

Testing will now become much easier. You may need to fix the order of the expected
results, but you can now automate your test and rely on it. Our code is now tested, and
we can return to `main.go` to print out the result.

3.3   *Print*

Back in the `main` function, we've loaded the data and nothing more. Let's call `find-`
`CommonBooks`. We now have a slice of books that we need to display correctly.
`fmt.Println` is nice, but we need to loop over the collection of `books`.

Let's write a function that prints out a list of `books`. You should be able to do it in five
lines of code.

Listing 3.19   `bookworms.go`: `displayBooks`

```
// displayBooks prints out the titles and authors of a list of books
func displayBooks(books []Book) {
    for _, book := range books {
        fmt.Println("-", book.Title, "by", book.Author)
    }
}
```

If you want to test this, you have to either write an `Example` or provide an `io.Writer`.
You'll see how to provide writers in chapter 4. We can now implement the third feature—printing the books—into the `main` function,.

Listing 3.20   `main.go`: The `main` function

```
func main() {
    bookworms, err := loadBookworms("testdata/bookworms.json")
    if err != nil {
        _, _ = fmt.Fprintf(os.Stderr, "failed to load bookworms: %s\n", err)
        os.Exit(1)
    }

    commonBooks := findCommonBooks(bookworms)

    fmt.Println("Here are the books in common:")
    displayBooks(commonBooks)
}
```

Before automating the test, let's run the program manually:

```
> go run .
```

> **Side quest**
>
> Use the flag from chapter 2, section 2.4, listing 2.17, to pass the file path as a parameter to your program.

You already know how to write an `Example` test. Feel free to play around with different book lists!

Listing 3.21 `main_internal_test.go`: **Testing** `main`

```go
package main

func Example_main() {
    main()
    // Output:
    // Here are the common books:
    // - The Handmaid's Tale by Margaret Atwood
}
```

3.4 Improvements

As we approach the end of this chapter, let's take a step further and explore how we can enhance the functionality of our program. These improvements focus on making the code more flexible and idiomatic, showcasing techniques that can be applied to broader projects. By refining how we handle sorting and optimizing file operations, we'll not only make our code more efficient but also learn valuable patterns to use in our future Go development.

3.4.1 Implement sort.Interface

To sort the books in the output of the `main` function, we used `sort.Slice`, which takes a function as the sorting strategy. There is a second option, which you may prefer. The `sort` package provides `sort.Interface`, which can be implemented to sort `slices` or user-defined collections. It becomes very handy when implementing custom sorting—in our case, by author and title. The `sort.Interface` interface exposes three methods where elements are referenced by an integer index. Note that you need to fully implement the interface, all three methods, even if you're not using all of them:

```go
// Len is the number of elements in the collection.
Len() int

// Less reports whether the element with index i
```

```
// must sort before the element with index j.
Less(i, j int) bool

// Swap swaps the elements with indexes i and j.
Swap(i, j int)
```

As this only applies to collections, we add an intermediate custom type representing a collection of Books and implement the methods on it. This type is named after the way it sorts. The following listing shows the implementation of sort.Interface with type byAuthor.

Listing 3.22 Implementing sort.Interface on Books

```
// byAuthor is a list of Book.
// Defining a custom type to implement sort.Interface
type byAuthor []Book

// Len implements sort.Interface by returning the length of the BookByAuthor.
func (b byAuthor) Len() int { return len(b) }          ◄──┐  Implements Len

// Swap implements sort.Interface and swaps two books.
func (b byAuthor) Swap(i, j int) {
    b[i], b[j] = b[j], b[i]              ◄──┐  Implements Swap by Book type
}

// Less implements sort.Interface and
// returns books sorted by Author and then Title.
func (b byAuthor) Less(i, j int) bool {
    if b[i].Author != b[j].Author {             ◄──┐  Orders by Author if
        return b[i].Author < b[j].Author              they are different
    }
    return b[i].Title < b[j].Title         ◄──┐  Orders by Title if
}                                                they are identical
```

The new function sortBooks can now directly call the sort.Sort implementation. It's important to note that sort.Sort doesn't return anything. Instead, it updates the contents of the slice with the same elements but in a sorted order (you can find the full code in the repository):

```
// sortBooks sorts the books by Author and then Title in alphabetical order.
func sortBooks(books []Book) []Book {
    sort.Sort(byAuthor(books))
    return books
}
```

3.4.2   *Exercise: Reading recommendations*

Now that you've gathered everybody's data, you can do some cheap data analysis. Knowing what books both your friend reads and you read is a good conversation starter, but we can go deeper. Let's write a program that will suggest a reading list from what other like-minded people read and hopefully liked. This should be something like the "Other Readers Bought" section of an online bookshop, even though buying, reading, and liking are three very different things.

In this section, we'll go for a simplified approach: assuming our bookworms only keep books on their shelves they appreciate. We don't know what happens to other books, but we hope they are traded for even more books or given to charity. We can assume, from now on, that books on a shelf are beloved and cherished, and for this reason, we'll take the shortcut of assuming that if Fadi has kept the same book on her shelf as Peggy did, she might be interested in what other books Peggy has kept on hers.

For each reader, we go through all other bookworms and retrieve the list of books they have read. This allows us to make a list of books, "similar" to every given book (shown in listing 3.23) when they appear on any bookshelf, compute a like-mindedness (or similarity) score. Then, if the similarity is greater than zero, we can add that score to each book that wasn't read by the target reader but was read by a similar person. Sometimes, writing in code can be clearer.

Listing 3.23 `recommendations.go`: **A possible implementation**

```go
func recommendOtherBooks(bookworms []Bookworm) []Bookworm {
    sb := make(bookRecommendations)

    // Register all books on everyone's shelf.
    for _, bookworm := range bookworms {
        for i, book := range bookworm.Books {
            otherBooksOnShelves :=
                listOtherBooksOnShelves(i, bookworm.Books)     // Lists the other books on the shelf
            registerBookRecommendations(
                sb, book, otherBooksOnShelves)                 // Marks these other books as similar to this one
        }
    }

    // Recommend a list of related books to each bookworm.
    recommendations := make([]Bookworm, len(bookworms))
    for i, bookworm := range bookworms {
        recommendations[i] = Bookworm{
            Name:  bookworm.Name,
            Books: recommendBooks(sb, bookworm.Books),         // Retrieves the list of books similar to those of that bookworm
        }
    }

    return recommendations
}
```

We need a type for the books read by our target. It must be able to quickly tell us whether it contains a book and make sure each book is only contained once:

```go
type set map[Book]struct{}

func (s set) Contains(b Book) bool {
```

```
    _, ok := s[b]
    return ok
}
```

Storing in a map, as we saw, is the best (i.e., fastest) way to tell whether the list (of keys) contains a given value. We're using the empty struct rather than, say, a Boolean because a Boolean takes up 1 bit of memory and the empty struct takes 0. This means the map won't take up more memory than a slice of the same size. Take your time to write, test, and play around with the rest of the code.

3.4.3   *Using bufio to open a file*

The first step we took in this chapter was to read the contents of a file. Let's take a closer look at how we did this. We first opened the file, which returned a file descriptor that implements the io.Reader interface:

```
f, err := os.Open(filePath)
if err != nil {...}
defer f.Close()
```

We then provided this reader to the json.NewDecoder function, and from that point on, the magic happened in the Decode method of the json package:

```
var bookworms []Bookworm

err = json.NewDecoder(f).Decode(&bookworms)
if err != nil {...}
```

But do we know how the reading actually happens? Accessing files, either for reading or for writing, makes system calls. System calls are at the junction between our program and the operating system. System calls are expensive, and we usually want to reduce their number, which, fortunately, is controllable when reading or writing a file.

First, we need to understand the problem: How many system calls do we go through when reading a 10 MiB file with our current implementation? The answer isn't obvious; it's hidden in the default buffer size of the file descriptor returned by os.Open, and we have no say in its value. Even worse, the os.File type is OS specific. So how can we improve this?

The answer lies in the bufio package, which provides a NewReaderSize function with the following description: "NewReaderSize returns a new Reader whose buffer has at least the specified size. If the argument io.Reader is already a Reader with large enough size, it returns the underlying Reader." This means if we call NewReaderSize with any io.Reader and give it a size of 1 MiB, we're guaranteed that the reading will happen by making system calls with chunks of 1 MiB. This way, we're able to tinker with our program to make it behave exactly as we want. Note that finding the best size for the buffer of a reader isn't an easy task—giving it 1 GiB would obviously make system calls less frequent, but it would also consume 1 GiB of memory that, perhaps, isn't fully used.

Let's make use of this nice feature and decide that our buffer should be of "an average size" for a file, something in the megabyte range. The following listing shows an example.

Listing 3.24 Reading a file with a buffered reader

```
f, err := os.Open(...)
if err != nil { ... }
defer f.Close()

buffedReader := bufio.NewReaderSize(f, 1024*1024)      ◄─── 1 MiB
// bufio.Reader doesn't implement Closer
decoder := json.NewDecoder(buffedReader)
err = decoder.Decode(...)
```

Finally, the `bufio` package also offers an implementation of `io.Writer`. The latter is obviously very useful when writing files, as it drastically reduces the number of system calls. Instead of writing line-by-line entries to a CSV file, we could be working with batches of 1 MiB.

But there's a very important point to keep in mind here: the `bufio.Write` method will only write data when its internal buffer is full. Most of the time, the last call to `bufio.Write` won't precisely fill the remainder of its buffer, and this last chunk could be lost! But don't panic. There is a way to flush the remaining bytes from the buffer to its destination, and it consists of making a simple call to `writer.Flush()`:

```
f, err := os.Create(...)
if err != nil { ... }
defer f.Close()

buffedWriter := bufio.NewWriter(f,1024*1024)      ◄─── 1 MiB
for _, data := contents {
  _, err = buffedWriter.Write(data)
  if err != nil { ... }
}

err = buffedWriter.Flush()      ◄─── Don't forget to flush
if err != nil { ... }                the remaining data!
```

Summary

- The JSON format is commonly used when representing structured data. It can hold `slices`, `maps`, and objects.
- The `encoding/json` package exposes two ways of decoding a JSON message: the `json.Decoder` type and the `json.Unmarshal` function. Most of the time, the `json.Decoder` should be used, as it can read from an `io.Reader` rather than from a complete `slice` of bytes. The `encoding/json` package also offers similar functions to encode a JSON message: `json.Encoder` and `json.Marshal`.

- Fields of Go structures must be exported if something has to be decoded into them, so the decoder can access them.

- Test data should live in a folder named `testdata`, which will be automatically ignored by the `go` tool when compiling the code.

- In Go, all loops are `for` loops; the keyword can be followed by a variety of different syntaxes. The most common are `for i := min; i < limit; i++ {`; and `for condition() {`.

- To loop over values stored in a `slice` or an `array`, use the `for index, value := range mySlice {` syntax. The `index` will start at `0`, and its last value will be `len(values)-1`. If you don't really need the index, you can iterate over the values with `for _, value := mySlice values {`. From time to time, you'll see the following syntax: `for index := range mySlice {`. In this case, only the index is retrieved. This can sometimes be useful, as it doesn't cause each value of the `slice` to be copied.

- To loop over all pairs of keys and values stored in a `map`, we again use the `for` keyword: `for key, value := range myMap {`. If you're only interested in values, you can, like we did with the `slice`, use `for _, value := range myMap {`. If, on the other hand, you're only interested in the keys of the `map`, then it's even shorter: `for key := range map {`.

- `Slices` are an abstraction of `arrays`. When in doubt, use `slices`.

- You can sort `slices` with the `sort` package one of two ways. First, you can give a sorting function as a parameter to `sort.Slice`. Alternatively, you can implement the package's `Interface`, which consists of a `Len` function that returns the length of the `slice`, a `Swap` function that permutes two entries, and a `Less` function that returns the comparison of two entries.

- The key of a `map` can be an `int`, a `string`, or even a `struct`. When it's a structure, the structure can't contain a pointer, a `slice`, a `map`, a channel, a function, or a field of type `interface{}`. Indeed, these types can't be compared with other values.

- If you want to discard repeated values from a `slice`—for instance, you want to have the list of bands that appear in your collection of CDs—you can use a `map[X] struct{}`. Iterate through your list, and write the elements you want to keep into the `map`. In the music example, we'd write `myMap[cd.Band] = struct{}{}`. At the end of the loop, the keys of the `map` will be the unique values you had in your original list.

- When you want to know whether an element appears in a `slice`, and you know you'll do the operation so many times that you can't afford to iterate through the `slice` every time, you can use `map[X]bool`. Start by adding keys to this `map` by iterating over your list once, and set their value to `true`. After that, you can check whether an element is in the `map` by running `found := myMap[element]`. If it was initially in the `slice`, then the value returned is `true`—what we set it to—and if the element wasn't in the `slice`, the value returned is the zero value of a Boolean: `false`.

- Remember to call `Close()` when you `Open` or `Create` a file. The `defer` keyword is your friend here.

- Use `defer` to keep together the code lines that make sense together but need to be executed at different moments.

- Using a `bufio.Reader` or a `bufio.Writer` will reduce the number of system calls your program executes and make it simpler to count such system calls.

- When using a `bufio.Writer`, always keep in mind that you must `Flush` the buffer before the data can be considered fully written.

A log story:
Creating a library

This chapter covers

- Implementing a three-level logger
- Using an integer-based new type to create an
  enum
- Publishing a library with a stable exported API
- Implementing external and internal testing
- Package-level exposition

It's late at night. You and your colleague Susan have been working on trying to fix a bug for 2 hours straight. You don't understand what's happening with a certain count variable that should have the value 1, but the result of the program seems to indicate that the value there is 2 instead. You try to read the code, but the problem isn't obvious to your tired eyes. Is count really 2? You decide to add a small line in the code and relaunch everything to get a better idea of what's going on. The line you add will help you at least understand what the variable's value is. You use

```
fmt.Printf("counting entries, current value is %d\n", count)
```

We've all been there. Having the code say something we can understand at specific steps is our easiest way of following the program as it executes.

Then, Susan notes, "Wouldn't it have been nice to have this information from the initial run, without needing to redeploy updated code?" But then, would we also want to deploy this unconditional `fmt.Printf`? (Hint: The answer is absolutely not.) Were there other options that could have made our life simpler?

Debugging isn't the only time we want to know what's happening in the guts of our program. It's also valuable to inform the user that "Everything is going extremely well. " (for you *2001, A Space Odyssey* fans), or that something bad has happened, but the system recovered. Any trace of what's happening might be useful, but that's also a lot of messages, and some aren't as important as others.

Keeping track of the current state or events via readable messages is called *logging*. Every piece of tracked information is a *log*, and *to log* is the associated action.

What is a logger?

In computer science, a *logger* is in charge of noting down log messages (an activity called *logging*, as mentioned earlier). Historically, a log relates to a ship's logbook, a document in which records of the speed and progress of the ship were written.

The logbook's name derives from a *chip log*, a piece of wood attached to a string that was tossed into the water to measure the speed of the vessel. The string had knots, at regular intervals, and measuring speed consisted of counting the number of knots that were unrolled during a given amount of time.

Every application needs a logger to write messages at specific moments in its execution so that they can be read and analyzed later, if necessary. Depending on the scenario, we'll want these messages to be written to a file, written to the standard output, written to a printer, or streamed through the network to an aggregating tool, such as a database.

However, not all messages carry the same amount of information. For example, "Everything is going extremely well" is very different from "I just picked up a fault in the AE-35 unit." We might want to emphasize critical messages or discard those of lesser importance. Humans have emphasized text with a higher degree of importance since at least ancient Egypt, where scribes would highlight specific sections of text by writing them in red (this is where the word *rubric* originates).

This chapter covers a specific need: write a piece of code that other projects can use. It's extremely common, as a programmer, to use existing code that we didn't write. As you can imagine, it would be painfully tiresome to write simple functions, such as `cosine` or `ToUpper`, over and over again, when they've already been written, thoroughly tested, and documented. Instead of copying and pasting code written by others, developers created *libraries*—code you can use but didn't write. In Go, libraries come in the shape of packages that we import. Go libraries are, of course, written in Go and are made of (always) exported and (almost always) unexported types and functions. The exported part of the library (both functions and types) is called its *application program-ming interface* (API).

Now, let's write a library that anyone can use and that you can reuse in any of your future projects. Susan will take care of the user code, and she'll interact with our code via its API. First, we want to define the API—exported functions and types—and agree with any already identified users that it covers their needs. Then, we'll be able to publish the API, even before implementing the logic. The sooner your library is out in the world, the sooner you can get feedback and improve it. Finally, we'll write the logging functions and test them. This project requires the following:

- A library that enables the user to log information of any type
- A library that makes available functions with signatures resembling that of `fmt` `.Printf`
- The ability for users to set the threshold of importance for logging messages from their code
- The ability for users to choose where logs are written

4.1 Defining the API

Defining the way a caller interacts with a library is essential for making it stable and easy to use. To make our users happy, the exported types and functions should have the following characteristics:

- *Easy to grasp*—People don't want to spend hours trying to figure out how to use our types and functions. To achieve this, making it small and simple is usually the better option: there should only be a single function to achieve each specific functionality.
- *Stable*—If you make evolutions, fix bugs, or add functionalities, users should be able to take the latest version without changing their own code.

What we'll export is an object that provides different methods to address criticality. For this, we'll first define the different importance levels of logging. Then, our library will provide an object and a function to create it. These tools will be implemented in a package.

4.1.1 Package summary

Go applications are organized in packages (i.e., collections of source files located in the same directory, each declaring the same package name). Go's convention states that the name of the package is the same as the name of the directory. As an example, we've used the `fmt` package in the previous chapter—it's located in Go's sources, in a directory named `fmt`.

In Go, packages are the way we isolate the scope of functions and types. As previously mentioned, when a symbol's name starts with an uppercase letter, it's visible outside the package. Exported symbols are available to users, and the rest remain inside the package. If you know Java, the package has roughly the same level of importance as a Java class as far as what you can do with it, but it's similar to a Java package in that it gathers together related types. What is public or exported should change as little as possible from version to version. This is especially important for packages intended to be consumed by other people. We want to preserve backward compatibility and avoid breaking our users' code. If you want to improve performance or fix bugs, what is private or unexported can change.

Rules of a Go package

The following rules apply to Go packages:

- A package is a collection of files located in the same folder that all share the same package name. Each Go file starts with the package declaration.
- It's customary to name the package after the name of the directory.
- Avoid overly long names if possible; a lowercase single word is best. If you compress the word, avoid abbreviations that make the package name more ambiguous.
- Any symbol (functions, types, variables, constants, etc.) starting with an uppercase letter will be exported outside the package and can be used by other packages, while those starting with a lowercase letter will not.
- Both camelCase and PascalCase are conventions used for functions, variables, constants, and types. Package names remain in lowercase.

Before you start coding, don't forget to `go mod init learngo-pockets/logger` your module. See appendix A, section A.4, if you've forgotten how.

> **DEFINITION** A *module* is a collection of Go packages stored in a file tree with a `go.mod` file at its root. The `go.mod` file defines the module's module path, which is also the import path used for the root directory, and its dependency requirements, which are the other modules needed for a successful build. Each dependency requirement is written as a module path and a specific version.

Create a folder named `pocketlog`. The name of the package reflects its purpose. In the `pocketlog` folder, create a file named `logger.go`. The name of the file should explicitly describe its contents. Here is a `tree` output command to help you understand the organization:

```
> tree
.
├── go.mod
└── pocketlog
    └── logger.go
```

In the `logger.go` file, we add the `Logger` struct, as shown in listing 4.1. Before we can start adding fields or methods to it, we need to think about the logging levels we want to support.

```
package pocketlog

// Logger is used to log information.
type Logger struct {
}
```

4.1.2 *Exporting the supported levels*

When using a logger, it's mandatory to assign an importance level to a message. This is the task of the user, who must determine how critical the information about to be recorded is. Loggers around the world have a wide variety of levels, which always follow the same pattern: they start with those of the lowest importance (usually `Trace` or `Debug`) and progress to those of greatest importance (usually `Error` or `Fatal`). The number of different log levels varies from project to project, but these three are quite common:

- `Debug`—Used by developers to help monitor any information (e.g., which way a message went, how long it took to process a request, or the URL of the request). It's usually used to print the contents of a single variable. In a production environment, we don't print `Debug` messages.
- `Info`—Used to track meaningful information (e.g., "Payment of amount X from account Y received").
- `Error`—Used when something goes wrong, before we try to recover. `Error` logs provide messages that are useful to help the maintainers investigate the source of problems (e.g., "Database not responding" or "Processing request would cause a division by 0").

We can declare these levels as an enumeration. The levels comprise a finite and defined list of possible values.

> **A matter of file size**
>
> Don't be afraid to keep your files small. When a type begins supporting more and more methods, think about splitting them into multiple files—the scope for declaring methods on a type or accessing its unexported fields is the package in which this type is declared. You can split by usage and business logic or keep exported methods together, for example. Make sure reading your file doesn't get overwhelming. Incidentally, spreading the code across several files reduces conflicts in your version control.

Create a file named `level.go`. Again, the first line of this file is the package we're developing: `package pocketlog`. Considering the targeted size of this new file, we could very well keep everything in the `logger.go` file, but we find it easier to open a file named `level` when looking for levels.

In this file, we declare a named type `Level` of the underlying type `byte`. We could use `int32` as an underlying type, as all we want is a number, but this would take four times more memory for no good reason. Other packages can use the type `Level`, as it's exported:

```
type Level byte
```

Wait! Experience and code reviews will tell you something is wrong. Any exported symbol requires a line of documentation—a commented sentence that starts with the name of the type, function, or constant you're documenting. Let's fix this:

```
// Level represents an available logging level.
type Level byte
```

Once we have a type for our levels, we can export them. Logging levels are constants that we declare as an *enumeration*—a finite list of entities of the same kind. This list of `Level`s belongs in the `level.go` file:

```
const (
    // LevelDebug represents the lowest level of log, mostly used for
    // debugging purposes.
    LevelDebug Level = iota
    // LevelInfo represents a logging level that contains information
    // deemed valuable.
    LevelInfo
    // LevelError represents the highest logging level, only to be used
    // to trace errors.
    LevelError
)
```

> **NOTE** The syntax here is to use `= iota` to let the compiler know we're starting an enumeration. `iota` allows us to create a sequence of numbers incremented on each line. We don't need to assign explicit values to these constants; the compiler does it automatically for us thanks to the `iota` syntax. `iota` can be used on any type that is based on an integer. The `iota`'s behavior is to increase on every line, which means we need to sort our levels by order of importance.

We now have three log levels, and each has its own purpose. If we decide to add a level later, we'll only need to add a line, without worrying about renumbering everything. Feel free to add more, such as `Warn` (between `Info` and `Error`) or `Fatal` (guess where).

4.1.3 Object-oriented Go: "GoOOP"?

Object-oriented programming (OOP) is a paradigm based on entities (the objects) that usually contain data (the fields or attributes). OOP is a common paradigm among backend languages—Java, C++, and Python are among its most popular examples. But how about Go? The official documentation reads, "Although Go has types and methods and allows an object-oriented style of programming, there is no type hierarchy." Go is, indeed, not natively an object-oriented language, but it has all the necessary functionalities. Most of the principles that apply to object-oriented languages can apply to Go. Go has no inheritance, but don't worry; it has other features that let you achieve similar goals, such as composition (more on that in chapter 10).

Let's head back to the `logger.go` file. What we've created here for our logger is the definition of a *structure*. We want it to log lines of text at different levels. The user will then be able to pass this object as a dependency to any function that needs to log something.

Let's take a look at two approaches that fulfill the expectation of exposing methods on a variable `l` of type `Logger`, each with a signature similar to that of `fmt.Printf`:

- *One method with a level parameter:* `l.Log(pocketlog.Info, "message")`—In this case, the caller passes the level of log as the first parameter.
- *As many methods as there are levels:* `l.Info("message")`—In this case, the caller decides which function to call.

We picked the second option, as it seems clearer and simpler than the former, which requires a lot of dot characters and text before we reach the interesting part of the line. Remember that code needs to be easy to read.

To declare a method that can be called on an object, we use receiver methods; these functions are attached to an instance of a struct. A receiver method is a function that operates on the structure specified in parentheses before the function's name. Receiver methods can accept a copy or a reference—a pointer—to the structure. For the difference between these, check appendix E. Since these methods operate on a `Logger` structure, the most intuitive place for them is in the `logger.go` file.

Listing 4.2   `logger.go`: Receiver methods

```
// Debugf formats and prints a message if the log level is debug or higher.
func (l *Logger) Debugf(format string, args ...any) {
    // implement me
}

// Infof formats and prints a message if the log level is info or higher.
func (l *Logger) Infof(format string, args ...any) {
    // implement me
}
```

As required, we've used the same signature as the `Printf` method of the `fmt` package, a signature that developers are already accustomed to. This is why we end the function name with the letter `f`. The receiver methods `Debugf` and `Infof` are called *variadic functions*.

> **DEFINITION**   Sometimes, you want to pass a variable number of parameters—none, exactly one, or more—to your function. In this case, the best approach is offered by Go's *variadic function* syntax. The last argument of a function can be of the type `args ...{some type}`. When calling such a function, the user

can provide any number of parameters—from zero to too many. Inside the function, we can access the parameters as we would access elements from a `slice`, using the `args[2]` notation. The most used variadic functions are the `fmt.Printf` ones, but we'll see more examples before the end of this chapter.

Side quest 4.1

Write the signature of the `Errorf` method on your logger. This should require a lot of copying and pasting, but make sure you understand what you're writing.

Our `Logger` does nothing, but it already can be called from Susan's code. Before we publish it to her (while she impatiently waits to use it), there is one thing we want to add.

4.1.4 The New() function

At the moment, a new logger can be created via these two completely equivalent lines of code:

```
var log pocketlog.Logger
```

or

```
log := pocketlog.Logger{}
```

The former explicitly defines a zero-value logger, while the latter leaves room for initialization, if we later want to add exported fields and give them a specific value. Picking one over the other is a question of how you think the code might need to change.

But as your logger evolves, there will be mandatory parameters, such as the threshold where it should start caring about messages. Go doesn't provide any constructor mechanism to gently convince users to stay up to date with evolutions, but we can write a `New()` method that builds a new instance. When outside of the `pocketlog` package, the method will be called with `pocketlog.New()`, so no need to name it `NewPocketLog`. Developers can still use the preceding syntax (they must make sure it's safe, as it will set every field of the structure to its zero value), but that's not recommended. We don't need to specify `Logger` in the name of that function because users will be calling the name of the `pocketlog` package first, making it clear that we're creating a new pocket logger. This way, we avoid the stuttering `pocketlog.Logger`, where `log` appears twice. As shown in the following listing, we add the `threshold` of the logger to the struct and define the `New()` method.

Listing 4.3 `logger.go`: Defining a new object

```
// Logger is used to log information.
type Logger struct {
```

```
      threshold Level
}

// New returns you a logger, ready to log at the required threshold.
func New(threshold Level) *Logger {
    return &Logger{
        threshold: threshold,
    }
}
```

This comma is required in Go. Adding a new field will only change a single line.

You've probably noticed that the `threshold` field of the `Logger` isn't exported. This is a decision we must make whenever we declare a new field in a structure. When in doubt, don't export; it's a lot safer than exposing everything. In this case, the user needs to define a logging threshold, which is done via the `New` function. The internal structure of the logger is none of the business of our library's callers.

We also made a second decision with this `New` function—we returned a pointer to a `Logger`, rather than a `Logger` itself. It's generally more useful for `New` to return a pointer. The `new` built-in function in Go also returns a pointer, with the bottom line being that returning a pointer makes it easier for the caller to share the resource—the `Logger`—in their program.

Our `Logger` still does nothing, but it can be used on Susan's development branch, and she won't need to change anything while you make it work. You can commit.

> **NOTE**   Every type in Go has a *zero value*. This includes basic data types, struct types, functions, channels, `interfaces`, `pointers`, `slices`, and `maps`. Basically, any type for which you can declare a variable has a zero value. The zero value of a type is the value held by a noninitialized variable of that type. Appendix C provides more details.

> **Side quest 4.2**
>
> What is the logging level of a logger defined with the `var log pocketlog.Logger` syntax?

4.1.5 *What about testing?*

We just committed, but we have no test. This is subpar! Earlier is always better when it comes to writing a unit test.

How can we test this? We have a very clear definition of how the `Logger` should behave from the user's point of view, but we don't know much yet about how it will work internally. This is the perfect situation for closed-box testing, where we test a system from the *outside*, meaning from another package. We could test it from the same package, but we'd be able to access fields or functions an external user won't be able to access.

Here, we'll start by creating a `logger_test.go` file; contrary to the previous chapter's open-box tests, this one isn't an internal test. As we want to test from the outside, the file will have to be part of another package—one that's different from the rest of the code but still in the same directory, for consistency:

```
> tree
.
├── pocketlog/
│   ├── level.go
│   ├── logger.go
│   └── logger_test.go
├── go.mod
└── main.go
    └── logger.go
```

This is package pocketlog.

This is package pocketlog_test.

Go will complain if we write two packages in the same directory, but there is an exception to this rule that allows for tests to be written close to the source code: we can have a `foo_test` package alongside a `foo` package. This is what we'll use here:

```
package pocketlog_test
```

To access `pocketlog` functions, we need to import it:

```
import "learngo-pockets/logger/pocketlog"
```

From this `pocketlog_test` package, we only have access to what the package `pocketlog` exports; hidden functions, variables, constants, types, and fields of exported types aren't accessible. As the logger is currently writing to the standard output, we can start with an `ExampleXxx` function to test it, as shown in listing 4.4. We're testing the `Debug` method of the `Logger` struct, so the signature of the testing function is `ExampleLogger_Debugf`. Optionally, we can add details about the expected output or the test scenario after yet another underscore (e.g., `ExampleLogger_Debugf_runes` or `ExampleLogger_Debugf_quotes`).

Listing 4.4 `logger_test.go`: **Testing the standard output**

```go
func ExampleLogger_Debugf() {
    debugLogger := pocketlog.New(pocketlog.LevelDebug)
    debugLogger.Debugf("Hello, %s", "world")
    // Output: Hello, world
}
```

Run the test. It should return an error because our `Logger` still does nothing. Fixing this error will be our next task. Then, we can add test cases because this one isn't covering enough of the use cases.

4.1.6 Documenting code

An important part of exposing a library is to document it, so other people understand how to use it. Comments on exported functions, methods, structs, or interfaces are extremely important; some IDEs will automatically show them as we hover over them. Tests are the second place other users might look for advice on how to use your library—sometimes, it's even comments in tests that resolve the biggest mysteries.

We've already seen previously that a comment on an exported type or function should be a line starting with the type or function name as the first word of the line. It's also good practice to end the sentence with a period:

```
// New returns you a logger, ready to log at the required threshold.
func New(level Level) *Logger {
```

A SPECIAL FILE: DOC.GO

An unofficial convention calls for writing a special file in each Go package that will describe the purpose of this package. This is almost like a README file, but it's intended for developers only. The doc.go file is called a *package header*. You'll find one in most packages you use, if you venture in there.

The doc.go file contains no Go code, only one uncommented line: the package. And before that line, there is a verbose description of what the package is about. This is where we can tell how to properly use the package, in which order to call functions, and what we shouldn't forget to defer, if need be.

Prior to the package name, there should be a multiline comment, where the first line starts with Package pocketlog, in our example. The uppercase first letter in Package matters for code linters. Write this file with every piece of information you deem important for the callers of our library. The following listing shows our pocketlog/doc.go file.

> #### Listing 4.5   doc.go: Documenting a package

```
/*
Package pocketlog exposes an API to log your work.

First, instantiate a logger with pocketlog.New, and giving it a
threshold level.
Messages of lesser criticality won't be logged.

Sharing the logger is the responsibility of the caller.

The logger can be called to log messages on three levels:
  - Debug: mostly used to debug code, follow step-by-step processes
  - Info: valuable messages providing insights to the milestones of a process
  - Error: error messages to understand what went wrong
*/
package pocketlog
```

THE GO DOC COMMAND

One of the tools Go is shipped with is the go doc command. We already briefly discussed this tool in the context of inspecting the contents of standard packages. The go doc command will give you the documentation of a package or symbol that the go command can find in the subdirectories. There is a minor limitation: `go doc` won't go looking on the internet—it's a local tool. This means you need to be working inside a project (with a `go.mod` file) for which the dependencies will have been downloaded— something that is achieved silently by some IDEs but that can always be done manually with a `go mod download` command. In our case, we retrieve the documentation of the `pocketlog` package and the `New` function in the `pocketlog` package by running the following commands:

```
> go doc path/to/repo/pocketlog
> go doc path/to/repo/pocketlog.Logger
> go doc path/to/repo/pocketlog.New
> go doc path/to/repo/pocketlog.Logger.Debugf
```

In any case, documentation should always be part of what you deliver in the form of comments, examples, or package headers. You can learn more about this here: https://go.dev/doc/comment. Now that we've explained how to use our library, it's high time to make it usable!

4.2 Implementing the exported methods

In the previous section, we published the API to Susan, and we wrote some failing tests. The next step, to comply with expectations, is to decide where the logger is going to do its deed and, finally, to log. We ask questions like these: Should it always write to the standard output and never the error one? How will it send a message to a ticket printer, write in a file, or send via the network to a different aggregating mechanism? Should we implement this functionality for every possible use case?

As we want this package to be usable in any situation, we'll leave the implementation of having a custom writer to the user's discretion. But Susan wants a default implementation that just spits out on the console (the standard output) so that she can focus on her business logic before improving her logging and monitoring (we may disagree on the priorities here, but the products team insisted). So, `stdout` it is. We'll improve it shortly.

4.2.1 Default implementation

The first implementation is the easy part (see listing 4.6). Think about how you would write the `Debugf()` method before spoiling your pleasure with the following solution. Remember that `Debugf()` should only log if the threshold level is `Debug` or lower.

Listing 4.6 `logger.go`: Default `Debugf` implementation of the console

```go
// Debug formats and prints a message if the log level is debug or higher.
func (l *Logger) Debugf(format string, args ...any) {
    if l.threshold > LevelDebug {        // ◄── Debug logs everything that is
        return                           //      even remotely interesting.
    }

    _, _ = fmt.Printf(format+"\n", args...)    // ◄── We use Printf, which formats
}                                              //      the arguments into a string.
```

When calling the `Debugf` function, the user expects the message to be printed if the level of the logger allows for it. So, the first thing to do in this function is to make sure that we should be logging a message. The `enum` we declared for the levels allows us to compare two levels, as the underlying `Level` type is an integer.

This method could be just three lines if we chose to log inside the `if` and invert the condition, but you should always choose to align the happy path unindented. Deal with errors and early exits inside your `if` blocks, and keep real business logic as far left as possible. This helps a lot when reading the code and makes extending it much easier.

Once we're sure we need to handle this message, we'll log it. For now, we'll use the `fmt.Printf` function. This whole library might look like a verbose wrapping of this `Printf` call, but rest assured, there's more to it than meets the eye.

> **Side quest 4.3**
>
> Implement `Info`, `Infof`, `Error`, and `Errorf` levels methods. In addition, implement all the other levels that you chose to add.

Now, our previous test should be green. Let's discreetly postpone the testing of the other methods; we want to write `TestXxx` methods, which give more flexibility, so we need to write to nonstandard outputs.

4.2.2 *Interfacing*

Writing bytes in various places is an extremely common use case in all computer programs. Whether writing JSON to an HTTP output, ones and zeros to a network router, bits into a digital port to turn a light on, encoded pixels to a printer, or letters on a console, everything we do has to output its result somewhere to be useful. Go has a set of standard interfaces for the most common uses, such as writing or reading bytes. This means that everyone who produces code that writes or reads bytes can use these existing interfaces.

IO.WRITER

Among the most commonly cited interfaces in the standard library, the `io` package holds two famous interfaces: `io.Writer`, to write to any destination, and `io.Reader`, to read from any source (e.g., an array of bytes, a file, a JSON stream). The following listing shows the declarations of these interfaces.

Listing 4.7 `io` interfaces

```
type Reader interface {
    Read(p []byte) (n int, err error)
}

type Writer interface {
    Write(p []byte) (n int, err error)
}
```

We want the user of our logger to define the destination. We can ask for an io.Writer and simply write into it. They will be responsible for providing an implementation of their choice.

> **TIP** One major difference between Go and the most-known object languages (e.g., Java and C++) is that interfaces in Go are implicit. To implement an interface, just add the methods your interface defines to an object, and the compiler will recognize it.

We can already add the output to the structure and the standard Writer to our New() builder. You can see this in the following listing.

Listing 4.8 logger.go: **Adding an output field to the struct**

```
// Logger is used to log information.
type Logger struct {
    threshold Level
    output    io.Writer
}

// New returns you a logger, ready to log at the required threshold.
// The default output is Stdout.
func New(threshold Level, output io.Writer) *Logger {
    return &Logger{
        threshold: threshold,
        output:    output,
    }
}
```

Note the slightly enhanced documentation. Alternatively, it could default to os.Stderr, which represents the default error output.

Lastly, each of the methods will need to use this new field (see listing 4.9). And let's make sure users who don't follow our recommendation of using New to create a Logger don't get nil pointer reference exceptions.

Listing 4.9 logger.go: **Adding the output field to the struct**

```
// Debug formats and prints a message if the log level is debug or higher
func (l Logger) Debugf(format string, args ...any) {
    // making sure we can safely write to the output
    if l.output == nil {
        l.output = os.Stdout
    }
    if l.threshold <= LevelDebug {
        _, _ = fmt.Fprintf(l.output, format, args...)
    }
}
```

In Go, the underscore symbol represents the *void*. In other words, assigning a value to the underscore will just discard the result. What is the point? Go likes to be explicit.

Here, we explicitly say to the next developer, including our future selves, "I know there are values returned by this function, but I don't need them."

Here, the function returns an `int`, the number of written characters, and sometimes an error. We don't want to deal with that error at the moment, so we explicitly ignore it.

4.2.3   Refactoring

You might have noticed when implementing the `Info` and `Error` methods that we're calling the same function `fmt.Fprintf` as our writing function. You also might have noticed that, unlike its `fmt.Fprintf` sibling, `fmt.Fprintln` appends an end-of-line character at the end of the string. In a way, the `printf` function allows you to do very fine craftsmanship, while the `println` function won't let you format everything exactly as you'd like it: no left padding before numbers or strings, no hexadecimal representation of numbers, and so on.

A newline is the guarantee that your log messages will be easily distinguishable in a console. As we want to export the `Printf` toolbox, we must add an explicit \n when we write the messages.

In our case, we need to add that newline three times, once in each of the functions. And whenever we want to make a change to the log message—for instance, add the logging level—we need to write the same lines three times. Should `Warn` or `Fatal` also be implemented, the count goes even higher. This (loudly) calls for a minor refactoring; we don't want to maintain the same code more than twice. Let's group all the lines together and alter a single line every time we want to adapt the logger.

Create a `logf()` method on the `Logger`, as shown in listing 4.10. For now, the method will have the same arguments as `Debug`, `Info`, and `Error`. These three will call `logf`, which is now the one method responsible for formatting and printing. The other three, the exported ones, are responsible for their log level and nothing more. There is no good reason to export this one.

Listing 4.10   `logger.go`: Refactoring the logging methods

```
// Debugf formats and prints a message if the log level is debug or higher.
func (l *Logger) Debugf(format string, args ...any) {
    if l.threshold > LevelDebug {
        return
    }

    l.logf(format, args...)
}

// logf prints the message to the output.
// Add decorations here, if any.
func (l *Logger) logf(format string, args ...any) {
    _, _ = fmt.Fprintf(l.output, format+"\n", args...)
}
```

Comments on unexported methods are usually for the next maintainer (including yourself).

Run the tests. The tests should fail by now, as we haven't updated them with the `os.Stdout` parameter for the `New` function. Once this is done, you can commit and inform your colleague that the code is ready to be used. However, Susan tells you that her logs should be written to a specific file rather than on the standard output because she already makes use of the standard output. Can the `Logger` achieve that by itself?

4.3 The functional options pattern

Default values are a subject of high debate among development theorists and theoreticians. Some people love using them because it makes everything discoverable and, therefore, easier to bootstrap. Other people hate them because they don't force you to know what you're doing. We believe default values are a good thing if used sparingly.

When we start developing, say, a new web service, we want to focus on the business logic. We want to make sure our logic works locally before making the service production ready. To decrease the cognitive load, we start with the default version of the logger—architecting a better logger can come later. Before writing the deployment code, we don't need anything but the standard output.

But very quickly, we deploy to a cheap cloud provider so that we can pitch our prototype and show it to the world. Reading the standard output isn't so trivial anymore. We pick a tool, such as an aggregating database, that happens to publish a Go driver. The developers of this driver were smart enough to have a structure in their library that implements the `io.Writer` interface.

We still want to keep this default implementation, writing to the standard output, but we want to provide the option of writing somewhere else. One common way of doing this is by using the functional options pattern.

4.3.1 Creating configurations

Create a new file, `options.go`, in the `pocketlog` package, where our configuration functions will be written. Define a type of function that can be passed to the `New()` function and that will be applied one after the other:

```
// Option defines a functional option to our logger.
type Option func(*Logger)
```

This function takes a pointer on our logger so that the function's body can change the pointed value directly. In our case, change the default output to whatever the user gave us.

Listing 4.11 `options.go`: An optional function to change the output

```
// WithOutput returns a configuration function that sets the output of logs.
func WithOutput(output io.Writer) Option {
    return func(lgr *Logger) {
        lgr.output = output
    }
}
```

This type of function can be passed to the `New()` function as variadic parameters: a list of zero or more arguments of the same type.

Listing 4.12   `logger.go`: Applying options

```
// New returns you a logger, ready to log at the required threshold.
// Give it a list of configuration functions to tune it at your will.
// The default output is Stdout.
func New(threshold Level, opts ...Option) *Logger {
    lgr := &Logger{threshold: threshold, output: os.Stdout}

    for _, configFunc := range opts {
        configFunc(lgr)
    }

    return lgr
}
```

Next time you want to add an option to your logger (e.g., a date formatter), just create a new `Option`, and you're set. It's important to notice here that adding configuration functions is easy and lets the user set specific behaviors without altering the API of our library. Our `New` function accepts as many configuration functions as the user needs, from the list we implement in this package.

A USAGE EXAMPLE

Susan wants to know how to use your library. There is a documentation file, but human interaction is always so much more efficient. You write a small example and send it to her.

Outside of the library, `go mod init` a new module and create a `main.go` file. Define a function `main()`, as you did in the previous chapter. In this function, instantiate a new logger, and call a few methods to showcase your work.

Listing 4.13   `main.go`: A usage example

```
package main

import (
    "os"
    "time"

    "learngo-pockets/logger/pocketlog"
)

func main() {
    lgr := pocketlog.New(pocketlog.LevelInfo, pocketlog.WithOutput(os.
        Stdout))

    lgr.Infof("A little copying is better than a little dependency.")
    lgr.Errorf("Errors are values. Documentation is for %s.", "users")
```

```
        lgr.Debugf("Make the zero (%d) value useful.", 0)

        lgr.Infof("Hallo, %d %v", 2022, time.Now())
}
```

4.3.2 *Testing our example*

We're already using the logger, but it's not fully tested. How unprofessional! Susan can use our library, but we don't want her to come back with possible bugs. The magic of interfaces means we can write a test helper that implements io.Writer and give it to our Logger under test.

TEST HELPER IMPLEMENTATION

At the end of logger_test.go, write a new testWriter struct, as shown in listing 4.14. Make it implement io.Writer, but instead of writing to a destination, it validates the output string. For example, you can keep a field in the struct where you concatenate the output, and you can validate that against the expected result.

> **Listing 4.14** logger_test.go: **Test helper implementation**

```
// testWriter is a struct that implements io.Writer.
// We use it to validate that we can write to a specific output.
type testWriter struct {
    contents string                          ┐ The receiver is a pointer,
}                                             │ so we can modify its
                                              ┘ contents field.
// Write implements the io.Writer interface.
func (tw *testWriter) Write(p []byte) (n int, err error) {
    tw.contents = tw.contents + string(p)    ◄── ┐ Concatenates each call to
    return len(p), nil                             ┘ your in-memory logger
}
```

This structure can be passed to the functional option higher in our test. At the end of the test, we can then check that the writer's contents are what we expect.

In practice, strings.Builder or bytes.Buffer can be used instead of the testWriter. Now, you know how to do a mock, in case the interface you need isn't standard.

UPDATING THE TEST

Now that we're not forced to check the standard output anymore, we can write a TestXxx function, one that will test all of the logging methods together, sequentially (see listing 4.15). We can have one test case per required logging level and check that the outputs are different and the Debugf() call is mostly ignored.

> **Listing 4.15** logger_test.fo: **A test function**

```
                                         ┐ Defines test strings; use
                                         ┘ your favorite sonnet.
const (
    debugMessage = "Why write I still all one, ever the same,"  ◄──
```

```
        infoMessage  = "And keep invention in a noted weed,"
        errorMessage = "That every word doth almost tell my name,"
)

func TestLogger_DebugfInfofErrorf(t *testing.T) {
    type testCase struct {
        level     pocketlog.Level
        expected string
    }

    tt := map[string]testCase{
        "debug": {
            level:    pocketlog.LevelDebug,
            expected: debugMessage + "\n" +
                      infoMessage + "\n" +
                      errorMessage + "\n",
        },
        "info": {...},
        "error": {...},
    }

    for name, tc := range tt {
        t.Run(name, func(t *testing.T) {
            tw := &testWriter{}

            testedLogger := pocketlog.New(tc.level, pocketlog.WithOutput(tw))

            testedLogger.Debugf(debugMessage)
            testedLogger.Infof(infoMessage)
            testedLogger.Errorf(errorMessage)

            if tw.contents != tc.expected {
                t.Errorf("invalid contents, expected %q, got %q",
                    tc.expected, tw.contents)
            }
        })
    }
}
```

It's your turn to write these two test cases!

Note the use of %q to help check for extra spaces.

Side quest 4.4

The test, as we've written it here, only tests the calls to functions in one order: `Debugf`, then `Infof`, and then `Errorf`. What if we decide to add a buffer and only consider writing everything in the `Errorf()` method? We won't see it in this situation, and `Debug` and `Info` messages might stay stuck.

Your logger is ready, fully functional, documented, and tested. The rest of the company starts using it, yet you keep dreaming up new functionalities for it. Let's explore a few, and see where they lead.

4.4   Additional functionalities

This tool offers endless optimization possibilities. The only limit, as always, will be the amount of time we're ready to spend on it. For example, this library isn't thread safe; when multiple goroutines use the same `Writer` without any protections, the outcome can be unexpected—we'll explore solutions to that in later chapters. In the meantime, let's look at a few interesting enhancements we can add to our `Logger`.

4.4.1   Logging the log level

Your service runs locally, with the lowest possible level of logs. You know everything that happens just by looking at your console, but now, you would like to see the errors in red. You add an old `awk` command to your log tailing, but how do you know what to color?

How can we know while reading the logs which message has which level? Well, let's add that as an exercise.

> **Side quest 4.5**
>
> Add the log level to your output. Hint: Change the contents of the `format` variable before printing, as we did when we added the current time.

4.4.2   Exposing the generic logging function

We chose from the start to export as many functions as there are logging levels to make the user's code easier to read. Now, imagine yourself in a situation where you only know what level to pick at runtime. You're logging the email address of your app's user, but on one platform, all the users are internal and the admins need to know who did what, whereas on another platform, email addresses are covered by data protection laws and shouldn't appear in logs, even in case of errors. You choose to have this information in your app's configuration and want to pass it directly to the logger, but you can't change the logging level for the whole application, as this might discard some of your unrelated and important messages. For this, we can add an exported `Logf()` function that takes a logging level as its first parameter.

Listing 4.16   `logger.go`: The exported `Logf` function

```go
// Logf formats and prints a message if the log level is high enough
func (l *Logger) Logf(lvl Level, format string, args ...any) {
    if l.threshold > lvl {
        return
    }

    l.logf(format, args...)
}
```

From there, why not refactor so that all the other exported methods simply call this one? Of course, having both options will make your APIs more cluttered and harder to understand and maintain. And, users can always write their own function with a simple switch, using a variable defined in their own domain.

> **Side quest 4.6**
> Add a test for this method.

4.5   *Logging: Best practices*

Now that we've completed this library, which you'll hopefully use and share, some recommendations might be necessary. What kind of information do we want to log? At what frequency do we want to log? Logging is a story of compromise as there are two factors to take into account: how much easier it is to understand errors when using logs and the high cost of log storage.

Logs are the trace of the past execution of a program, and as soon as the need for logs arises (usually when questions like, "What was the value of count at this moment?" or "How long did this request take to process?" arise), the need to keep these logs safe also appears on the stage. Whether stored in a file, a database, a bucket in the cloud, or anywhere, persistent logs cost money. Having more logs makes it easier to understand what went wrong and quickly fix it, but that also is expensive.

Every company has its own policy regarding what should and shouldn't be logged as well as the level at which they should be categorized. However, we share a few recommendations next.

WRITING CLEAR MESSAGES

Although it might be very tempting to simply log "step 1," "step 2," and so on inside a function with no further explanation, these messages won't help you on the next day. Think about what happened in step 1: Was the document inserted in the database? Was the email sent? Help your future self by writing clear messages. When a function has only one possible execution, the only value of a log message is the comforting reassurance that we've finished this or that piece of logic. Valuable information here includes knowing how long it took to process the function or something similar.

AVOIDING LONG MESSAGES

The amount of data written to the logs is directly related to the amount of money that will be spent to keep these messages. If your variable is a map, potentially with thousands of keys, printing the map will be costly. Instead, wouldn't having its size or whether a specific key is present be just as valuable? If your data is a piece of an image or a song recording, the logger isn't the place to keep a copy of the bytes being processed. Instead, write a function to save the image or the song.

LOGGING AT MILESTONES AND HEEDING LOOPS AND RECURSION

Functions can be complex and span hundreds of lines. When this happens, the most important question is to identify which sections really deserve a log and which simply don't. If we return early because we found no item to process, should we say so? Maybe not, but we could always log the number of items found instead.

When retrieving items from a database and processing every one in a loop, do we want to know that we're at item 5,567 out of 81,543; and then 5,568, and so on? If the normal flow doesn't require this level of detail, maybe we can simply log a message every 10,000 items, to get a rough idea of how much of this big list of data has already been processed.

LEARNING TO TRUST THE CODE

Logging shouldn't be a tool to debug the code. Most of the time, when you scratch your head wondering what's going on when the input of this or that function has this or that value, it's because the code is unclear. There are three ways of addressing this:

- *Write clearer code.* Split logical blocks into more and smaller functions.
- *Write better documentation.* Use comments, variable names, and so on.
- *Write more tests.* Errors don't happen on the happy path; they happen when something is wrong. Make sure you cover as many edge-case scenarios as possible.

STRUCTURED MESSAGES

In the modern world, most logs aren't processed by humans. They are mostly read by programs that use the logs to generate information displayed in dashboards—for instance, representing the number of errors that happen per minute over the course of time or the time it took to process a request.

For this, we need to tell these computers how to parse the logs—which piece of information is valuable, which isn't to be taken into account, and so on. And the simplest solution is to format the log messages into structured entities. A common structured log message format is JSON (displayed here on several lines for readability by humans):

```
{
    "time": "2022-31-10 23:06:30.148845Z",
    "level": "warning",
    "message": "platform not scaled up for request"
}
```

Some existing logging libraries offer several additional features. One such example is letting users include their own set of keys and values to the logged message.

Side quest 4.8

Update the log function to print logs of the format discussed in this section (you can ignore the "time" part for now, as we need a bit more than what we've covered to validate it in the tests). This will require making use of the encoding/json package and the Marshal function it contains. This function will have to be called on a new type, which we'll define as a structure that contains a Level and a Message. One of the most common traps when using the Marshal (or Unmarshal) function is to forget that the json package needs to access the fields of the structure. It's tempting for newcomers to keep these fields unexported, but this makes them precisely unexported to the functions in charge of reading and writing them. We'll cover this further when we start implementing services. (The concepts in this side quest are explained in chapter 5.)

Summary

- A library in Go is a package containing exported types and functions (its API) that clients can use directly.
- A library should only export what is necessary for its users, keeping internal details unexposed to maintain simplicity and encapsulation.
- Use explicit names and replicate familiar patterns or existing function signatures in your library to make it intuitive for users.
- Define domain-specific types, rather than relying on primitive ones, such as int or string, for improved readability and maintainability. For example, replacing int with a UserID type can make code clearer.
- Use enumerations with iota when defining types with a small, finite set of possible values, such as states or modes. This approach ensures type safety and readability.
- Implementing a New() method allows you to enforce required parameters during object initialization, ensuring a clean and consistent setup for users of your library.
- Use the functional options pattern to initialize optional fields or set default values for struct fields, improving flexibility while avoiding excessive constructors.
- When implementing and testing your library, rely on closed-box testing to validate behavior through its public API rather than internal details, ensuring robust and client-focused design.
- Write smaller files to make code easier to navigate and read, especially in larger projects. Splitting logically distinct pieces of functionality into separate files improves maintainability.
- Be selective about what you log. Focus on logging meaningful information, avoiding unnecessary clutter or sensitive data.

5

Gordle: Play a word game in your terminal

This chapter covers

- Building a game that runs in a terminal
- Retrieving runes from the standard input
- Getting a random number in a `slice`
- Propagating errors
- Reading the contents of a text file

CLAUDIO—One word, good friend. Lucio, a word with you.
LUCIO—A hundred, if they'll do you any good.

—*Measure for Measure*, William Shakespeare

This chapter is about a love story. During the 2020 pandemic, Mr. Wardle, a passionate software developer, created a new game named Wordle for his partner Ms. Shah, a word-game addict. After introducing the game to his relatives and seeing how welcomed it was, he decided to publish it. This is how the famous Wordle game began its journey before going public and rising like a rocket. Now, a new word is released daily, which most people across the world call "today's Wordle." There are many variations, based on geography, math, Shakespeare terms, Tolkien, or Taylor

89

Swift, along with even more adaptations in different languages throughout the world (beyond time and space, ancient Greek, Quenya, and Klingon are offered).

The game is pretty basic: you must guess a word of five characters in six attempts. After each attempt, the game tells you, for every character, whether it belongs to the solution and whether it has the correct position.

The goal of this chapter is to create our own game called Gordle (just a bit of word-play). The game will be a configurable version of Wordle; whereas the official version has five characters per word, our game can pass longer or shorter words, as well as change the number of attempts before a player's game is over. Lucio will be our developer, while Claudio, the player, will execute a command that will start the game. In our code, we'll progress step by step, starting with a simple function reading from the input and printing Claudio's attempt. Then, we'll iterate and have the game evolve to give feedback to the player. Adding a corpus (a list of words) from which to pick a random solution will make the game more replayable. Finally, we'll support more languages and tweak the parameters as needed.

For the sake of simplicity, this version will only support writing systems where one character never needs more than one code point in Unicode. Supporting other writing systems is out of the scope of this chapter, but you can find extending ideas in the extras at the end. This project requires the following:

1 Write a program that picks a random word in a list.
2 Read the player's guesses from the standard input.
3 Give feedback on whether the characters are correctly placed or not.
4 Recognize that the player wins if they find the correct word or loses after the maximum number of unsuccessful attempts is reached.

5.1   *Basic main version*

The default approach to any coding exercise is always to simplify the problem to its absolute simplest version. We'll have time to improve it later. First, let's start with a basic version of the main function that will have a hardcoded solution. We'll allow only one guess, and the program will answer ok or not ok. As we did in previous chapters, we first initialize our module:

```
> go mod init learngo-pockets/gordle
```

Then, we create a new package named after the game gordle next to the main.go file. This package is where we'll implement the game. Our project will have the following structure:

```
> tree
.
├── go.mod
├── gordle
│   └── files in package gordle
└── main.go
```

The package `gordle` will expose a structure `Game` to which we'll progressively add the needed methods to build a full game.

5.1.1 Mini main

Lucio begins simply, with an empty structure named `Game` in the `gordle` package. We know that this program will need more than 50 lines of code, so it's a good idea to split responsibilities over several files. Anything that relates to the game will be in the `gordle` package. We know, for instance, that we'll have to keep the secret word somewhere. This leads us to the creation of a structure that will contain game information.

> **Listing 5.1** `game.go`: `Game` **structure**

```
// Game holds all the information we need to play a game of gordle.
type Game struct{}
```

As we've seen in chapter 4 with the logger, there are several ways to create an object. In listing 5.2, we expose a `New()` method, which is the recommended entry point into the library, guaranteeing the creation of the `Game` object with all of its dependencies. Note that it's a good habit to ensure the proper behavior of your library.

By convention, `New()` will return a pointer to `Game`, similarly to Go's built-in function `new`, which returns a pointer too.

> **Listing 5.2** `game.go`: **Using** `New` **to create a** `Game` **structure**

```
// New returns a Game, which can be used to Play!
func New() *Game {
    g := &Game{}

    return g
}
```

We didn't write `return &Game{}` because we'll add some code before this `return g` line to configure our game. We next attach a `Play` method to the `Game` type, as shown in listing 5.3. `Play` will run the game. In our first implementation, let's simply print the instructions. Creating a method on an object in Go is achieved by writing a pointer receiver on the `Game` structure. We'll explore this topic further later in the chapter.

> **Listing 5.3** `game.go`: **Using** `Play` **to run the game**

```
// Play runs the game.
func (g *Game) Play() {
    fmt.Println("Welcome to Gordle!")

    fmt.Printf("Enter a guess:\n")
}
```

This is enough for our first version. Let's call these new methods in the `main` function. For this, we need to import the `gordle` package in the `main.go` file:

```
import (
    "learngo-pockets/gordle/gordle"
)
```

In the `main` function, we need two steps to start the game—create a new Gordle game, and launch it:

```
func main() {
    g := gordle.New()
    g.Play()
}
```

The aggregated `main` file is shown in the following code.

Listing 5.4 `main.go`: `main` function and package

```
package main

import (
    "learngo-pockets/gordle/gordle"
)

func main() {
    g := gordle.New()
    g.Play()
}
```

After these initial steps, we can run our program and verify that it behaves as expected. Now is also a good time to commit these files to your favorite version control system, before you add some content into the `Game` structure. We now await Claudio's guess of the secret word!

5.1.2 *Read player's input*

Because this is a game, we have a player, Claudio. Let's ask him for a suggestion. Claudio has access to the keyboard, and we'll be reading his attempts through the standard input. After reading the attempt, we can check it against the solution.

GAME STRUCTURE

Depending mostly on what we want to read, there are several ways of reading from the standard input. Some functions read a `slice` of bytes. Some read strings. In this case, the player will type characters and then press the Enter or Return key. We, therefore, want to read a line until we hit the first end-of-line character.

The `bufio` package has a useful method to achieve this on its `Reader` structure, as described in the documentation: "`ReadLine` tries to return a single line, not including the end-of-line bytes." The documentation also states that it's not the best reader in the world for most reading use cases, but for one word from the standard input, it's perfect. The good thing is that the `bufio.Reader` implements the `io.Reader` interface! We don't want to overengineer our solution.

Our `Game` object will hold a pointer to a `bufio.Reader`, as shown in listing 5.5. We use a pointer and not a simple object because the `bufio` package exposes a `NewReader` function that returns a pointer to a `bufio.Reader`. In addition, we'll be calling `Read-Line` a lot, so it's useful to immediately have a variable of the type of that method's receiver—a pointer.

Listing 5.5 game.go: Using `Game` with a reader

```
// Game holds all the information we need to play a game of gordle.
type Game struct {
    reader *bufio.Reader
}
```

But wait, how do we initialize this reader? Should we do it as part of the `New()` function? Although this is a valid option, we soon realize that `NewReader` itself requires an `io.Reader` parameter, so where should that parameter come from? Because `io.Reader` is a very simple interface, we can pass a variable implementing it to our `New` function, and create the `bufio.Reader` inside `New`.

Listing 5.6 game.go: Using `New` with the reader as parameter

```
// New returns a Game variable, which can be used to Play!
func New(playerInput io.Reader) *Game {
    g := &Game{
        reader: bufio.NewReader(playerInput),
    }

    return g
}
```

Before we dive into reading a player's input, we need to answer a question: How does Go deal with characters?

If we want to play using another language, or even play in English with words that come from another language, we need Unicode for full support of writable characters. Would it be fair to repudiate words such as *canapé, façade, dürüm,* or even the old-fashioned *rememberèd?*

Go natively uses Unicode. All the source files need to be encoded in UTF, and Go even has a specific primitive type called `rune` that serves to encode a Unicode code point.

For example, let's take the default line that appears on the Go playground and look at the length of the string (including the comma and the whitespace):

```
fmt.Println(len("Hello, 世界"))
```

This prints out 13. Indeed, UTF-8 requires 3 bytes to encode each of these non-Latin characters. On the other hand,

```
fmt.Println(len([]rune("Hello, 世界")))
```

outputs 9. We're measuring the number of runes and not the number of bytes necessary to encode them. Keep that in mind whenever iterating over a string's elements: you can either access its byte representation with `[]byte(str)` or access its rune representation with `[]rune(str)`, which is the default behavior. The following listing shows how to display these various lengths.

Listing 5.7   **Printing the string and rune lengths**

```
package main

import "fmt"

func main() {
    fmt.Println("Hello, 世界")
    fmt.Println(len("Hello, 世界"))
    fmt.Println(len([]rune("Hello, 世界")))
}

Console Output:

Hello, 世界
13
9
```

THE ASK METHOD

There's a variable that allows us to read from the standard input once the game is set. Let's politely ask Claudio for his next word. Because the feature of retrieving an attempt provided by the player through the reader can be summarized in a sentence without having to explain how it works, it's a great candidate for a function. We'll call it `ask`, for clarity and simplicity (see listing 5.8). Because it needs to read from a `Game`'s reader, the `ask` method will accept a `Game` receiver. The `ask` method will also return a `slice` of runes—the word proposed by the player. This will guarantee we have a valid suggestion.

Listing 5.8   `game.go`: `ask` **method signature**

```
// ask reads input until a valid suggestion is made (and returned).
func (g *Game) ask() []rune {
    // ...
}
```

You may have noticed that we use a pointer receiver here. There are two reasons for this. The first is simple: we'll be modifying the state of our `Game` structure via many of its methods, so they will all require a pointer receiver. It's good Go practice to avoid having both pointer and nonpointer receiver methods on a type for consistency. The second reason is a bit more complex and is motivated by the `Game` structure having a field—the `output` field—that is a pointer. Appendix E covers the problems that can arise when using value receivers with pointer fields.

Inside this `ask` method, we read the line using the reader. Should an error occur, we'll print it using `Fprintf`, but we decide to continue anyway and wait for a new attempt. In other words, a jammed line won't cause the game to crash, but merely cause it to ask for another word. `Fprintf` allows us to write to the standard error.

We'll see how to better deal with errors when completing the `Play` method. The hard truth is that they shouldn't be ignored, most of the time. However, deciding that an error isn't blocking is a good moment to leave a comment for your future self explaining this decision.

We can add an easy check on the length of the word. For the moment, we play with the same parameters as the original Wordle, with five-character-long words. We can define a constant at the package level and use that constant everywhere we need it.

A constant serves two purposes. The first one is to address a developer's laziness: by reusing a constant, we won't have to update several lines of code should the value change. The second purpose is to make the code clearer and avoid typing errors by giving a name and a purpose to a value (just like we do with variables): `connectionTimeout` is more explicit than `5*time.Minute`. So please don't call your constant `time5minutes`. Making the value a constant is an unambiguous way of telling the reader of the code that this value isn't expected to change. The following listing shows the implementation of the `ask` method.

Listing 5.9 `game.go`: `ask` method with the reader

```go
const solutionLength = 5

// ask reads input until a valid suggestion is made (and returned).
func (g *Game) ask() []rune {
    fmt.Printf("Enter a %d-character guess:\n", solutionLength)

    for {
        playerInput, _, err := g.reader.ReadLine()      // Reads the attempt
        if err != nil {                                  //   from the player
            _, _ = fmt.Fprintf(os.Stderr,
                "Gordle failed to read your guess: %s\n", err.Error())
            continue       // We failed to read this line, but
        }                  //   maybe the next one is better.
                           //   Let's give it a chance.
        guess := []rune(string(playerInput))

        // TODO Verify the suggestion has a valid length.
    }
}
```

The `ReadLine` method will give us the user's input as a `slice` of bytes. We'll then need to convert this byte `slice` into a `rune slice`. Converting each byte into the rune representing that byte would be a major mistake because everything not ASCII would break. To properly convert a `slice` of bytes that we know represents a string to a `slice` of runes, we need to first convert the `byte slice` into a string and then into a rune `slice`.

The built-in method `len()` returns the length of a `slice` (or array). We can use it to compare the length of Claudio's word against the `solutionLength` constant. We should be polite and return a message if it fails. However, to clarity that we aren't returning "happy path" information, we'll use the standard error output available via `os.Stderr`.

Listing 5.10   `game.go`: ask method with the reader

> **Converts a byte array into a rune array**

> **Verifies the suggestion has a valid length, assuming, again, that each character is one Unicode code point**

```go
guess := []rune(string(playerInput))    ◄────────

if len(guess) != solutionLength {    ◄─────
    _, _ = fmt.Fprintf(os.Stderr, "Your attempt is invalid with Gordle's
solution! Expected %d characters, got %d.\n", solutionLength, len(guess))
} else {
    return guess
}
```

LET'S TEST THE ASK METHOD

The `ask` method uses its receiver's reader and returns a `slice` of runes. Let's declare these in the test case definition, as shown in listing 5.11.

Because we're using the standard library's `bufio.Reader`, we can use a reader to any stub mimicking the player's input. A stub is a very simple way of implementing a dependency over a third party (in our case, Claudio). Think of a few original test cases that use your favorite alphabet (e.g., the Latin script, used in English, where each letter represents a consonant or a vowel), abjad (e.g., the scripts used for Arabic or Hebrew languages, where only consonants are written, and vowels are optional or written separately), abugida (e.g., the Devanagari script, where consonants are written independently, and vowels modify them), syllabary (e.g., Hiragana or Cherokee scripts, where each character represents a syllable), or even emoji from the Unicode list of supported characters.

Listing 5.11   `game_internal_test.go`

```go
package gordle

import (
    "errors"
    "slices"
    "strings"
    "testing""
```

```
)

func TestGameAsk(t *testing.T) {
    tt := map[string]struct {
        input string
        want  []rune
    }{
        "5 characters in english": {
            input: "HELLO",
            want:  []rune("HELLO"),
        },
        "5 characters in arabic": {
            input: "مرحبا",
            want:  []rune("مرحبا"),
        },
        "5 characters in japanese": {
            input: "こんにちは",
            want:  []rune("こんにちは"),
        },
        "3 characters in japanese": {
            input: "こんに\nこんにちは",
            want:  []rune("こんにちは"),
        },
    }

    for name, tc := range tt {
        t.Run(name, func(t *testing.T) {
            g := New(strings.NewReader(tc.input))

            got := g.ask()
            if !slices.Equal(got, tc.want) {
                t.Errorf("got = %v, want %v", string(got), string(tc.want))
            }
        })
    }
}
```

You might have noticed that the first line of our test function is somewhat different from those in the previous chapters. Indeed, we used to declare a testCase structure that encapsulated all the fields we needed—but now it's gone! Or, rather, it's been replaced with an *anonymous structure*. This implementation is very common in Go tests, and we'll be using it from now on. However, if you prefer the previous way of declaring the testCase structure, that's also perfectly valid. For comparison, both are shown here. The implementation with the explicit structure looks like this:

```
type testCase struct {
    input string
    want  []rune
}
testCases := map[string]testCase
```

The popular anonymous structure implementation looks like this:

```
testCases := map[string]struct {
    input string
    want  []rune
}
```

Note that, with the current implementation of `ask`, if we have an input of only three runes, the `ReadLine` method waits forever, after ignoring the invalid three-character-long line and waiting for more. What's happening here is that when `ReadLine` hits the end of the input, it returns a specific error to let the caller know that there's nothing to be read.

Why are we not using `==` to compare `slices`? We can for `arrays`, after all! Remember that `slices` hold a pointer to their underlying `array`. Array values are comparable if values of the `array` element type are comparable. Two `array` values are equal if their corresponding elements are equal. But when it comes to `slices`, structs, and `maps`, `==` simply won't work. It's not that using `==` will produce random results, but that Go simply won't let you compare two `slices`—not even a `slice` with itself. The only entity that we can compare with a `slice` is the `nil` keyword.

This might sound a bit harsh, but it's really more of a safeguard than a restriction. It's possible, in tests, to use method `reflect.DeepEqual`, but it wasn't designed for performance, so you should avoid it in production code. Instead, write the simple loop.

Is your code compiling and your test passing now? We can move on.

PLAY

We're now able to read Claudio's guess. Let's make great use of this ability, and plug it in the `Play()` method, which looks like the following listing.

Listing 5.12   `game.go`: `Play` method

```
// Play runs the game.
func (g *Game) Play() {
    fmt.Println("Welcome to Gordle!")

    // ask for a valid word
    guess := g.ask()

    fmt.Printf("Your guess is: %s\n", string(guess))
}
```

There's one missing update in the `main` function; can you spot it? Because the `New()` method takes a reader as a parameter, we need to pass `os.Stdin` to wait for the player's input.

Listing 5.13   `main.go`: `main` function updated with `os.Stdin`

```
package main

import (
    "os"
```

```
    "learngo-pockets/gordle/gordle"
)

func main() {
    g := gordle.New(os.Stdin)
    g.Play()
}
```

You can test it manually in your console. Here is an example of a game:

```
> go run main.go
Welcome to Gordle!
Enter a 5-character guess:          First input with a
four                                four-character word
Your attempt is invalid with Gordle's solution!    Checks on the number
Expected 5 characters, got 4.                       of characters fails
apple
Your guess: apple      The check passed!    Second attempt with a
                                            five-character word
```

You may have noticed the ask() method is now responsible for reading the input, standardizing it, and validating the guess. It's best to separate the concerns, so let's refactor!

5.1.3 *Isolate the check*

There's no specific rule concerning the responsibilities of a method, but when you start having multiple operations of different natures, it might be best to have one function for one action. Small functions are also easier to test and maintain, while making sure the code is robust.

Let's move the word length validation to another method, adequately named validateGuess. Notice that we did say method, and not function. This validateGuess method will have a receiver over the Game type. The reason for this won't be visible here, but in the next pages, we'll want to get rid of that solutionLength constant in favor of a test against the real secret word's length, which will be part of the Game structure. This validateGuess method is in charge of the validation: it takes the guess as a parameter and returns whether the word is valid.

There are two common ways to indicate a successful check: either return a Boolean value or return an error, which is in a Go value, representing the problem we found (or nil, if everything was fine). Returning a Boolean is simple, but it doesn't allow for fine behavior. What if we need to specify that we faced an unrecoverable error (at least for this validateGuess's concern)? Although there's no granularity with Booleans, errors offer a lot more variations that will allow the caller—in our case, the ask method—to determine the behavior if there's any error. We'll also see how it makes the code easier to test.

ERROR PROPAGATION

Unfortunately, most programs will face errors. A file could be missing, a connection could be closed, a value could be an unexpected zero, and so on. Go's take on error handling is to use functions that return one or more values, the last one (if any) being an error. The first line that follows the call to such a function is the most common line of any Go source code: `if err != nil {`. It's so common, we have a macro to paste it in our IDEs.

When we retrieve an error, the best thing to do is handle the error as much as possible. Then, if there's nothing this layer can do about it, we propagate the error to the upper layer, nicely wrapped. Wrapping the error will provide context to the layer that can finally decide how to handle the error. The simplest way to wrap an error is to call `fmt.Errorf("... %w ...", ..., err, ...)`, where the `%w` stands for "wrap the error." For example:

```
err := myFunction()
if err != nil {
    return fmt.Errorf("an error occurred in myFunction: %w", err)
}
```

In this code, `fmt.Errorf` returns the wrapped error. Listing 5.14 holds the new method and its attached error. The method is declared outside of the `validateGuess` method to enlarge its scope and use it in unit tests later, validating that we retrieved the proper error.

Listing 5.14   `game.go`: `validateGuess` method

```
// errInvalidWordLength is returned when
// the guess has the wrong number of characters.
var errInvalidWordLength = fmt.Errorf("invalid guess, word doesn't have the
    same number of characters as the solution")        ◄── The dedicated variable
                                                            for the error message
// validateGuess ensures the guess is valid enough.
func (g *Game) validateGuess(guess []rune) error {
    if len(guess) != solutionLength {
        return fmt.Errorf("expected %d, got %d, %w",
            solutionLength, len(guess), errInvalidWordLength)
    }

    return nil
}
```

We decided to keep the validating function simple. Every implementation of the original Wordle will feature its own validator—some will ensure that the attempt has the right length, and others will ensure that the attempt is a word that exists in a dictionary or in a list provided by the developers. There are as many implementations of this as you can think of. Be sure to replace the validation with the call to `validateGuess` in the `ask` method, as shown in the following listing.

Listing 5.15 `game.go`: **Call to** `validateGuess` **in ask method**

```
err = g.validateGuess(guess)
if err != nil {
    _, _ = fmt.Fprintf(os.Stderr,
        "Your attempt is invalid with Gordle's solution: %s.\n",
        err.Error())
} else {
    return guess
}
```

◄── **Prints a message to Claudio**

TESTING VALIDATEGUESS()

Extracting the validation into a dedicated method is one way to test unitary behavior. As we did previously, we'll use table-driven tests to cover several cases without too much repetition. Let's test this new function.

First, we need a new `Game` object in our test to be able to call the `validateGuess` method. Then, we build the structure holding all the parameters needed for our execution and validation phase—in this case, the attempted word and the expected error. Then, it's time to add test scenarios to our table. Finally, in the execution phase, we call `validateGuess` with the test case word and verify the error is as expected.

The `errors` package provides an important function, `errors.Is(err, target error) bool`, which reports whether any error in the `err`'s chain matches the `target` error. `errors.Is` is very handy when dealing with wrapped errors, as it will unwrap all the errors and the chains to verify the presence of a specific error. Wrapped errors are similar to matryoshkas (stacking dolls), and `errors.Is` is similar to letting you know if any of the stacked dolls is of this or that kind.

Now that you're familiar with table-driven tests, you should be able to write the first test scenario without checking the solution, which we provide anyway in the following listing.

Listing 5.16 `game_internal_test.go`: **Testing the** `validateGuess` **method**

```
package gordle

import (
    "errors"
    "testing"
)

func TestGameValidateGuess(t *testing.T) {
    tt := map[string]struct {
        word     []rune
        expected error
    }{
        "nominal": {
            word:     []rune("GUESS"),
            expected: nil,
        },
```

◄── **Defines the required input and the expected output**

◄── **Writes your scenarios, happy paths, and unhappy paths**

```
        "too long": {
            word:      []rune("PCCKET"),
            expected: errInvalidWordLength,
        }
    }
}

    for name, tc := range tt {
        t.Run(name, func(t *testing.T) {
            g := New(nil)

            err := g.validateGuess(tc.word)
            if !errors.Is(err, tc.expected) {
                t.Errorf("%c, expected %q, got %q",
                    tc.word, tc.expected, err)
            }
        })
    }
}
```

Only one method is called, and it doesn't require the reader. We can give it a nil.

Call to the method using the g Game object

Verifies if the error is as expected using the errors package

%c can be used to print the contents of a slice.

Side quest 5.1

Here, we cover the happy path case with a five-character word and one unhappy path when the word is too long. Add new test cases to cover more invalid paths. What happens if the attempt has fewer characters, is empty, or is nil?

INPUT NORMALIZATION

In this section, we aim to standardize how input is processed by converting it to uppercase characters. This ensures that our program can handle all mixes of uppercase and lowercase inputs uniformly. Additionally, by encapsulating this logic in a function, we make it easier to extend support for other writing systems in the future.

For instance, instead of processing a string such as "Go" or "go" directly, we normalize it into a consistent format, such as "GO" by using the splitToUppercaseCharacters function. Let's refactor the following line:

```
guess := []rune(string(suggestion))
```

We accept all kinds of uppercase and lowercase mixes. Later, it will be simple to take care of the not-yet-supported writing systems if we put this into a new small function called splitToUppercaseCharacters.

Listing 5.17 game.go: Split characters

```
// splitToUppercaseCharacters is a naive implementation to turn a string
// into a list of characters.
func splitToUppercaseCharacters(input string) []rune {
    return []rune(strings.ToUpper(input))
}
```

All we have left to do is replace the line `guess := []rune(string(suggestion))` with a call to our new `splitToUppercaseCharacters` function. You can also check that the input was correctly normalized by writing a test over the function.

5.1.4 Check for victory

We've built the foundations of the game. The next step is to verify if Claudio's attempt is the solution. If it isn't, he gets to try again. We'll also limit the number of attempts to make the game more challenging. A game of Gordle ends when either the word is found or the maximum number of attempts is reached.

To give Claudio more attempts at finding the solution, we need to enrich the `Game` structure, as it holds all the information required to play a game. We keep the solution in the same type as the attempt, a `slice` of runes, to make the comparison and the manipulation easy. We can either have the `gordle` package select that solution or, for now, have it as a parameter of the `New` function. To make sure the player can still try new words, we need to store the maximum number of attempts in a variable somewhere. We could make it a constant of the package, but it's better to embed the variable within the `Game` structure to avoid creating unnecessary constants and to keep the door open if we want to allow for more attempt.

Listing 5.18 `game.go`: Adding the solution and max attempts

```
// Game holds all the information we need to play a game of Gordle.
type Game struct {
    reader      *bufio.Reader
    solution    []rune        // Adds the solution as a slice of runes
    maxAttempts int           // Adds the max number of attempts allowed before losing
}
```

Let's update the `New` function by passing both the solution and the maximum number of attempts as parameters, for the time being:

```
// New returns a Game variable, which can be used to Play!
func New(playerInput io.Reader, solution string, maxAttempts int) *Game {
    g := &Game{
        reader:      bufio.NewReader(playerInput),
        solution:    splitToUppercaseCharacters(solution),
        maxAttempts: maxAttempts,
    }

    return g
}
```

We take the solution as a string, which is easier to use, and reuse the function we just wrote before. We're also normalizing the solution given to our package by setting all letters to uppercase, which again only makes sense in a limited number of alphabets.

In the `Play` method, we can add a loop to let Claudio suggest a second word, a third word, and so on. The criterion to end the loop will be that Gordle has received a number of attempts equal to the maximum allowed. That loop starts by asking for a word, ensures its validity, and then checks if the attempt is equal to the solution. The following listing shows the new version of the `Play()` method.

Listing 5.19   `game.go`: Adding a check on victory

```
// Play runs the game.
func (g *Game) Play() {
    fmt.Println("Welcome to Gordle!")                    Break condition: we've
                                                          reached the maximum
                                                          number of attempts.
    for currentAttempt := 1; currentAttempt <= g.maxAttempts;
currentAttempt++ {
        guess := g.ask()            ◀── Asks for a valid word

        if slices.Equal(guess, g.solution) {
            fmt.Printf("🦄 You won! You found it in %d guess(es)!
The word was: %s.\n", currentAttempt, string(g.solution))
            return
        }
    }
    fmt.Printf("😔 You've lost! The solution was: %s. \n",       We've exhausted
        string(g.solution))                                      the number of
}                                                                allowed attempts.
```

Using emojis

To insert emojis, use Ctrl-Cmd-Space on Mac or Win-period on Windows. Typing Ctrl-Shift-U on Linux will let you enter Unicode typing mode; write the hexadecimal code value, and press Enter to see it appear. `1F984` is the code of a unicorn. You can find the list of all available codes here: https://mng.bz/XxBG.

With the solution now embedded in a `Game` object, we can remove the constant `solutionLength` everywhere and replace it with the length of the solution: `len(g.solution)`.

Listing 5.20   `game.go`: Example of replacement

```
// Before the replacement
fmt.Printf("Enter a %d-character guess:\n", solutionLength)
// After the replacement
fmt.Printf("Enter a %d-character guess:\n", len(g.solution))
```

ARE OUR TESTS STILL PASSING?

It's been a long time . . . are our tests still passing? Well, for now, they don't even compile because we changed the signature of `New`. As you can see, it forces the user to provide the mandatory fields:

```
g := New(strings.NewReader(tc.input), string(tc.want), 0)
```

The `ask` method doesn't use the max number of attempts, so we can give the zero value as a parameter and tell the next maintainer that it's useless in this context.

This should do it! We can continue to update the rest of the code, starting with the `main.go` file. As mentioned earlier, we need a solution word to play. For now, we'll hardcode this in the `main.go` as shown in the following snippet of code, along with the default maximum number of attempts.

Listing 5.21   `main.go: main` **hardcoded solution and updated** `New()`

```
package main

import (
    "os"

    "learngo-pockets/gordle/gordle"
)

const maxAttempts = 6

func main() {
    solution := "hello"

    g := gordle.New(os.Stdin, solution, maxAttempts)

    g.Play()
}
```

LET'S PLAY A ROUND OF GORDLE!

Here's an example of the game when the player finds the solution. This illustrates the game when Lucio plays his game and gets an easy win on the first attempt! Remembering what he wrote and hardcoded in `main` a few minutes earlier did help here:

```
> go run main.go
Welcome to Gordle!
Enter a 5-character guess:
hello
🎉 You won! You found it in 1 attempt(s)! The word was: HELLO.
```

However, if Lucio lets his friend play the game, it's a lot more difficult to win! With no hints to guide Claudio to the solution, this game is almost impossible to win (unless one plays it twice, but changing the solution every time the game is played is work for later):

```
> go run main.go
Welcome to Gordle!
Enter a 5-character guess:
sauna
```

```
Enter a 5-character guess:
pocket
Your attempt is invalid with Gordle's solution: expected 5, got 6, invalid
guess, word doesn't have the same number of characters as the solution.
[...]
Enter a 5-character guess:
phone
😞 You've lost! The solution was: HELLO.
```

The game would be quite a bore if it didn't give the players some information about how close they are to the solution in the form of hints as to which characters are properly located and which are misplaced. It's time to give Claudio some feedback.

5.2   *Providing feedback*

Claudio just submitted a word. Our task now is to let him know which characters of that word are in the correct position, which are in the wrong position, and which don't appear in the solution at all. This will help him find the secret word that Gordle initially chose.

Good feedback should return a clear hint for every character of the input word that explicitly informs the player about the correctness of the character in this or that position. The initial Wordle game uses background color, behind each character of the player's input. While this was great for most of us, an application that provides feedback to the user should take user accessibility into account. A common impairment is color vision deficiency, where making out the difference between green and orange isn't as obvious as it would seem. An option was added to Wordle that allows players to use colors with high contrast instead of the default colors. Let's see what we can do here.

5.2.1   *Define character status*

We've determined that feedback will be a list of indications that can have three values: correct, misplaced, and absent. To easily manipulate the feedback for a character, we create the type `hint` to represent these hints of the type `byte`—the smallest type Go offers—regarding memory usage. The `iota` keyword allows us to automatically number them from 0 to 2. Using underlying numbers will make it easier when it comes to finding the best hint we can provide the player. Define this `hint` type in a new file, `hint.go`, in the package `gordle`.

Listing 5.22   `hint.go`: `Hint` character type and enum

```
// hint describes the validity of a character in a word.
type hint byte

const (
    absentCharacter hint = iota        ◄─────  absentCharacter = 0
    wrongPosition                      ◄─────  wrongPosition = 1
    correctPosition                    ◄─────  correctPosition = 2
)
```

Ordering values in an enum

In our example, we have values that we want to list in an enum. There are 3! ("factorial 3," equal to 3 × 2 × 1) overall possible permutations of three elements, which is six ways of ordering them.

In Go, the best practice is always to make best use of the zero value, and to sort the elements of the enum in a logical way—in our case, from worst to best. We could have had `unknownStatus` as the zero value of our enum, but as we'll see later, using the zero value for `absentCharacter` will come in handy.

These hints will be printed on the screen to help Claudio make the best guess he can on his next attempt. We need to find a representation of these hints that is both simple and explicit. Because this is the 21st century, what's better than emojis to convey a message that we can all understand and agree upon? We want to attach one emoji to each hint, and the Go way of implementing this is through a `switch` statement.

Let's now think about how to call the method that will provide a `string` representation of a `hint` both literally and practically: How do we want to name it, and how do we want to make calls to it?

The Stringer interface

One of the important interfaces to keep in mind while writing Go code is the `Stringer` interface defined in the `fmt` package. Its definition is simple: `String() string`. This means any type that exposes a parameterless method named `String` that returns a `string` implements this interface.

So far, so good—but there's a key aspect that still has to be mentioned here. If we look at the `fmt.Printf` functions, we can read that "Types that implement `Stringer` are printed the same as strings." This means, to print a variable of a type that implements `Stringer`, we only need to use `%s`, `%q`, or `%v` in a `Printf` call, and this will, itself, call the `String()` method.

As shown in listing 5.23, implementing the `Stringer` interface will save a lot of time—reusing a well-known convention is better than trying to be smart. In addition, it won't require an extra layer of knowledge from future developers who will later work on this code.

Listing 5.23 hint.go: String() method

```
// String implements the Stringer interface.
func (h hint) String() string {
    switch h {
    case absentCharacter:
        return "⬜" // grey square
    case wrongPosition:
```

```
        return "●" // yellow circle
    case correctPosition:
        return "♥" // green heart
    default:
        // This should never happen.
        return "♥" // red broken heart
    }
}
```

Note that if your terminal doesn't display emojis properly, you can replace them with numbers or regular characters such as "." for absent, "x" for misplaced, and "o" for correctly placed characters. Although this version is less fun, at least it's more readable than squares.

Providing a hint for a single character is good, but we'll need to do so for every character of the word. We'll represent the feedback of a word as a structure. It will hold the hint for each attempted character compared to its position in the solution. We name this new type feedback. We could place the definition of feedback in a feedback.go file, but because it'll be very tightly linked to a hint and these two types won't have more than one method over them, we can place them in the same file.

Listing 5.24   hint.go: feedback type

```
// feedback is a list of hints, one per character of the word.
type feedback []hint
```

You might wonder what the benefit of having an alias for a slice of status really is. This is an interesting question, and its answer is simple: we can define methods over that alias. In particular, here, we want to print the feedback so Claudio can next make an informed guess. And, as we've seen a few lines earlier, the best way to provide a nice string from a structure is to have its type implement the Stringer interface. All we have to do is write a small function that will print the feedback of each character.

BENEFITS OF A STRINGS BUILDER

Our first and naive implementation of the String method on the feedback type is to create a string and append the status representation as we go through the feedback's statuses.

Listing 5.25   Naive implementation of building a string

```
// StringConcat is a naive implementation to build feedback as a string.
// It is used only to benchmark it against the strings.Builder version.
func (fb feedback) StringConcat() string {
    var output string
    for _, h := range fb {
        output += h.String()
    }
    return output
}
```

However, there's an important lesson here: you should never concatenate Go strings in a loop. We've written this function here only for teaching purposes.

In Go, strings are immutable and constant. We can't alter them. We can't even replace a character in a string without casting something to a `slice`, and something back to a string. This makes string manipulation quite painful, especially for what would seem the simplest task—sticking two strings together. When we use the + operator on two strings, Go will allocate memory for a new string of the correct size and copy the bytes of each operand into that new string.

While this is simple and clear when concatenating two strings together, it becomes slower as soon as we have several strings to merge. Keep in mind that, when the number of strings to connect exceeds two, there are two quite common alternatives that are worth checking:

- `strings.Join(elems []string, sep string) string`—This returns a string of the elements separated by the separator (usually a whitespace or a comma). This works only if you already have a `slice` of strings, which isn't our case here.

- `strings.Builder`—Although slightly more complex, this alternative is a lot more versatile. Under the hood, a `strings.Builder` stores the characters in a `slice` of runes, which is a lot easier to grow than a rock-solid string. This is the option we use in our example.

The `strings` package provides the type `Builder` that lets you build a `string` by appending pieces of the final string, while minimizing the number of memory allocations and reallocations every time we add some characters.

To use the `Builder`, we declare a new variable and fill the string, as shown in listing 5.26. This type exposes several methods that can be used to append characters to the string being built: `WriteString`, `WriteRune`, `WriteByte`, and the basic `Write`, which takes a `slice` of bytes. In our case, the `WriteString` method is the most appropriate because we know how to make a `string` from a `status`. Once we're done feeding data to the builder, calling `String()` on it will return the final string.

> **Listing 5.26** `hint.go: String()` **on feedback type**

```
// String implements the Stringer interface for a slice of hints.
func (fb feedback) String() string {
    sb := strings.Builder{}
    for _, h := range fb {
        sb.WriteString(h.String())
    }
    return sb.String()
}
```

Want to check the difference? See appendix D for how to benchmark your code.

Once we've selected which implementation we'd rather use, let's not forget to test this method. Testing `feedback.String()` will cover `hint.String()`, which will be enough, so there's no need to also test the `hint.String()` method.

We're now ready to send feedback to Claudio, but we're missing a small piece of information here. We don't know yet which characters are correctly—or incorrectly—located! This will be our next task before the game can be enjoyed.

5.2.2 *Checking a guess against the solution*

This section is about approaching a new problem. Whatever the language you use, there will be times when you need to roll away from the screen, take a piece of paper and pen, and think about the best way to solve your problem. In our case, we want to make sure the hints we give are accurate. A letter in the correct position should always be marked as in the correct position. A letter in the wrong position should only be marked as such if it appears unmatched elsewhere in the word. We need to make sure we cover double letters properly; for instance, what should the feedback be to the word "SMALL" if the solution is "HELLO"?

As this book isn't about algorithms, we'll start with the pseudo-code of the check function that implements our solution. Feel free to think about it yourself before jumping to our solution.

Pseudo-code is an intermediate representation of the code's logic with sentences and words rather than instructions. Pseudo-code doesn't have an official grammar—sometimes, the loops end with END FOR or sometimes with a curly brace. It's up to you to decide how you want to write it. Reading your own pseudo-code should be at least as clear as reading code, and you'll have access to operators that might not exist for a given programming language. Pseudo-code magically offers any functions that you can dream of (although you might have to implement them later on). In listing 5.27, we highlight the use of a "fake" operator such as `mark`.

Our pseudo-code's syntax will be close to that of Go, with curly braces, because we think it makes more sense in this book. We had previous drafts of pseudo-code that used boxes, arrows, and loops.

Listing 5.27 Pseudo-code of `computeFeedback()`

```
func computeFeedback(guess, solution) feedback {

    for all characters of the guess {          ◀———  Initializes variables
        mark character absent
    }

    for each character of the attempt {                    ◀———  First, marks the
        if the character in solution and guess the same {        characters in the
            mark character as seen in the solution               correct position
            mark character with correct position status
        }
    }
```

```
for each character of the guess {
    if current character already has a hint {
        skip to the next character
    }

    if character is in the solution and not yet seen {
        mark character as seen in the solution
        mark character with correct position status
    }
}

return the hints
}
```

Finally, marks all misplaced characters as such, if they are

Once we've written the pseudo-code, we can shoot some examples at the code and see how it behaves. By first iterating over correctly placed characters and then over those that are misplaced, we get the expected output for "SMALL" vs. "HELLO":

```
S M A L L
H E L L O
```

We need to think about how to implement the different parts that are still "pseudo-code magic." How do we mark a character with a hint? How do we mark a character as seen in the solution? There are lots of ways of implementing this, but we'll go with a simple approach here. We'll use a slice of hints to mark characters of the guess with their appropriate hint, and we'll use a slice of Boolean to mark characters of the solution as either seen or not yet seen, as shown in listing 5.28. We recommend you give it a try before checking the solution.

Listing 5.28 `game.go:` `computeFeedback()` **method**

```go
// computeFeedback verifies every character of the guess against
// the solution.
func computeFeedback(guess, solution []rune) feedback {
    // initialise holders for marks
    result := make(feedback, len(guess))
    used := make([]bool, len(solution))

    if len(guess) != len(solution) {
        _, _ = fmt.Fprintf(os.Stderr, "Internal error! Guess and solution" +
            " have different lengths: %d vs %d", len(guess), len(solution))
        return result
    }

    // check for correct letters
    for posInGuess, character := range guess {
        if character == solution[posInGuess] {
            result[posInGuess] = correctPosition
            used[posInGuess] = true
        }
    }
```

Naturally initialized with the zero-value absentCharacter

Initialized with false (not seen)

Makes use of the zero value

```
        }

        // look for letters in the wrong position
        for posInGuess, character := range guess {
            if result[posInGuess] != absentCharacter {
                // The character has already been marked, ignore it.
                continue
            }

            for posInSolution, target := range solution {
                if used[posInSolution] {
                    // The letter of the solution is already assigned
                    // to a letter of the guess.
                    // Skip to the next letter of the solution.
                    continue                            ◄──────┐  Continues the inner
                }                                              │  for loop over the solution

                if character == target {
                    result[posInGuess] = wrongPosition
                    used[posInSolution] = true
                    // Skip to the next letter of the guess.
                    break                               ◄──────┐  Ends the inner for
                }                                              │  loop over the solution
            }
        }

    return result
}
```

A tricky part here is handling the case when the guess and the solution have different lengths. Because this is our code, we know this can't happen as it's been checked earlier. But if somebody changes the code later (including future Lucio who forgot everything he wrote and why), it will end in a segfault during runtime; we can't even warn him with a unit test. For this reason, we decide to recheck the length of the guess against the length of the solution here.

Alternatively, we could modify the computeFeedback function to return both feedback and an error. Such assumptions are acceptable in internal functions, where we control the inputs, but they would be unacceptable in exposed functions, as we can't control the range of values passed to them.

Congratulations, you implemented the most difficult part! Now, let's add some tests.

TESTING COMPUTEFEEDBACK()

To properly test the method computeFeedback, we need to provide a guess, a solution, and the expected feedback. Once we have these, we can call computeFeedback and verify that the received feedback is the expected one.

To easily compare two feedbacks, we write a helper method next to the feedback definition, as shown in listing 5.29. The package github.com/google/go-cmp/cmp from Google provides some insights as to how we should name this method: "Types with an Equal method may use that method to determine equality."

Listing 5.29 `hint.go`: `Equal()` **helper**

```go
// Equal determines equality of two feedbacks.
func (fb feedback) Equal(other feedback) bool {
    if len(fb) != len(other) {
        return false
    }

    for index, value := range fb {
        if value != other[index] {
            return false
        }
    }

    return true
}
```

Earlier, to compare two slices, we used the golang.com/x/exp/slices package. As always, when writing code, there's more than one way of doing things. Here, we offer a different take, which is as valid as the previous one. You'll find arguments for both all over the internet. Our recommendation is to use whichever is clearer to you. If you're curious, checking the implementation of slices.Equal is worth the time, but it requires some understanding of generics, which is a topic for later.

You now know how to write a test in a table-driven way. First, we define our structure holding the required elements for our test case, inputs, and expected outputs. Then, we write our use cases, and, finally, we call the method and check the solution. Here, for the sake of clarity and to avoid unnecessary clumsiness, we've decided to use strings instead of slices of runes in the structure of our test case for the guess and the solution. The conversion from a string to a slice of runes is simple and safe enough to be performed during the test execution. On the other side, we want to explicitly check the contents of the returned feedback, and, for this reason, we have a feedback field in the test case.

Listing 5.30 `game_internal_test.go`: `computeFeedback()` **tests**

```go
package gordle

import "testing"

func TestComputeFeedback(t *testing.T) {
    tt := map[string]struct {
        guess            string
        solution         string
        expectedFeedback feedback
    }{
        "nominal": {...},
        "double character": {...},
        "double character with wrong answer": {...},
        "two identical, but not in the right position": {
            guess:            "hlleo",
```

```
            solution:          "hello",
            expectedFeedback: feedback{
                correctPosition,
                wrongPosition,
                correctPosition,
                wrongPosition,
                correctPosition},
        },
    }

    for name, tc := range tt {
        t.Run(name, func(t *testing.T) {
            fb := computeFeedback([]rune(tc.guess), []rune(tc.solution))
            if !tc.expectedFeedback.Equal(fb) {
                t.Errorf(
                    "guess: %q, got the wrong feedback, wanted %v, got %v",
                    tc.guess, tc.expectedFeedback, fb)
            }
        })
    }
}
```

Side quest 5.2

Part of the fun of a project is coming up with some edge case scenarios. Try to find some that would push the logic to its limits.

Finally, we need to integrate the computeFeedback call in the Play function, as shown in listing 5.31. This isn't too difficult, especially as we only want to print the feedback to Claudio.

Listing 5.31 `game.go`: Updating `Play()` to display the feedback

```
[...]
    for currentAttempt := 1; currentAttempt <= g.maxAttempts;
currentAttempt++ {
        guess := g.ask()

        fb := computeFeedback(guess, g.solution)        ◀─── Checks the guess
                                                              against the solution
        fmt.Println(fb.String())                         ◀─── Prints the feedback
                                                              to the player
        if slices.Equal(guess, g.solution) {
            fmt.Printf(" You won! You found it in %d guess(es)! The word
was: %s.\n", currentAttempt, string(g.solution))
            return
        }
    }
[...]
```

Finally, this is what playing the game looks like:

```
> go run main.go
Welcome to Gordle!
Enter a 5-character guess:
h a i r y
♥ ■ ■ ■ ■
Enter a 5-character guess:
h o l l y
♥ ♥ ♥ ♥ ■
Enter a 5-character guess:
h e l l o
♥ ♥ ♥ ♥ ♥
```

**First attempt with the first
character at the right position
and the other characters absent**

**Second attempt with three
characters at the correct position
and one at the wrong one**

**Third attempt with
correct characters**

🏆 You won! You found it in 3 attempt(s)! The word was: hello.

We now have a solution checker and we're able to give Claudio some well-deserved feedback! Feedback makes it a lot easier for the player to find the solution. However, there's a small final detail we still need to address that will provide even more fun: How about Claudio getting a different word every time he plays Gordle? We proved that our implementation works with a hardcoded solution, so it's time to add a corpus and add randomization to our game.

5.3 Corpus

In linguistics, a *corpus* is a collection of sentences or words assumed to be representative of and used for lexical, grammatical, or other linguistic analysis. Our corpus will be a list of words with the same number of characters.

Until now, we've used a hardcoded solution and ensured our algorithm was working as expected. In this section, we'll focus on adding randomization to our game by picking a word from a given list. Let's first retrieve a list of words and then pick a random word from the list as the solution of the game.

5.3.1 Create a list of words

First, we create a corpus directory with a file named english.txt. This file contains a list of uppercase English words, one per line. Our corpus was built while playing other versions of the game. Feel free to use the adequate list for your own game. Adding a new corpus for a different language or for a different list of words (e.g., six characters long) is now simple: all we have to do is add a file here and have the program load it.

5.3.2 Read the corpus

Parsing a file is a very common task that most programs face. It could be a configuration file with default values to load, an input file as we have here, a database query, an image, a video file, or anything that comes to your mind. If it exists on a disk, a program is going to read it. In our case, we want to read the corpus file as a list of words that we'll store in a slice of strings.

Start by creating a new file, corpus.go, where all methods related to the corpus will live. How can we read the corpus? As it happens, the os package provides a ReadFile method that takes the path to a file on disk as a parameter, reads it, and returns its contents as a `slice` of bytes. It reads the whole file or returns an error if something bad happened. Following is the signature of method `os.ReadFile`:

```
func ReadFile(name string) ([]byte, error)
```

It's good to keep in mind that files, when written on disk, are nothing but a chunk of bytes. Nice characters, spaces, tabulation, tables, and so on are rendered by file editors. This book was saved as some 0s and 1s. This is why we don't immediately have a list of lines out of the `ReadFile` function. We have to implement that logic at reading time. We know that some of these bytes are the newline character, but let's not rush to an easy solution, such as splitting this `slice` of bytes on \n. What if the byte representation for \n (0x0a) was in fact a byte part of a representation of a non-ASCII longer character? Or, what if the file was encoded differently, with a newline character not represented by \n, but rather \r\n?

Manipulating an array of bytes in our case isn't very practical, so we'll convert it to a string to split on any whitespace, including the newline characters. The `strings` package exposes `Split` and its siblings `SplitAfterN`, `SplitN`, `Cut`, and `Fields`. These functions come in handy when the need to split strings arises. In our case, the basic `Fields` is enough, as it will split the string into a `slice` of its substrings delimited by all default whitespaces, which relieves us from the trouble of knowing them. This `slice` of substrings is our list of words eligible to become a solution. The signature of the function `strings.Fields` is as follows:

```
func Fields(s string) []string
```

The full code of the `ReadCorpus` method is shown in the following listing.

Listing 5.32 `corpus.go`: `ReadCorpus` method

```go
const ErrCorpusIsEmpty = corpusError("corpus is empty")

// ReadCorpus reads the file located at the given path
// and returns a list of words.
func ReadCorpus(path string) ([]string, error) {
    data, err := os.ReadFile(path)
    if err != nil {
        return nil, fmt.Errorf("unable to open %q for reading: %w",
            path, err)
    }

    if len(data) == 0 {
        return nil, ErrCorpusIsEmpty
    }

    // we expect the corpus to be a line- or space-separated
    // list of words
    words := strings.Fields(string(data))
```

```
    return words, nil
}
```

Sentinel errors

Error management is at the heart of software development, whatever your chosen language and whatever application you're making. Say you try to read a file line by line: the file may not exist, you might be missing the adequate rights to read it, the file may be empty or incomplete, or the file may be accessible, allowing you to read it to the end. In all these cases, even the successful one, you get an error back from the reader; your program's reaction will be different depending on which error case you fall into. To check the error that was returned, we use a line of code such as `err == ErrNoSuchFile` or `err == EOF` (i.e., End of File, which is the successful case).

Sentinel errors are a type of recognizable error. In Go, the phrase "errors are values" means that errors carry a meaning. Sentinel errors must behave like constants, but Go will only accept primitive types as constants, and not method calls. Unfortunately for us, the two default ways to build an error are by calling either `fmt.Errorf` or `errors.New`. And these don't produce constant values; instead, they produce the output of a function, which isn't known at compile time, only at execution time. This implies that errors generated by `fmt.Errorf` or `errors.New` will always be variable. So, how do we get the constant errors we'd like? We declare our own type and have it implement the `error` interface.

> **Listing 5.33** `errors.go`: Sentinel error `corpusError`

```
package gordle

// corpusError defines a sentinel error.
type corpusError string

// Error is the implementation of the error interface by corpusError.
func (e corpusError) Error() string {
    return string(e)
}
```

Here, we can declare a `corpusError` that is a constant (it's as primitive as a string) and still implements the `error` interface.

> **Don't create global exposed variables**
>
> If you look at `io.EOF` in the code, you'll realize it's a global and exposed variable that was generated at execution time by a call to `errors.New`. Don't do that at home. Imagine a pesky colleague were to do this:
>
> ```
> io.EOF = nil
> ...
> if err == io.EOF { // oops
> ```

TEST THE READING

Now, we can test if we can actually read a file full of words into a string `slice`. Let's add a nominal case reading from the corpus we created for the English list of words, verifying the length and the associated error, if any.

Listing 5.34   `corpus_test.go`: Testing `readCorpus()`

```go
func TestReadCorpus(t *testing.T) {
    tt := map[string]struct {          // The structure embedding the
        file   string                  // needed values for the test
        length int
        err    error
    }{
        "English corpus": {            // The nominal and
            file:   "../corpus/english.txt",   // error use cases
            length: 34,
            err:    nil,
        },
        "empty corpus": {
            file:   "../corpus/empty.txt",
            length: 0,
            err:    gordle.ErrCorpusIsEmpty,
        },
    }

    for name, tc := range tt {
        t.Run(name, func(t *testing.T) {
            words, err := gordle.ReadCorpus(tc.file)   // Calls the ReadCorpus
            if !errors.Is(tc.err, err) {               // method and tests the
                t.Errorf("expected err %v, got %v", tc.err, err)  // output and the error value
            }

            if tc.length != len(words) {
                t.Errorf("expected %d, got %d", tc.length, len(words))
            }
        })
    }
}
```

We're now happy: we have our corpus in a handy form, and it's reading from a file that can be updated in the simplest way possible—just add a new word to it as a newline. Gordle now knows a list of words. If we pick one—and try to make it different every time—Claudio will face a different challenge every time he plays the game.

5.3.3   *Pick a word*

Every game of Gordle needs a random word for the player to guess. We have a corpus, so all that's left is to select one word from our list.

Libraries implementing random number generators are under a lot of pressure, as they need to comply with very strict requirements. We expect, for instance, a random number generator to generate numbers with the same probability and amount of time.

Go's math/rand package provides a random number generator, but another package called crypto/rand also achieves this in Go's standard packages. The main difference is that the crypto package guarantees truly random numbers, while the math package generates pseudo-random numbers. The tradeoff? The crypto/rand package is significantly more expensive because it relies on system-level entropy sources, which involve accessing hardware or the operating system to gather randomness. As a rule of thumb, for small noncritical applications, using the math package is perfectly fine. When it comes to passwords, tokens, or security-related objects, using the crypto package is recommended.

Both of Go's rand packages expose, among others, an Intn(n int) function that returns a number between 0 (included) and n (not included). These packages are built on algorithms using a base value called source that can be overridden. Overriding it with something that changes every time will ensure we get a random number out of the library. Earlier versions of Go (prior to 1.20) required the rand package to be seeded with a call to rand.Seed(seed). The random number generator is now seeded randomly when the program starts—there's no real point in calling it. We'll keep this rand .Seed in the code for those who aren't using the latest version of Go.

Now that we know how to get a random number, picking a random word in a list is straightforward—simply get the word at the random index:

```
index := rand.Intn(len(corpus))
```

The pickWord function is implemented as shown in the following listing.

Listing 5.35 corpus.go: pickWord() **method**

```
// pickWord returns a random word from the corpus
func pickWord(corpus []string) string {
    index := rand.Intn(len(corpus))

    return corpus[index]
}
```

How to Test a Random Function

You know the importance of testing the core methods to make sure they are working properly before calling them into higher methods. pickWord will follow that trend, but there's a minor problem. When we execute tests, we usually want to compare an output to a reference. pickWord, by design, has a nondeterministic output. When this happens, we have two solutions. The first option is to change the behavior of the random number generator from the test (but then we're not testing anything). The second option is to assert a truth about the output: what we really want to test is whether the method returns a word from the list, or the results we get when calling the random function a lot of times follows the expected distribution. So, we'll go for the second approach and ensure that the word `pickWord` returns is indeed in the initial list. For this, we won't use a table-driven test, as we won't have a wide variety of cases.

Let's first write a helper function to verify a word is present in a list of words, as shown in listing 5.36. There's no special trick here: we have to range over the list and, if the word corresponds to the input, immediately return `true`. Otherwise, we return `false`. Like the previous two functions that compared `slices`, this function is also a very common one that we can make more generic.

Listing 5.36   `corpus_internal_test.go:` **Helper** `inCorpus()`

```go
func inCorpus(corpus []string, word string) bool {
    for _, corpusWord := range corpus {
        if corpusWord == word {
            return true
        }
    }
    return false
}
```

Earlier, we ventured into the standard `slices` package to use the `Equal` function. That `slices` package also offers a `Contains` function with a signature very similar to our `inCorpus`. Practice makes perfect, so it doesn't hurt to have your tiny implementation close by. With the help of this small function, we can now add a test that will ensure `pickWord` returns a word from the input `slice`.

Listing 5.37   `corpus_internal_test.go:` **Testing** `pickWord`

```go
func TestPickWord(t *testing.T) {
    corpus := []string{"HELLO", "SALUT", "ПРИВЕТ", "ΧΑΙΡΕ"}
    word := pickWord(corpus)

    if !inCorpus(corpus, word) {          // Confirms a truth about the output word
        t.Errorf("expected a word in the corpus, got %q", word)
    }
}
```

Now that we've done the implementation and covered the testing, we're ready to wrap it up. Do you remember that nasty hardcoded solution in the `Game` structure creation? It's time to replace it by calling the `pickWord` method and passing the corpus as a parameter of `New()`. Don't forget to update it with the `maxAttempts` too.

We want Gordle to be independent and reusable by anyone with a list of words. For this reason, we'll pick the solution in `New` rather than have it provided by the rest of the world. Even the `main` function doesn't know the hidden word! However, we must now ensure that the corpus is valid; that is, it should have at least one word. If the corpus is empty, the `New` function won't be able to create a playable game, and we need to return an error. This will change the `New()` function's signature.

We're now also reaching the moment where `New()` does a lot. Not only does it create a `Game`, but it also initializes it. We won't push it any further and instead consider that it might be time to split `New()` into two distinct functions, each with its own responsibilities. For now, let's just add that final cherry on top of the `New()` function.

Listing 5.38 `game.go`: **Updating** `New()` **with a corpus**

```
// New returns a Game variable, which can be used to Play!
func New(reader io.Reader, corpus []string, maxAttempts int) (*Game, error) {
    if len(corpus) == 0 {
        return nil, ErrCorpusIsEmpty
    }

    g := &Game{
        reader:      bufio.NewReader(playerInput),
        solution:    []rune(
            strings.ToUpper(pickWord(corpus))),    ◀─┤ Picks a random
        maxAttempts: maxAttempts,                       word from the corpus
    }

    return g, nil
}
```

Now, everything's ready. Claudio's been waiting a long time to play, so let's adjust the call in the `main` function and give him the keyboard!

5.3.4 *Let's play!*

There's very little left to do before the game is complete. Only a few changes in the `main` function remain to apply. We need to parse our corpus and feed it to Gordle's `New()` function. Because this `New()` function now returns an error, we should take care of it. Let's write a message on the error output and leave the `main()` function with a `return`.

Listing 5.39 `main.go`: **Calling** `readCorpus()` **in** `main`

```
package main

import (
    "bufio"
    "fmt"
    "os"

    "learngo-pockets/gordle/gordle"
)

const maxAttempts = 6

func main() {
```

```
    corpus, err := gordle.
        ReadCorpus("corpus/english.txt")
    if err != nil {
        _, _ = fmt.Fprintf(os.Stderr, "unable to read corpus: %s", err)
        return
    }

    // Create the game.
    g, err := gordle.New(bufio.NewReader(os.Stdin),
        corpus, maxAttempts)
    if err != nil {
        _, _ = fmt.Fprintf(os.Stderr, "unable to start game: %s", err)
        return
    }

    // Run the game ! It will end when it's over.
    g.Play()
}
```

Reads the corpus in English and retrieves the list of words

Passes the parsed corpus to the New() game structure

That's enough typing from our side; it's time to let Claudio smash these keys freneti-cally in search of one of Gordle's secret words:

```
> go run main.go
Welcome to Gordle!
Enter a 5-character guess:
s a u n a
▓▓▓▓▓
Enter a 5-character guess:
w a s t e
▓▓▓▓▓
Enter a 5-character guess:
h e l l o
▓▓▓▓▓
Enter a 5-character guess:
t e r s e
▓▓▓▓▓
Enter a 5-character guess:
c r e p t
▓♥♥▓▓
Enter a 5-character guess:
f r e e d
♥♥♥♥♥
🎉 You won! You found it in 6 attempt(s)! The word was: FREED.
```

5.4   *The limit of runes*

Claudio enjoyed this so much that he wants to submit his list of words. He wants to share Gordle with his friend Mithali, who lives in India. He writes a small list of words, to make sure the program behaves as expected, using the Devanagari characters (used to write in Hindi, just like Latin characters are used to write in English). The first word he writes is नमस्ते—"namaste," meaning "hello." It's composed of four characters, but after updating the `main` function and reading from this new `hindi.txt` file, Claudio gets prompted with `Enter a 6-character guess:`. He comes back to you, unhappy with the program. What's happening?

Devanagari, as opposed to Latin, isn't an alphabet. Instead, it's an abugida—a system in which (simply put) vowels alter consonants. To better understand how Devanagari works, let's break down the word नमस्ते ("namaste"), and inspect its different sections:

- न is pronounced "na."
- म is pronounced "ma."
- स्ते is pronounced "ste," like "stay."

That last part of the word is actually the combination of the "sa" letter, written स, without its "a" part, and the "ta" section, written त. Here, it's actually written ते because the sound "e" must be present, as represented by the *matra*, a descending bar above the *shirorekhā*, the horizontal line.

The word combination here also is important: even though the spelling न + म + स् + ते would pronounce the same sound, the rules of Devanagari combine the last two symbols, "s" and "te," into one: स्ते "ste." Now, let's see how Go deals with the "नमस्ते" string in the following listing.

Listing 5.40 Understanding the नमस्ते case

```
func main() {
    s := "नमस्त"
    for _, r := range []rune(s) {
        fmt.Print(string(r) + " ")
    }
}
```

Running this small program produces the following output:

```
न म स ् त े
```

We can see that Go did indeed split the string into six runes. We've already seen four of them, those with the *shirorekhā*: they are called *swars* in Hindi. The other two are a bit cryptic—they represent a dotted circle with a decoration—called a diacritic. In Devanagari, this is one way of representing *matras* (which include, but aren't restricted to, vowels). Diacritics are alterations to existing characters; they don't exist on their own. English has some diacritics, mostly in borrowed words such as *déjà-vu* or *señor*: the accents on the first word's vowels can't be written without their supporting vowel, and the same goes for the tilde, which needs a letter to sit on.

As we can see, Go won't merge the diacritic ् with the character स when splitting the string into runes. This character remains two different runes for Go. So, what can Lucio do to help Claudio? Unfortunately, this is the limit of what the native `rune` type of the Go language can support. But this is precisely what the `golang.org/x` packages are for—extending the limits of what Go natively accepts. In our case, the package `golang.org/x/text/unicode/norm` provides a type `Iter` that can be used for these strings.

Despite its name, `norm.Iter` doesn't just iterate—it's a specialized tool for normalizing and combining Unicode characters, ensuring they are treated as a single unit. With a bit more work on the code, Mithali will be able to play Gordle too!

5.5   *Conclusion*

Finally, we've completed our objective! We've written a command-line game that lets a user interact with it via the standard input. Our game reads data from a file containing words, selects one at random, and has the player guess the word. After each attempt, we provide visual feedback to help the player toward the solution. Whatever happens, we've tried to print clear messages for players so they don't get lost with what to do next.

Summary

- A `switch/case` statement is a lot more readable than a long sequence of `if/else if/else` statements. A `switch` can even be used instead of an `if` statement. If you need an `else` statement, you're better off with a `switch` block.

- A command-line tool often needs to read from the console input. Go offers different ways of doing it, but in this chapter, we used the `bufio.ReadLine` method, which reads an input line by line.

- Sentinel errors are a simple way of creating domain errors that can be exposed for other packages to check. It's a cleaner implementation than creating exposed errors with `errors.New()` or `fmt.Errorf()`. To declare a new sentinel error type, declare a new type that is defined as a `string` (this makes creating new errors simple).

- Propagating an error to the caller is the way Go handles anything that steps out of the happy path. Functions that propagate errors have their last return value of their signature be an error. In the implementation of these functions, `fmt.Errorf("... %w", ... err)` is the default way of wrapping errors. The w in `%w` stands for "wrap."

- Any structure with a method with the `String() string` signature implements the `fmt.Stringer` interface. Any structure that implements the `Stringer` interface will be nicely printed by `fmt.Print*` functions.

- The `os` package provides a `ReadFile` function that loads a file's contents as a `slice` of bytes. This function can be used for plain-text files, media files, files in XML or HTML format, and so on.

- The `slices` package contains useful tools such as the `Equal` function or the `Contains` function. As we've seen, implementing the function for a specific use case isn't too complex.

- A Go `string` can be parsed as either a `slice` of bytes or as a `slice` of runes. The latter is recommended when iterating through the characters that compose it. Use `[]rune(str)` to convert the `str` string to a `slice` of runes. However, even this solution isn't perfect and won't always work. First check the language you're dealing with to select the best libraries to parse any text.

- All receivers of a specific type should be either pointer or value receivers. Using value receivers is only interesting if the structure is small in memory, as calling the method will copy the receiver. When in doubt, use pointer-receiver declarations.

- When writing table-driven tests, it's a very common practice to use a `map[string]struct{...}`. The key of the `map`, the `string`, describes the test case, and the `struct` is an anonymous structure that contains the fields necessary for your test case.

- Getting a random number can be achieved by both the `math/rand` and the `crypto/rand` packages. Anything related to security, cyphering, or cryptographic data should use the `crypto/rand` package, while the `math/rand` is cheaper to use.

- When working with random numbers, make sure you're using Go 1.20 or later. Otherwise, be explicit about setting the seed with a call to `rand.Seed()`. A usual choice for the seed value used to be the current nanosecond, retrieved with `time.Now().Nanosecond()`, but since Go 1.20, it is no longer necessary to manually seed the `rand` library.

- Taking a step back away from your screen, writing pseudo-code, and drawing diagrams that connect components with arrows are valuable for helping you see the bigger picture and imagining tricky scenarios that might prove or disprove an algorithm.

Money converter: CLI around an HTTP call

This chapter covers
- Writing a command-line interface
- Making an HTTP call to an external URL
- Mocking an HTTP call for unit tests
- Grasping floating-point precision errors
- Parsing an XML-structured string
- Inspecting error types

Thousands of websites nowadays expose useful APIs that can be called via HTTP. Common examples include the famous open source system Kubernetes for automating deployment, weather forecast services, international clocks, social networks, online databases such as BoardGameGeek or the Internet Movie Database (IMDb), and content managers such as WordPress. Some of them also provide a command-line tool that calls these APIs. Why? Even though nice and clickable interfaces are wonderful, they are still very slow. Here's an example: when we look up a sentence in our favorite search engine, it still takes an extra click to access the first link that isn't an advertisement or the first one we haven't opened yet. The terminal shell, on the other hand, allows us to manipulate inputs and outputs of programs—and even to combine them—reducing the number of command lines and helping automate more of our work.

In this chapter, we'll create a command-line interface (CLI) tool that can convert amounts of money. Starting with a broad view of what we want our tool to achieve, we'll begin by defining the main concepts: What is a currency, and how do we represent it? What does it mean to convert money? How do we get the required exchange rate? What should our input and our output be? How do we parse the input? As you'll see, some precaution is required when manipulating floating-point precision numbers.

> **WARNING** An early disclaimer is required here: this project is a tutorial project and shouldn't be used for real-life transactions.

This project requires the following:

- Writing a CLI tool that does the following:
  - Takes two currencies and an amount
  - Returns the converted amount
  - Safely rounds to the precision of the given currencies
- Providing currency according to the ISO-4217 standard

This project has the following limitations:

- The input amount must be defined with digits only and one optional dot as a decimal separator. This can be extended later with spaces, underscores, or apostrophes.

- Only decimal currencies are supported (sorry, ariaries and ouguiyas).

Here's a usage example of how we'd like to call the tool:

```
> change -from EUR -to USD 413.9
```

We expect the program to return a value of something like `427.66`.

6.1 Business definitions

One approach to building software is to start with the business definitions. Understanding what you're trying to achieve is a good way to avoid having to solve a different problem. The business terms we'll use are highlighted in the following big picture description of our scenario: we need a command-line tool that takes an *amount* of money expressed as a *quantity* in its original *currency* and then *converts* that amount into a different target currency as its output.

As we want to convert a certain amount of money between two currencies, we'll start this section by defining types called `Currency` and `Amount`, and then we'll export a `Convert` function that takes these as input.

Before we get to that though, we need to initialize a new module. To do so, create your folder, and initialize it as follows:

```
> go mod init learngo-pockets/moneyconverter
```

Let's start simple and create a `main.go` file at the root of the project, with the package name `main` and the usual `func main()`. As long as we're only having a single binary, it's fine to have the `main.go` file at the root directory. For tools that expose several binaries, the common place for the `main` function is in `cmd/{binary_name}/main.go`.

6.1.1   Converting money

While the `main` function is responsible for running the executable in a terminal, reading input, and writing output, most of the logic will reside inside a subpackage called the `money` package. The scope of this package is the heart of our domain logic. The `main` package will be in charge of calling this `money` package. As a general rule, imagine that the package can be reused; for example, you might start writing a fancy UI without overengineering it until you know what you actually need.

We now create a folder named `money` containing one file that will expose the converter's entrypoint of the package, the `Convert` function. We can start writing the contents of `convert.go`: it has to be an exposed function.

Listing 6.1   `convert.go`: **Signature of the converter's entrypoint**

```
package money

// Convert applies the change rate to convert an amount to a target currency.
func Convert(amount Amount, to Currency) (Amount, error) {
    return Amount{}, nil          ◄─── Returns dummy
}                                        values for now
```

The two parameters are hopefully self-explanatory. We want to convert a given amount into the currency `to`. The function will return an amount of money or, if something goes wrong, an error.

To make our project compile, we need to define the two custom types: `Amount` and `Currency`. We can already anticipate that they will hold a few methods, for example, `String()` to print them out. This calls for a file for each of the types, ready to hold their future methods.

CURRENCY TYPE

The ISO-4217 standard associates a three-letter code to every currency used out there in the real world, for example, USD or EUR. As this will be our input, we can start by using that three-letter code to define our `Currency` type that will represent the currency code with a field of type `string`. Create a `currency.go` file in the same package and add the structure in the following listing.

```
// Currency defines the code of a currency.
type Currency struct {
    code string
}
```
◀── **Uses the three-letter code of the currency**

IMMUTABILITY

The `code string` is hidden inside the `struct` for any external user. We'll continue building all of our types so that they stay immutable, meaning that once they are constructed, they can't be changed.

We do that to make the code more secure for the package's users (i.e., us): if we have 10 euros, they won't suddenly become 19.56 deutsche marks because we called a function on them. Immutability also makes the objects inherently thread safe.

AMOUNT AND DECIMAL STRUCT

As our tool will convert money, we need to be able to represent a quantity of money in a given currency to convert. This is what the `Amount` type needs: a decimal value and a currency. Let's create the `amount.go` file in the package `money` and add the structure in the following listing.

```
// Amount defines a quantity of money in a given Currency.
type Amount struct {
    quantity Decimal
    currency Currency
}
```
◀── **Stores "40.00" for an amount of 40.00 USD**
◀── **Stores "USD" for an amount of 40.00 USD**

Why is `quantity` not simply a float? For a start, if we want to attach some methods, it needs to be a custom type. Second, as you'll see in the "Floating-point numbers" section later, floats are dangerous. There are many possible ways to save this number, and if we want to make room for later optimization, we need to hide the entrails behind a custom type.

As we don't know yet how we'll write these internal details, let's leave it empty for now, as shown in listing 6.4. It's not necessary to have one struct per file or name the files after the main structs they contain, but it's a good way for maintainers to find what they are looking for.

```
// Decimal is capable of storing a floating-point value.
type Decimal struct {
}
```

At this point, your project's tree should have one directory and a total of five Go files:

```
> tree
.
├── go.mod
├── main.go
└── money
        ├── amount.go
        ├── convert.go
        ├── currency.go
        └── decimal.go
```

Everything should now compile with the `go build -o convert main.go` command. Congratulations, we've defined the business entities of our money-converting library. Before we start filling it up, let's write a test on its one function: `money.Convert`.

TESTING CONVERT

You might think testing a function that does nothing is pretty preposterous, but if you can't write a test that's easy to understand and to maintain, your architectural choices are on the wrong path. If writing the test is a mess, rethink your code organization even before starting to work on the business logic. Unfortunately, easy testing isn't a guarantee of a good architecture, or the world would be a better place. More for learning reasons than anything else, we chose to use a validation function here.

VALIDATION FUNCTION

In chapter 2, we learned about writing table-driven tests, where you define a list of test cases, each in its instance of a custom structure. The expected return value is directly in the structure in each case. Usually, you'll see a function returning a decimal . value and error pair. A validation function can ensure that a returned result is valid on a case-by-case basis. Sometimes, you want to dig deep into the returned value; other times, you may want to focus on ensuring the returned error is the expected one. Most of the time, it's pointless to fully check both the returned value *and* the error—only one of them will be set.

A validation function is a field from the test case structure that takes parameter `*testing.T` and all necessary parameters for the check. This approach centralizes the logic for checking results, ensuring consistency across test cases. It doesn't return an error but fails directly if something wrong happens. For our `Convert` function, we'll need the value we got and the error:

```
tt := map[string]struct {
    // input fields
    validate func(t *testing.T, got money.Amount, err error)
}{
```

Now wait a second—is that field actually a function? Yes! Go allows for the definition of variables of many types, including functions of specific signatures. This is particularly useful in table-driven tests because each test case can have unique validation logic. By storing a function directly in the test case structure, we allow each test to define how it should validate its own results. For example, some test cases may only need to validate the returned value, while others might need to focus on ensuring that an error is correctly handled. Having a different function for each test case enables you to tailor the validation logic without cluttering the main test function. You can see examples of what it looks like in the test cases in the following listing.

Listing 6.5 `convert_test.go`: **Checking the testability of design choices**

```
package money_test

import (
    "learngo-pockets/moneyconverter/money"
    "reflect"
    "testing"
)

func TestConvert(t *testing.T) {
    tt := map[string]struct {
        amount   money.Amount
        to       money.Currency
        validate func(t *testing.T,                      ← Validation function
            got money.Amount, err error)                   (see section 6.3.2)
    }{
        "34.98 USD to EUR": {
            amount: money.Amount{},                      The name of the test is phony until we put
            to:     money.Currency{},                    some actual data into these structures.
            validate: func(
                t *testing.T,                            A test case–specific
                got money.Amount,                        validation function makes
                err error) {                           ← the loop below shorter.
                if err != nil {
                    t.Errorf("expected no error, got %s", err.Error())
                }
                expected := money.Amount{}             ← This empty value
                if !reflect.DeepEqual(got, expected) {   will change soon.
                    t.Errorf("expected %v, got %v", expected, got)
                }
            },
        },
    }
    for name, tc := range tt {
        t.Run(name, func(t *testing.T) {
            got, err := money.Convert(tc.amount, tc.to)
            tc.validate(t, got, err)                   ← Validates the test
        })                                               with a single line
    }
}
```

Enough suspense! Let's code this `Decimal`.

6.2   *Representing money*

How should we represent a given amount of money? For example, should we use 86.33 Canadian dollars, or should we use 86.33 CAD, which is the ISO-4217 standard? One idea that comes to mind is to simply use a floating-point number. Unfortunately, there are two problems in this naive approach.

First, we aren't preventing anyone from declaring 86.32456 CAD, which bears no real-world meaning. The smallest subunit of this Canadian dollar is the cent, a hundredth of a dollar. Anything smaller than 0.01 CAD must be rounded one way or another. We want to prevent this nonsense from happening *by design*. This means that the way we build this `Decimal` struct should prevent it from ever happening, not because of safeguards that we may accidentally remove, but because it should simply be impossible. The second problem relates to the precision of the floating point numbers, which is worth diving into.

6.2.1   *Floating-point numbers*

Using integers in computer programming is straightforward—all you need to pay attention to is whether they're not too big. Using floating-point numbers is a very different story—always assume you won't get exactly what you expect if you use them.

The IEEE-754 standard, adopted by Go, defines an implementation of floating-point numbers arithmetic. Go offers two flavors of floating-point numbers: `float32` (encoded as 4 bytes) and `float64` (encoded as 8 bytes). Due to the implementation of IEEE-754, these two types have a precision—a number of guaranteed correct digits—when written in base 10.

For `float32`, the precision is only six digits. This means anything farther down the line from the first nonzero digit, in a `float32` variable, can safely be considered gibberish. Here are two examples:

- `123_456_789` *(around a hundred million)*—The first nonzero digit is the leading 1, and the seventh digit is the 7. If we write `fmt.Printf("%.f", float32(123_456_789))`, we get the output `123456792`. As you can see, the correct digits are lost after the 7.

- `0.0123456789`—The first nonzero digit is the 1 in the hundredth (second after the decimal separator) position. If we write `fmt.Printf("%.10f", float32(0.0123456789))`, we get the output `0.0123456791`. Again, only the first seven nonzero digits were safely encoded; the rest are lost.

When using `float64` variables, the precision is 15 guaranteed digits. With that many digits, a measurement of the distance between the Earth and the Moon (around 384,400 km) would be precise down to the micrometer. You might think this is way too accurate to ever be imprecise—sometimes, it simply isn't: using a `float64` to represent the mass of Earth would make the weight of all the gold on Earth a negligible part of these gibberish numbers.

Some numbers will have an exact representation in IEEE-754—numbers that are combinations of inverses of powers of 2—up to a certain point. For instance, 0.625, which is ½ + ⅛, prints as 0.625000 . . ., and all digits after the 5 are zeros. But most fractions can't be written as sums of inverses of powers of 2, so most decimal numbers will be incorrectly represented when using `float32` or `float64`.

We can reach the limits of `float32` rather early: the following line doesn't print the expected 1.00000000. Even though the first seven digits are correct (0.9999 . . . is equal to 1), the eighth isn't:

```
fmt.Printf("%.8f", float32(1)/float32(41)*float32(41))
```

Sometimes, a precision of seven significant digits will be enough. When averaging grades, using `float32` works perfectly. Similarly, an error of a millionth of a dollar would seem tolerable if we were to use `float32`s in our project, wouldn't it? But what if the amount to convert isn't 1 dollar, but 10 million dollars? In this case, the error we introduce by using `float32` would already be a few dollars. Would that still be acceptable?

6.2.2 *Back to money*

To represent an amount of money, it's always preferable to default to a fixed precision, unless you know for certain that the floating point won't cause any harm—arithmetic operations on integers are correct to the unit—as long as they're not too big. If we want to represent billions, which is close to the maximum value of a `uint32`—that is, 2^32, or around 4 billion—the package `big` has a few types to represent really big numbers, for example, `big.Int` or `big.Rat`, respectively, for integers and rationals. In our case, let's keep it simple and use regular integers: we'll accept the fact that we aren't decillionaires as a limitation.

When it comes to operations, there are a few things we can take for granted, and others that we should not. We'll take a look at those next.

6.2.3 *Floating-point number operations*

Multiplying or dividing floating-point numbers is usually fine. The problems start happening when adding one to another and subtracting one from another. Here's a simple scenario: a bank has encoded the money in its customers' accounts with `float32`. A very, very rich customer decides to buy ice cream with a credit card. The ice cream costs 1 euro. At that moment, the customer had 100 million euros in their account. On the bank's side, the operation `float32(100_000_000) - float32(1)` is executed. The customer is surprised to realize they still have 100 million euros, as if the payment of 1 euro had never happened. This occurs because we have 8 significant digits in the customer's bank account before we reach the unit, and the subtraction of 1 is lost in the noise of `float32`'s precision, which guarantees only 7 correct digits.

One of the most common mistakes programmers make when using floating-point numbers is using the `==` operator as a comparator. Because a floating-point number isn't properly represented, how can we hope it will be equal to another badly represented number? The safe way of comparing floating-point numbers is to take into account the precision: if two floating-point numbers are within the precision range of the largest, they should be considered equal; otherwise, they should be considered different. Here's a quick trigonometric example. Don't worry, we won't go too far. The sine function returns 0 when evaluated on any multiple of π. Let's see how this looks when calling the `math.Sin` function (it returns a `float64`) in Golang:

```
fmt.Println(math.Sin(math.Pi))
```

This returns a very small, but clearly not null, value of 1.2246467991473515e−16. Any mathematician would be offended by this result. However, as computer scientists, we know that, instead of comparing this number to the exact 0, we should compare it to 0 within the range of the precision of a `float64`. This is how we could check if $\sin(\pi)$ is close enough (to the precision of 15 digits) to 0 that we can consider them indistinguishable:

```
fmt.Println(math.Abs(math.Sin(math.Pi)-0) < math.Pow(10, -15))
```

6.2.4   *Implementing decimals*

That was a lot of theory. Knowing all this, there are a number of different possibilities for implementing this `Decimal` struct. We chose to split the integer and decimal parts. Fortunately, as the contents of the struct are private to the package, users don't depend on our implementation, and it should be possible to revert this decision anytime without breaking our exposed API.

This is another reason why hiding the internal details behind a custom type is generally a good idea. In practice, we could start with imprecise floats and refactor later. Let's not, though, because we already know that floats can introduce imprecision.

Integer and decimal parts are two different numbers. But how do we know what this decimal represents in the currency? The satoshi is currently the smallest unit of the bitcoin currency recorded on the blockchain, and it's 100 millionth of a single bitcoin (0.00000001 BTC), far from the generally accepted hundredth of euro, franc, hryvnia, or rupee. We'll keep this precision of the decimal part as a power of 10. This precision is a number that will range between 0 (we'll always want to be able to represent 1.0) and a value that isn't too big. Because we don't need to represent numbers bigger than 10^30, we don't need to store an exponent of 10 that is bigger than 30. For small numbers such as this, using a `byte` is a safe choice. A `byte`'s maximum value is 255, and we're definitely not going to need that power of 10. The following listing shows the implementation using subunits and precision.

Listing 6.6   `decimal.go`: Decimal struct implementation

```
// Decimal can represent a floating-point number with a fixed precision.
// example:
// 1.52 = 152 * 10^(-2) will be stored as {152, 2}   ◄─┐ Provides an example
type Decimal struct {                                    │ to aid understanding
    // subunits is the amount of subunits.
```

```
    // Multiply it by the precision to get the real value
    subunits int64
    // Number of "subunits" in a unit, expressed as a power of 10.
    precision byte
}
```

The decimal value

**Precision of the decimal value,
as the exponent of a power of 10**

We should be able to update the test to add real quantity (as a `Decimal`) and currency (as a `Currency`) values to it. But can we?

CONSTRUCTING THE DECIMAL

The fields of the structs aren't exposed, and we really want to keep it that way. We need a building function for `Decimal` and `Amount`.

Let's start with the one with no dependency: `Decimal`. What will it take as parameters, though? If we ask for three `int`s for the integer part, decimal part, and precision, there will be no way of changing this `int`-based implementation later. We can expect the amount to be expressed as a string in the caller's input to avoid floating-point imprecision from the start.

One common way of creating a struct in Go is the `New` function, as shown previously in chapter 4. Another, when everyone carries strings around, is the `Parse` keyword, as found, for example, in `time.ParseDate` or `url.Parse`. Our `Decimal` is a good candidate for this pattern. Let's write a function that will take a string as its parameter and return a `Decimal` that the string represents.

PARSE A DECIMAL NUMBER

Write a `ParseDecimal` function in the `decimal.go` file that returns a `Decimal` or an error. Don't forget to write a test. You'll need `strconv.ParseInt` to convert strings to integers, and you'll need `strings.Cut` to split a string on a separator. In a terminal, you can run `go doc strconv.ParseInt` and `go doc strings.Cut` for some inspiration. Remember, we want to use an `int64` to represent the value, as this is the largest of the basic types. Here's a short description of the various steps we need to go through in `ParseDecimal`:

```
ParseDecimal(string) (Decimal, error)
// 1 - find the position of the . and split on it.
// 2 - convert the string without the . to an integer. This could fail
// 3 - add some consistency check
// 4 - return the result
```

There are several ways of splitting the string `"18.95"` into `"18"` and `"95"`, and the strings package offers two: `Cut` and `Split`. We are using `strings.Cut` and not `strings.Split` because we appreciate the simplicity of the former, and it's a lot more convenient to use when the separator isn't present in the input string.

On one hand, `Cut` will break the string into two parts, right after the first instance of the given separator, and return a Boolean telling whether the separator was found. If the string doesn't contain the separator, the function returns the full string, an empty string, and `false`.

On the other hand, Split breaks the string into substrings, delimited by separators, and returns a slice of these substrings. If the separator doesn't appear, Split returns a slice with only one string. Finally, if the separator or the string is empty, it returns an empty slice.

Table 6.1 shows an example of the behavior of strings.Cut and strings.Split on three different strings: one where the separator doesn't appear, one where the separator appears once, and one where the separator appears more than once.

Table 6.1   Examples of strings.Cut and strings.Split

Value	Output of (strings.Cut("{Value}", "p"))	Output of (strings.Split("{Value}", "p"))
banana	"banana", "", false	[]string{"banana"}
grape	"gra", "e", true	[]string{"gra", "e"}
apple	"a", "ple", true	[]string{"a", "", "le"}

You can see on the grape example for strings.Split that the length of the resulting slice is the number of "p" + 1. It's also interesting to notice that strings.Split won't discard empty strings, as you can note on the apple example. Because ParseDecimal can return an error, let's take some time to go through what error types are and how to check them.

ERROR TYPES

The fact that there might be problems is nearly part of the definition of parsing. If the user sends us letters, what can we do? Return an error. The errors package exposes a useful method as

```
errors.As(err error, target any) bool
```

that reports whether err's concrete value is assignable to the value pointed to by the target. It becomes very handy when you're using a library and want to compare the type of error with the domain error, for example, when asking if this error comes from the money package. When you're the writer of the library, it's polite to expose a domain error for the users so that they can adapt the behavior in their code if the error is coming from your library.

In our case, we're the polite writers of the library, so we'll expose a domain error type in the package money and implement the interface Error from the standard errors package. Let's create a package-specific error type.

Listing 6.7   errors.go: Custom error type for the money package

```
package money

// Error defines an error.
type Error string
```

```
// Error implements the error interface.
func (e Error) Error() string {
    return string(e)
}
```

That didn't require a lot of effort, and it's worth the simplicity in usage. Finally, before we start writing code, let's think of errors that consumers will be able to understand. The first error will be returned if the string to parse isn't a valid number. The second error will be raised if we try to deal with values that are too big. Having a limit is a good idea because it will help ensure that we don't exceed the maximum value of an `int64`, especially when multiplying two `Decimal` variables together, which is bound to happen. The following listing shows the declaration of each of these errors.

Listing 6.8 `decimal.go:` **Exposing errors**

```
const (
    // ErrInvalidDecimal is returned if the decimal is malformed.
    ErrInvalidDecimal = Error("unable to convert the decimal")

    // ErrTooLarge is returned if the quantity is too large
    // this would cause floating point precision errors.
    ErrTooLarge = Error("quantity over 10^12 is too large")
)
```

Now that we've exposed the errors we could think of, let's write the function. The code for the function is shown in the following listing.

Listing 6.9 `decimal.go:` `ParseDecimal` **function**

```
// maxDecimal value is a thousand billion, using the short scale -- 10^12.
const maxDecimal = 1e12

// ParseDecimal converts a string into its Decimal representation.
// It assumes there is up to one decimal separator,
// and that the separator is '.' (full stop character).
func ParseDecimal(value string) (Decimal, error) {
    intPart, fracPart, _ := strings.Cut(value, ".")

    subunits, err := strconv.ParseInt(
        intPart+fracPart, 10, 64)
    if err != nil {
        return Decimal{}, fmt.Errorf("%w: %s",
            ErrInvalidDecimal, err.Error())
    }

    if subunits > maxDecimal {
        return Decimal{}, ErrTooLarge
    }

    precision := byte(len(fracPart))
     return Decimal{subunits: subunits, precision: precision}, nil
}
```

Cuts the integer and decimal parts, and checks whether the latter was found

Parses the value

If parsing isn't possible, returns an error

The precision is the number of digits given after the decimal separator.

How does our precision variable work? Let's look at a few examples in table 6.2.

Table 6.2   Precision examples

Value (String)	Precision
5.23	2
2.15497	5
1	0

As you can see, the precision of the parsed number is simply the number of digits after the decimal separator. If the user gives us 1.1 dollars, it's a bit weird but valid. Note that converting it to dollars will give $1.10 back, with one more digit, because dollars are divided in hundredths.

TESTING PARSEDECIMAL

To check the results, we need to access the unexposed fields of the `Decimal` structure. To achieve this, our test needs to reside in the same package and be aware of the implementation. The test can look like the following listing.

Listing 6.10   `decimal_internal_test.go`: Testing `ParseDecimal`

```
func TestParseDecimal(t *testing.T) {
    tt := map[string]struct {
        decimal  string            ◄──────┐ Default value: useless for the
        expected Decimal                  │ code, useful for the reader
        err      error
    }{
        "2 decimal digits": {
            decimal:  "1.52",
            expected: Decimal{subunits: 152, precision: 2},
            err:      nil,
        },
        "no decimal digits": {...},
        "suffix 0 as decimal digits": {...},      A handful of
        "prefix 0 as decimal digits": {...},      nominal test cases
        "multiple of 10": {...},
        "invalid decimal part": {...},
        "not a number": {                  ◄────── A handful of error
            decimal: "NaN",                        test cases
            err:     ErrInvalidDecimal,
        },
        "empty string": {                  ◄──────
            decimal: "",
            err:     ErrInvalidDecimal,
        },
        "too large": {                     ◄──────
            decimal: "1234567890123",
            err:     ErrTooLarge,
        },
    }
```

```
    for name, tc := range tt {
        t.Run(name, func(t *testing.T) {
            got, err := ParseDecimal(tc.decimal)
            if !errors.Is(err, tc.err) {
                t.Errorf("expected error %v, got %v", tc.err, err)
            }
            if got != tc.expected {
                t.Errorf("expected %v, got %v", tc.expected, got)
            }
        })
    }
}
```

Let's take a look, in particular, at the test named `"suffix 0 as decimal digits"`. In this test, we parse the value `1.50`, and it gets converted to a `Decimal` with 150 subunits and a precision of 2. This is correct, but is it really the best we can do? We're dealing with a decimal number here, so there's no point in keeping these extra zeros, as they don't provide any information. Let's simplify a decimal with the use of a new method for the `Decimal` type called `simplify`. This method will be tested via the tests on `Parse-Decimal`. The `simplify` method will remove zeros in the rightmost position as long as this doesn't affect the value of the `Decimal`; for example, 32.0 should be simplified to 32, but 320 should remain 320.

Listing 6.11   `decimal.go`: Method `simplify`

```
func (d *Decimal) simplify() {
    // Using %10 returns the last digit in base 10 of a number.
    // If the precision is positive, that digit belongs
    // to the right side of the decimal separator.
    for d.subunits%10 == 0 && d.precision > 0 {
        d.precision--
        d.subunits /= 10
    }
}
```

That was an important first step. Remember to run tests and commit regularly—with explicit messages—especially on completion of a piece of the deliverable. After this complex logic, writing the `Currency` builder will be easy.

6.2.5   *Currency value object*

To understand what this input number means, we need a currency. As mentioned before, each currency has a fixed precision and can't express any value smaller than this precision: 0.001 CAD isn't an amount that we want to represent, as it doesn't exist in real life (it may be used in very particular use cases such as statistics, but not in transactions). There's no way to guess each currency's precision. We could retrieve this information through a service, read a database, read a file, and so on, or we could simply keep a hardcoded list of the exceptional currencies and default to the hundredth, which most use. Hopefully, currencies won't start using new subunits too often. After all, this is just a pet project, and we aren't planning (yet) to support funky historical currencies.

First, we need to add the currency's precision to the struct, as shown in the next listing, which will be a value between 0 and 3. A `byte` is again a good choice here.

Listing 6.12 `currency.go`: Adding precision

```go
// Currency defines the code of a money       Don't forget to update
// and its decimal precision.                  the docstring.
type Currency struct {
    code      string                          Adds the precision
    precision byte                            of the currency
}
```

We can use the `Parse` prefix, as we take a `string` in and return a valid object or an error. Let's consider the error(s) we might have to return. If an invalid code currency is given, we should be able to return an error. Let's create a new constant, `ErrInvalidCurrencyCode` of `Error` type, as shown in listing 6.13. As you can see, the proposed name of the error begins with an uppercase letter, meaning it's exposed, which allows this package's consumer to check against it. Then, we can create a function named `ParseCurrency` that will take the given currency code as a string and return a `Currency` object and an `error`. The first validation consists of checking whether the code is composed of three letters; if it isn't, we can directly return our new error. Otherwise, we'll switch on the possible code currencies and return the `Currency` object with their respective precisions. We'll assume that the default case is 2, as most of the currencies have a precision of two digits.

Listing 6.13 `currency.go`: Function for supported currencies

```go
// ErrInvalidCurrencyCode is returned when the currency
// to parse is not a standard 3-letter code.
const ErrInvalidCurrencyCode =
    Error("invalid currency code")               Exposes the error in case the
                                                  consumer wants to display a
                                                  friendly message in this case
// ParseCurrency returns the currency associated to
// a name and may return ErrInvalidCurrencyCode.
func ParseCurrency(code string) (Currency, error) {
    if len(code) != 3 {
        return Currency{}, ErrInvalidCurrencyCode    Checks that the currency
    }                                                 has three letters,
    switch code {                                     according to ISO-4217
    case "IRR":
        return Currency{code: code, precision: 0}, nil
    case "CNY", "VND":
        return Currency{code: code, precision: 1}, nil    Go supports several
    case "BHD", "IQD", "KWD", "LYD", "OMR", "TND":          cases on a single line.
        return Currency{code: code, precision: 3}, nil
    default:
```

```
        return Currency{code: code, precision: 2}, nil
    }
}
```

> **All other circulating currencies use a hundredth division, according to ISO-4217.**

Again, don't trust this tool in production. Validating the currency in real life should be done against a list that can be updated without touching the code. To avoid making this project too big to fit in a pocket, we can make sure uppercase Latin letters are used.

> ### Side quest 6.1
>
> Make sure the currency code is three letters between A and Z. You can use the `regex` package if you want to make things complicated or check that the three bytes between `'A'` and `'Z'` are included.

Have we properly tested everything? Not yet. Try writing a test for the parser yourself before looking at our version shown in the following listing.

Listing 6.14 `currency_internal_test.go: TestParseCurrency` **function**

```
package money

import (
    "errors"
    "testing"
)


func TestParseCurrency_Success(t *testing.T) {        // Success cases
    tt := map[string]struct {
        in       string
        expected Currency
    }{
        "hundredth EUR": {
            in: "EUR",
            expected: Currency{code: "EUR", precision: 2}},
        "thousandth BHD": {...},
        "tenth VND": {...},
        "integer IRR": {...},
    }
    for name, tc := range tt {
        t.Run(name, func(t *testing.T) {
            got, err := ParseCurrency(tc.in)
            if err != nil {
                t.Errorf("expected no error, got %s", err.Error())
            }

            if got != tc.expected {
                t.Errorf("expected %v, got %v", tc.expected, got)
            }
```

```
        })
    }
}


func TestParseCurrency_UnknownCurrency(t *testing.T) {      ◀─────┐ Error cases
    _, err := ParseCurrency("INVALID")
    if !errors.Is(err, ErrInvalidCurrencyCode) {
        t.Errorf("expected error %s, got %v", ErrInvalidCurrencyCode, err)
    }
}
```

This time, we aren't using validation functions but separating the success cases from the one error case. It's mostly a matter of taste because the only criteria, as usual, are whether the next reader will understand what we're testing and find it easy to add or change a test case. By calling t.Run, we also make sure that all test cases can be run separately. If your tests pass, don't forget to commit. We now have a number and a currency that we can put together and make an Amount of money.

6.2.6   *NewAmount*

An amount is a decimal quantity of a currency. As mentioned before, a decimal can be incompatible with a currency if its precision is too large. For instance, we shouldn't allow for the creation of an amount of decimal quantity 19.8875 (a number with a precision of 4) Canadian dollars because a Canadian dollar's subunit is a cent (a precision of 2). Building an object that isn't valid makes no sense: it's the role of the NewAmount function to return either something valid or an error. The following listing shows the implementation of the NewAmount function.

> **Listing 6.15** `amount.go`: `NewAmount` **function**

```
const (
    // ErrTooPrecise is returned if the number is
    // too precise for the currency.
    ErrTooPrecise = Error("quantity is too precise")
)                                                          Checks that the
                                                     precisions are compatible
// NewAmount returns an Amount of money.
func NewAmount(quantity Decimal, currency Currency) (Amount, error) {
    if quantity.precision > currency.precision {         ◀────────┘
        // In order to avoid converting 0.00001 cent, let's exit now.
        return Amount{}, ErrTooPrecise          Ensures we use the full
    }                                           precision of the currency,
    quantity.precision = currency.precision     ◀── not the input value

    return Amount{quantity: quantity, currency: currency}, nil
}
```

The test should be quite straightforward, so we won't give you our version here. Of course, you can still find it in the book's code repository. Don't forget to cover the error case and run the test with coverage to validate you didn't miss anything:

```
> go test ./... -cover
```

Now, the last step before writing the actual conversion is to update the `Convert` test. This tests `Convert` but not `ParseDecimal`, `ParseCurrency`, or `NewAmount` (already covered by their own internal tests), so how do we handle the potential errors? It's not the role of the `TestConvert` function to check the different values that `ParseNumber` and friends can return, but it needs to deal with the errors.

One option to avoid dealing with these errors is to write a function that builds the required structures without checking anything because you know that your test cases are valid. To build them, your function needs to live in the `money` package and be exposed to the `money_test` package. But then, what would prevent consumers from using that test utility function to send you invalid values? It completely invalidates the actual builders that we wrote in this section. Let's not choose this dangerous option. An alternative is to call the function and ignore the error:

```
number, _ := money.ParseDecimal("23.52")
```

This is practical and doesn't expose anything dangerous, but it raises a problem: if we give our test an invalid value by mistake, there's no way to detect it. We would be testing on the zero values returned by the function alongside the error without knowing it, resulting in flaky tests. Again, let's not choose this option.

As we need to call a chain of different builders, we'll instead write a test helper function, and we'll tell Go about it (see listing 6.16). The `testing.T` object that we use for unit testing has a `Helper` function, of which the documentation (access with `go doc testing.T.Helper`) says the following: "`Helper` marks the calling function as a test helper function. When printing file and line information, that function will be skipped." This means that you'll be able to see which test broke, rather than this helper function's line number.

Listing 6.16 `convert_test.go`: **Helpers to parse** `Currency` **and** `Amount`

```go
package money_test

import (
    "testing"

    "learngo-pockets/moneyconverter/money"
)

func mustParseCurrency(t *testing.T, code string) money.Currency {
    t.Helper()                                          ◄─── Skips this function
                                                              in the call stack
    currency, err := money.ParseCurrency(code)
    if err != nil {
        t.Fatalf("cannot parse currency %s code", code) ◄─── Doesn't just fail the test,
    }                                                        but stops dead, right here
```

```
        return currency
}

func mustParseAmount(t *testing.T, value string, code string) money.Amount {
    t.Helper()                              ←———  Skips this function
                                                  in the call stack
    n, err := money.ParseDecimal(value)
    if err != nil {
        t.Fatalf("invalid number: %s", value)
    }

    currency, err := money.ParseCurrency(code)
    if err != nil {
        t.Fatalf("invalid currency code: %s", code)
    }

    amount, err := money.NewAmount(n, currency)
    if err != nil {
        t.Fatalf("cannot create amount with value %v and currency code %s",
            n, code)
    }

    return amount
}
```

As you can see we aren't using t.Fail but t.Fatal, which stops the test run immediately. We can now give actual values to the Convert function's test, as shown in the next listing. The return value is still nothing, though.

Listing 6.17   `convert_test.go`: Calling `mustParse` in the test case

```
"34.98 USD to EUR": {                                          ←——— Input amount
    amount:     mustParseAmount(t, "34.98", "USD"),
    to:         mustParseCurrency(t, "EUR"),                   ←——— Input currency
    validate: func(t *testing.T, got money.Amount, err error) {
        if err != nil {
            t.Errorf("expected no error, got %s", err.Error())
        }
        expected := money.Amount{}
        if !reflect.DeepEqual(got, expected) {
            t.Errorf("expected %q, got %q", expected, got)
        }
    },
},
```

Does it compile? Does it run? Does it pass tests? Good job! This is a good time to commit your work.

6.3   *Applying conversion logic*

We're happy (or at least OK) with the API of this package, and the objects that we have in hand are guaranteed valid and supported. Let's now have it actually convert the money. For the first version, until we can run the tool, we'll hardcode an exchange rate.

After validating the base logic, we can call a distant server holding the truth. For this distant server, we've decided to use the European Central Bank, which offers a free service, doesn't require authentication, and is likely to still be around in a couple of years.

6.3.1 Applying an exchange rate

Of all the different entities that we built, which is responsible for applying an exchange rate? This logic could belong to the `Amount` structure as it would know how to create a new `Amount` with a new value. Of course, amounts should be immutable, and we need to make sure that the input amount isn't modified by the operation. But does this option make sense conceptually? Would you expect a sum of money in a given currency to tell you what it's worth in another? Would you expect your 10 sterling pound note to tell you "Hey, I'm worth roughly 10 US dollars today"? Probably not. You would go to an exchange office, hand over your note, and expect another back with a handful of coins. If it doesn't make sense conceptually, then it will be harder to understand for future maintainers. Instead, let's write the exchange office as a function that will be called by `Convert`.

IMPLEMENTING APPLYEXCHANGERATE

As mentioned earlier, we don't want to use `float64` for this piece of the logic. It's the most sensitive, and we want to ensure we do the exact math, without losing any precision on the values we handle. On one side, we have our `Amount`'s `quantity` field of type `Decimal`, and on the other side, we have an exchange rate that will be retrieved in a remote call. We must also provide the target currency, as that is where the precision of the output amount is stored.

How should we express that rate? Exchange rates published by the European Central Bank have up to seven figures, which means we could safely store it in a `float64` variable. A `float32` might not be enough for currencies that use seven digits (who knows why an eighth digit wouldn't be added). We've already created `Decimal` as the specific type for floating-point numbers with high precision, so it's better to use that. Because this variable won't represent a "normal" decimal number, we might as well use a specific type to best describe its purpose. We can even create a new file for it, but at this point, even the most adamant advocate for small files among these authors will admit that the type can also live in the `convert.go` file, just after the exposed method (see the following listing).

> **NOTE** You always want to have the exposed method first in a file, as it's easier to read code from its entrypoint. If you have multiple exposed functions in the same file, you may want to start with an exposed function and keep the private functions it calls just after.

Listing 6.18 `convert.go`: `ExchangeRate` **type**

```
// ExchangeRate represents a rate to convert from one currency to another.
type ExchangeRate Decimal
```

This leads to an explicit signature for the function: `applyExchangeRate` is in charge of multiplying the input quantity by the exchange rate and returning an `Amount` compatible with the target `Currency`. We'll first need a function to multiply a `Decimal` with an `ExchangeRate`, and then we'll have to adjust the precision of that product to match the `Currency`'s.

To multiply a decimal with an exchange rate, we converted the exchange rate to a `Decimal` and performed some math: the result of the multiplication is the product of the values, and the precision of the returned decimal is the sum of the precisions. We've done the following:

```
20.00*4.0 = {subunits: 2000, precision:  2}*{subunits: 40, precision: 1}
          = {subunits: 2000*40, precision: 2+1}
          = {subunits: 80_000, precision: 3}
```

The first point to notice here is that we've obtained 80 by using a lot more digits than necessary. Although 80 is equal to 80.000, we don't really need this precision. We can make use of the method `simplify` here again when performing the multiplication

The second point to notice is that we have a precision that doesn't yet take into account any information about currencies. All we've done so far is multiply decimal numbers. In `applyExchangeRate`, we'll therefore need to adjust the result of `multiply` to give it the precision of the target currency. For this, we'll have to multiply (or divide) by the difference of precision between our target currency and the result of the exchange rate multiplication. Of course, we could have a direct call to `math .Pow(10., precisionDelta)` here, but this would be costly, with lots of casting to and from floats or integers. Instead, we'll delegate that task to a function named `pow10`. In the function, we'll hardcode some common powers of 10 as quick-win solutions and default to the expensive call to `math.Pow` only for values out of the expected range of exponents, as shown in listing 6.19. Overall, this `pow10` function could be implemented with an exhaustive `map` or a `switch` statement. We decided to go with the latter, but both options are valid.

Listing 6.19   decimal.go: pow10()

```go
// pow10 is a quick implementation of how to raise 10 to a given power.
// It's optimised for small powers, and slow for unusually high powers.
func pow10(power byte) int64 {
    switch power {
    case 0:
        return 1
    case 1:
        return 10
    case 2:
        return 100
    case 3:
        return 1000
    default:
```

```
        return int64(math.Pow(10, float64(power)))
    }
}
```
◄─── **Calling math.Pow is a lot slower than simply returning a value.**

Let's write the code for this first part, and then we can implement the mysterious `multiply` function, as shown in listing 6.20. The `switch` is here to adjust the result with the precision of the target currency.

Listing 6.20 `convert.go: applyExchangeRate`

```
// applyExchangeRate returns a new Amount representing the input
// multiplied by the rate.
// The precision of the returned value is that of the target Currency.
// This function does not guarantee that the output amount is supported.
func applyExchangeRate(a Amount, target Currency, rate ExchangeRate) Amount {
    converted, err := multiply(a.quantity, rate)
    if err != nil {
        return Amount{}
    }

    switch {
    case converted.precision > target.precision:
        converted.subunits =
    converted.subunits / pow10(converted.precision-target.precision)
        case converted.precision < target.precision:
            converted.subunits =
    converted.subunits * pow10(target.precision-converted.precision)
    }

    converted.precision = target.precision

    return Amount{
        currency: target,
        quantity: converted,
    }
}
```

- `multiply(a.quantity, rate)` ◄─── **Applies the rate to the input quantity**
- `switch {` — **Checks both precisions**
- `case converted.precision > target.precision:` ◄─── **We need to chop off some digits.**
- `case converted.precision < target.precision:` ◄─── **We need to append some zeros.**

The returned `Amount` isn't constructed using the function that validates it. Instead, we prefer to return an amount that the `Convert` function has to validate before returning it to the external consumer. Note that we're being explicit in the documentation: if a future maintainer (you included) wants to start exposing this function for some reason, they will need to change it to return an error if needed.

Finally, the core of this chapter resides in the multiplication function, so let's implement it! Remember, we don't want to multiply floats together, as this could lead to floating-point errors. This means we'll have to convert our `ExchangeRate` into a `Decimal`, as shown in the next listing. The rest is quite straightforward.

Listing 6.21 `convert.go: multiply`

```
// multiply a Decimal with an ExchangeRate and return the product
func multiply(d Decimal, r ExchangeRate) Decimal {
```

```
dec := Decimal{
    subunits:  d.subunits * rate.subunits,
    precision: d.precision + rate.precision,
}
// Let's clean the representation a bit. Remove trailing zeros.
dec.simplify()

return dec
}
```

Now that we have a function to convert an amount to a new currency, where should we call it? Before we answer that question, let's test what we've written.

TESTING applyExchangeRate

This is the heart of the logic. It requires a lot of testing to make sure that everything works fine and will keep working fine if we ever decide to change any implementation.

Before writing the test, you can start thinking about all the possible test cases. Table 6.3 shows a few examples.

Table 6.3   Possible test cases

Amount	Rate	Target currency precision	What we are checking
1.52	1	2	Output must be exactly identical to the input.
2.50	4	2	The decimal part becomes 0, but precision should be that of the target.
4	2.5	0	The decimal part becomes 0, and the precision is 0.
3.14	2.52678	2	A real-life exchange rate
1.1	10	1	Keeping the precision of 1
1_000_000_000.01	2	2	Keeping the precision in large numbers
265_413.87	5.05935e-5	2	Very small rate
265_413	1	3	Adding extra precision in the output when there was none
2	1.337	5	Increasing the precision in the output
2	1.33 * 10^16	5	Rate is too high.

The number of different test cases and how fast we can think of new corner cases calls for a table- or map-based test. Of course, as the function isn't exposed, the test will have to be internal, which requires a new file. The implementation of the test can look like the following listing.

Listing 6.22 convert_internal_test.go: Testing applyExchangeRate

```go
package money

import (
    "reflect"
    "testing"
)

func TestApplyExchangeRate(t *testing.T) {
    tt := map[string]struct {
        in             Amount
        rate           ExchangeRate
        targetCurrency Currency
        expected       Amount
    }{
        "Amount(1.52) * rate(1)": {          ◄─── The test case is named
            in: Amount{                            with the parameters.
                quantity: Decimal{
                    subunits:  152,
                    precision: 2,
                },
                currency: Currency{code: "TST", precision: 2},
            },
            rate:           ExchangeRate{subunits: 1, precision: 0},
            targetCurrency: Currency{code: "TRG", precision: 4},
            expected: Amount{
                quantity: Decimal{
                    subunits:  15200,
                    precision: 4,
                },
                currency: Currency{code: "TRG", precision: 4},
            },
        },

        // add test cases
    }

    for name, tc := range tt {
        t.Run(name, func(t *testing.T) {
            got := applyExchangeRate(tc.in, tc.targetCurrency, tc.rate)
            if !reflect.DeepEqual(got.number, tc.expected) {
                t.Errorf("expected %v, got %v", tc.expected, got)
            }
        })
    }
}
```

Finally, Convert can now return something useful to the consumer. We don't have exchange rates right now, so let's hardcode a rate of 2 for now and keep the fetching of exchange rates for later in this chapter.

> **Listing 6.23   convert.go: First implementation of Convert**

```
// Convert applies the change rate to convert an amount to a target currency.
func Convert(amount got. Number, to Currency) (Amount, error) {
    // Convert to the target currency applying the fetched change rate.
    convertedValue := applyExchangeRate(amount, to, 2)    ◄──┐ Calls the function
    return convertedValue, nil    ◄──┐                          that applies the rate
}                                    └ Returns the new value
```

Congratulations, you broke the test for this function! We're now returning something so you can fix it by calling `mustParseAmount` to define the expected output. Now that we trust the heart of the conversion, we can make sure that what is returned to the consumer can be used again by our own library.

6.3.2 *Validating the result*

Because we have so many limitations in the supported values, it seems wise to check that we'll get the expected output, as shown in listing 6.24. Following are the limitations:

- The number can't be higher than 10^{12}, or it will lose precision due to the floats.
- The number's precision must be compatible with the currency's precision.

Contrary to the conversion logic, this can be the responsibility of the `Amount` structure. An amount can be valid or not, and an `Amount` should know about its validity. After all, pound notes and dollar bills are covered in the necessary fancy decorations to attest their authenticity.

> **Listing 6.24   amount.go: validate method implementation**

```
// validate returns an error if and only if an Amount is unsafe to use.
func (a Amount) validate() error {
    switch {
    case a.quantity.subunits > maxDecimal:    ◄──┐ const and errors were
        return ErrTooLarge    ◄──┐                   defined when we
    case a.quantity.precision > a.currency.precision:   parsed the number.
        return ErrTooPrecise    ◄──┘
    }

    return nil
}
```

Listing 6.25 shows what the `Convert` function finally looks like. It's pretty small, so not much needs to be tested internally.

> **Listing 6.25   convert.go: Convert implementation**

```
// Convert applies the change rate to convert an amount to a target currency.
func Convert(amount a.quantity. Subunits, to Currency) (Amount, error) {
    // Convert to the target currency applying the fetched change rate.
    convertedValue := applyExchangeRate(amount, to, 2)
```

```
    // Validate the converted amount is in the handled bounded range.
    if err := convertedValue.validate(); err != nil {
        return Amount{}, err
    }

    return convertedValue, nil
}
```

Check your tests: do you have a convincing coverage of the finalized library? You can check the coverage of your test.

Now that we have the whole structure and logic of our library and it's tested, let's plug it in because code isn't fun if you don't run it! After that, we'll fetch some real-life exchange rates and finish the tool. Having an executable in which we keep adding features allows us to showcase an early version of our product that we can improve on.

6.4 Writing the CLI

In this section, we'll write the `main` function: let's not forget that we aren't writing a library, but a CLI. This means we'll be parsing, validating, and passing input parameters on to the `Convert` function. But before we implement all of these safety nets, we want to run our application.

6.4.1 Flags and arguments

Take a step back. What should our program do? Let's look at the usage we wrote in the requirements at the beginning of the chapter:

```
> change -from EUR -to USD 413.98
```

Note that we have two flags (the in and out currencies) and an argument (the amount we want to change).

CURRENCY FLAGS

To read flags from a command line, as we saw in chapter 2, Go has the explicit `flag` package. After importing it in our `main.go` file, we can start with the first few lines to ensure that we properly read from the command line.

As mentioned in chapter 2, the `flag` package exposes useful methods to retrieve values from flag parameters. In listing 6.26, we'll use the `flag.String` method to retrieve the two currencies' source and target: `from` and `to`.

The `flag.String` method takes the name of the flag as an argument, the default value (which can be empty), and a brief description. It returns the contents of the flag `-from` as a variable of type `*string`. As we've already mentioned in chapter 2, calling the `Parse` method is necessary after all flags are defined and before values are accessed. Here, we leave the default value empty for the `-from` flag, but we set it for the `-to` flag to the string `EUR`. Should the user not provide the `-from` flag on the command line, the value of the `from` variable will be an empty string. Similarly, if the `-to` flag is absent, the value will be `EUR`.

Listing 6.26   `main.go`: Parsing the flags

```go
package main

import (
    "flag"
    "fmt"
)

func main() {
    from := flag.String("from", "", "source currency, required")
    to := flag.String("to", "EUR", "target currency")

    flag.Parse()

    fmt.Println(*from, *to)
}
```

You can use your local currency as default value.

Prints to check what it does

Now, we can run it. Do you remember how to run a program from the terminal after all of this library development?

```
> go run . -from EUR -to CHF 10.50
```

This first implementation of the `main` function doesn't call the `Convert` function, but it does print the source and destination currencies. They should appear on the screen.

VALUE ARGUMENT

The next step in implementing our CLI is to retrieve the value that we have to convert. If it's absent from the command line, we'll exit with an error.

RETRIEVING ARGUMENTS FROM THE COMMAND LINE

When running an executable, most of the time, we need to specify the input, the behavior, the output, and so on. These parameters can be provided explicitly via the command line, or they can be provided implicitly via preset environment variables or configuration files at known locations. When it comes to explicit settings, there are two ways of passing user-defined values to the program: arguments and flags.

Arguments refer to a sequence of parameters that starts at 0 and proceeds. Arguments are anonymous and ordered. Exchanging their position can completely change the behavior of the program. Arguments, most of the time, are mandatory and have no default value. The only argument of the `go build` command is the directory, file, or package containing the `main` function.

Flag parameters, on the other hand, aren't sorted. They can appear in any order in the command line without altering the behavior of the program. They can have default values (used when the flag is absent from the command line) like our `-to` has. An example of a flag that controls behavior that you may have used is the `-o {binaryPath}` option of the `go build` command.

In Go, the parameters of the command line can be retrieved with `os.Args` or with the `flag` package. The following example shows the differences between these two:

```
> ./convert -from EUR -to JPY 15.23
```

In this line, the `os.Args` returns a list of six strings, each entry representing a word of the command: `{"./convert", "-from", "EUR", "-to", "JPY", "15.23"}`. The `flag.Args`, on the other hand, returns only the arguments to the command line that weren't in flags: `{"15.23"}`.

Depending on which information we want to access, using `flag.Args` or `os.Args` is more meaningful. In our case, we only want to access the command-line parameters, and we don't care which flags were set. Using the first parameter that isn't part of a flag is simple: we can use `flag.Arg(0)`.

Listing 6.27 `main.go`: **Retrieving the first argument of the program**

```go
func main() {
    from := flag.String("from", "", "source currency, required")
    to := flag.String("to", "EUR", "target currency")

    flag.Parse()

    value := flag.Arg(0)        // If no argument, returns
                                //    an empty string
    if value == "" {
        _, _ = fmt.Fprintln(            // Ignores the output of Fprintln
            os.Stderr, "missing amount to convert")
        flag.Usage()
        os.Exit(1)              // Prints error and
    }                          //    usage of the tool

    fmt.Println(*from, *to, value)    // Prints to check that
}                                     //    you read everything
```

The inputs are in. They are strings, and we aren't sure that the values are valid. Fortunately, we have the perfect functions for that already.

6.4.2 *Parse into business types*

The `Convert` function takes values as parameters that are already typed for its usage, and the package exposes ways to build them. This strategy optimizes flexibility in the consumer's logic, as `main` is free to use the type through any other logic that it can add, to use its own different types and `Parse` at the last minute, or to use strings and `Parse` whenever required.

We aren't doing much more than converting in this chapter (feel free to add to it later). We just need to parse them all.

Listing 6.28   `main.go`: Parsing `Currency` and `Amount`

```go
package main

import (
    "flag"
    "fmt"
    "os"

    "learngo-pockets/moneyconverter/money"
)

func main() {
    from := flag.String("from", "", "source currency, required")
    to := flag.String("to", "EUR", "target currency")

    flag.Parse()

    fromCurrency, err := money.ParseCurrency(*from)      // Parses the currencies
    if err != nil {
        _, _ = fmt.Fprintf(os.Stderr,
            "unable to parse source currency %q: %s.\n",
            *from, err.Error())
        os.Exit(1)
    }

    // TODO: repeat for target currency

    // TODO: read the value argument, as seen above

    quantity, err := money.ParseDecimal(value)      // Parses the quantity
    if err != nil {
        _, _ = fmt.Fprintf(os.Stderr,
            "unable to parse value %q: %s.\n", value, err.Error())
        os.Exit(1)
    }

    amount, err := money.NewAmount(                 // Transforms the value into
        quantity, fromCurrency)                     // an amount with its currency
    if err != nil {
        _, _ = fmt.Fprintln(os.Stderr, err.Error())
        os.Exit(1)
    }

    fmt.Println("Amount:", amount,                  // Quickly displays
        "; Currency:", toCurrency)                  // the result
}
```

Run the code and enjoy the show. You should have some gibberish, like this:

```
> go run . -from EUR -to CHF 10.50
Amount: {{10 50 2} {EUR 2}}; Currency: {CHF 2}
```

For someone who doesn't know the structures we use, this is hard to understand. It's therefore polite for the library to expose some `Stringer`s on its types.

6.4.3 *Stringer*

If you look into the `fmt` package, you can find a very useful interface that all the package's formatting and printing functions understand: the `Stringer`. It follows a Go pattern where interfaces with only one method are named with this method followed by -er, as in `Reader`, `Writer`, and so on. Let's look at how it's defined:

```
type Stringer interface {
    String() string
}
```

`fmt.Stringer` is implemented by any type that has a `String` method, which defines the "native" formatting for that value. The `String` method is used to print values passed as an operand to any format that accepts a string or to an unformatted printing function such as `Print`. To implement an interface in Go, a type only needs to have the right method(s) attached to it.

> **Listing 6.29** `currency.go`: **Implementing the** `Currency Stringer`

```
// String implements Stringer.
func (c Currency) String() string {
    return c.code
}
```

Magically, your `Currency` is now a `Stringer`. Anyone calling a printing function with a currency as a parameter will call this. Try it:

```
> go run . -from EUR -to CHF 10.50
Amount: {{10 50 2} EUR}; Currency: CHF
```

The target currency is now properly readable. Let's do the same with `Decimal`. We already have a method on the type `Decimal`, and it receives the `simplify` method as a pointer. Go doesn't like having both pointer and nonpointer receivers for methods of a type, so let's have `String()` accept a pointer receiver. We need a pointer receiver for `simplify`.

Here, we chose to use a double-formatting trick: we're using the precision to create the formatting string, and then using this to format the number. For example, for a precision of two digits, the format variable will be `%d.%02d`, which pads the decimal part with zeros. We don't want to print 12.5 when the currency has cents; instead, we want to print 12.50. This trailing 0 is added by padding it in the `%02` formatting string.

However, not all currencies have a precision of two digits, and we must build this `%02` string using the precision of the currency. For this, we can use a function provided by the package in charge of string conversions, which is adequately named `strconv`. The function we use is `strconv.Itoa`, which you can think of as the reverse `strconv.Atoi`:

```
decimalFormat := "%d.%0" + strconv.Itoa(int(d.precision)) + "d"
```

Immediately, we notice an edge case when the precision is 0. Because this is a simple test with a simple output, we'll start our `String()` function by checking this scenario.

We have all the bricks to write the implementation of the `Stringer` interface for the `Decimal` type. The output of `pow10` gives us the number of subunits in a unit of the currency, which means we can retrieve the fractional part and the integer part by simply dividing by the number of subunits. Finally, we can return the printed output using the formatting `decimalFormat`.

Listing 6.30   `decimal.go`: Implementing the `Decimal` `Stringer`

```go
// String implements stringer and returns the Decimal formatted as
// digits and optionally a decimal point followed by digits.
func (d *Decimal) String() string {
    // Quick-win, no need to do maths.
    if d.precision == 0 {                              ◄——  Early exit if there are
        return fmt.Sprintf("%d", d.subunits)                no fractional parts
    }

    centsPerUnit := pow10(d.precision)                 ◄——  Converts "2" to "100"
    frac := d.subunits % centsPerUnit                        or "3" to "1000"
    integer := d.subunits / centsPerUnit

    decimalFormat := "%d.%0" +                          Creates the formatting
        strconv.Itoa(int(d.precision)) + "d"            string "%d.%0{2}d"
    return fmt.Sprintf(decimalFormat, integer, frac)

}
```

Even if `Currency`'s `String` method can arguably skip the unit test requirement, this method needs one. Take a minute to write it and check your coverage. Remember that coverage doesn't check that you're covered, as you could have perfect coverage and still miss a lot of cases; instead, it tells you where you're not covered, and you can decide whether it's worth the effort to extend coverage.

Finally, `Amount` should also implement the `Stringer` interface. This could be adapted to different language standards, but we chose `22.368 KWD` as the output format in the following listing.

Listing 6.31   `amount.go`: Implementing the `Amount` `Stringer`

```go
// String implements stringer.
func (a Amount) String() string {
    return a.number.String() + " " + a.currency.code
}
```

Is your output more legible now? See what you think:

```
> go run . -from EUR -to CHF 10.50
10.50 EUR CHF
```

Now that we have all the `Stringer` code implemented, we can call the `Convert` function.

6.4.4 *Convert*

The only thing left to do in the main function is to call `Convert`. The code in the following listing compiles and can be run—it's beautiful.

Listing 6.32 `main.go`: **End of the** `main` **function**

```
func main() {
    // ...

    convertedAmount, err := money.Convert(amount, toCurrency)
    if err != nil {
        _, _ = fmt.Fprintf(os.Stderr,
            "unable to convert %s to %s: %s.\n",
            amount, toCurrency, err.Error())
        os.Exit(1)
    }

    fmt.Printf("%s = %s\n", amount, convertedAmount))
}
```

There's a final problem we need to address here, though. Despite our heavy testing, we've missed something quite obvious—did you spot the bug? If you've tried running the tool, you might've noticed it. When we pass the input amount with a lower number of decimal digits than the currency's precision, we display that amount with its input number of digits and not its currency's! Here's an example:

```
> go run . -from BHD -to CHF 12.5
12.5 BHD = 25.00 CHF
```

If we check the switch in the `ParseCurrency` code, we see that there are 1,000 *fulūs* in 1 Bahraini dinar, so we should be writing `12.500 BHD = 25.00 CHF` with three digits after the decimal point for the dinar.

The root of this problem resides in the `NewAmount` function. Let's fix it by taking into account the currency's precision and add a test to cover this bug.

Listing 6.33 `amount.go`: **Fixing the** `NewAmount`

```
// NewAmount returns an Amount of money.
func NewAmount(quantity Decimal, currency Currency) (Amount, error) {
    switch {
    case quantity.precision > currency.precision:
        // In order to avoid converting 0.00001 cent, let's exit now.
        return Amount{}, ErrTooPrecise
```

```
    case quantity.precision < currency.precision:
        quantity.subunits *= pow10(currency.precision - quantity.precision)
        quantity.precision = currency.precision
    }
    return Amount{quantity: quantity, currency: currency}, nil
```

}

There's a teeny tiny problem, though. Our code-converting amounts don't work properly: it applies a constant conversion rate of 2, regardless of currencies we set on the command line. We need real exchange rates. We're ready to call the bank.

6.5   *Calling the bank*

We have a working solution, but for one problem: we aren't using the real exchange rates. We need to call an external authority to get them. Here, we chose to implement a solution based on the API of the European Central Bank because it's free of charge, it doesn't need any identification protocol, and it's very likely to still be running with the same API in a year or even two. An unreliable API from a data provider is something we don't want to face.

Fetching and using the data are two separable concerns, and any separable logic should be separated to make testing and evolving easier. The bank will be a dependency of our program: an external resource on which it relies to work. It's an accepted best practice in software design, whatever the language you use, to use inversion of control (IoC) for multiple design purposes:

- Decoupling the execution of a task from the implementation
- Focusing a module or package on the task it's designed for
- Freeing systems from assumptions about how other systems do what they do and instead relying on contracts
- Preventing side effects when replacing a module

More concretely, the money package shouldn't know where the exchange rate is coming from, as this is beyond its scope. Another package will be responsible for calling the bank when needed, dealing with the bank-specific logic, and returning the required information. This other package is therefore a dependency that the consumer (here, our main function) is providing via a contract in the shape of an interface. This way, the consumer decides what source of data is the best, and the money conversion isn't touched.

For example, let's say that while you're writing the tool, somebody else in another team is writing the banking service. You can't access the service yet, but you can create a dependency that Convert can understand, where you simply return hardcoded values. When the service is finally here, you just need to replace the plug with a call to the new API. Everything else is already tested and runs smoothly. Replacing dependencies with stubs during development is just one use of this pattern. Another might be adding a cache: replace a call to the API with a similar function that checks in memory whether the value is already known and avoids a network call.

In our case, the dependency's role is to fetch the exchange rate between two currencies. Think of an errand boy cycling to the bank a few streets away and returning with the information while the clerk responsible for computations is waiting. Even though the API returns the whole list of currencies that it knows and exchange rates for 1 euro, the tool doesn't need the full list, only the `to` and `from` currencies. The details of the API should stay inside the dependency's package.

6.5.1 *Dependency injection: Theory*

There are two ways in Go to provide a dependency: one is more object-oriented; the other looks like functional programming.

OBJECT DEPENDENCY

The first option requires the consumer to have in hand a variable of a type that implements an interface. If you know any object-oriented language, such as the Java family, you'll be familiar with this approach.

In this version, as shown in listing 6.34, we create a structure with a `FetchRates` function attached to it, and we pass a variable of this type to `Convert`. `Convert` expects any variable that implements the expected interface. In this implementation, the `main` function is in charge of creating the variable that implements the interface.

> **Listing 6.34   Dependency injection via an interface**

```
type ratesFetcher interface {
    FetchRates(from, to Currency) (ExchangeRate, error)    ◀── Signature of the
}                                                              dependency's
                                                               expose method

func Convert(..., rates ratesFetcher) {                    ◀── Convert expects the interface
    ...                                                        as parameter and calls it.
    rate, err := rates.FetchRates(from, to)                ◀──
    ...
}

...

func main() {
    ratesRepo := newRatesRepository()                      ◀── Creates the variable and
    money.Convert(..., ratesRepo)                              passes it to Convert
}
```

FUNCTION DEPENDENCY

The second option, as shown in listing 6.35, is more verbose, but it also works and can be preferred in some cases. The `Convert` function's last parameter is a function's definition rather than an object implementing an interface. The rest is relatively similar.

Listing 6.35   Dependency injection via a function

```
func Convert(...,
    rates func(from Currency,              The last parameter
        to Currency) (ExchangeRate, error),   is a function.
) (Amount, error) {
    ...                                    A different way to
    rate, err := rates(from, to)     ◄──── call the parameter
    ...
}

                                                 Similar instantiation
func main() {
    ratesRepo := newRatesRepository()    ◄──    Passes the relevant
    money.Convert(..., ratesRepo.FetchRates)  ◄── function without calling it
}
```

The `main` function is passing the `FetchRates` method directly that `Convert` will be calling. You can even name the function's signature by declaring a type:

```
type getExchangeRatesFunc func(from, to Currency) (ExchangeRate, error)

func Convert(..., rates getExchangeRatesFunc) (Amount, error) {
    ...
}
```

Alternatively, the consumer is free to create any function on the fly, relying on variables of the outside scope if needed.

Listing 6.36   Dependency injection via a local function

```
func main() {
    config := ...

    fetcher := func(from Currency,              Declares an anonymous function if
        to Currency) (ExchangeRate, error){     you need access to local variables
        return config.MockRate, nil     ◄──
    }                                           Here, you can access config.

    money.Convert(..., fetcher)
}
```

As you can see, the function dependency option is a bit less intuitive for beginners (why would a function be a parameter?), but also leaves more room for the consumer to implement the dependency. The option doesn't fix the name of the function, nor does it require the function to be a method on an object. Additionally, mocking a function for tests is slightly easier. The function dependency option often leaves more freedom for the implementation, which means that mistakes are easier to make.

For example, you can have two different methods on one object and pick the one you want to use depending on the context. Imagine an API where you can have daily exchange rates for free or rates updated every minute when you're logged in. Both functions have the same signature with different names, and they are methods of the same object, which contains configurations valid for both calls. The following listing shows how to override a default function based on a configuration setting.

Listing 6.37 Using different fetchers depending on the environment

```
func main() {
    ratesRepo := newRatesRepository()
    apiKey := getAPIKey()                          This can return
                                                   an empty string.

    fetcher := ratesRepo.FreeRates               Uses a default value
    if apiKey != "" {
        fetcher = ratesRepo.WithAPIKey(apiKey).    Overrides with a
            LoggedInRates                          different function
    }

    money.Convert(..., fetcher)
}
```

In the rest of the chapter, we chose to implement the rate retriever with the first approach presented, the interface dependency, mostly because it's easier to read, explain, and understand.

6.5.2 *ECB package*

Let's create a new package that will be responsible for the call to the bank's API. There's no point in trying to make it sound generic: the package will only know how to call this one API from the European Central Bank, so let's call it ecbank. As we've seen, the new package should expose a struct with one method attached, and probably a way to build it.

Let's talk a little about the method's signature. We assume that it will take two currencies and return the rate or an error. It shouldn't return a Decimal because Decimal represents money values and has the associated constraint that nothing exists below the cent (or agora or qəpik). It should return an exchange rate, for which we happen to already have a business type.

What are we going to call the structure? In real physical life, to get the information, your errand boy would walk to the bank and ask. In our code, this object does what the bank does, so we can safely call it a bank.

Listing 6.38 ecb.go: Client struct and its principal method

```
// Client can call the bank to retrieve exchange rates.
type Client struct {
}

// FetchExchangeRate fetches the ExchangeRate for the day and returns it.
func (c client) FetchExchangeRate(source, target money.Currency,
```

```
)  (money.ExchangeRate, error) {
     return money.ExchangeRate{}, nil
}
```
You need to import
the money package.

Arguably, we could build completely independent packages and not rely on money's types. The architectural decision instead is to base everything on the autonomous money package. Others are allowed to rely on it, but it needs to rely on nothing else. In Go, if package A relies on package B and B on A, the compiler will stop you right there: import cycles, also known as cyclic dependencies, aren't allowed. Cyclic dependencies are a compiler's version of our chicken or egg dilemma. Even though some languages might manage how to build with cyclic dependencies, Go forbids it from the start. This makes the architecture cleaner, in our opinion.

This `FetchExchangeRate` method will build the request for the API, call it, check whether it worked, and—if it did—read the response and return the exchange rate between the given currencies. The whole logic is articulated around the HTTP call. Let's see how Go natively deals with these steps.

6.5.3   HTTP call: Easy version

The European Central Bank exposes an endpoint that lists daily exchange rates. You can first try calling the API in your favorite terminal to see what it looks like:

```
> curl "http://www.ecb.europa.eu/stats/eurofxref/eurofxref-daily.xml"
```

As you can see, it returns a large XML response. We'll have to parse it and find the desired value, but first, let's retrieve this message in our code!

Go's `net/http` package provides server and client utilities for HTTP(S) calls. It uses a struct called `Client` to manage the internals of communicating over HTTP and HTTPS. Clients are thread-safe objects that contain configuration, manage the transmission control protocol (TCP) state, handle cookies, and so on. Some of the package's functions don't require a client (e.g., the simple `Get` function) and use a default one:

```
http.Get("http://example.com/")
```

We'll start with this easy call. Design is about what you allow and what you prevent.

Making calls to external resources

Anything that calls something that isn't your code should be handled with extreme care and precaution. Anything generated or returned by third-party apps, libraries, or services should be considered untrusted until explicitly validated. Hope for the best, but prepare for the worst. Here's your chance to be creative: What's the worst that could possibly happen when calling someone else's code? Making a call to a library could, potentially, lead to a panic in the worst-case scenario.

When it comes to network calls, we could get errors from the network (e.g., unable to resolve the URL of the resource) or server-related problems (timeouts, unavailability). Never assume that an external service will always respond as expected.

It's your responsibility, as the developer, to decide which problems will and won't be handled by your code. Be explicit in your documentation about what is covered and what isn't. For instance, if you decide to not set a timeout for your request, you implicitly accept that the call you make could hang on to your connection forever, resulting in your application being frozen.

WHERE TO DECLARE THE PATH

We declared the path to the resource as a constant. This is OK for now because maintainers can change it in one single place if the API changes (imagine the case of a version change in the path, even if it's not the case here). Ideally, the client package should know about the relative path, and the consumer should tell the package, as a configuration, what URL to call. This leaves space for test environments. This configuration is out of the scope of our chapter, but feel free to think up a cleaner solution.

You can declare the constant just before the function, but you can also reduce its visibility and prevent anything else inside the package from reaching the constant by declaring it inside the `FetchExchangeRates` function, as shown in the following listing. The compiler will still replace the constant wherever it's found.

Listing 6.39   `ecb.go`: `FetchExchangeRates` first lines

```
const path =
    "http://www.ecb.europa.eu/stats/eurofxref/eurofxref-daily.xml"

resp, err := http.Get(euroxrefURL)
if err != nil {
    return money.ExchangeRate{}, fmt.Errorf("%w: %s",    ◄─── Returns an error
        ErrServerSide, err.Error())
}
```

Note that in production code, it's considered a bad idea to stick to the default client that `http.Get` is using. You'll learn more about clients later in section 6.2.5.

ERRORS, AGAIN

Keeping in mind that the consumer—the `main` function—shouldn't have to deal with implementation details, we shouldn't directly propagate the `net/http` package's error to our consumer. If the consumer wants to check what type of error is returned, they would also have to rely on the `net/http` package. Then, if we change the implementation and use another protocol, we break the consumer's code, which isn't nice.

We'll instead declare the same four lines as the `money` package's errors, but these will be specific to our `ecbank` package. Consumers will be able to check the value of the error with `errors.Is()` and know its meaning.

In listing 6.40, we don't really need to expose the error type we define because it brings no value to the customers. We only need to expose the sentinel errors, as we want to allow for error checking.

Listing 6.40   `errors.go`: Possible errors

```go
// ecbankError defines a sentinel error.
type ecbankError string

// ecbankError implements the error interface.
func (e ecbankError) Error() string {
    return string(e)
}
```

We then declare our constant and exposed errors close to where they can be returned. This list will be enriched as we add more code:

```go
const (
    ErrCallingServer = ecbankError("error calling server")
)
```

The `http.Get` function returns an `http.Response`. One of `Response`'s exposed fields is its `Body`, which implements `io.ReadCloser`. Before even looking at the documentation, you can see from its name that it exposes a `Read` and a `Close` method. Whatever you do, don't forget to close it, or you'll create all kinds of memory leaks. To clear your mind from that as soon as possible, Go has the `defer` keyword: what you put after `defer` will be done just before any return. It means you can use the response, read it, have fun, and return errors when you have to, and whichever branch the code runs through will close the response body before returning:

```go
defer resp.Body.Close()
```

Now, we can look at what we received from the bank.

6.5.4   *Parse the response*

Before parsing the body of the response, we first want to check the status code. The status code describes how the remote server handled our query. There's no point in reading the response if we know that the call was unsuccessful.

CHECK STATUS

The standard of the hypertext transfer protocol defines a long list of possible status codes distributed in five classes:

- *1xx (100 to 199) informational response*—The request was received, and the server continues to process.
- *2xx (200 to 299) successful*—The request was successfully received, understood, and accepted.

- *3xx (300 to 399) redirection*—Further action needs to be taken to complete the request.
- *4xx (400 to 499) client error*—The request contains bad syntax or can't be fulfilled.
- *5xx (500 to 599) server error*—The server failed to fulfill an apparently valid request.

To carry on, we need something that starts with 2—more specifically, we know that we want a 200. But we also want to check for 4xx and 5xx, as shown in listing 6.41: in the first case, we made a mistake with our query, and in the second, it's not our fault.

Because we currently only really care about the class of the status code, in case of a problem, we can use a division to check just the first figure. It's perfectly fine to have a function dedicated for only this division.

Listing 6.41 `ecb.go`: Function handling the HTTP status code

```go
const (
    clientErrorClass = 4
    serverErrorClass = 5
)

// checkStatusCode returns a different error
// depending on the returned status code.
func checkStatusCode(statusCode int) error {
    switch {
    case statusCode == http.StatusOK:                        // All clear
        return nil
    case httpStatusClass(statusCode) == clientErrorClass:    // Error 4XX
        return fmt.Errorf("%w: %d", ErrClientSide, statusCode)
    case httpStatusClass(statusCode) == serverErrorClass:    // Error 5XX
        return fmt.Errorf("%w: %d", ErrServerSide, statusCode)
    default:                                                 // Any other status code
        return fmt.Errorf("%w: %d", ErrUnknownStatusCode, statusCode)
    }
}

// httpStatusClass returns the class of a http status code.
func httpStatusClass(statusCode int) int {
    const httpErrorClassSize = 100
    return statusCode / httpErrorClassSize
}
```

The `FetchExchangeRate` function can call this checker and forward the error without wrapping it: we already made sure we knew what type of error would be returned. When calling functions from the same package, it's your responsibility to decide whether you want to wrap the error or not. Errors coming out of exposed functions should all be documented and of known types, but you have the choice of where you create them.

We now know that the HTTP call caused no error, and we can ensure that the server returned a valid response. Let's now take a look at the XML contained in this response.

XML PARSING

To parse XML, we'll use the encoding/xml package of Go. As we saw in chapter 3, there's a good list of different encodings supported by Go's standard library's packages,, including JSON, CSV, and Base64.

DECODING AND ENCODING XML (OR JSON)

Both the encoding/json and encoding/xml packages offer two ways of decoding a message. They both expose an Unmarshal function that can convert a slice of bytes into an object. They also both allow for the creation of a Decoder through a function called NewDecoder. This constructor takes an io.Reader as its parameter, from which calls to Decoder will read and convert data to the desired object. The decision of which function you should use is simple. If you have an io.Reader, use a Decoder; if you have a []byte, then using Unmarshal or NewDecoder is fine.

Similarly, when encoding JSON or XML, if you have access to an io.Writer, use an Encoder. Otherwise, use Marshal. We'll show three examples of how to parse a slice of bytes. Example 1 shows data as a byte slice:

```
type person struct {
    Age    int    `json:"age"`   # Must be exposed to be decoded
    Name string `json:"name"`
}
data := []byte(`{"age": 23, "name": "Yoko"}`)
```

Example 2 uses json.Unmarshal:

```
p := person{}
err := json.Unmarshal(data, &p) // This requires the whole data slice
if err != nil {
    panic(err)
}
```

Example 3 uses json.NewDecoder:

```
p := person{}
dec := json.NewDecoder(bytes.NewReader(data)) // Or use an io.Reader
err := dec.Decode(&p)
if err != nil {
    panic(err)
}
```

The response.Body is of type io.Reader—isn't that convenient! It therefore makes complete sense to use a Decoder here. We can then Decode into the right structure. To do this, we first define a type (covered in the next paragraph) and pass a pointer to a variable of that type to the decoder. Declaring the variable will allow it to exist in memory, and the decoder will access its various fields to fill them with what can be found in the Reader. It's paramount to provide a pointer to the Decoder (see appendix E for a more detailed explanation):

```
decoder := xml.NewDecoder(resp.Body)

var xrefMessage theRightStructure          ◄─────┐  The decoding structure
err := decoder.Decode(&xrefMessage)
```

What exactly is this "right" structure? It's the structure that matches the response format and specifies how each XML field should map to a Go field, using tags.

To define this structure, let's start by looking at the response. Since the European Central Bank is responsible for euros, everything is based on euros.

Listing 6.42   XML response from the API

```
<?xml version="1.0" encoding="UTF-8"?>
<gesmes:Envelope                                            ◄─────┐  Envelope
    xmlns:gesmes="http://www.gesmes.org/xml/2002-08-01"
    xmlns="http://www.ecb.int/vocabulary/2002-08-01/eurofxref">
    <gesmes:subject>Reference rates</gesmes:subject>
    <gesmes:Sender>
        <gesmes:name>European Central Bank</gesmes:name>
    </gesmes:Sender>
    <Cube>                                          ┌─  Contains the list of
        <Cube time='2023-02-20'>              ◄─────┘   rates at a given date
            <Cube currency='USD' rate='1.0674'/>  ◄─┐
            <Cube currency='JPY' rate='143.09'/>    │  The values we
            <Cube currency='BGN' rate='1.9558'/>    │  want to extract
            <Cube currency='CZK' rate='23.693'/>
            <Cube currency='DKK' rate='7.4461'/>
            [...]
        </Cube>
    </Cube>
</gesmes:Envelope>
```

We can keep the name of the response and create a structure called `envelope`. However, the XML node name `Cube` isn't explicit enough, so we'll use `currencyRates`.

While the parsing objects themselves, `envelope` and `currencyRate`, don't need to be exposed, their fields must be accessible to the `encoding/xml` package, so they have to be exposed.

The way Go tells the `encoding/*` packages (`encoding/csv`, `encoding/json`, `encoding/xml`, `encoding/gob`) how to encode or decide each field is by defining a tag at the end of the line declaring this field's name in the structured language. Tags are always declared between backticks and are composed of their name followed by a column and a value in double quotation marks. If you need multiple tags on the same field, separate them with commas inside the backticks, for example:

```
type Movie struct {
    Title       string `xml:"Title",json:"title"`  ◄──┐  Exposes the title
    ReleaseYear int    `json:"year"`            ◄──┐   │  in both formats
}                                                 │
                                    XML users don't have access
                                    to the release year.
```

To retrieve the attributes of an XML node, you just need to tell the decoder to look for an attribute. Go offers the possibility to "unnest" nodes by using the > syntax. Here, we don't want to retrieve the time attribute of the intermediate Cube node, only its inner Cube nodes. We "skip" from the root to the level that contains the data we want with Cube>Cube>Cube, where the first one is a child of the Envelope, and the last one contains our exchange rate.

Listing 6.43   envelope.go: Structures used for XML decoding

```
type envelope struct {
    Rates []currencyRate `xml:"Cube>Cube>Cube"`        ◄─── Travels into the XML tree
}                                                            faster with the > sign

type currencyRate struct {
    Currency string             `xml:"currency,attr"`    ◄─── Decodes from the
    Rate     money.ExchangeRate `xml:"rate,attr"`             attribute into the
}                                                             type we want
```

There are a couple of fields that we don't need, such as the time or the subject. Be minimal when you're declaring tags, and only retrieve what you need.

COMPUTE EXCHANGE RATE

Now, we need to compute the exchange rate between the source and target currencies. Remember that the European Central Bank's exchange rates are all answers to "which quantity of currency X do I get for 1 euro?" This means that the euro can be used as a "transition" currency, or, even better, that the rates to convert from a currency to another are simply computed with a hop in euro-world. The rate from CAD to ZAR (South African Rand) is, by transitivity, the rate from CAD to EUR multiplied by the rate from EUR to ZAR. We only have access to the EUR-to-CAD exchange rate, but we'll assume, in this project, that the CAD-to-EUR exchange rate is the inverse of the EUR-to-CAD exchange rate.

How do we retrieve our two exchange rates from the decoded list? One approach is to go through the list and retrieve them. We'll need to stop as soon as we find both of them. If, when we reach the end of the list, we haven't found them, then we can send an error. This implementation will work, but it doesn't make the easiest code to read.

Considering the very low performance requirements in our situation, we prefer to optimize for maintainability rather than memory footprint and go with another solution: store all the decoded currencies and their exchange rates in a map, and add the euro (it's absent in the payload from the European Central Bank). Then, when necessary, we can get the interesting values from the map. Registering the values has an $O(N)$ time and memory complexity because we go through the list once; and getting a value from a map is, in our case, an $O(1)$ in time complexity. It adds a little memory footprint larger than only storing two values, but there aren't millions of currencies in the world, even if we consider all of human history. We should be fine.

The map key is the currency, and the value is the rate. Note that we could improve readability by naming the currency code something other than string, but as the money package didn't deem it necessary to expose the type, let's follow suit and roll with a simple `string`, as shown in listing 6.44.

We could write a function that takes an `envelope` as its input and returns the `map`, or we could write a method. Both implementations would be clear here. Using a method implies that we may be changing the object that holds it, whereas using a function shouldn't. It's more a convention than a real constraint.

Listing 6.44 `envelope.go`: **Mapping the rates for easy search**

```go
const baseCurrencyCode = "EUR"

// exchangeRates builds a map of all the supported exchange rates.
func (e envelope) exchangeRates() map[string]money.ExchangeRate {
    rates := make(map[string]money.ExchangeRate,
        len(e.Rates)+1)                              // The map size is the length of
                                                     // the list + a space for euros.
    for _, c := range e.Rates {
        rates[c.Currency] = c.Rate
    }

    rates[baseCurrencyCode] = 1.    // Adds EUR to EUR rate

    return rates
}
```

From there, it becomes easy to compute the desired exchange rate. The code is shown in the following listing.

Listing 6.45 `envelope.go`: **Computing the exchange rate**

```go
// exchangeRate reads the change rate from the Envelope's contents.
func (e envelope) exchangeRate(
    source, target string) (money.ExchangeRate, error) {
    if source == target {
        return 1., nil          // No exchange rate for the same
    }                           // source and target currencies

    rates := e.mappedChangeRates()

    sourceFactor, sourceFound := rates[source]     // Looks for source
    if !sourceFound {
        return 0, fmt.Errorf("failed to find the source currency %s",
            source)                                 // These errors are wrapped
    }                                               // in the caller function.

    targetFactor, targetFound := rates[target]     // Looks for target
    if !targetFound {
        return 0, fmt.Errorf("failed to find target currency %s", target)
    }

    return targetFactor / sourceFactor, nil    // Returns the rate
}
```

We're using the shortened syntax for currencies in input, where multiple parameters have the same type; this type is only declared once at the end of the list. Compare the following:

```
source, target string

source string, target string
```

Don't forget to test! You don't need us for this one. While sometimes it's OK to skip a unit test on some intermediate layers, this kind of computation should raise a test flag and sirens. Coming back to change an implementation detail may result in this division being switched around, and the next thing you know, the FBI is after you for illegal money exchange. But who would ever switch a division around? You'd be surprised. Once you're done, it's time to write the function that reads from the response body and returns the exchange rate.

Listing 6.46 `envelope.go`: Reading the exchange rate

```go
func readRateFromResponse(
    source, target string, respBody io.Reader) (money.ExchangeRate, error) {
    // read the response
    decoder := xml.NewDecoder(respBody)

    var ecbMessage envelope
    err := decoder.Decode(&ecbMessage)
    if err != nil {
        return 0., fmt.Errorf("%w: %s", ErrUnexpectedFormat, err)
    }

    rate, err := ecbMessage.exchangeRate(source, target)
    if err != nil {
        return 0., fmt.Errorf("%w: %s", ErrChangeRateNotFound, err)
    }
    return rate, nil
}
```

As you can see, we're limiting the scope of the arguments to `strings` and `io.Reader`. Although it may be tempting to send the full `money.Currency` and `*http.Response` that the main function actually has in hand, it makes testing harder and blocks future changes for no good reason.

The last thing we need to do for the exposed method of the package is call this last function:

```
readRateFromResponse(source.ISOCode(), target.ISOCode(), resp.Body)
```

The ISO codes of `source` and `target` aren't exposed, though. They are accessible via the `String()` method, so it would be tempting to use that, but how do we know the stringer will always return the ISO code? For example, if somebody wants to make the CLI nicer and print the full name in English, they would just have to change the stringer and—boom—nothing works anymore.

We can instead add an ISOCode method in the money package that provides the ISO code and whose behavior isn't going to change for the sake of the presentation. The final exposed function should look something like the following listing.

Listing 6.47 ecb.go: **Fetching the exchange rate**

```
// FetchExchangeRate fetches the ExchangeRate for the day and returns it.
func (ecb EuroCentralBank) FetchExchangeRate(
    source, target money.Currency) (money.ExchangeRate, error) {
    const path =
        "http://www.ecb.europa.eu/stats/eurofxref/eurofxref-daily.xml"

    resp, err := http.Get(path)
    if err != nil {
        return 0., fmt.Errorf("%w: %s", ErrServerSide, err.Error())
    }

    // don't forget to close the response's body
    defer resp.Body.Close()

    if err = checkStatusCode(resp.StatusCode); err != nil {
        return 0., err
    }

    rate, err := readRateFromResponse(
        source.Code(), target.Code(), resp.Body)
    if err != nil {
        return 0., err
    }

    return rate, nil
}
```

TESTING AROUND HTTP CALLS

Now, this part is pretty important for our tool, so how do we test it? The code is explicitly calling a hardcoded URL. Do we really want to make an HTTP call every time we run a unit test? What if the remote server isn't responding, and what if we lost the connection? Unit tests should be local and fast. We certainly don't want to have a real call during unit testing.

The httptest package exposes the infrastructure to set up a small HTTP server for the tests. It can run a very tiny mock HTTP server for the milliseconds when your test requires it. Then, you just need to pass the server's URL to the caller and define what you expect as a response. Any query to that server's URL will always return a specific message, as we'll see in section 6.2.5.

But, wait, in our code, the URL is a constant. As mentioned before, in a production environment, we would want to make this configurable and make it part of the Client object. Let's do that. Add a field path to the object, as shown in listing 6.48. Ideally, a New function would be tasked with taking this path as a parameter and creating the object, but we can take a small shortcut.

Listing 6.48   `ecb.go`: Fetching the exchange rate with mockable path

```
// Client can call the bank to retrieve exchange rates.
type Client struct {
    url string                  ◀──────┐ Adds a field
}

// FetchExchangeRate fetches today's ExchangeRate and returns it.
func (c Client) FetchExchangeRate(
    source, target money.Currency) (money.ExchangeRate, error) {
    const euroxrefURL =
        "http://www.ecb.europa.eu/stats/eurofxref/eurofxref-daily.xml"

    if c.url == "" {                  ◀──────┐ Uses the const if
        c.url = euroxrefURL                  │ the field is empty
    }

    resp, err := http.Get(c.url)
// ...
```

This should work the exact same way if you test it manually. The only difference is that now you can automate the test.

In your test, start by creating a server using the `httptest` facilities. `NewServer` takes a function of the type `HandlerFunc`, which is the standard HTTP handler in Go, defined not in the `httptest` but in the real `http` package:

```
ts := httptest.NewServer(
    http.HandlerFunc(func(w http.ResponseWriter, r *http.Request) {
    fmt.Fprintln(w, "...")
}))
defer ts.Close()          ◀──────┘ Don't forget to stop the server.
```

Here, the parameter is an anonymous function that we cast into the `HandlerFunc` type. The server just writes the expected response into the `ResponseWriter` every time a query is sent to its URL. We can then pass this server's URL to our `EuroCentralBank`, and the rest of the test is quite easy for you by now.

Listing 6.49   `ecb_internal_test.go`: Testing the `Fetch` function

```
func TestEuroCentralBank_FetchExchangeRate_Success(t *testing.T) {
    ts := httptest.NewServer(
        http.HandlerFunc(func(w http.ResponseWriter, r *http.Request) {
        fmt.Fprintln(w, `<?xml...>`)
    }))
    defer ts.Close()          ◀──────┐ Creates and defers the
                                      │ closing of the server
```

```
ecb := Client{
    path: ts.URL,
}
```
Sets the path to your test object

```
got, err := c.FetchExchangeRate(mustParseCurrency(t, "USD"),
    mustParseCurrency(t, "RON"))
...
```
Reuses mustParseCurrency by copying it here

You may be wondering why we're copying `mustParseCurrency` in two places. Many times, a small copy is better than a big dependency. This way, both can evolve independently. To keep only one, you would need to expose it in a nontest file. Let's stop there and copy a handful of lines.

Of course, the example test that we're giving here is just one test case. Don't forget to add more cases, including error cases. Instead of writing a pretty XML response into the `ResponseWriter`, try this line:

```
w.WriteHeader(http.StatusInternalServerError)
```

What would you expect if the XML is broken?

6.5.5 *Integration in the money package*

Now, we can retrieve the rate. Back in `main`, how do we use our European Central Bank client with `Convert`?

INTERFACE DEFINITION

In some common languages, an interface is a contract that every implementation must satisfy. In Go, it's quite the opposite. We don't write interfaces as long as we don't need them. And we start needing them when they make our life simpler. We have a saying in Go that could be counterintuitive if you come from a strongly object-oriented language such as Java or C++, where interfaces are implicit: interfaces should be discovered, not designed. What does that mean? We've written a dependency for `Convert` without first defining the contract between the two packages: `money.Convert` has to use something from the `ecbank` package. It's never too late, so to tell `Convert` what rates provider to expect, we can use the function signature we already have, which is generic enough to be mocked in tests. Let's put it in an interface for `Convert` to use, as shown in the next listing. As usual, put it where you need it: you can declare it next to `Convert` itself.

> **Listing 6.50 exchangerates.go: Interface definition**

Don't expose it.

```
type exchangeRates interface {
    FetchExchangeRate(source, target Currency) (ExchangeRate, error)
}
```

We don't need to expose the interface because other packages won't use the interface. We don't want anyone else to rely on this interface; it's ours in this package. If someone else needs to call the same API, they will define their own one-line interface and mock it the way they want. It reduces coupling drastically. Next, let's see how we can use the interface.

USING FETCHEXCHANGERATE IN CONVERT

We can now add the dependency to `Convert`'s signature and call it to retrieve the current rate, as shown in listing 6.51. As the caller is responsible for providing the implementation of the rates provider, it will know about all the kinds of errors that it can return. If anything wrong happens, we can simply wrap the error that we get and bubble it up.

Listing 6.51   `convert.go`: Final implementation

```
// Convert applies the change rate to convert an amount to a target currency.
func Convert(
    amount Amount, to Currency, rates exchangeRates) (Amount, error) {
    // fetch the change rate for the day
    r, err := rates.FetchExchangeRate(amount.currency, to)      ◀── Fetches the
    if err != nil {                                                  exchange rate
        return Amount{}, fmt.Errorf(                                 for the day
            "cannot get change rate: %w", err)      ◀──
    }                                                   │ Wraps with %w

    convertedValue := applyExchangeRate(amount, to, r)

    if err := convertedValue.validate(); err != nil {
        return Amount{}, err
    }

    return convertedValue, nil
}
```

FIX THE TEST

Time to fix your test. If you want to be fast, the smallest thing that implements your local interface is `nil`. Let's try the following:

```
got, err := money.Convert(tc.amount, tc.to, nil)
```

The test compiles, but if you try to run it, you'll get a full-fledged panic attack:

```
panic: runtime error: invalid memory address or nil pointer dereference
```

This message means you're trying to access a field or a method on a pointer that is clearly wrong, which is the case of our `nil` value. The C family of languages calls this a segmentation fault, and the Java family calls it a `NullPointerException`. At runtime, your machine is trying to access a function on an object whose address is nothing (recognizable by the value `zero`). In Go, this causes the runtime system to raise a panic signal.

Wasn't that fun to watch? Thankfully, this happened in a test environment and not on a production platform. Meeting with these runtime errors is always valuable. Once you've experienced a few, you know precisely what you're looking for when investigating a problem. Did we access a `slice` past its bounds? Did we dereference an invalid pointer? Did we just divide by 0? Let's fix this by implementing a stub in the test file: a very minimal struct that implements our interface and returns values that we require for testing (see listing 6.52). If you require a mock in a bigger project, there is a handful of tools out there that can generate one from the interface definition, for example, minimock or mockgen. The difference between a mock and a stub is that the mock will check whether it has been called and make the test fail if the expected calls don't match the actual ones. A stub will only imitate the expected behavior when called, but can't validate anything.

Listing 6.52 `convert_test.go`: **Stubbing the dependency**

```go
// stubRate is a very simple stub for the exchangeRates.
type stubRate struct {
    rate money.ExchangeRate
    err  error
}

// FetchExchangeRate implements the interface exchangeRates with the same
// signature but fields are unused for tests purposes.
func (m stubRate) FetchExchangeRate(
    _, _ money.Currency,          ◄——— Explicitly ignores the
) (money.ExchangeRate, error) {         parameters you don't need
    return m.rate, m.err
}
```

Side quest 6.2

Update the rest of the unit test. You need to add the stub to the test case scenario and give the rate that you expect to get from the dependency.

6.5.6 *Dependency injection in main*

The last missing piece consists of building the `EuroCentralBank` and passing it to `Convert`, as shown in the following listing. For this, the zero value will do, as the `FetchExchangeRate` already knows the URL to ask for the rates.

Listing 6.53 `main.go`: **Using the conversion rate**

```go
[...]
rates := ecbank.EuroCentralBank{}
```

```
convertedAmount, err := money.Convert(amount, toCurrency, rates)
[...]
```

Try it out. Just because we're all tired by now, here's an example command again:

```
> go run . -from EUR -to JPY 15.23
```

You can try invalid currencies and numbers, and just have fun with it—it's not your money anyway.

6.5.7 *Sharing the executable*

While the `go run .` command is nice, sometimes you don't want to share the source code with other people, but only want to share the compiled binary. Generating the executable file in Go is achieved with the following command:

```
> go build -o bin/convert main.go
```

This command generates an executable binary file, `convert`, in the `bin` directory. Of course, the location can be changed. The -o flag has a default value, as all flags do, of the current directory. Then, we can execute it as follows:

```
> ./convert -from EUR -to JPY 15.23
```

6.6   *Making improvements*

There are a lot of tiny problems with the implementation we presented here. The goal of the chapter was to reach a working solution, not a perfect one. Let's go over a few ideas and implement one of them to make an improvement.

6.6.1 *Caching*

First, we're calling the bank for every run of the tool, which is a waste of resources. For example, you might be tempted to write a script that reads a long list of amounts from a file, and, for each line, changes the amount to Philippine pesos. Currently, there would be an identical HTTP call for each line, which is quite time consuming.

A solution is to dump the rates in a temporary file with the date in the name. The `ecbank.Client` struct will have a pointer to that file. If the file doesn't exist, fetch the rates and dump them. If the file is too old, do the same; otherwise, load from the file. You then need to provide a way to flush the cache with a different flag.

6.6.2 *Timeout*

You might someday be in the situation of one of the authors of this book: trying to get the exchange rate between euros and British pounds, but there's some sea above your head as you travel undersea by train, and you've lost the 4G signal. (Fun fact, the world's longest undersea section for trains is 37.9 km, and the fastest train can only go at 160km/h inside.) What happens when you make an HTTP call, and the server never answers? Nothing happens, unless you plan for it by the means of a timeout.

In our `FetchExchangeRate` function, we're calling `http.Get`. Under the hood, this makes use of the default client available in the `net/http` package. Although this is perfectly fine for a small example such as the one in this chapter, it's certainly not good enough for production code. Running `go doc http.Client` shows that one of the fields of the `Client` structure is `Timeout`. As expected, setting this will take care of interrupting calls exceeding a given amount of time. The default value of this field, which is the default value of the `http.DefaultClient`, is zero, which means "no timeout" per the documentation, as shown in listing 6.54. Using `http.Client{Timeout: 5*time .Second}` would, for instance, create a client with a specific timeout that can be safely used instead of the default client. If you look at how the client is defined in the code, you'll see a lot of default zero values.

> **Listing 6.54** `net/http/client.go`: **Implementation of the `DefaultClient`**

```
// DefaultClient is the default Client and is used by Get, Head, and Post.
var DefaultClient = &Client{}
```

It's a pointer, so anyone changing it will make the change for the whole program. This is actually a design choice: you can start the program by setting a timeout on this variable, and the rest of the program can rely on it and use that timeout value. But it's a global variable that the rest of the program can change, so you have to hope that none of your libraries sets a different timeout than your timeout inside the `DefaultClient`. If you want to fathom how annoying this would be, simply imagine that your smartphone has unfortunately inverted the phone numbers of two of your contacts, and you have to figure out a way to find out who is who.

Instead, we can declare our own `http.Client` that will only be used in our `EuroCentralBank` structure and use the `Get` method of the client, as shown in the next listing. This lets us set a timeout that will be used during, and only during, our calls to the European Central Bank.

> **Listing 6.55** `ecb.go`: `timeout` **example**

```
// Client can call the bank to retrieve exchange rates.
type Client struct {
    client http.Client          ◄─┐ Adds the field to
}                                  │ the structure

// NewBank builds a Client that can fetch exchange rates
// within a given timeout.
func NewClient(timeout time.Duration) Client {    ◄─┐ Adds a function
    return Client{                                   │ for bank building
        client: http.Client{Timeout: timeout},
    }
}
```

```go
// FetchExchangeRate fetches the ExchangeRate for the day and returns it.
func (c Client) FetchExchangeRate(
    source, target money.Currency) (money.ExchangeRate, error) {
    const path =
        "http://www.ecb.europa.eu/stats/eurofxref/eurofxref-daily.xml"

    resp, err := c.client.Get(path)         ◄─────┐ Uses our own client
    [...]
```

The `main` function will have to adapt:

```go
rates := ecbank.NewBank(30 * time.Second)
```

We're now ready to handle undersea tunnels. The `http.Get` function will immediately return an error (and an unusable response) if the timeout is reached, and it'll be up to the caller to decide what to do. The `net/http` package warns us in the `http.Get` documentation that the errors returned are of type `*url.Error` (the pointer information is very important) and that we can use the returned error to determine whether the call timed out. This is a nice opportunity to discover a useful function of the `errors` package.

We've already seen that we can test if an error is of a specific flavor with `errors.Is`. Sometimes, we want to inspect the error a bit further, especially when we know there is something more than an error message that can be extracted from the error. In this case, we're informed that the error returned is, in fact, of a specific type. This means we could cast it to that type:

```go
urlErr, ok := err.(*url.Error)
```

This would then allow us, provided the `ok` variable is `true`, to access fields and methods of the `*url.Error` structure. Let's have a look at what's over there: `go doc url.Error`.

As we can see, there are several exposed fields in that structure: the operation that was attempted, the URL that was requested, and the error itself. For us, the interesting bit is that we can call a `Timeout` method that returns a Boolean value. This is how we can ensure we did indeed reach a timeout:

```go
if urlErr.Timeout() {
```

This is nice, but there is a nicer and more idiomatic way of performing this operation: we can make use of the `errors.As` function. Its signature is simple: it takes an error and a target, and it returns a Boolean indicating whether it succeeded. When successful, the target contains the value of the original error.

Because `errors.As` is writing to its `target` parameter, we need to provide it as a pointer to a variable that will receive the value, just as we had to do earlier with the `Decode` method of the `encoding/xml` package. In our case, we want to pass a pointer to a variable of type `*url.Error`. Yes, that's a pointer to a pointer. But it's important to understand that we merely pass the address of a variable, and the fact that this variable is itself a pointer has nothing to do with it—we only retrieved this information from the `http.Get` documentation. Then, if everything goes as expected, we can use the (now populated) `*url.Error` to check if it is indeed a timeout.

Listing 6.56 `ecb.go`: **Checking for** `timeout`

```
func (c Client) FetchExchangeRate(
    source, target money.Currency) (money.ExchangeRate, error) {
    [...]
    resp, err := c.client.Get(path)
    if err != nil {                              We don't care about initializing
        var urlErr *url.Error                    it; errors.As will fill it.
        if ok := errors.As(err, &urlErr); ok && urlErr.Timeout() {
            // This is a timeout!
```

It's now up to you to decide what should be done when a timeout is reached. It could be interesting to retry after a few moments (maybe we're out of that undersea tunnel and the 4G coverage is better). Or we could decide that any error we face is fatal for the process of converting money, and it's not our converter's responsibility to choose how to deal with network errors.

BEYOND TIMEOUTS

As we've seen, our `http.Client` structure can be tuned with a timeout. But a timeout isn't the only value we can set for our client. For instance, here, we've not overwritten the `Transport` field of our `http.Client`, which means we'll be using the `http.DefaultTransport` in our client. The arguments for using a specific `http.Client` applies here again, and we might also want to tune the `Transport` within our `Client`.

TESTING OUR IMPLEMENTATION

We can't reuse the same test as previously because we were only passing the URL of the bank to the `Client`. This time, we need to use a client that will proxy to the server's URL. We can do this with the `Transport.Proxy` field of the `http.Client` structure. The implementation for this is shown in the following listing.

Listing 6.57 `ecb_internal_test.go`: **Testing exchange rates**

```
func TestEuroCentralBank_FetchExchangeRate_Success(t *testing.T) {
    ts := httptest.NewServer(...)
    defer ts.Close()

    proxyURL, err := url.Parse(ts.URL)
    if err != nil {
        t.Fatalf("failed to parse proxy URL: %v", err)
    }

    ecb := Client{
        client: &http.Client{
            Transport: &http.Transport{              Client calls the
                Proxy: http.ProxyURL(proxyURL),       server's URL.
```

```
        },
        Timeout: time.Second,          ◄─── Sets a timeout
    },
}
got, err := ecb.FetchExchangeRate(
    mustParseCurrency(t, "USD"), mustParseCurrency(t, "RON"))
...
```

The rest of the test is the same as before, but this only tests the happy path, so let's also test the case where a timeout occurs! For this, we'll change the behavior of the New-Server we build in the test, and, instead of writing an XML message to the response, we'll instead simulate a long wait with time.Sleep, as shown in listing 6.58. We'll reuse a similar client as in the successful test, and this time, we'll check the error that is hopefully returned!

Listing 6.58 `ecb_internal_test.go`: Testing `timeout`

```
func TestEuroCentralBank_FetchExchangeRate_Timeout(t *testing.T) {
    ts := httptest.NewServer(
        http.HandlerFunc(func(w http.ResponseWriter, r *http.Request) {
            time.Sleep(time.Second * 2)          ◄─┐
    }))                                             │  The server will take 2
    defer ts.Close()                                │  seconds to respond.

    proxyURL, err := url.Parse(ts.URL)
    if err != nil {
        t.Fatalf("failed to parse proxy URL: %v", err)
    }

    ecb := Client{
        client: &http.Client{
            Transport: &http.Transport{
                Proxy: http.ProxyURL(proxyURL),
            },
            Timeout: time.Second,          ◄─┐ The client will timeout
        },                                   │ after 1 second.
    }

    _, err = ecb.FetchExchangeRate(
        mustParseCurrency(t, "USD"), mustParseCurrency(t, "RON"))
    if !errors.Is(err, ErrTimeout) {          ◄─┐
        t.Errorf("unexpected error: %v, expected %v", err, ErrTimeout)
    }
}                                             Checks that we get
                                              the appropriate error
```

TIMEOUT'S VALUE

When it comes to choosing a "good" timeout value, you want to think about the call you're executing. Your timeout is your patience. You don't want to think about what the remote service has to do to execute your query because you shouldn't know. Its implementation and performance might change without you having to change your code. A rule of thumb when making calls to external resources is that a call that leaves your environment—whether a local network or a cloud platform—should be allowed up to a few seconds. You need to account for all of these time-consuming network handshakes. When running locally, a few seconds are only tolerable for big processes, and the usual value is less than a second. These numbers aren't set in stone, as they need to be tuned for your own use cases. Allowing only 20 milliseconds for a call over the internet is too short, and if your timeout for a local query is 30 minutes, there's something fishy in the architecture.

6.6.3 *Alternative tree*

In your everyday developer life, you'll be led to import external libraries from the open source world. This is very frequent for most libraries. In general, they are organized with the exposed types at the root of the module as it minimizes the path to reach the required package for users. Compare `github.com/learngo-pockets/money` to `github.com/learngo-pockets/moneyconverter/money`.

We've created a folder named `money` containing one file, exposing all the methods and types to the users and having everything at the root. If you need a `main`, it's common to create it in a folder called `cmd` for command. Here's an example of a project importing our library:

```
> tree
.
├── cmd/main.go
├── money
│       └── money.go
└── go.mod
```

Congrats! You're done! It was a tough chapter with different concepts that we'll practice again over the following chapters.

Summary

- The `flag` package exposes functions that allow us to retrieve both arguments and optional parameters from the command line. We can even set default values to our flags. Remember to call `flag.Parse()` before checking the values of the flags.
- When implementing a functionality, it's good to declare types that mirror the core entities that we'll have to handle. In our case, we created a `Currency`, a `Decimal`, and an `Amount`, and we defined what `Convert` should do before writing a single mathematical operation or calling a single function. We also knew from the start how to organize our code, including which types and functions should be exposed.
- The simple `fmt.Stringer` interface makes printing complex structures easy.

- Floating-point numbers are inaccurate, at best. There should always be room for margin when comparing two floating-point numbers. Operations on floats will sometimes seem nonsensical because of the precision limitation. Knowing their precision and the precision of the computation they're used for will help make a choice between `float32`, `float64`, `big.Float`, or something else.

- A package is most often built starting with its API and finishing with its unexposed functions.

- Go's `net/http` package offers functions to perform HTTP calls, such as GET or POST requests, over the network. It offers a default client, which can be used for prototyping, but shouldn't be kept in production-level code for security reasons.

- An HTTP call will return a response that contains a status code. Checking this status code is mandatory—the code informs how meaningful the body of the response is. Status codes are divided into five classes, but the most important are 200 (and 2xx), which means everything went fine; 400 (and 4xx), which means the request might be incorrect (some fields missing, some authentication wrong, etc.); and 500 (and 5xx), which means the server faced a problem and couldn't process the request.

- Testing HTTP calls should be agnostic to external behavior. Go provides an `httptest` package to mock HTTP calls by providing an infrastructure to set up an HTTP server for tests. The `httptest.NewServer` function is particularly useful to simulate real HTTP interactions.

- Clean code separates the responsibilities of each package. Retrieving data isn't the same task as computing data, and it should be handled in a separate piece of code. Go offers extremely simple interfaces that allow for dependency injection. Dependency injection makes code simple and makes tests even simpler.

- Stubs are a nice way of implementing interfaces. Simply declare a struct where you need to implement an interface—usually in a _test.go file—and have it implement the interface. Stubs are useful when trying to improve test coverage, but they can only be used for unit tests, as they don't check the whole logic of the call.

- Exposed functions, in a package, should return sentinel errors. This makes using a package clean and simple. Within the implementation of the package, the decision of creating the sentinel errors in exposed functions or in unexposed functions is left to the developer.

- Using `errors.Is` is how we test if an error is a sentinel. Using `errors.As` is how we access an error's fields and methods.

- Go's `encoding/xml` package provides a function and a method to decode an XML message. To be able to decode some bytes into a structured variable, Go's syntax requires that the fields we want to decode are described with the XML path where their value can be read. It's even possible to skip layers by using the `>` character in that path.

- The toolchain offers the `go build -o path/to/exec .` command, which generates an executable file at the specified location.

Caching with generics

7

Think back to your school days. Did you ever suddenly remember you had a homework assignment due the next day that you hadn't even started? Maybe you phoned a friend and asked if they had the answer to question 2.b, just to get you a head start and allow you to spend more time on some other part of the homework. Teachers frowned on this kind of thing, of course.

Computers, on the other hand, won't judge you for taking shortcuts. A cache is such a shortcut: it's a key-value storage which can access data that has at least been computed once in the past—as long as it makes sense to access the data. Caches are often used when we know a slow function returning a value will be called several times with the same input—and that the output value should be the same every time. There are cases when we want to use a cache. For instance, say you know that "the city with the longest name is: Bangkok." This isn't something that you need to check every morning. There are cases when we specifically don't want to use a cache ("The current exchange rate of the Algerian dinar to Euros is: ?"); in these cases, an outdated response could lead to confusion. And, sometimes, using a cache could be acceptable ("The total population of Ethiopia is: 123,967,194") because the question doesn't really require an instantaneous answer; that is, the value from last week has the same magnitude as that of this week.

In this chapter, we'll present generics and implement a naive cache. Through tests, we'll show how our first approach isn't good enough and needs to be strengthened. Then, we'll add a "time to live" to values in our cache, to make sure we don't store outdated information. Finally, we'll cover some good practices for using caches. This project requires the following:

- Write a cache storing pairs of keys and values.
- You should be able to store, read, and delete data in the cache.
- Make sure the cache is concurrency safe.

7.1 A naive cache

Let's start with a short definition. A *cache* is storage for retrieving values that were previously saved. To access these values, the user of the cache will use the same key as they did when they registered the value the first time. There are three important notions regarding a cache that need to be evoked here:

- A cache should be able to store any new pair of key and value.
- When retrieving a value using a key, the cache should return what was previously stored in the cache.
- Usually, the whole reason for using a cache is speed, so a cache needs to be fast.

Here are two examples of pairs of keys and values a cache could hold:

- *Phone number* (`string`)—Name (`string`)
- *Year* (`uint`)—All the medalists, per country, at these Olympics (`map[Country][]Athlete`)

Through these examples, we'll show that a key can take many forms and that a value can take even more. We'll cover this in detail later, but for now, we need to understand generics and how to write them in Go, so we can write our first implementation of a cache.

We need to start with a bit of theory, but we'll try to keep it short. We're here primarily for hands-on projects, after all.

7.1.1   *Introduction to generics*

Go is strongly typed by design, which means every variable has to have an explicit type. You can determine by looking at the code which variable is a string and which is an `int` to understand how they interact and what the code does. If your function takes a `float64`, there's nothing else you can give it than a `float64`:

```
func prettyPrint(f float64){
    fmt.Printf("> %f", f)
}

prettyPrint(.25)
```

This is nice and clear, but how can we write a function that prints an `int`? Do we have to copy these three lines and change a few characters? Well, believe it or not, ancient generations of gophers (Go programmers) remember the time when yes, you indeed had to copy all of these little functions around. But generic types, also known as generics, arrived and saved us from so much boilerplate.

Generics let you write code without explicitly providing the type of the data a function takes or returns. The types are instead defined later when you use the function. Functions are just an example. You can't fathom the amount of boilerplate code (and bugs) that got swept away by this great feature. But like all good things, we shouldn't overuse them, and we should know what we're doing with them.

How does it work? Instead of specifying a real type, like `float64` shown earlier, we define a generic type and give it a *constraint*. The least-constraining type constraint is the keyword `any`, which really means what it says: any type at all. Following is an example of a single function that first accepts a `float64` as its parameter `t`, and then accepts a `string` as the same parameter `t`. Notice that the signature of the function is somewhat different—we've used square brackets between the name of the function and its parameters. We've declared in these square brackets that `T` is a placeholder for the type constraint `any` for the scope of this function's declaration. The type `T` is set when we call the function:

```
func prettyPrint[T any](t T){
    fmt.Printf("> %v", t)          ◄────┐  %f was used for floats;
}                                       │  use %v instead.

prettyPrint[float64](.25)          ◄────┐  Calls the function
prettyPrint[string]("pockets")          │  with various types
```

In this example, we can no longer use the `%f` verb in `Printf`, as this is only usable with floating-point numbers. When we call the function, we specify what the type `T` should be.

But what is type `T`, specifically? It depends on what we decide to pass to the function when it's called. The function is *parameterized*; that is, compilation time, the required flavors, here a `float32` and a `string`, will both be generated and compiled like any concretely typed function. The only difference is the reusability of your code, which is now much better.

TYPE INFERENCE

If the type `T` appears in the parameters of the function, the Go compiler is able to detect which type it represents each time the function is called and doesn't need the hint we're giving it by using square brackets when we call the function. For instance, because the parameter of the function is precisely of type `T` in the previous example, the Go compiler will notice that we call this function with a `float64` and with a `string` parameter. The earlier code lines can be simplified to the following:

```
func prettyPrint[T any](t T){
    fmt.Printf("> %v", t)
}

prettyPrint(.25)                    ◄──────┐ Type inference: T==float64
prettyPrint("pockets")    ◄──────────┘ Type inference: T==string
```

Type inference might make generics seem a bit magical. It's worth noting that type inference will only happen on input parameters, not on returned types.

TYPE CONSTRAINTS

We saw that `any`, introduced by Go 1.18 along with generics, is a keyword that can be used as a type constraint for, actually, no constraint at all. It's equivalent to `interface{}`. The only other built-in constraint is called `comparable` and is implemented by all comparable types, that is, all types that support comparison of two elements using `==` or `!=`. Into this category fall Booleans, numbers, strings, pointers, channels, `arrays` of comparable types, and structs whose fields are all comparable types. `Slices`, `maps`, and functions aren't comparable. If you create a `map` and want its key to be generic, it will have to be `comparable`. We'll provide more on that in section 7.1.3.

We've seen in the previous chapters how interfaces work and how any structure can implement an interface as long as it has all methods attached with the right signature. Type constraints are interfaces, and, of course, you can declare your own. As `%v` isn't exactly formatting prettily, here's a different version:

```
func prettyPrint[T fmt.Stringer](t T){
    fmt.Printf("> %s", t)          ◄──────┐ Using %s calls .String()
}
```

The difference here is that now we can't give floats and integers to our function anymore because they don't implement the `Stringer` interface, but we can give any structure that does implement it. If you remember the `Amount` from our previous chapter's money converter—it did implement this interface, so we can call the following:

```
amount, err := money.NewAmount(...)
prettyPrint(amount)
```

GENERIC TYPES

Let's say we want to define a group of `Amounts` so that we can perform some specific operations on them:

```
type Group []Amount

func (g Group) PrettyPrint() {
    for _, v := range g {
        prettyPrint(v)
    }
}

func main() {
    var g Group
    g.PrettyPrint()
}
```

Suppose we want to do the same to pencils, clouds, and dresses. We would decide to make this group generic:

```
type Group[T any] []T
```

`Group` is parameterized: it's a group of `T`, and it's an alias for a `slice` of `T`. Go won't allow us to write a method with a receiver of type `slice` (`func (s []string) Do()`); the compiler would complain with an `Invalid receiver type` message. But using our `Group`, we're able to write a method on that parameterized type:

```
func (g Group[T]) PrettyPrint() {
    for _, v := range g {
        prettyPrint(v)
    }
}
```

The receiver of the method needs to be parameterized too. Indeed, the variable `v` in the loop will be of type `T`, and the compiler needs to know where to look for what `T` means. Until we instantiate a `Group`, it means nothing:

```
var g Group[Cloud]
g.PrettyPrint()
```

The compiler can now create a version of the `Group` that supports clouds, and only clouds.

DECLARING YOUR OWN CONSTRAINTS

Finally, what if you want to support multiple integer types? Or you want to support `int` and your own `PocketInt` but nothing else? You can't make primary types implement an interface, but you can define union interfaces:

```
type summable interface {
    int | int32 | int64
}
```

This means that any function that can take a summable as parameter will accept `int`, `int32`, or `int64`, and will be able to use the + operator. However, now, if you define a new type that is an `int` (in other words, a new type whose underlying type is `int`), it won't be included. For example:

```
type age int
```

To support all things that are actually `int`s, we use the `~int` (with a tilde) syntax to include all types whose underlying type is `int`. The following interface includes the type `age` shown just previously:

```
type summable interface {
    ~int | ~int32 | ~int64
}
```

If your program is about astronomy and you specifically need an `int64` to represent a star's age, you can change your type and everything will fall into place. Enough with theory; let's write this cache.

7.1.2 *Project initialization*

Because this project is about creating a library, we'll use a common organization of our files. In chapter 4, we exposed a module that contained a package called `pocketlog`. Although this was nice when we needed to introduce packages, most open source libraries will expose their types at the root of the module, as this prevents having cumbersome import paths. Here, we want our users to import our cache package with minimum effort, and this means placing our cache as early as possible. Following is our file organization:

```
> tree learngo-pockets/genericcache
.
├── cache.go
└── go.mod
```

This will allow anyone to use our library by importing our module and then using `genericcache.Cache`. Of course, other files will be required, but these are the bare necessities that our users will need.

Start by creating a `genericcache` directory, and then run the following line in that directory to initialize the module:

```
> go mod init learngo-pockets/genericcache
```

7.1.3   *Implementation*

As we've seen earlier, a cache is a place to store data in a way we can retrieve it easily. In our case, we decided to have a key-value storage that could be used for almost any type of key and any type of value. We need our keys to be comparable—that is, we need to know if two keys are considered equal. This is achieved with the constraint `comparable`.

In our tests, we use simple cases where the key is an integer and the value a string, but feel free to use other types instead. If you're unsure, you can always take a peek at the provided code for some inspiration.

Create a type `Cache` in your package in a `cache.go` file, as shown in the next listing. It's a `struct` holding one field: a `map`. The types of the keys and values are parameterized.

Listing 7.1   `cache.go`

```
// Cache is key-value storage.
type Cache[K comparable, V any] struct {
    data   map[K]V
}
```

As you can see, we've defined two types, giving them one-uppercase-letter names per convention. `K` for key and `V` for value seem as self-explanatory as we can get.

Already we face a decision: Should we store a `map[K]V` or a `map[K]*V`? In human terms, should our cache store copies of the user's values, or should we only store pointers to them? There are pros and cons to each choice, and a tradeoff has to be found between using more memory (with copies of the values) and using more CPU (because of pointer indirection having to be resolved). We decided to go with the implementation just shown—after all, if a user wants to use a type `V` that is a pointer to their values, they can still do it! This also means that our cache is fully responsible for its memory and that once a value has been added to the cache, it can't be updated without a call to the cache.

NEW

Because our `Cache` contains a `map`, we need to initialize the `map` before it can be used. A side effect of using a `map` in a structure is that its zero value (an uninitialized `map`) can't be used directly without causing runtime errors, such as `nil` pointer dereferences. To avoid this, we define a constructor function, `New`, that initializes the `map` for us, as shown in listing 7.2. By exposing the `Cache` type but not its `map` directly, we enforce the use of the constructor, ensuring that all instances of `Cache` are properly initialized. This design reduces the risk of bugs caused by uninitialized `map`s while keeping the internal implementation details of the cache encapsulated.

Listing 7.2   `cache.go`

```
// New creates a usable Cache.
func New[K comparable, V any]() Cache[K, V] {
    return Cache[K, V]{
```

```
        data: make(map[K]V),
    }
}
```

READ

The most common operation executed on a cache is usually to read from it, as that's
the whole point of our cache. Let's write the Read method to achieve this, as shown in
listing 7.3. This method accepts a key of the adequate type and returns the value—also
of the adequate type. It's up to us to decide what to return when the key isn't found in
the cache, which is the case when the value hasn't been stored there yet. As a reminder,
Go's default map implementation returns a value and a Boolean, so that's what we'll
be using here. Should you want to use errors, you'll have to decide how to return the
error: via a constant and a local type or via an exposed variable. You can also, as usual,
call errors.New directly in your return line, but it will be harder for users to compare
with a known value and decide what to do next. Having the same interface as a map
makes things clearer for the end user.

Listing 7.3 `cache.go`: **Implementing the** Read **method on the cache**

```
// Read returns the associated value for a key,
// and a boolean to true if the key is absent.
func (c *Cache[K, V]) Read(key K) (V, bool) {
    v, found := c.data[key]
    return v, found
}
```

The most-used function is written. We could unit test it, but in this situation, an integration test involving multiple operations seems a better idea. If we write a unit test
now, it will be tied to the implementation choices and won't help us in any future
refactoring. We would end up testing whether Go can read from a map, which is already
covered by the Go developers. To write the integration tests to read from the cache, we
need to first be able to write something into it.

UPSERT

If we want to read a value from our cache, we need to expose a way of adding it in
there. This leads to the following question: Should we let the user insert the same key
several times? In most caches, a more recent value is usually more interesting than an
older value, so we decided to silently overwrite any previously existing values in our
cache. However, other implementations might decide to return an error if the key is
already present when we try to add it in the map.

Because we're overwriting any potentially existing data, we can name our method
Upsert—a combination of "insert" and "update"—as shown in listing 7.4. It guarantees
the key will be present in the cache associated with the specified value.

Upsert could return an error. For instance, we might want to limit the number of
elements in our cache—hitting a limit would be a valid reason to divert from the happy

path. Let's keep this door open from the start. After all, returning an error is perfectly normal in Go.

Listing 7.4   cache.go: Implementing the Upsert function on the cache

```go
// Upsert overrides the value for a given key.
func (c *Cache[K, V]) Upsert(key K, value V) error {
    c.data[key] = value

    // Do not return an error for the moment,
    // but it can happen in the near future.
    return nil
}
```

We're nearly there. You can start writing a unit test that writes, reads, checks the returned type, checks the returned value for an absent key, writes another value for the same key, and so on. There are a lot of different situations that can already be covered.

DELETE

The last operation we need is deleting a key from the cache for when we know that this value is stale. For example, say we're precomputing the list of group conversations that each user is part of. Someone creates a new conversation and invites five people. Each person will need a new computation of the listing, but only when they open the messaging app. We can invalidate their keys and let the system recompute the next time the list is required.

> **NOTE**   Most caches grow with no real limit. At the end of this chapter, we'll expose a few ways to keep the cache manageable.

Let's expose a method to ensure an item is no longer present in a cache. This method will take a key and remove the entry from the cache. But what if the key isn't present in our cache to begin with?

Go's answer to this question—at least for maps—is to be idempotent: rather than considering that we're trying to remove an entry, we think of this action as ensuring that this entry isn't in the map after the execution of delete. We decided to follow the same philosophical approach with our Delete method, as shown in the following listing. If the key isn't in the cache, our method performs no operation—commonly shortened as "no-op."

Listing 7.5   cache.go: Implementing the Delete method on the cache

```go
// Delete removes the entry for the given key.
func (c *Cache[K, V]) Delete(key K) {
    delete(c.data, key)
}
```

To test or not to test

Unit testing a one-liner like this is a question that a dev team needs to answer as a group: What is the level of testing we want to have on this; are we testing our own code or the Go map itself? Because we didn't add any logic on top of the map, we decided that our code—so far—didn't need unit tests. This doesn't prevent us from writing some small functional tests—a list of calls ensuring that we inserted values in our cache and that we're able to retrieve them.

Our first implementation of the cache seems to cover our needs—we can store data, retrieve values using the keys that were used to insert them, and remove some data, if need be. The world seems perfect. That's precisely the moment when someone in your team makes a comment in the code review: Is this thread safe?

This is an excellent question, and, to answer it, we need to understand how we'll be able to prove it is (or isn't) safe. *Thread safety* is invoked when several threads—parallelized parts of a program—access the same resource simultaneously and try to alter it. To imagine a real-world parallel, suppose you're having dinner with a friend, and both of you are suddenly thirsty. You both want to grab the bottle of water to fill your glass. If you were to grab the bottle at the same time and pour in different glasses at the same time, there would probably be water all over the place, and you wouldn't be sure your glass is full by the end of it. For our cache, this would mean, for instance, having two threads try to write a different value for the same key. How do we know this won't break anything?

7.2 *Introducing goroutines*

Let's return for a moment to the basics of what a computer is—a set of devices connected together. We've got a processor (CPU), the central unit in charge of performing the actual computing; some memory bars to store values used by the computing module; a power source; and many extra parts, such as a hard drive to store persistent data, a motherboard to connect everything together, and so on. Here, we'll focus on the processor.

A processor is in charge of running the binary code that was generated by the compiler. Each program, when launched, is loaded in the memory and then executed on the processor. Does that mean a processor can only run a single program at a time? The answer is no, for two reasons. First, programs run on cores, which are parts executing the binary code in the processor. In the 2000s, processor manufacturers started shipping their processors with two or more cores. Each core can dedicate its activity to only one task at a time. If you have more cores, they can run multiple tasks at the same time independently on a single computer. Second, our operating system, which is also a program, coordinates different tasks and programs to run on these cores. The UI has to run somewhere, some running piece of code must read input from the keyboard, and something must communicate with your hard drive.

To prevent a computer from freezing because a core is running a program that won't end, computer scientists have implemented schedulers for CPUs—a way of "pausing" a program to let another one run. Schedulers are how multiple programs are able to run simultaneously on a single-core computer. Since the early 2000s, computers with multiple cores have become cheaper and more common, bringing real parallelism to users.

For many programmers, the fact that several cores were present on a machine meant that there were more resources that could be used to run a program. After all, if the load could be balanced on two cores instead of one, maybe the program could run twice as fast! Let's douse your hopes right now—in most cases, this doesn't work.

How can we use this feature? Pieces of a program that run independently at the same time are called threads, coroutines, fibers, or—in Go—goroutines. In this section, you'll learn what goroutines are, as well as how to create and manage them.

7.2.1   *What's a goroutine?*

Many other programming languages use the term "thread" when they describe a task that is launched for parallel execution. In Go, we see things differently. First, we don't use system threads directly; instead, we use Go's goroutines. They are managed by the Go runtime layer that runs alongside your Go program. There are many differences between goroutines and threads, but this isn't a topic for this book. Instead, just remember that a goroutine is a way of launching a piece of code in the background:

```
a = taskA()          │ Only executed when the
b = taskB()       ◄──┘ previous has finished
```

Of course, most of the time, we want our program to execute sequentially—we want the second task to be run after the first. But sometimes, we don't *need* the first task to have successfully returned before we run the second one.

Here's a real-world comparison: suppose you're preparing a curry. You have a pot with curry sauce and a pot with rice. The recipe tells you that each one should cook for 10 minutes. You could first cook the sauce for 10 minutes, and, when it's ready, cook the rice for 10 minutes—but the sauce is getting cold. You'd spend 20 minutes preparing your dish, when you could have cooked both pots at the same time—provided you had enough burners—reducing that total time to around 10 minutes.

This is what goroutines address. They allow you to run several tasks simultaneously—provided you can launch them. This last bit usually isn't a problem—goroutines are really light to handle, and unless you start creating millions of them, you should be fine.

Now, there's a word that has been used in this section that needs a closer look. We've used "in parallel," "simultaneously," "in the background," and "concurrently" to represent the idea that a goroutine doesn't block its caller. Over the years, these words have sometimes been used interchangeably. Fortunately, Rob Pike, the co-creator of Go, wrote some proverbs (https://go-proverbs.github.io/) scattered through this chapter that can help.

GO PROVERB   Concurrency isn't parallelism.

According to Pike, concurrency and parallelism aren't interchangeable terms. Having two (or more) goroutines doesn't guarantee any simultaneous execution on parallel cores but that they will be executed independently, for better or for worse. Concurrency should focus on how to write code to support goroutines, while parallelism is what happens when the code is executed.

7.2.2 *How to launch a goroutine*

Let's remember that Go was created with the idea in mind that running goroutines should be simple. The creators of Go made it extremely straightforward: if you want a function to run in the background, you simply prefix its call with `go`. That's it. It doesn't require any specific import or compilation options. The following listing shows a simple example.

Listing 7.6 `parallel.go`: Example of a program running goroutines

```
package main

import (
    "fmt"
    "time"
)

func printEverySecond(msg string) {
    for i := 0; i < 10; i++ {
        fmt.Println(msg)
        time.Sleep(time.Second)
    }
}

func main() {
    // Run two goroutines
    go printEverySecond("Hello")     ◀── Launches a first goroutine in the background
    go printEverySecond("World")     ◀── Launches a second goroutine in the background

    var input string
    fmt.Scanln(&input)               ◀── Waits for a keypress to end the program
}
```

When the execution reaches the `fmt.Scanln` line, we have our three goroutines running at the same time—the main one, and those printing messages every second. But there's a small drawback to using goroutines: they're launched in the background, which means they finish without letting the caller know! This is what the problem looks like for our previous example, in lines of code:

```
go cookCurrySauce()
go cookRice()
// how do I know the food is ready?
```

There are two major ways of dealing with this—the first one is to use channels, and the second one is to use a library that solves the problem.

7.2.3   *Using channels to communicate that a goroutine has ended*

Go has a specific type called channels that it can use for communication between goroutines. A channel is how goroutines communicate in Go. We can send information such as triggers, new data, results, errors, and so on between goroutines through channels.

> **GO PROVERB**   Don't communicate by sharing memory; share memory by communicating.

A channel can be seen as a conduit to which data can be sent—and from which data can be retrieved. In Go, a channel is declared for a specific type of message it will contain. For instance, if a channel were to be used to convey integers, we'd write the following line:

```
var c chan int
```

Channels, like `maps` and `slices`, need to be instantiated with the `make` function. When instantiating them, we can decide whether we want a channel to be *buffered* (only able to contain up to X elements) or *unbuffered* (you can't write a message in the channel if no goroutine is reading from it):

```
c := make(chan int, 10)
c := make(chan int)
```

Buffered channel that can hold up to 10 elements
Unbuffered channel

A buffered channel that has reached its capacity becomes "blocking" on writing attempts. In other words, as long as no message is read from the channel when it has reached its capacity, any sending to the channel will wait for a spot in the queue, blocking the goroutine. The syntax to write to and read from a channel uses arrows:

```
c := make(chan int)
c <- 4
i := <- c
```

Creates a channel for integers
Writes an integer to the channel
Reads one integer from the channel

The power of channels in Go comes from the fact that items are read from the channel in the same chronological order they were sent—in other words, *first in, first out.*

Finally, when no new messages are expected, a channel should be marked as closed for writing. For this, we use the built-in function `close`. It's still possible to read from a channel after it's closed:

```
c := make(chan int)
c <- 4
```

```
close(c)
i := <- c
```
Prevents anyone from writing again into c

Reading from a channel is a blocking call. If there are no messages in the channel, the execution waits till we find one. As a result, we can use a channel to notify that a goroutine is done:

```
c := make(chan struct{}, 1)
```
Our channel will receive no more than one message.

```
go func(doneChan chan <- struct{}) {
    defer func() {
        log.Println("done")
        doneChan <- struct{}{}
        close(doneChan)
    }
    // run task
}(c)

_ = <- c
```
Defers sending a message to the channel until end of execution

Functions in charge of writing to a channel are in charge of closing it.

Passes the channel to the goroutine

Synchronization point, waiting for end of goroutine

We introduced two commonly used notions in this example. First, a channel can be used to notify its listeners. Here, we only want to notify that we're done—and for this, we use the Go trick of empty structures (`struct{}`) because empty structures are very light (they have a memory footprint of 0 bytes). We don't need a convoluted structure that would transport data around, so we don't use one. There's no point in overdoing it here.

The second interesting part is the signature of the function we run as our goroutine. A small arrow `<-` squeezed its way between the words `chan` and `struct{}`. When we declare a function, we can be a bit more specific than "here's a channel for you to use": we can specify in the signature of the function whether a channel should be used for reading messages from it, for writing messages to it, or for both. If a function should only read from a channel of strings, its signature can be written as `func read(c <- chan string)`. Visually, the arrow points out of the channel, an indication that messages will be read from the channel. If we want to specify that we want to write to a channel in a function, we can use the `func write(c chan <- string)` syntax. Visually, the arrow helps us understand that strings will be sent into the channel.

If we want to both read and write from a channel, the syntax is simply `func rw(c chan string)` with no arrows this time. However, we discourage passing a channel for both reading and writing to a function because this suggests the function's scope is too big. We should be able to extract the reading and the writing into two different functions.

Finally, a channel should be closed when the job is done to tell listening goroutines that no more data will arrive. When a single function is in charge of writing to a channel, that function should be in charge of closing the channel. Leaving it open isn't a problem if you don't want to signal listeners that you're done.

Let's take a final look at how we'd write our synchronization point if we have to handle several goroutines (bon appétit!):

```
numRoutines := 2
c := make(chan struct{}, numRoutines)        ◄──┐  Creates the buffered
                                                 │  channel of the right size

go cookRice(c)          ┌─────────────────────────  Each goroutine will send a message
go cookCurry(c)         │                            to the channel when done.

for i := 0; i < numRoutines; i++ {   ◄──┐  Synchronization point: we
    _ = <- c                            │  need to read two messages.
}
```

7.2.4   *Running goroutines and having a synchronization point*

While using channels works perfectly well, it always feels like reinventing the wheel, which is fine if you need custom wheels, but it so happens that Golang provides two libraries that replace these channels nicely. One is present in the standard library, while the other is (still) in the experimental packages of the Go sources.

USING SYNC.WAITGROUP

Let's take a look at the `sync` package—in particular, its `WaitGroup` type. The `go doc sync.WaitGroup` tells us that `WaitGroups` can be used to wait for goroutines to finish, which is exactly what we're trying to do here. The `WaitGroup` type exposes three methods:

- `Add(delta int)`—Registers a number of new goroutines to wait for. This can be called several times.
- `Done()`—Used by a goroutine to notify the `WaitGroup` that it has completed its task. This should be called in a `defer` statement.
- `Wait()`—The synchronization point, called after `Add()` and after the goroutines have been launched.

Let's give these a try with our cooking example.

Listing 7.7   Cooking example using `sync.WaitGroup`

```
package main

import (
    "fmt"
    "sync"
)
                                            ┌──  Uses a pointer to pass the work
                                            │    group to other functions
func main() {
    wg := &sync.WaitGroup{}      ◄──────────┘
    wg.Add(2)        ◄──┐  Sets the correct size
```

```
    go cookRice(wg)
    go cookCurry(wg)                    Launches the goroutines

    wg.Wait()              ◄────── Synchronization point
}

func cookRice(wg *sync.WaitGroup) {
    defer wg.Done()                           Each goroutine should finish by
    fmt.Println("Cooking rice...")            telling the WaitGroup it's done.
    // prepare rice
}

func cookCurry(wg *sync.WaitGroup) {
    defer wg.Done()
    fmt.Println("Preparing curry sauce...")
    // prepare curry
}
```

In this example, we created a default `WaitGroup`. Because `WaitGroups` don't expose any fields, they will always be created with the exact same line: `wg := &sync.WaitGroup{}`—well, not always, as you could name yours differently, but `wg` is a common name for a `WaitGroup`.

The second step is to set the number of goroutines that this `WaitGroup` will be in charge of. Here, we made a single call to `Add`, but it's perfectly fine to call `Add(1)` several times. This is quite common when you have to deal with loops. We could have written our code this way, which makes it easier to refactor, if you want bland rice or just the sauce:

```
wg.Add(1)
go cookRice(wg)

wg.Add(1)
go cookCurry(wg)
```

Then, the important part is to defer a call to `wg.Done()` in each function we call. This is why we need to pass a pointer to the `WaitGroup` in the signature of each of these functions. If we had passed a copy, each function would call `Done()` on a copy of the `WaitGroup` `wg`, and the original `wg` (in `main` in our code) would never be notified. In this case, a call to `Wait()` will eventually result in a `panic`. For more details on passing values by copy or by reference, see appendix E.

Finally, we call `wg.Wait()`, which will return after the same number of `Done()` methods have been called as the sum of all the `Add(n)` methods we've performed on this `WaitGroup`.

`WaitGroup` is a very commonly used way of synchronizing goroutines that we've launched into the wild. Under the hood, to keep track of how many goroutines aren't completed yet, it uses a field of type `atomic.Uint64`. It's interesting to know that Go exposes types that can serve for atomic operations—but we won't dive into this world here. They work great for functions that do their thing on their own. However, if anything goes wrong and an error needs to be captured, the only way is through an error channel that we pass to each goroutine and from which we read after the call to `Wait`:

```
wg := &sync.WaitGroup{}
wg.Add(2)
errChan := make(chan error, 2)

go cookCurry(wg, errChan)
go cookRice(wg, errChan)

wg.Wait()

// handle the error, if any
select {
case err := <- errChan:
    // deal with the error
default:
    continue
}
```

As you can see, we can retrieve some errors from the goroutines with an error channel. Unfortunately for us, we had to pass a channel around to read errors, and the whole point of using a `WaitGroup` was to not have to use channels in the first place. Well, guess what? There's a library that allows us to handle errors when we're using goroutines.

USING GOLANG.ORG/X/SYNC/ERRGROUP

The `errgroup` package isn't in the standard Go library. This means that to use it, we need to start by importing the package as a dependency of our module: `go get golang .org/x/sync/errgroup`. Now, let's take a look at what this package exposes:

```
> go doc golang.org/x/sync/errgrcup
```

We can find a type `Group` in there and four methods—we'll only cover three of them here, as they're the most commonly used. But, first, to create a `Group`, we can either use a zero value—eg : = errgroup.Group{}—or we can use the `errgroup .WithContext(ctx)` function. In our simple example, we don't have contexts, so we'll go with the first option, but, in the vast majority of cases, using the second option is recommended, as you'll have a variable of type `context.Context` close by. (We'll cover contexts in a later chapter.) Internally, an `errgroup.Group` is a `sync.WaitGroup` with extra fields at its disposal—mostly to handle context and errors.

Now, what can our `Group` do? It has a `SetLimit(n)` method, which reminds us of the `Add(n)` method of the `WaitGroup`. They are different, though, in that when we called `Add(n)`, we needed to have n equal to the number of goroutines we were launching (and for which we'd later call `Done()`). `SetLimit` doesn't work the same way: instead of immediately defining how many goroutines will be launched (the `errgroup.Group` tracks this internally), we specify a maximum number of goroutines allowed to be running at the same time. Most of the time, you'll want this value equal to the number of goroutines you're running, which is the default value, but sometimes your goroutines make use of a resource that doesn't scale well with load—maybe each of your goroutines calls the database, and the database can only handle 10 calls at a time. In such cases, it's perfectly valid to have a hardcoded limit in your `Group`.

`errgroup.Group` has a `Wait()` method, also similar to that of the `WaitGroup` type, except that it returns an error. This is important, as you'll soon see. And, finally, `Group` has a `Go` method that takes as its parameter a function returning an error. This `Go` method is in charge of launching the goroutine and letting the `Group` know when this function finishes.

As we know, many functions written in Go can return an error. In our example, `cookCurry` could, for instance, return an `ErrIngredientNotFound` error. All of our functions could return an error, and we don't want to deal with the problems of retrieving all of them. The `Wait()` method of the `errgroup.Group` type returns an error that happened in one of the goroutines. It doesn't return just any error that happened there—it returns the (chronologically) last one. Now that we know how to use an `errgroup.Group`, let's use it in our cooking example.

Listing 7.8 Cooking example using `errgroup.Group`

```go
package main

import "golang.org/x/sync/errgroup"

func main() {
    var g errgroup.Group          // Creates the group
    g.SetLimit(2)                 // Sets the max number
                                  // of parallel goroutines

    g.Go(func() error {           // Launches the
        cookRice()                // goroutines
        return nil
    })
    g.Go(cookCurry)

    err := g.Wait()               // Synchronization point
    if err != nil {
        // handle error
    }
}

func cookRice() {
    // cook rice here
}

func cookCurry() error {
    // cook curry here—this may return an error
    return nil
}
```

That's it! We've now seen three ways of controlling the synchronization of goroutines. While we can use channels to notify that a function is returning, it's common to use `sync.WaitGroup` when we want to launch any number of simultaneous calls or to use `errgroup.Group` when we also want to retrieve any error from these calls.

7.3   *A more thread-safe cache*

But let's get back to the initial question—is our cache thread safe? Now that we know how to run goroutines, let's test the cache! But before we run any tests, we need to keep a very important quote regarding testing in mind:

> *Program testing can be used to show the presence of bugs, but never to show their absence!*
>
> —Edsger Dijkstra

First, let's look at the test we currently have and notice one thing: it's extremely linear, which means if we do a specific operation before another one, then the output is predictable. However, it doesn't run anything in goroutines, so it proves absolutely nothing about thread safety.

Our cache could possibly be used by several goroutines during the execution of a program; for instance, several incoming requests could be processed at the same time, causing the cache to be updated in a very short window. Let's start by writing a test that simulates these "simultaneous" calls.

7.3.1   *Using goroutines*

We'll use the `sync.WaitGroup` to run goroutines and make sure they've all finished before returning from the test. To make things "problematic," let's have each of the goroutines write a different value in the same cache every time for the same key. The following listing shows what we write.

Listing 7.9   **Testing the cache with goroutines**

```
func TestCache_Parallel_goroutines(t *testing.T) {
    c := cache.New[int, string]()                    One cache, used
                                                      by all goroutines

    const parallelTasks = 10
    wg := sync.WaitGroup{}                            Sets the max number
    wg.Add(parallelTasks)                             of parallel goroutines

    for i := 0; i < parallelTasks; i++ {
        go func(j int) {                              Launches the goroutine
            defer wg.Done()
            c.Upsert(4, fmt.Sprint(j))                Each goroutine calls Upsert.
        }(i)
    }

    wg.Wait()                     Synchronization step
}
```

In this test, we launch 10 goroutines, and each one is in charge of writing a different value for the same key in our cache.

7.3.2 Using t.Parallel()

Alternatively, we can use the `testing` package to execute parallel tests. This feature is particularly useful in two scenarios: when you want to reduce the time your tests will take because you know some steps are independent and can be run simultaneously, and when you want to make sure you don't have data races.

The gist is that if a test function contains the line `t.Parallel()`, the Go test framework will run it along with other functions in the same scope that also have the `t.Parallel()` line. In other words, the execution of this function won't be blocking for the execution of other test functions.

Let's write a test using the `t.Parallel()` feature. In our test, we want the same index of our cache to be written at by two different calls, with different values in each case.

Listing 7.10 Cooking example using `t.Parallel()`

```
func TestCache_Parallel(t *testing.T) {
    c := cache.New[int, string]()          ◄─── One cache, used
                                                 by all goroutines
    t.Run("write six", func(t *testing.T) {
        t.Parallel()                        ◄─── This goroutine can be
        c.Upsert(6, "six")                       executed along with another.
    })

    t.Run("write kuus", func(t *testing.T) {
        t.Parallel()                        ◄─── This goroutine can also be
        c.Upsert(6, "kuus")                      executed along with another.
    })
}
```

Now let's run it and see what happens: everything seems fine with `go test`. However, we're cheating here—we've written this test because we know something should go wrong. We know that upserting two different values at the same time is precisely a data race, and we want it to be caught. But how can we achieve this?

7.3.3 Using go test -race .

The `go test` command comes with several flags. To find them, use `go help test`, which returns a short list—namely, `-args`, `-c`, `-exec`, `-json`, and `-o`—but it also informs us that the flags from the `build` command are inherited by the `test` command. Let's take a look at the output of `go help build`: one of the first flags provided is `-race`, which enables race detection and is precisely what we're looking for.

Let's run our test again, but this time with the `-race` flag: `go test -race .`. We get the following output:

```
> go test --trimpath -race .
===================
WARNING: DATA RACE
Write at 0x00c0000a53e0 by goroutine 13:
```

```
runtime.mapassign_fast64()
    runtime/map_fast64.go:93 +0x0
learngo-pockets/genericcache.(*Cache[...]).Upsert()
    learngo-pockets/genericcache/cache.go:28 +0x124
learngo-pockets/genericcache_test.TestCache_Parallel.func1()
    learngo-pockets/genericcache/cache_test.go:73 +0x97
learngo-pockets/genericcache_test.TestCache_Parallel.func2()
    learngo-pockets/genericcache/cache_test.go:74 +0x47

Previous write at 0x00c0000a53e0 by goroutine 20:
  runtime.mapassign_fast64()
    runtime/map_fast64.go:93 +0x0
learngo-pockets/genericcache.(*Cache[...]).Upsert()
    learngo-pockets/genericcache/cache.go:28 +0x124
learngo-pockets/genericcache_test.TestCache_Parallel.func1()
    learngo-pockets/genericcache/cache_test.go:73 +0x97
learngo-pockets/genericcache_test.TestCache_Parallel.func2()
    learngo-pockets/genericcache/cache_test.go:74 +0x47
```

As you can see, Go was able to detect that we were writing at the same index twice, at the same time. This constitutes a data race, which would make our cache not thread safe.

You might notice that we didn't describe the `--trimpath` flag here. The default behavior of Go's test framework is to output the absolute path of failing tests (and the stack that leads there). Using `--trimpath`, we tell Go to only output the path from the root of our module. This makes the output clearer when sharing it.

We can now answer our question from earlier by stating that our implementation of the cache isn't thread safe. This is a severe flaw in design and security, so we need to work on it.

7.3.4 *Add a mutex*

When it comes to restricting synchronized access to a resource, computer scientist Edsger Dijkstra introduced the notion of semaphores. A *semaphore* is a counter that keeps track of a number of threads accessing a given resource. Semaphores are used to allow a specific number of threads to simultaneously access a variable, a connection, a socket, and so on. We can push the semaphore to the extreme and allow up to exactly one thread to access a resource. A semaphore that ensures mutual exclusion to a resource is suitably named *mutex* (short for mutual exclusion). Go allows us to use mutexes through the type `Mutex`, defined in the standard library's `sync` package.

GO PROVERB   Channels orchestrate; mutexes serialize.

THE SYNC.MUTEX TYPE
Here's how to declare a simple mutex in Go:

```
var mu sync.Mutex
```

Before diving into usage, let's first understand a little more about what a mutex is. A mutex is a synchronization primitive that prevents multiple goroutines from accessing a shared resource at the same time. Think of it as a lock on a door: only one goroutine can enter the locked section at a time, ensuring exclusive access.

When using a mutex, always remember that it protects access to a specific resource. For clarity and safety, place the mutex in your code as close as possible to the resource it's meant to protect.

Let's take a look at go doc sync.Mutex. We see there that a Mutex exposes Lock(), Unlock(), and TryLock(). However, a glance at its documentation go doc sync.Mutex .TryLock reveals that resorting to TryLock() often indicates a deeper design problem, as it's rarely the best solution for synchronization. We can lock our mutex when we want a piece of code to have exclusive access to the resource and then unlock it afterward.

We're almost ready to use our mutex, but there's a final line of the documentation that is worth remembering: "A Mutex mustn't be copied after first use." Copying a mutex by passing it as a parameter to a function is a mistake that usually leads to unexpected behaviors when locking or unlocking the mutex. Mutexes and the structures containing them need to be passed as pointers.

The zero value of a Mutex is to be unlocked. Using mutexes requires paying special attention to the structure of the code. It's a common source of error to forget to unlock a mutex because the function exits early. As a best practice, we recommend always deferring (via defer) the Unlock() call right after calling Lock(). There will be a few cases when this isn't exactly what you need, but they are exceptions to the general rule of deferring unlocking.

Let's return to the code and add a mutex to our cache. First, we'll add a mutex next to the resource we want to protect—the data map, within the Cache structure.

> **Listing 7.11** `cache.go`: **Caching with a** Mutex

```
type Cache[K comparable, V any] struct {
    mu    sync.Mutex
    data map[K]V
}
```

Each method on the Cache type will ensure only a single goroutine can enter it at a time by having the same two lines:

```
c.mu.Lock()
defer c.mu.Unlock()
```

We can now rerun go test -race .: we should no longer see any data race detected. The mutex seems to have done the job. However, using mutexes isn't free—there's a cost in time execution every time we lock (and unlock). For this reason, it's worth checking we weren't overzealous in our usage of mutexes. In our example, while we're ensuring that no two goroutines update the contents of the cache simultaneously, we're also preventing two goroutines from reading from our cache, which isn't a conflicting operation.

THE SYNC.RWMUTEX TYPE

To address this specific need, the standard library exposes another mutex—the RWMutex, a read-write mutex—also in the sync package. This mutex is very similar to the basic Mutex—it also exposes Lock() and Unlock()—but on top of that, it also has RLock() and RUnlock() methods that are used when we only want to use the mutex to read data. Any number of goroutines can call RLock() without blocking each other, but as soon as Lock() is called, no goroutine can access the resource for reading or for writing.

We can update our code—the mutex in the cache should be a RWMutex. The Read method should only call RLock and RUnlock, as it doesn't modify the contents of the cache. Upsert and Delete will still need a regular Lock and Unlock call. As a general rule, sync.Mutex is the way to go, and sync.RWMutex should only be considered if you're facing performance problems—even then, caution should be the rule. Because of its richer interface, accidentally calling RLock instead of Lock will have a disastrous effect on the code—and the compiler won't tell you. Don't blindly believe that RWMutex is faster than Mutex; instead, benchmark it for your specific use case, and use the appropriate one.

Running go test -race . once more should give us confidence we didn't add a data race. We now have a fully operational, thread-safe, generic cache!

7.4   *Possible improvements*

Even though our cache looks perfect, there are a couple of optimizations we could add. The first one represents the idea that no value is frozen in time forever. After all, in the near future, the last person to have walked on the Moon could very much not be Gene Cernan. Sometimes, it's best to ignore outdated values, and the cache should tell us whether a value has reached its expiration date.

The second optimization we'll present is about handling the cache's memory footprint. If the user doesn't call Delete(), the cache will only grow, storing more and more items. Not having a limit on the cache size is dangerous—it could end up using too much memory, causing some slowdown in the application.

7.4.1   *Adding time to live*

As we mentioned previously, values retrieved in the past can become outdated. One way of ensuring that our values are never too ancient is to give each one of them a "best before" date. Once this timestamp has passed, we shouldn't trust the value any longer. In computer science, this timestamp is called a *time to live* (TTL). To implement it in our cache, we need to attach a "best before" to each of our values.

ADD THE TIMESTAMP

Thanks to generics, we can add an expiration date to any value by defining a new type—an entry with timeout:

```
type entryWithTimeout[V any] struct {
    value   V
    expires time.Time // After that time, the value is useless.
}
```

Our cache is in charge of setting the `expires` value when we upsert an item in our cache. We'll provide a TTL to our cache as a field. This TTL could be a hardcoded parameter of the cache, but this isn't very user friendly. When writing a library, you don't know what use will be made of it. Our cache can be used for varying values such as "most trending posts on social media" or for stable values such as the list of capitals of countries of the world. It's best to expose this TTL as a mandatory parameter of our `New` function.

> **Listing 7.12** `cache.go`: **Creating a cache with a TTL**

```
type Cache[K comparable, V any] struct {
    ttl   time.Duration

    mu    sync.Mutex
    data  map[K]entryWithTimeout[V]
}


func New[K comparable, V any](ttl time.Duration) Cache[K, V] {
    return Cache[K, V]{
        ttl:      ttl,
        data:     make(map[K]entryWithTimeout[V]),
    }
}
```

UPDATE THE METHODS

Let's now consider what will happen in our `Read()`, `Upsert()`, and `Delete()` methods. The easiest one is `Delete`: there's nothing to change there. A key can be removed, regardless of whether the associated value has reached its expiration date. Regarding `Upsert`, we used to either insert the data or override the value. Things aren't very different now—upon insertion, we'll add the data with the correct `expire` value, and upon updating, we'll override not only the value but also its `expires` field.

> **Listing 7.13** `cache.go`: `Upsert` **with a TTL**

```
func (c *Cache[K, V]) Upsert(key K, value V) {
    c.mu.Lock()
    defer c.mu.Unlock()

    c.data[key] = entryWithTimeout[V]{
        value:   value,
        expires: time.Now().Add(c.ttl),     ◄── Uses the cache's TTL
    }                                             for each value inserted
}
```

Finally, we're left with the trickier `Read()` method. This is where we'll check whether an entry is no longer valid, as shown in listing 7.14. We need to add a second check on top of the present one that verifies our cache has a value for the requested key. If the value is still valid, we can return it. But what if it's not? In this case, in our implementation, we decided that the user doesn't need to know why the value isn't in the cache—after all, what matters is that it couldn't be found.

Listing 7.14   `cache.go`: Read with a TTL

```
func (c *Cache[K, V]) Read(key K) (V, bool) {
    c.mu.Lock()
    defer c.mu.Unlock()
                                            A zero value is useful for
    var zeroV V          ◄────────────      our return statements.

    e, ok := c.data[key]

    switch {
    case !ok:
        return zeroV, false
    case e.expires.Before(time.Now()):
        // The value has expired.
        delete(c.data, key)
        return zeroV, false
    default:
        return e.value, true
    }
}
```

By implementation, our `Read()` method now has to alter the contents of the `map`. As a result, we can't rely on a `RWMutex` as we did in section 7.3. Instead, we use a regular `sync.Mutex`. This will have a small effect on performance—two `Read()` methods can no longer be executed simultaneously.

In the implementation of our `Read()` method, we start by defining a noninitialized value of type `V`. This is very common in generic functions that return a constraint—indeed, we can't `return V{}`, as this would require `V` to have a concrete type representation at runtime.

Now that we've written the code, we should test it. Our scenario here is to create a cache with a small TTL to insert an item and then to wait longer than our cache's TTL, as shown in the next listing. Checking immediately if the item is available shouldn't return an error, but checking after a while should.

Listing 7.15   `cache_test.go`: Testing Read with TTL

```
func TestCache_TTL(t *testing.T) {
    t.Parallel()

    c := cache.New[string, string](5, time.Millisecond*100)
    c.Upsert("Norwegian", "Blue")
```

```
    // Check the item is there.
    got, found := c.Read("Norwegian")
    assert.True(t, found)
    assert.Equal(t, "Blue", got)

    time.Sleep(time.Millisecond * 200)

    got, found = c.Read("Norwegian")

    assert.False(t, found)
    assert.Equal(t, "", got)
}
```

We start our test with a call to `t.Parallel()`, and we're fine running this test along with others. We recommend using this in every "light" test. If a test requires a lot of resources—CPU, RAM, disk, network—then you might not want to have it run with others. In our case, there's no reason not to run this test.

SCHRÖDINGER'S CONUNDRUM

You might have noticed that we discard expired items only when we try to access them via `Read()`. This means that items could expire long before we look at them, unbeknownst to us. The side effect is that our cache might be using chunks of memory for useless data. How do we deal with that?

Well, bluntly put, we decided not to. If we were to implement something that regularly checks each item and gets rid of the items that we know are no longer usable, we'd basically be writing a garbage collector for our cache. We'd need to start a goroutine in `New()`, and that goroutine's only task would be to endlessly scan the `map` and delete items that have reached their TTL. Instead of implementing this, we've decided to address a slightly related problem—controlling the size of our cache.

7.4.2 *Add a maximum number of items in the cache*

To prevent too many items from being added to the cache, we'll set a limit to our cache's size. This will be a property of the cache, an unexposed unsigned integer keeping track of how many items were added and removed.

ARCHITECTURAL DECISIONS

We'll need to make a decision when we try to add a new value into the cache and the maximum number of items is reached. In our implementation, we decided to allow this operation—and discard another entry. There are lots of interesting choices to determine which entry to remove from the `map` in this case; eligible candidates could be the oldest entry in the cache, the most recent entry in the cache, the least read entry in the cache, the entry that hasn't been read for the longest time, and so on. Each of these implementations requires storing extra information in our cache. The choice of which one to use is highly dependent on the information stored in the cache. Here, we'll decide to remove the entry that is the oldest in the cache, and we consider that overriding a value should reset its timestamp—as it does for the TTL.

For this, we need to keep track of the order in which items were inserted. Let's look at which options Go offers to implement this:

- *Use a channel*—This is the most intuitive implementation of a first in, first out list in Go. When we Upsert a new entry, we register the key in the channel. The first item in the channel is the oldest. However, this won't work because we don't cover the cases where the user calls Delete or Upsert. In these two cases, we have to move an item from "somewhere" in our channel to its tail. Because channels in Go don't support suppression of an element, this implementation isn't good enough.
- *Use a* slice—After all, slices can handle the suppression of some element in the middle of the slice without too much effort. When we Upsert an element that is present, we add it to the slice; when we want to override the element with another Upsert, we can move it to the end; and we can use Delete to remove the element from the slice.
- *Use other available options*—We can use a binary search tree, for instance.

In this instance, we choose the slice because it covers most of our needs. Because we want our cache to hold up to a maximum number of items, we already know that we can give an upper bound to our slice's capacity. We'll initialize it with the following syntax:

```
chronologicalKeys := make([]K, 0, maxSize)
```

To check whether we've reached the maximum number of items, we can either store the maxSize value as a field of our cache, or we can use the cap built-in function on the chronologicalKeys slice. In this book, we decided to go with the former for the sake of clarity, but this adds the cost of storing this value in our structure:

```
if len(c.data) == maxSize
if len(c.data) == cap(c.chronologicalKeys)
```

This last parameter is here to tell the capacity of our slice at execution. When an element is appended to a slice, if that slice's length is equal to its capacity, the whole slice needs to be reallocated elsewhere in memory. Setting the correct capacity to our slice prevents these reallocations. Now, just as we did for the TTL, let's take a look at the effect of having this slice in our cache for each of our exposed functions.

IMPLEMENTATION

New() should take another parameter: the maximum size of the cache (see listing 7.16). Having a default value doesn't really make sense here—a cache of 10 integers wouldn't be the same size as a cache of 10 extremely complex structures with lots of fields. The reflect package could help us set a maximum memory size to our cache based on the memory footprint of a single item, but this would be overkill. Instead, let's have the user specify a size they think is good enough. Then, any memory consideration is left to them.

```
type Cache[K comparable, V any] struct {
    ttl                 time.Duration

    mu                  sync.Mutex
    data                map[K]entryWithTimeout[V]

    maxSize             int
    chronologicalKeys   []K
}

// New creates a new Cache with an initialised data.
func New[K comparable, V any](
    maxSize int,
    ttl time.Duration) Cache[K, V] {        Passes the maximum size of
    return Cache[K, V]{                     the cache as a parameter
        ttl:                ttl,
        data:               make(map[K]entryWithTimeout[V]),
        maxSize:            maxSize,
        chronologicalKeys:  make([]K, 0, maxSize),
    }
}
```

Next, we notice that adding an entry to our cache will no longer be as simple as adding a key-value pair to a map. We now need to update the `chronologicalKeys` slice by adding, removing, or moving one of its elements every time we update the map by inserting, deleting, or updating one item, respectively.

As a result, we refactor our code to avoid duplicating logic. We need both a small function that adds a key-value pair to our cache and a function that removes a key from it. Both functions should be in charge of updating both our map and our slice. Let's start with these, which is also a good opportunity to use a feature added in Go 1.21—the `slices` package. This package is a helper for most common operations on `slices`. Here, we'll use it to delete all items that have a specific value from the slice with its `DeleteFunc` function, as shown in the following listing. This function returns a slice that has dropped all items that returned `true` in the provided callback (it doesn't update the slice).

```
// addKeyValue inserts a key and its value into the cache.
func (c *Cache[K, V]) addKeyValue(key K, value V) {
    c.data[key] = entryWithTimeout[V]{
        value:   value,
        expires: time.Now().Add(c.ttl),
    }
    c.chronologicalKeys = append(c.chronologicalKeys, key)
}

// deleteKeyValue removes a key and its associated value from the cache.
```

```
func (c *Cache[K, V]) deleteKeyValue(key K) {
    c.chronologicalKeys = slices.DeleteFunc(
        c.chronologicalKeys,
        func(k K) bool { return k == key })
    delete(c.data, key)
}
```

Now that we have these helping functions, we can update the code in `Read()` first, as shown in listing 7.18. All we have to do now is update how we remove an entry when it reaches its TTL, as shown in listing 7.19.

Listing 7.18   `cache.go`: `Read` **with the new helper functions**

```
func (c *Cache[K, V]) Read(key K) (V, bool) {
    ...
    case e.expires.Before(time.Now()):
        // The value has expired.
        c.deleteKeyValue(key)            Refactors using the
        return zeroV, false              new helper function
    ...
```

Listing 7.19   `cache.go`: `Delete` **with the new helper functions**

```
func (c *Cache[K, V]) Delete(key K) {
    // Lock the deletion on the map
    c.mu.Lock()
    defer c.mu.Unlock()

    c.deleteKeyValue(key)
}
```

And, finally, we have to update the `Upsert()` function. This one is slightly trickier, as this is where the core of the feature we want to implement resides—we want to limit the number of items that are stored in our cache at a given time. Because this number only grows when we upsert items, it makes sense that this function will be the most affected one. Let's have a look at the possibilities when the user calls `Upsert()`:

- *The cache already has a value for that key.* In this case, we want to reset the whole entry with the new value and the new TTL. We need to also update the position of the key in our chronological `slice`. We can achieve this by deleting the old pair and adding the new one.

- *The cache doesn't have a value for that key.* In this case, if we haven't reached the maximum capacity of our cache, then we can simply insert the new pair. However, if we've reached the maximum capacity, we need to clear some space for the new entry—this means discarding the item that has been there for the longest. This item is at the beginning of our `slice` of keys.

Now that we know how our method should behave, let's implement it. The necessary code is shown in the following listing.

Listing 7.20 `cache.go`: `Upsert` with the new helper functions

```
func (c *Cache[K, V]) Upsert(key K, value V) {
    c.mu.Lock()
    defer c.mu.Unlock()

    _, alreadyPresent := c.data[key]
    switch {
    case alreadyPresent:
        c.deleteKeyValue(key)                        ◀── Discards any previous reference
    case len(c.data) == c.maxSize:
        c.deleteKeyValue(c.chronologicalKeys[0])     ◀── There's no room left in our map.
    }

    c.addKeyValue(key, value)                        ◀── Inserts the item
}
```

There's one last chance for optimization here. When we need to replace an existing entry, but the cache is at maximum capacity, we don't need to discard the oldest entry because we can discard the value we're about to replace to create enough room for the new entry. Go's `switch/case` statement has a very specific behavior that we used in our implementation: when several `case` statements are valid, only the first eligible one will be executed. That's an implicit rule that most people know without knowing it—it also applies to `default`: if we enter a `case` statement, we won't execute the `default` block. We used that behavior here to delete only the pair we need to update. Should you ever need to enter more than one `case` statement, you could consider using the keyword `fallthrough`. However, it will likely be clearer to write a list of `if` statements in that case.

TEST THE CACHE

Our cache is no longer a plain `map`. We've added logic by age with our list of items, and this new logic is invisible to the end user. As a result, it's worth adding a few internal tests to just make sure we're doing everything right.

Finally, let's think of an end user test scenario for our new feature. We can validate it by adding items to our cache beyond its limit, as shown in listing 7.21. We also need to check that updated items have their insertion timestamp updated. For this, we'll create a cache with a small maximum capacity, insert items to the brim, upsert the oldest, and then insert a new key. We should then be able to retrieve the upserted value, and we should no longer be able to retrieve the second value we added in our cache.

Listing 7.21 `cache_test.go`: Testing the maximum capacity of the cache

```
// TestCache_MaxSize tests the maximum capacity feature of a cache.
// It checks that update items are properly requeued as "new" items,
// and that we make room by removing the most ancient item for the new
// ones.
```

```
func TestCache_MaxSize(t *testing.T) {
    t.Parallel()                                          Use this everywhere.

    // Give it a TTL long enough to survive this test
    c := cache.New[int, int](3, time.Minute)              Short maxSize and
                                                          long TTL for this test
    c.Upsert(1, 1)
    c.Upsert(2, 2)
    c.Upsert(3, 3)

    got, found := c.Read(1)
    assert.True(t, found)
    assert.Equal(t, 1, got)

    // Update 1, which will no longer make it the oldest
    c.Upsert(1, 10)

    // Adding a fourth element will discard the oldest - 2 in this case.
    c.Upsert(4, 4)

    // Trying to retrieve an element that should've been discarded by now.
    got, found = c.Read(2)
    assert.False(t, found)
    assert.Equal(t, 0, got)
}
```

Congratulations! We've now written a generic library that we can share with other developers. We started with a naive implementation that covered our needs, and then we strengthened it by adding thread safety. Even though there was quite a lot of theory presented in this chapter, we managed to cover practical requirements for a cache.

7.5   *Common mistakes*

In *100 Go Mistakes and How to Avoid Them* (https://mng.bz/QDjw), Teiva Harsanyi dedicates 20 of the 100 lessons to concurrency and parallelism. We highly recommend the book to dive deeper into Go. In the meantime, here's our short list of common mistakes to avoid.

7.5.1   *When to use channels in a concurrency situation*

Channels are very specific to Go, which means developers new to the language don't master them as easily as the rest of the language. They are, arguably, the one feature in the entire language that requires a learning curve and some practice.

Because they can be tricky at first, don't use them if you don't need them. Although your situation might look like a good place to use this shiny feature, think twice. Channels should be used when you need to communicate into or out of a goroutine.

7.5.2   *Concurrency effect of a workload type*

Given a concurrency situation, you first need to determine the type of workload: not all types lead to the same solution. Loads can be CPU, memory, or IO-bound. Running a merge sort algorithm is typically high on CPU, whereas making REST API calls is a lot of input/output.

Take, for example, a program that counts the number of lines in a bunch of files. Opening and closing files would be the bottleneck here because it's IO-bound. The number of goroutines that can work in parallel will be determined by the operating system's limit or the rules of your server if the files are remote. You don't want to crash your system or get banned by hitting your server too much.

On the other hand, if you're encoding a video on a single machine, a task that is typically high on CPU, then you need to look at the architecture of your machine. The GOMAXPROCS environment variable is an interesting hint. Its default value is the number of cores of your CPU. The variable represents the maximum number of goroutines that could actually run simultaneously. Any extra goroutine will have to share a CPU with existing goroutines. Too often, parallelizing the work actually makes things worse because you've already hit the max load of your CPU. The size of a buffered channel can be a good thing to benchmark in your performance tests, which should be executed on a machine with a similar architecture as that's where your code will be executed.

7.5.3 *Finish your goroutines*

Goroutines are easy to start, but don't let them leak. As we've seen, a program should only exit when all of its child goroutines are finished. Once you're done writing to your goroutines, close them so that their readers know when to stop listening.

Explore the sync package for tools to make your life easier. Most of the types there shouldn't be copied, though, so be careful.

Summary

- A cache is a key-value storage facility. Caches are commonly used when getting the value associated with a key is costly (timewise or in the number of resources) and when getting a previously retrieved or computed value is OK.
- When writing a library, you should always ask if the library is thread safe. The answer is either "Yes, and I know why," or "No, it's not." There's no middle ground—the worst-case scenario is usually also the most dangerous.
- Go implements genericity with, well, generics. Structures, variables, and functions can be declared using generics.
- A constraint is a requirement for a generic type. Common constraints are any (quite explicit); comparable, which allows the use of == between two values; or golang.org/x/exp/constraints.Ordered, which allows the use of >, <, >=, or <= between two values.
- Constraints are passed in square brackets after the name of the generic entity:
  - type fieldWithName [T any] struct { value T, name string }
  - var hashIndex [T myConstraint] map [uint] T
  - func sortSlice [T constraints.Ordered] (t []T) ([]T, error)

- Constraints can be omitted in the declaration of functions when the compiler can infer which type it should be using: `sortSlice([]int{1,4,3,2})`.

- Go uses goroutines for concurrency. Goroutines are similar to what other languages usually call threads, except they're not. Threads live at an OS level, while goroutines live farther from your silicon—they exist in the runtime environment of Go.

- In Go, goroutines are launched with the keyword `go`, and `go do()` runs the `do` function in a new goroutine.

- Channels are used to communicate data between different goroutines. When passing a channel to a function, make it explicit in the signature that the function will either read from the channel, with the syntax `func f(c <- chan string)`, or that it will write to the channel, with the syntax `func f(c chan <- string)`. If you need to both read from and write to a channel in a single function, there's probably a design flaw.

- Two types are commonly used when we need to synchronize goroutines: `sync.WaitGroup` and `errgroup.Group`. When using `sync.WaitGroup`, start by calling `Add(n)` with the number of goroutines that will be executed. Each goroutine is in charge of calling `Done`. The synchronization is achieved by calling `Wait()`. When using `errgroup.Group`, start by setting a maximum number of parallel goroutines with `SetLimit(n)`. Launch each goroutine with a call to `Go(...)`. The synchronization is achieved with a call to `Wait()`, which returns an error if one of the goroutines returns an error.

- The choice of `sync.WaitGroup` or `errgroup.Group` is often driven by the necessity to check for errors in at least one goroutine. Use `sync.WaitGroup` when errors don't need a specific treatment. Use `errgroup.Group` if you want to handle errors.

- Mutexes are used whenever we want to protect a variable from concurrent writing—or reading. In Go, we can create a mutex variable by using the `sync.Mutex` type: `var myMutex sync.Mutex`. A mutex should never be exposed; instead, use it in exposed functions. A mutex should always be written close to the variable or field it protects.

- You can call `mu.Lock()` on a mutex, but we highly recommend immediately following this with `defer mu.Unlock()`. Debugging locked mutexes is a pain.

- Use `t.Parallel()` in your tests to let the framework know that a test isn't blocking for the execution of other tests.

- Use the `-race` flag when testing to try to detect data races, but remember that the failure to detect a data race doesn't mean there are no data races.

- Use the `--trimpath` flag when testing to only output paths relative to the root of the module.

- A `switch/case` statement will only execute the first valid `case`; any subsequent case will be ignored.

Gordle as a service

8

This chapter covers

- Creating and running an HTTP server that listens to messages on a given port
- Listening to endpoints with GET and POST verbs
- Building a response with a status code
- Decoding different sources of data: path and query parameters, bodies, and headers
- Testing using regular expressions

In 1962, J. C. R. Licklider mentioned the possibility of having computers communicate one with another over a network. Since then, computer science has traveled a long way, first through this Intergalactic Computer Network (coined by Licklider), then the pioneering network of Advanced Research Projects Agency Network (ARPANET), and, today, the internet. Networks are now used on a daily basis—when you pick up your phone to check the weather, the news, or even the time. The possibility of using a server from a remote location was paramount when, in 2020, the whole planet went into lockdown during COVID.

A server, in the end, is really just a machine that listens to communications on a given set of ports and is able to answer messages that it receives. In this chapter, we'll implement such a server. To make things interesting, our server will have an API that allows a user to play a game of Gordle. In this chapter, we'll focus on the server-side implementation rather than on the algorithmic aspect, which has already been covered in chapter 5.

In the first part of this chapter, we'll create the REST API and test it with simple tools such as an internet browser or a command. In the second part, we'll integrate the game of Gordle—which will require a few updates to comply with how we want to use it in the server. Finally, we'll mention a few security tips.

> **NOTE** Further steps, such as containerization and deployment, are not in the scope of topics for this chapter. For more information, check out *Kubernetes in Action* by Marko Lukša and Kevin Conner (Manning, 2017, www.manning .com/books/kubernetes-in-action).

The project has the following requirements:

- Play Gordle on a web service.
- Run a service that exposes at least the following endpoints:
  - `NewGame` creates a session and returns a gamer ID. This will be used for counting the number of attempts.
  - `GetStatus` returns, well, a game's status, including how many guesses are still allowed, previous hints used, and so on.
  - `Guess` takes a word as a parameter and returns the feedback and the status of the game.
- Include, in a second step, some tracking of the players' sessions. Many online resources use some kind of user identifier—most of the time, authentication. You'll see how we can convey this information.

The following are not required for this project: monitoring, logging strategy, and scalability (yet).

8.1   Empty shell for the new service

A web service can be thought of as a daemon—it's always running, waiting for queries that are sent to a port of the computer hosting it. In this chapter, we'll start our development from the outside in: we'll first create a service that listens to a port but does nothing; then add empty endpoints, one per feature; and, finally, we'll add their logic. This strategy is best when some other team members, for example, frontend developers or other teams altogether, are waiting for your work. It's possible to return a static mocked response that other people can use while you develop and where they can give you feedback. Having a service that returns something, even when it's constant or irrelevant, is often enough to help other people design, develop, test, or deploy their solutions. Before we begin writing a few lines of code, it's important to introduce some vocabulary and understand a few theoretical notions.

8.1.1 Server, service, web service, endpoints, and HTTP handlers

A *server* can be thought of as a computer, running somewhere. We usually keep servers running, as they host *services*, which are applications that expose an API. Usually, we want services to be permanently running because a stopped service is of no use. A *web service* is a particular kind of service that makes use of the web protocol to receive and send communications with the outer world.

> **NOTE** Keep in mind, for later steps of this chapter, that a service isn't supposed to end its execution. In other words, it's running until the user decides to stop it.

Endpoints are the access points for the exterior into a service. For web services, endpoints are mapped to specific URLs, as you'll soon see. A web service, behind the scenes, will use an HTTP handler to deal with requests. *HTTP handlers* receive HTTP requests and generate HTTP responses.

> **NOTE** Be aware that the terms *web service* and *endpoint* are used in different contexts with slightly different definitions, but we'll use the definitions just mentioned in our discussions in this chapter.

8.1.2 Let's code

Let's start by creating the module for our service. Keeping in mind that we'll be running Gordle in an HTTP server, we can come up with a relevant name. Remember that if you're pushing your code to a code repository, it's always better to declare the full path of your repository as a module:

```
> go mod init learngo/httpgordle
```

Once we've created the `go.mod` file, we can start writing the `main` function, which will be responsible for creating and running a server (see listing 8.1). For this, we'll need some help from the `net/http` package that we've already seen in chapter 6. Its documentation is quite long, but just the first lines of `go doc net/http` state that "Package `http` provides HTTP client and server implementations." For now, we're only interested in the server side.

A server listens to a specific port, so find any free port on your host machine. The default port for HTTP is 80, but for development purposes, we prefer to use another, such as 8000 or 8080, as 80 will probably be used on your machine by something else. A function in the `net/http` package seems to achieve exactly what we need—`ListenAndServe`.

Listing 8.1   `main.go`: Creating the server

```go
package main

import "net/http"

func main() {
    // Start the server.
    err := http.ListenAndServe(":8080", nil)   ◄——————  Use any free port here.
    if err != nil {
        panic(err)          ◄——————  It's OK to panic in
    }                                 the body of main.
}
```

We hope this wasn't too frightening. We've given `ListenAndServe` two parameters. The first one is the address we want our web service to be listening to—`localhost:8080` (the `localhost` can be omitted) is a popular choice. If you're on Windows, consider using a port other than 8080 to avoid the Windows Firewall pop-up. The second parameter is the handler that can deal with requests (discussed next)—for now, we can keep it `nil`, but that's where the logic will be implemented. We said panicking was OK in the body of the `main` function, but actually that's only partly true. `panic` dumps the whole stack trace, which could be confusing for users. It would be more polite to dump the error and exit with a proper code such as the following snippet (the downside is not having the guarantee that all the `defer` calls have been executed):

```go
if err != nil {
    fmt.Fprintln(os.Stderr, err)
    os.Exit(1)
}
```

Let's run it:

```
> go run .
```

You might notice that the execution hangs. That's because the `ListenAndServe` function never returns. After all, that's exactly how we want it to behave: the service is running!

To test an HTTP server manually, many tools are available. Here are four of them:

- *Internet browser*—Browsers are designed to send HTTP requests. Setting some parameters, such as the body of the request, its headers, or the verb we want to use, might be a little tricky, but it should do the trick for this first implementation.

- *Postman*—This tool has a GUI that allows for finer usage than a web browser when it comes to sending formatted messages over the network.

- *curl*—This command-line tool exposes everything we want to use. This is our preferred option: not only is it simpler to share the execution command line in a book, but also using command-line tools rather than clickable interfaces will make testing a lot more automatable. curl is shipped with every version of Linux or macOS, and with Windows 10 and above.

- *Go program*—You can write a program in Go that creates a client to speak with our server, as we did in chapter 6.

The `nil` handler we provided can't really do much, but still, we can see it in action. If you open your favorite web browser and enter the URL `localhost:8080`, you'll see a response from the default HTTP handler in the form of a 404 message.

If you want to use curl, here's the same request as a command line:

```
> curl http://localhost:8080
```

It will also return a 404 message. We'll make more extensive use of `curl` in our next tests.

We've successfully implemented our first HTTP server. Before we move on to the next section, we need to kill our server. In the shell where we executed `go run .`, press Ctrl–C. This sends an interrupt signal to the current process, which terminates it. There are other ways of terminating a running program, either via your computer's task manager or by using the `kill` command, if you know the process ID of the program you want to terminate. Once this is done, we can commit our work before moving on to the next part—getting rid of this `nil` handler.

8.2 Adding endpoints

For this project, we're implementing a web service that allows people to play a game of Gordle. Let's take a look again at the requirements: we need to be able to create a game, to play a guess, and to retrieve the status of a game. We can immediately see our service will be dealing with "game" entities—creating them, using them, and displaying them. We also need to access these games—either to play a guess or display their status. For this, we'll need some way of identifying a game and storing it. Storing will come later, as we work from the outside in.

An endpoint on an HTTP server is a pair of a path and an HTTP method. The path should reflect which resource is being used. In our case, we'll be dealing with games, which makes the path `/games` a good start. When we need to identify a single game, we can use `/games/{game_id}`.

An *HTTP method* (or verb) describes the action we want to execute as we call an address. There are several methods defined, but we'll focus on the following:

- `GET`—Used when accessing a resource.
- `POST`—Used when creating a resource or asking for data to be processed.
- `PUT`—Used to update a resource.
- `DELETE`—Used to delete a resource.

Some of these endpoints—`GET`, `PUT`, and `DELETE`, in this list—should be idempotent; that is, several consecutive calls should all return the same response and should all leave the resources in the same state as calling them just once. If your API isn't idempotent, you need to explicitly tell your users in the documentation. GET, PUT, and DELETE should simply not be used for non-idempotent endpoints—use POST instead. We're now ready to implement our first endpoint.

8.2.1 *Create a new game*

Creating a game is the first thing a player will do. Let's start by considering the goals we need to achieve. We don't really need any input to create a game of Gordle. If you remember chapter 5, we launched a game with go run main.go. As we're adding a new endpoint, we need a pair of a path and an HTTP method. The resources we'll want to use are the games—the /games path seems perfect.

Which HTTP method should we use? In this case, because we're creating a game, we should use a POST. In some situations, you may already know the identifier of the resource to create. For instance, if we're dealing with books, we could use the ISBN to create a book resource with the method PUT on the following address: /books/9781633438804.

For Gordle, we only need to create an empty game. However, to keep track of it, it's paramount that we return the game's identifier, which will be used in the GetStatus and Guess endpoints. An identifier can take the form of a series of digits (e.g., a phone number is a digit-only identifier) or characters (e.g., a license plate is a car's identifier). There are some good libraries that provide unique identifiers, such as https://github.com/google/uuid. We'll stick to random integers, as we've already covered this topic in chapter 5 when we needed to get a random word from a list.

We've now defined the API for this endpoint. We know the path, the verb to associate with it, and the expected response—an identifier. The documentation starts like this:

```
POST /games - creates a new game and returns its ID.
```

Now, let's get back to the code!

PROJECT ORGANIZATION

There's no official rule on how to organize files within a module, nor how to organize modules within a project. However, there are common practices that are worth mentioning. The first important point is that a few folder names have specific behaviors in Go:

- testdata—We've already mentioned in chapter 3 that directories named testdata won't be examined by the Go tool. Code inside the directories won't be compiled by go build or go run, tests written inside won't be executed by go test, and documentation won't be visible through go doc.
- internal—It's now time to introduce another special name for a directory: internal. An internal directory can contain code for the current module to use, but this code won't be visible to other modules. For instance, the module golang.org/x/text has an internal package where the type Inheritance-Matcher is defined. However, even though this type is exposed (due to the

uppercase letter), we can't create a variable of this type in our module. The scope of types and functions defined in a directory named `internal`—or a subdirectory of an `internal` directory—is limited to the current module (in our example, the `golang.org/x/text` module). An `internal` directory is a good place to put code you don't want other people to use. In the case of a service, most of the code will reside there.

- `vendor`—We mention the `vendor` directory for historical reasons only. We won't go through the whole history of the language, but earlier versions of Go used to have "versioned" dependencies—copies local to each module. These copies would be placed inside a `vendor` directory—and it was a good idea to always ignore the contents of that directory in your favorite versioning tool. It's best to simply never name a directory `vendor`, for compatibility reasons. If you really must, use `vendors` instead.

- `pkg`—You might encounter packages located in a `pkg` package, at the root of the module: `module/pkg/my_package`. In `pkg`, you can expect to find libraries that could be used outside of your project. We don't encourage the use of `pkg` because it's not a Go standard. It's rather a historical artifact or a `golang-standards/project-layout`, which isn't the official standard from the Go team.

These were strict rules, and we can add some suggestions that you're free to follow. We like to expose the API of a service in an `api` package—a directory at the root of the module.

FILE ORGANIZATION OF THE SERVICE

We're now prepared to organize our code, create an `api` directory at the root of our module, and create an `internal` directory into which we'll write all sorts of things, including our HTTP handlers in a subdirectory. How we implement an endpoint won't be of any use to external developers, so we might as well hide this within an `internal/handlers` directory.

We chose to create a package for each handler. In our case, a simple package for all of them would be perfectly fine as well, however, by having multiple packages, we can show how we would structure a larger project without actually writing a large project. Depending on the situation, you can sometimes do everything in the same package (albeit in different files for clarity) or spread the logic across different packages. Here, we chose to keep the logic (validations, calling the storage, etc.) inside the handlers (responsible for everything related to the HTTP API), which means we prefer to have a package per endpoint. As usual, think about how each package will scale and grow when you add functionalities as you make this type of decision.

Finally, it's important to take into account the notion of coupling. Some structures and functions are coupled by nature and will need to be updated together. The more coupled pieces of code are spread into different packages, the more difficult it is to maintain code quality. As usual, you need to find a balance, and later updates will provide opportunities to refactor the organization if it no longer fits your needs.

The HTTP API of our service can be exposed in an `http.go` file, while the initial handler for a new game will be in a `newgame/handler.go` file. We'll bind the API to the handler in the `router.go` file. Here's our file organization at this point:

```
> tree
.
├── go.mod
├── internal
│   ├── api
│   │   ├── doc.go
│   │   └── http.go
│   └── handlers
│       ├── doc.go
│       ├── newgame
│       │   └── handler.go
│       └── router.go
└── main.go
```

DEFINING THE **REST API**

REST is a set of conventions that help define an API on an HTTP server. It defines collections of resources and ways to interact with them.

Let's start with the `http.go` file. It should contain everything that we need to expose to allow someone else to use the `NewGame` endpoint that we'll implement next. By everything, we mean which URL should be used and which method. If there's anything more, such as parameters to the query, we include them in this file. Let's create the `http.go` file in the package `internal/api`.

> Listing 8.2   `api/http.go`: Defining necessities for the `NewGame` endpoint

```go
package api

import "net/http"

const (
    // NewGameRoute is the path to create a new game.
    NewGameRoute  = "/games"
)
```

We now have the necessary constant for the `NewGame` endpoint that we're about to implement. What should callers of this endpoint expect in return? Sometimes creation endpoints only return an ID. Here, we want to be more verbose and return the full game that we created: the client of our Gordle game needs to know the number of characters in the secret word and the maximum number of attempts allowed. As we're defining what a `Game` is in the API, we should think of every field that we want to include. We can also tell the status of the game to let players know whether they can keep playing and whether they won or lost already. Finally, having a list of the previous attempts will help in the display. Let's define the shape of this JSON game as follows:

```
{
  "id": "1225482481867118141",
  "attempts_left": 4,
  "word_length": 5,
  "status": "Playing",
  "guesses": [
    {"word":"slice","feedback":""}
  ],
}
```

This translates easily into a Go struct with JSON tags, as shown in previous chapters and in the following listing.

Listing 8.3 `internal/api/http.go`: **Defining the game's API structure**

```
package api

// ...

// GameResponse contains the information about a game.
type GameResponse struct {
    ID           string `json:"id"`
    AttemptsLeft byte   `json:"attempts_left"`
    Guesses      []Guess `json:"guesses"`        ◄── Guesses come as a list
    WordLength   byte   `json:"word_length"`          of previous attempts.
    Solution     string `json:"solution,omitempty"`  ◄── The solution is only
    Status       string `json:"status"`                  given when the
}                                                         game is over; it's
                                                          omitted otherwise.
// Guess is a pair of a word (submitted by the player)
// and its feedback (provided by Gordle).
type Guess struct {
    Word     string `json:"word"`
    Feedback string `json:"feedback"`
}
```

Note that all types are primary types; we're not imposing any strong typing to our consumers. We chose to express the feedback as a string. We'll talk more about this when we start filling up the feedback. We now have the structure, and it's officially published to consumers, so it's time for the server to actually expose the endpoint.

HTTP MULTIPLEXER, HANDLE, AND HANDLER

If you remember the first section, we provided a `nil` handler to the `ListenAndServe` function. Let's take a closer look at this function's second parameter, which is an `http.Handler`. This type is declared as follows:

```
type Handler interface {
    ServeHTTP(ResponseWriter, *Request)
}
```

There are several ways of implementing a `Handler` that can be passed to `ListenAnd-Serve`. For instance, we could define a structure and have it implement the interface:

```
type newGameHandler struct {}

func (h *newGameHandler) ServeHTTP(
    w *http.ResponseWriter, req *http.Request) {
    ...
}
```

And, in the `main` function, use the following:

```
err := http.ListenAndServe(":8080", newGameHandler{})
```

This would do the trick. However, there's a minor problem here: creating a handler this way only allows for one endpoint to be defined. As we know, we want to implement several endpoints—at least three.

Take a look at another type provided by the `net/http` package: `ServeMux`. A quick `go doc http.ServeMux` command shows that it's a *request multiplexer*. This means that a `ServeMux` is in charge of routing requests based on the URL they were sent to. Multiplexers (commonly called muxes) are the foundation of an HTTP service.

There are two other important points to highlight with `ServeMux`: first, it allows the registration of endpoints with the `HandleFunc` method, which is what we want to achieve. Second, `ServeMux` has a method called `ServeHTTP` with the correct signature. It implements the `Handler` interface, and we can pass a `ServeMux` to the `ListenAndServe` function.

MULTIPLEXER

Let's start by writing the multiplexer. We'll then look at the signature of what it accepts to register an endpoint.

We need to build an `http.Handler`, which will only take a few lines at first, but as soon as the service grows, it will grow fast. This is why we write a function that builds it and returns it, as shown in listing 8.4. All the logic of building the mux will be isolated here.

The function creates a new instance, makes it listen to our future endpoint, and returns it. We haven't defined yet what the endpoint will look like, so let's put a placeholder here first. If you want to compile to check that everything else makes sense, `nil` is perfectly acceptable; although, if you use `nil`, don't expect a request to your service to do anything but panic.

Listing 8.4   `internal/handlers/router.go`: Handler to URL association

```
package handlers

import (
    "net/http"

    "learngo-pockets/httpgordle/internal/api"
    "learngo-pockets/httpgordle/internal/newgame"
```

```
)

// Mux creates a multiplexer with all the endpoints for our service.
func Mux() *http.ServeMux {
    mux := http.NewServeMux()
    mux.HandleFunc(api.NewGameRoute, newgame.Handle)
    return mux
}
```

◀── Connects a URL to a handler

We can finally use this `Mux` in the `main` function, replacing the previous `nil` handler.

Listing 8.5 `main.go`: Using the new `Mux()` function

```
package main

import (
    "net/http"

    "learngo-pockets/httpgordle/internal/handlers"
)

func main() {
    err := http.ListenAndServe(":8080", handlers.Mux())
    if err != nil {
        panic(err)
    }
}
```

Now, what's left is to implement that `newgame.Handle` handler that we passed in the `mux`. We'll take care of that next.

HANDLER FOR THE NEWGAME {ENDPOINT}

The `mux.HandleFunc` method has the following signature:

```
func (mux *ServeMux) HandleFunc(
    pattern string, handler func(ResponseWriter, *Request))
```

This method registers a handler—the anonymous function we pass as the second parameter—for the provided path. The benefit of this method over `http.Handle` is that we don't have to write a new `http.Handler`; we simply have to provide the handler itself, the function in charge of dealing with the request and writing the response.

For the simplest implementation, we can call the `Write` function on the `Response-Writer` and say something to the client. Let's write the handler in the file `internal/handlers/newgame/handler.go`.

Listing 8.6 `handler.go`: Empty `newgame` handler

```
package newgame

import "net/http"
```

```
func Handle(w http.ResponseWriter, req *http.Request) {
    _, _ = w.Write([]byte("Creating a new game"))
}
```

This is the very first version. We're not even checking errors, but we will as we get closer to our final version.

Right, we're getting there! We can now go run . this code and check how it behaves. There is a final step we need to complete before we can move on to the next section. Let's discover it together.

If you open a browser to localhost:8080/games or run curl http://localhost:8080/games while the service is running, you should get a message letting you know that a game is being created. There's an invisible parameter that is passed by these tools—we didn't specify which HTTP method to use, and both tools chose and sent a GET by default. We want our NewGame endpoint to only accept POST requests. Let's implement this.

A REQUEST IS RECEIVED

Even though it might sound evident, a server should be able to serve several clients at a time. The fact that someone is using an endpoint shouldn't prevent others from also calling it. Behind the scenes, this means that the server won't wait till a task is complete before serving a new call. In Go, this is achieved with goroutines. Goroutines are Go's version of concurrent programming—the closest equivalent ideas, in other languages, are usually called threads, coroutines, fibers, or green threads. Goroutines, however, are different from threads, and we'll cover goroutines more extensively in chapter 9.

When a server receives a request, it starts a goroutine that will execute the handler. Even though this might seem wonderful and extremely handy, it comes with limitations. The last section of this chapter, covering correctness, will present two important topics—race conditions and ensuring the server doesn't explode when attempting to serve two requests at the same time. As discussed in chapter 7, instead of running go test ., we'll add the flag -race.

HTTP CODES AND HEADER

A game of Gordle should only be created when a POST request is received. But what should we do when we receive the wrong method, and how do we implement this?

The answer to the first question is clear: we should reject the message. There's actually a specific HTTP code for wrong verbs, so we might as well use it: http.Status-MethodNotAllowed (see table 8.1). As to where we should make this check, the only logical place is within the Handle function.

HTTP response headers are set by a call to WriteHeader with an adequate status code. If we receive a request for anything other than what we declared in the API, we can terminate the call there immediately. The following listing shows the implementation of the check in the newGameHandler function, in the file internal/handlers/newgame/handler.go.

Listing 8.7 `handler.go`: **Rejecting requests that use the wrong method**

```go
func Handle(w http.ResponseWriter, req *http.Request) {
    if req.Method != http.MethodPost {
        w.WriteHeader(http.StatusMethodNotAllowed)
        return
    }
    _, _ = w.Write([]byte("Creating a new game"))
}
```

As you can see, this isn't really the same error handling as in "regular" Go. We have to adapt to HTTP, and this means communicating errors through status codes. Because there's no point in trying to process a request that was invalid, we can safely return from our handler. The error—invalid method—has been dealt with, and there's nothing else we want to do.

Let's run our previous test of starting the service and checking the `http://localhost:8080/games` page through various tools. Depending on your browser, you may or may not see a 405 error. Firefox didn't display anything in our tests, whereas Google Chrome did. Let's take a look with curl:

```
> curl localhost:8080/games
```

Nothing is returned—a completely empty response. This is problematic because it makes checking our implementation more difficult. Fortunately for us, curl also comes with options, and an interesting one is `--verbose`, or `-v`, which prints a lot more information. Let's give it a try—you should get a somewhat similar output:

```
> curl -v localhost:8080/games
    Output:
*    Trying 127.0.0.1:8080...
* Connected to localhost (127.0.0.1) port 8080 (#0)
> GET /games HTTP/1.1
> Host: localhost:8080
> User-Agent: curl/7.81.0
> Accept: */*
> < HTTP/1.1 405 Method Not Allowed
< Content-Length: 0
<
* Connection #0 to host localhost left intact
```

Now that's more like it. Lines starting with > are header data sent by the client. Lines starting with < are header data returned by the service. The first line to notice here is the first header data sent—we did send a GET method. curl uses a default verb when sending a request if none was explicitly provided—in this case, a GET method. The other interesting line from this output is the first found in the response section: we can see the server returned a 405 status code and its explicit meaning Method Not Allowed, which is what we expected.

curl allows for specific methods to be used via the `--request`, or `-X`, option. In Postman, you'd simply change the method used via the dropdown box. From a web browser, things are getting a bit tricky. Sometimes, it's achievable to send a `POST`—or a `PUT`, a `DELETE`, or anything you'd like—using the developer's settings, but, in most cases, we've reached the limits of what browsers offer for our purposes. From now on, we'll limit the scope of testing with external tools to curl—Postman is quite intuitive for all basic uses and doesn't need guidelines. Let's shoot a `POST` on our endpoint:

```
> curl -v -X POST localhost:8080/games
```

Here's the output:

```
*    Trying 127.0.0.1:8080...
* Connected to localhost (127.0.0.1) port 8080 (#0)
> POST /games HTTP/1.1
> Host: localhost:8080
> User-Agent: curl/7.81.0
> Accept: */*
>
< HTTP/1.1 200 OK
< Content-Length: 19
< Content-Type: text/plain; charset=utf-8
<
* Connection #0 to host localhost left intact
Creating a new game
```

This is almost exactly what we wanted. We say almost because there's a rule in HTTP: an action that creates a resource should return a status describing that the resource was created. Here's what grabbed our attention in the pair of exchanged headers: the status code of the response is `200`, which stands for `OK`. This status code shouldn't be used when creating a game; instead, according to HTTP standards, we should be using `201`, which stands for `Created`.

Table 8.1 describes the most common HTTP status codes from the HTTP Semantics RFC9110 documentation (https://mng.bz/yWPG). This documentation contains the full details regarding protocols, standards, and status codes in HTTP. Make sure to look up the meaning of `418` and where it comes from.

Table 8.1 Most common HTTP status codes

Code	Meaning
200	OK—The server is returning what the client asked for.
201	Created—The Server processed the request and sent the newly created resource as response.
202	Accepted—The server will treat the client's demand later—typically used for asynchronous processes.

Table 8.1   Most common HTTP status codes (*continued*)

Code	Meaning
204	OK, nothing to return—The server correctly fulfilled the request and there's no content to return. It's used by POST, PUT, and DELETE commands.
400	Bad Request—The server can't process due to something that's perceived to be a client error (e.g., malformed request, missing mandatory fields).
401	Unauthorised—The client isn't allowed to do that action; the request lacks valid authentication credentials for the target resource.
403	Forbidden—The client needs to authenticate to access this resource; in other words, the server understood the request but refuses to fulfill it.
404	Not Found—The server didn't find a current representation for the target resource or isn't willing to disclose that one exists.
500	Internal Error—The server encountered an error and doesn't know how to deal with it.

Let's bring this final change to the code before we can wrap it up and move on to the next endpoint. The function in charge of writing this status code is the handler. So, let's open `newgame/handler.go` and include the call to write the status code, as shown in listing 8.8. This code appears in the response, and we'll use the `WriteHeader` method, which only takes a single parameter—the status code to be carried with the response body—in the file `internal/handlers/newgame/handler.go`.

Listing 8.8   `handler.go`: Setting the status code of the successful response

```
func Handle(w http.ResponseWriter, req *http.Request) {
    [...]
    _, _ = w.Write([]byte("Creating a new game"))
    w.WriteHeader(http.StatusCreated)
}
```

Now, if we restart our server and run

```
> curl -v -X POST http://localhost:8080/games
```

we should see that the response status code is now 201, shouldn't we? Well, unfortunately, it's not. It's still 200. What's happening? Well, if we have a look at the terminal in which the server is running, we should see a line similar to these lines:

```
http: superfluous response.WriteHeader call from
learngo-pockets/httpgordle/internal.newGameHandler (newgamehandler.go:16)
```

What does this mean? We only have one call to `WriteHeader`, so how can it be superfluous? It turns out that the `w.Write` call is already setting a header with a default `http.StatusOK` code. The good thing is that `WriteHeader` will ignore any subsequent calls once the header is set, which means it's basically a regular ordering bug between `w.Write` and `w.WriteHeader` to determine which code will be set. It's a rigged race because we're in charge of it, and we control which one is called first. Let's adapt the preceding code to complete this section in the same file, `internal/handlers/newgame/handler.go`.

Listing 8.9   `handler.go`: Setting the response message

```
func Handle(w http.ResponseWriter, req *http.Request) {
    if req.Method != http.MethodPost {
        w.WriteHeader(http.StatusMethodNotAllowed)
        return
    }
    w.WriteHeader(http.StatusCreated)
    _, _ = w.Write([]byte("Creating a new game"))
}
```

Great! After restarting it, we can observe that the server now behaves as expected: it returns the correct status code and tells us it's creating a game. We've checked that it only accepts POST requests. The pesky line about superfluous calls to `WriteHeader` is now gone. We can happily commit and move forward, but there's a way to make our code shorter.

OPEN SOURCE MULTIPLEXERS

In the previous section, we made an assumption. We assumed that the list of endpoints was set in stone and that we would never have to implement anything else. This meant that we were able to associate a path to each endpoint. But suppose we're now informed that we need a new endpoint, something to track the games currently being played. The best URL for this is /games, and the method to use is GET. Up to Go 1.22, there was the rub. Go used to only accept one handler per path, regardless of the verb, which meant we couldn't use the same /games for both creation of a new game and retrieval of a player's sessions. Fortunately, we can now use the standard library to implement our needs. For this reason (and a few others that we'll cover as we meet them), writing a personal implementation of the `http.Server` interface has been quite common, and many of the most-starred Go projects on GitHub are about this. Here are some popular picks of open source libraries implementing a mux supporting more than what the `net/http` package used to offer:

- `github.com/go-chi/chi`—This library allows for simple implementation of endpoints.
- `github.com/gorilla/mux`—This library is very complete and robust.
- `github.com/gin-gonic/gin`—This library is the most popular mux on GitHub.

If you wanted to use `chi`, for instance, here are the steps you have to perform. First, you need to get the dependency. For this, tell the `go` tool to add it to the `go.mod` file with the following command:

```
> go get -u "github.com/go-chi/chi/v5"
```

You might notice that there's a v5 trailing here (use whichever version is the latestfrom their repository). If you try to access this URL in a browser, it will return an error. However, this GitHub repository has been tagged with v5.0.0 at some point (and will have more tags as time passes), so using /v5 in the go get command ensures the version is compatible with v5—it could be v5.0.0 or v5.0.8; both offer the same API.

Each of these libraries offers something different. Some support thousands of parallel requests. Some offer extremely fast responses. We believe, however, that because Go's standard library offers the feature that caused most of them to be created in the first place, we might as well explain how that one works. Although these open source libraries are popular, there's no guarantee that they'll still be maintained by the time you read these lines. As a matter of fact, gorilla/mux had its maintenance paused and then resumed as we were writing this book. That interruption of support was one of the factors that got the Go team to implement a more complete version in the standard library. We can then update the router to add the method directly in our HandleFunc call.

Listing 8.10 `internal/handlers/router.go`: **Setting the verb and path**

```go
package handlers

import (
    "net/http"

    "learngo-pockets/httpgordle/internal/api"
    "learngo-pockets/httpgordle/internal/handlers/newgame"
)

// NewRouter returns a router that listens for requests
// to the following endpoints:
//    - Create a new game;
//
// The provided router is ready to serve.
func NewRouter() *http.ServeMux {
    r := http.NewServeMux()
    r.HandleFunc(http.MethodPost+" "+api.NewGameRoute,    // Registers the NewGame
        newgame.Handle)                                    // endpoint with the POST verb


    return r
}
```

Now that the path is part of the pattern of the endpoint, we can remove the check for the method in our NewGame handler, as shown in the next listing. We can even use the occasion to actually return a game, as defined by the API.

Listing 8.11 `newgame/handler.go`: **Returning a** Game **response**

```go
func Handle(w http.ResponseWriter, req *http.Request) {    // Tells the consumer that
    w.Header().Set("Content-Type", "application/json")     // we're sending JSON
```

```
w.WriteHeader(http.StatusCreated)

apiGame := api.GameResponse{}
err := json.NewEncoder(w).Encode(apiGame)
if err != nil {
    // The header has already been set. Nothing much we can do here.
    log.Printf("failed to write response: %s", err)
}
}
```

Defines an empty response

Encodes the game into JSON

If the encoding failed, it's an internal error.

Try it. Now we need to test the handler.

TESTING THE GAME CREATION

This new, shorter version of the handler should be easier to test: fewer lines of code means fewer bugs. What could be blocking is that it takes two rather complicated parameters that we need to mock or stub.

Lots of people are writing services, and this is why several libraries were developed to make implementing services easier. Lots of people are testing these libraries, so we don't need to stub them ourselves. It's always good to limit tests to the code you've written.

We can easily create a request with `http.NewRequest`. For the writer, Go has the built-in package `httptest` with a `Recorder` type and `NewRecorder` build function.

We're making use of two well-used testing packages: `require` and `assert`. Their use can be controversial because some purists will recommend calling only the standard library; nevertheless, we'll use these packages so you can get familiar with them. They are found in the module `github.com/stretchr/testify`, so let's start by adding this module to our project with `go get github.com/stretchr/testify`.

THE TESTIFY LIBRARY: ASSERT AND REQUIRE

The `testify` library is very popular for testing Go code. It offers a lot of validation tools, the most commonly used ones being its two packages `assert` and `require`. Each package offers similar functions—check whether an error is `nil` or if two values are equal—but they behave very differently:

- If a function in the `assert` package notices something wrong, a message will be displayed, and the execution of the test carries on.
- If a function in the `require` package notices something wrong, a message will be displayed, and the execution of the test is immediately terminated..

This helps drive which library we want to use: the former when we need to check several values, and the latter when we know there's no point in continuing the test if something is wrong. You should have everything in hand now to write the test to the nominal behavior.

Listing 8.12 `newgame/handler_test.go:` **Testing** `Handle`

```
func TestHandle(t *testing.T) {
    req, err := http.NewRequest(
```

```
        http.MethodPost, "/games", nil)          ◄────┐ Creates a request
    require.NoError(t, err)

    recorder := httptest.NewRecorder()            ◄────┐ Creates a response recorder

    Handle(recorder, req)                         ◄────┐ Calls the function

    assert.Equal(t, http.StatusCreated, recorder.Code)   ◄────┐
    assert.Equal(t, "application/json",                         │ Asserts that the
        recorder.Header().Get("Content-Type"))         ◄────┤ response is as
    assert.JSONEq(t, `{"id":"",...}`,                           │ expected
        recorder.Body.String())                       ◄────┘
}
```

This was our first endpoint—our service now supports the creation of (empty) games. That was a big step, but we've covered a good many important aspects of web services. Before we start playing, our next task is to ensure that we can get the status of a game given its identifier.

8.2.2 Get the game status

Here's the picture so far: we have a service that allows for the creation of Gordle games. Of course, the end goal is to have players make guesses, but the second endpoint we'll describe here is the GetStatus one. It contains a tiny bit more than the first one, as it introduces only a single new notion: reading a variable input from the user. This time, we can't just always return "a game"—we need to be able to identify which game the user wants to view.

PROVIDING PARAMETERS TO AN HTTP API

There are four main ways for a user to communicate parameters (or variables) to an HTTP web service. We'll see that they are each appropriate for specific use cases:

- Path parameters
- Query parameters
- Request bodies
- Metaparameters

Path parameters are used when we want to target a single resource. In our Gordle server, an identifier can be used to target an instance of a game. The path to target a game should be /games/{gameID}. Using the curly braces here means we're attributing a wildcard identifier to the path parameter—different users will call our endpoint with different values for {gameID}.

It's a common practice to use /items/{itemID} in REST APIs (more than the singular version, /item/{itemID}). Sometimes, we can accept more than one path parameter. Twitter, for instance, uses https://twitter.com/{user}/status/{messageID} to display a message by a user. Similarly, Wikipedia uses path parameters to access its articles: http://jp.wikipedia.org/wiki/金継ぎ, where the identifier of the article is 金継ぎ. Our GetStatus endpoint will implement this for the Gordle service.

Query parameters are used to filter the resources we want to target with our request. A filter is a list of pairs of keys and their associated values. There could be zero, one, or many results—we don't know, and we can't make any assumptions. These query parameters are passed in the URI of the request, but at the end of it, they are separated from the URL by a ? character. These parameters aren't specific to an endpoint and could be used in several places in the API. Their syntax is {path}?key1=value1&key2=value2. The most common example is Google's search engine: as there can't (reasonably) be a dedicated resource for every possible query that people pose to Google, each query is sent to their servers as a query parameter, where the key is q and the value was keyed in by the user: www.google.com/search?q=金継ぎ. We'll show how to use a query parameter at the end of this chapter to improve the NewGame endpoint by allowing the caller to specify which language they want to use.

While the path and query parameters should be used to specify which resources we want to operate on (retrieve, delete, update) or what characteristics these resources should have, we sometimes need to provide parameters inherent to the request itself. When we need to send data to the service, we use *body parameters*. This name derives from the fact that they will be transmitted to the service as part of the request's body. So far, we haven't seen request bodies, but this will be the point of the third endpoint—Guess.

Finally, some parameters are *metaparameters*—they don't affect the execution, but, for instance, they affect the format of the output or describe some information about the caller. These parameters are passed in the *headers* of the query—just as the status code is passed in the headers of the response. Headers are usually the place where we store authentication information. That's enough theory, let's start implementing our new endpoint!

DEFINE THE HTTP API FOR GETSTATUS

As we did earlier, we need to declare the path to this new endpoint and the method that we expect when it's called. We place these two values in the api package to make them visible to other users. We want to retrieve the status of the game resource without changing it, so a GET will do. But the path is a bit more complex! In a REST API, every request must contain all the information to identify which resource it's targeting. In our case, this means the request needs to contain the ID of the game. As we've seen previously, a path parameter is a common way of providing this identifier:

```
/games/{game_id}
```

How do we represent a path that isn't constant? That's where the default net/http package used to be a bit too strict, which was one of the problems that pushed developers into writing their own routing libraries, such as chi. We want to be able to access a game's status via the path /games/8476516, where 8476516 is the game's identifier. Obviously, we can't create billions of routes—one per identifier—so, instead, we'll let the standard library make use of the curly braces of our route to determine how a path parameter should be handled.

Before we start listening to the `GetStatus` route, there's one more definition we want to specify in our documentation: What is the expected response status code? This request is asking for a resource, so the possible responses should be `"200 here it is"` or `"404 not found"` if the game doesn't exist. Of course, `"500 internal server error"` is always a possibility, but we want to avoid it as much as possible.

IMPLEMENT GETSTATUS

Create a package for the new handler, ideally, `internal/handlers/getstatus`, with a file for the principal `Handle` function. If you decide that copy-pasting from the `newgame` package is a good option, don't forget to rename the package in both new files (in all three files, if you dutifully added a `doc.go`).

For now, the implementation of the `GetStatus` endpoint will be limited to only printing the game identifier that the caller passes as a path parameter: we don't have any storage yet, we just want to make sure that we know how to parse the ID. Let's start by updating our `api` package with the new endpoint's path.

Listing 8.13 `api/http.go`: **Adding a new endpoint route**

```
const (
    // GameID is the name of the field that stores the game's identifier
    GameID = "id"

    // NewGameRoute is the path to create a new game.
    NewGameRoute = "/games"
    // GetStatusRoute is the path to get the status
    // of a game identified by its id.
    GetStatusRoute = "/games/{" + GameID + "}"
}
```

The first thing to notice in this file is that we defined a constant for the game ID. We don't just want to define the route to the `GetStatus` endpoint—we also want to be able to retrieve that path parameter later on, and this will require using that `GameID` constant.

Next, add the path to the router. There's no specific priority when adding handles to a mux. Grouping things based on resources and related behavior is usually what makes the most sense:

```
. . .
    r.HandleFunc(http.MethodPost+" "+api.NewGameRoute,
        newgame.Handle)                                      ◄──┘ Previous endpoint
    r.HandleFunc(http.MethodGet+" "+api.GetStatusRoute,
        getstatus.Handle)                          ◄───┐ Adds the new endpoint
. . .
```

Now we need to write this `getstatus.Handle` function. It must have the same signature as in the first endpoint because it's a `HandlerFunc`. To retrieve the path parameter,

we can use `request.PathValue(api.GameID)`. If anything goes wrong, we'll call `http`
`.Error`, which writes a message and a status code to the response writer. Remember to
always `return` after a call to `http.Error` to prevent any writing to the response. Let's
write in the file `internal/handlers/getstatus/handle.go`.

> **Listing 8.14   `handle.go`: Status endpoint handler**

```
func Handle(
    w http.ResponseWriter, request *http.Request) {     ◄─── Follows the required signature
    id := request.PathValue(api.GameID)                  ◄─── Parses the parameter
    if id == "" {                                        ◄─── Checks that the ID isn't empty
        http.Error(writer, "missing the id of the game",
            http.StatusBadRequest)
        return
    }
    log.Printf("retrieve status of game with id: %v", id)

    apiGame := api.GameResponse{
        ID: id,
    }
    // ... encode into JSON
}
```

For the sake of simplicity, we decided to use the standard `log` package, which isn't
thread safe. So keep in mind that it can lead to unordered logs and complicate later
testing.

The validation of the ID could be more thorough: we could check that it's only digits
or that it follows whatever constraints we've put in for security. We'll forget this for the
sake of keeping our project pocket-sized, but keep it in mind if you push something to
production.

Run the server, and call the endpoint. Does it return the ID you passed in the URL?
Congratulations—you can commit. But wait, what about the test? Good thing you
asked.

TESTING GETSTATUS

The test here isn't much different from the `newGame` version. We only need to add
the ID to the list of URL parameters. To create a request that has the path parameter,
we first need to create a request targeting our endpoint—using the correct verb and
route—and then we can set the path value.

> **Listing 8.15   `getstatus/handler_test.go`: Testing handle**

```
func TestHandle(t *testing.T) {
    req, err := http.NewRequest(http.MethodGet,
        "/games/", nil)                               ◄─── Using "/games/123456" wouldn't work here.
    require.NoError(t, err)

    // add path parameter
```

```
req.SetPathValue(api.GameID, "123456")


recorder := httptest.NewRecorder()                 ◀─── Creates the response
                                                         receiver
Handle(recorder, req)

assert.Equal(t, http.StatusOK, recorder.Code)
assert.JSONEq(t, `{"id":"123456","attempts_left":0,"guesses":[],
    "word_length":0,"status":""}`, recorder.Body.String())
}
```

The rest, you can guess. We can now create games and retrieve them. This allows us to make sure everything is ready for our third and last endpoint—guessing!

8.2.3 Guess

Finally, to play, the player must be able to send a query with their word and get a feedback message. What will the API of the third endpoint be?

REQUEST DEFINITION

Adding a new endpoint means choosing a new pair of path and method. Because we're changing an already existing resource, PUT is in order. The path is fairly straightforward—/games/{game_id}, similar to the getStatus endpoint, as that's the resource we'll be interacting with.

But then, the endpoint needs to receive parameters. It will read the guess from the request body, encoded in JSON because we're following HTTP and REST standards. In some cases, updating a resource requires sending its full description. In that case, we would have the same JSON structure for the response of the POST and GET and the request of the PUT. Here, changing the status of a game requires only sending a word, as long as we're providing the ID, so we'll go for the simplest JSON object:

```
{"guess":"hello"}
```

This translates into a Request that we can define in the api package for others to use.

Listing 8.16 api/guess.go: Request definition

```
// GuessRequest is the structure of the message used when submitting a guess.
type GuessRequest struct {
    Guess string `json:"guess"`     ◀─── Uses JSON tags for encoding
}
```

Add the path to the endpoint to this file. The path is the same as for GetStatus, but nothing guarantees that it will always be, so we need another constant. Using the same path constant means forcing them to always be identical, by design. We don't want that because each endpoint deserves to have its path as a constant:

```
GuessRoute = "/games/{" + GameID + "}"
```

What we do want to force by design is the consistency of the `GameResponse` structure. Both `GetStatus` and `Guess` endpoints return a full game, and we don't want the definitions to diverge. For this, we can simply use the same structure as the response in both endpoints.

DECODING A REQUEST BODY

We have an API, so it's time to write a new handler in a new package and plug it into the router. We don't need to explain anything new here, so go ahead and prepare the handle function. You can even run it with a simple `log.Printf` to make sure it works as expected.

This new handler will first parse the ID of the game, exactly like we did in the previous endpoint, which is no surprise. Second, it will parse the body of the request. You already know from previous chapters how to decode JSON messages into a Go structure. In a flash of genius, somebody thought that the `Body` field of an `http.Request` should implement the `io.Reader` interface—let's make use of that.

> **Listing 8.17 `guess/handler.go`: How to read a request body**

```go
// Read the request, containing the guess, from the body of the input.
r := api.GuessRequest{}
err := json.NewDecoder(request.Body).Decode(&r)    ◀──── Instantiates the
if err != nil {                                     ◀──── request struct
    http.Error(writer, err.Error(),
        http.StatusBadRequest)                      ◀──── Decodes the body
    return                          If the JSON doesn't
}                                   parse, it's a bad request.
```

Print out your findings into the logs, and check what happens when you shoot a curl at the service (when using curl, we don't specify path parameters, we simply write them):

```
> curl -v -X PUT "http://localhost:8080/games/123456" -d '{"guess":"hello"}'
```

Note the `-d` flag for passing a body. You can also use `-d@file.json` if your request body is saved in a file. Does everything show properly on the logs? Did you write a test?

TESTING WITH A REQUEST BODY

If we run the same test on this handle function as we have in `GetStatus`, it will panic: the body of our request is `nil`, so we're trying to decode from a `nil` reader, and this doesn't end well. The only change that needs to be made is quite short: the `http.NewRequest` function that we've used to create requests so far takes, as its third parameter, an `io.Reader`, which is easy to create from a string in Go (remember to use backticks ` to wrap a string that contains double quotation marks " without having to escape them):

```
body := strings.NewReader(`{"guess":"pocket"}`)
req, err := http.NewRequest(http.MethodPut, "/games/", body))
req.SetPathValue(api.GameID, "123456")
```

We now have the full structure of our service: three endpoints that return something. This is a good time to deploy the service to a testing environment and have other people play with it. It's the situation where you send a link to your shiny new service to the rest of the team with a long message asking them to try it, warning them that it does nothing yet, and wait for somebody to reply saying "Hey, nice work, but I found a bug: How come it always returns an empty game?" Well, let's fix that.

8.3 *Domain objects*

Each player's game must be stored somewhere, commonly referred to as a *repository* (repo, for short). Out of the very many options, the cheapest and fastest is to store it in memory. This has a lot of downsides: if you decide to scale up a little and deploy more than one instance, the game will only be stored in one, meaning that if your Guess query hits an instance on which your game isn't registered, you get a 404. In addition, if the instance goes down for any reason, your game is lost.

We want this project to fit in a pocket, so we'll go for this option for now. In a bigger project, we'd use a proper database.

SEPARATION OF CONCERNS

One of the main ways to tell whether a project's code is *clean* is the *separation of concerns*. In theory, each package and each structure should have a defined role that can be explained in one sentence, and this sentence is the first line of its documentation. Most of the time, one sentence is enough to cover everything. In practice, this rule can introduce complicated communication between highly coupled ideas. As mentioned before, there's always a tradeoff to find between separating and keeping things together.

If the responsibilities of a package don't fit into a handful of words, it's generally a red flag: future maintainers won't know where to find what piece of logic and will end up throwing everything away and rewriting it—and not necessarily in a better way. Sometimes, we rewrite code only to understand what is going on.

Whether you choose hexagonal architecture, lasagna-style MVC, or any other chimera that fits your needs, most of the time, you want to isolate the data storage management from the API details. You'll see some cases where data storage and API design need to co-evolve to be performant, but they aren't in the majority.

Software theorists often give an example of the perfect data-storing package: "Look, you're using MariaDB, and you just need to change this package import and boom, you're using DynamoDB." That's nice, but it never happens: no one simply changes their storage system. What they do a lot, however, is maintain it, and knowing that all the database-related things are here and all the non-database-related things are not here will help everyone in the long run.

8.3.1   *Domain types*

You can create a new package for the data repository. Do you want other modules—other developers—to use it? No. That means `internal/repository` will do. This package is responsible for storing and retrieving games. Here, that was a one-sentence documentation. Figure 8.1 shows the structure of our code so far.

We have an `api` package that other modules can import, and an internal `handlers` package directly called by our `main`. To approach this development with a hexagonal architecture (aka ports and adapters) mindset, we should aim for a design similar to what is shown in figure 8.2, where the data access repository, the Gordle library, and the handlers all work independently, using the domain as a common language.

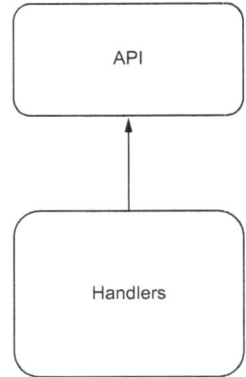

Figure 8.1   **Structure of the service**

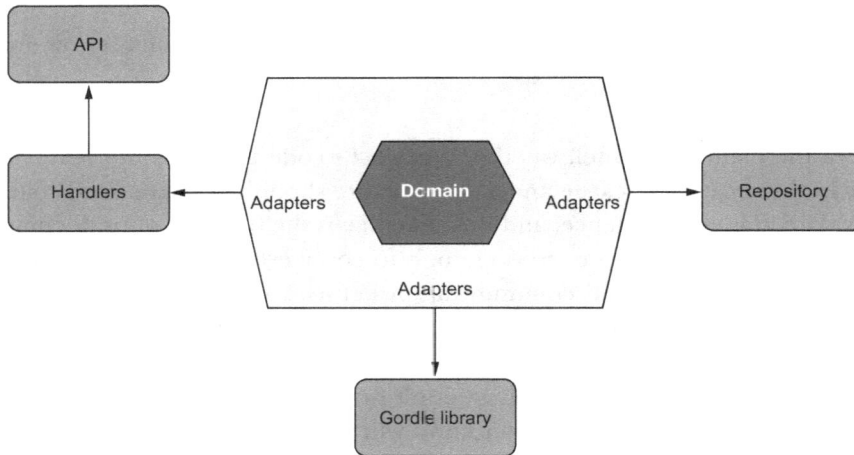

Figure 8.2   **Target structure of the service**

This is a bit too complex for the size of the service, so we'll keep the domain logic inside the `handlers` package. However, keep in mind that the core logic and the API details should be two distinct things, with an easy-to-draw boundary. Each different layer of our design should serve a specific purpose.

What we call the *domain* here is the core of the service, the business logic of our program. All adapters should be able to rely on the domain, and it should rely on none of them. This way, we prevent circular dependencies in the code and circular knots in our brains.

The package can be simply called domain, core, or with a more specific but limiting name. In our case, we find that it deals with a player's session.

In an internal/session package, create a Game struct. This should contain everything that the service needs to interact with Gordle games. We know we want to respond to the API's needs with a Game structure.

Listing 8.18 internal/session/game.go: Defining the Game structure

```
// Game contains the information about a game.
type Game struct {
    ID           GameID
    AttemptsLeft byte
    Guesses      []Guess
    Status       Status
}
```

As shown in this listing, we need new types, so let's define the GameID and Status in the same file as just used.

Listing 8.19 game.go: Defining the identifier and status types

```
// A GameID represents the ID of a game.
type GameID string                          ◄─── Game ID is a simple string.

// Status is the current status of the game and
// tells what operations can be made on it.
type Status string #B

const (
    StatusPlaying = "Playing"     ◄─── Enum-like type and its
    StatusWon     = "Won"              list of constants
    StatusLost    = "Lost"
)
```

We also want to expose the guesses, as we need to carry them around, store them, and return them. The following listing does the trick.

Listing 8.20 game.go: Defining the type Guess

```
// A Guess is a pair of a word (submitted by the player) and
// its feedback (provided by Gordle).
type Guess struct {
    Word     string
    Feedback string
}
```

That's a good start. It's not yet enough to play, but that will happen in the next section.

One thing we can already add to the domain is a business error: if the player sends a new guess after the game is over, we should be explicit about the problem. You can either define a custom error type or do it the short way:

```
// ErrGameOver is returned when a play is made but the game is over.
var ErrGameOver = errors.New("game over")
```

One of the authors really doesn't like exposing global variables, but you can decide for yourself.

8.3.2   *API adapters*

Now that we've defined the domain entity, we can start plugging it in each part of our hexagonal architecture. Let's start with the API side.

NEWGAME

Take, for example, the first endpoint: NewGame. This is how the handler currently creates the API version of the game:

```
func Handle(w http.ResponseWriter, req *http.Request) {
    w.Header().Set("Content-Type", "application/json")       Encodes the
    w.WriteHeader(http.StatusCreated)                        response headers

    apiGame := api.GameResponse{}                 Creates the game
    err := json.NewEncoder(w).Encode(apiGame)
    if err != nil //...                           Encodes the response body
}
```

The responsibility of the Handle function is to deal with the API details. If the client needs a different flag or a different format, this is where it should happen.

We decided to keep the business logic in the same package, but that doesn't mean we should keep it in the same function. Instead, we want a function that creates and saves the game somewhere, and another to reshape it into what the clients want. Following is the code for this.

Listing 8.21   `newgame/handler.go`: Using `session.Game`

```
func Handle(w http.ResponseWriter, req *http.Request) {
    game, err := createGame()                              Creates the game
    if err != nil {
        log.Printf("unable to create a new game: %s",
            err)
        http.Error(w, "failed to create a new game",       Logs any error for
            http.StatusInternalServerError)                future debugging
        return
    }                                           Don't forget to stop there.

    w.Header().Set("Content-Type", "application/json")
    w.WriteHeader(http.StatusCreated)                  Encodes for HTTP headers
```

```
    apiGame := response(game)
    // ...
}
```
Transforms the game into the API format

```
func createGame() (session.Game, error) {
    return session.Game{}, nil
}

func response(game session.Game) api.GameResponse {
    return api.GameResponse{}
}
```

This way, each function has a well-defined job, and we can test units rather than big blobs. It also becomes easier to parallelize the work inside a team, merge changes made by multiple people, and, most importantly, understand what we're reading.

GetStatus

Let's move on to the GetStatus endpoint. The response format is identical, which means the response function can be reused. Should it live in the newgame package and be exposed to the getstatus package? That would make very little sense to the next person looking for it to make changes.

The more straightforward solution here is to have the endpoint in an internal/api package with this function, as shown in listing 8.22. We avoid import cycles, and others coming after us will understand what's inside.

Now the name response doesn't make sense anymore. It converts a session.Game into a GameResponse. We can already write most of its logic too, and even start testing it.

> Listing 8.22 convert.go: Adapter between the API and domain

```
// ToGameResponse converts a session.Game into an GameResponse.
func ToGameResponse(g session.Game) GameResponse {
    apiGame := api.GameResponse{
        ID:           string(g.ID),
        AttemptsLeft: g.AttemptsLeft,
        Guesses:      make([]Guess, len(g.Guesses)),     // Inits the slice
        Status:       string(g.Status),
        // TODO WordLength
    }

    for index := 0; index < len(g.Guesses); index++ {
        apiGame.Guesses[index].Word =
            g.Guesses[index].Word                        // Accesses the slice elements directly
        apiGame.Guesses[index].Feedback = g.Guesses[index].Feedback
    }

    if g.AttemptsLeft == 0 {                             // Shows a solution if the game is over
        apiGame.Solution = ""// TODO solution
    }
                                                         // This is for later; we don't have the data yet.
    return apiGame
}
```

Testing this presents no trick: we need to check that an input game would come out as expected in a new shape. You can use go test -cover or your IDE's UI. The -cover option measures the percentage of code that your tests execute, helping you identify any untested branches or paths in your code. This ensures you're not missing edge cases and that your tests comprehensively cover the functionality of your program.

Update the GetStatus handler and run its tests. Are you still happy? If in the previous version, your guess slice was nil and it's now initialized, it should fail. You should be able to fix it by replacing the JSON value null with an empty array [].

GUESS

Finally, we've reached the last endpoint. Let's take a look at what the handler does here:

```go
func Handle(w http.ResponseWriter, req *http.Request) {
    // ... decode request

    apiGame := api.GameResponse{
        ID: id,
    }

    // ... encode response
}
```

We can already replace this naive initialization of an api.Game with two calls: a new local (unexposed) function with the business logic and a conversion into the API structure. The necessary code is shown in the following listing.

Listing 8.23   guess/handler.go: Using session.Game

```go
// Handler returns the handler for the game creation endpoint.
func Handle(w http.ResponseWriter, req *http.Request) {
    id := req.PathValue(api.GameID)
    // ...
    r := api.GuessRequest{}
    // ...

    game, err := guess(id, r)        ◄──────┘  Plays the game
    if err != nil {...}

    apiGame := api.ToGameResponse(game)       ◄──────┘ Adapts for API exposition

    w.Header().Set("Content-Type", "application/json")
    // ...
}

func guess(id string, r api.GuessRequest) (session.Game, error) {
    return session.Game{
```

```
        ID: session.GameID(id),
    }
}
```

The order of things is always the same: decode the request, validate any input that requires validation, call the business logic, convert the returned domain type into API-readable structures, and encode the response.

If your tests pass, you can commit. Try running the service and shooting a few curls at it to see how the service behaves. If you deploy again to the testing environment, that unhappy teammate who didn't read your warning will still be unhappy because the games are still as empty as before.

8.4 Repository

At this point, we must think about our priorities. We still have two main tasks at hand: saving the game and allowing clients to play. Which one should we tackle first?

To make this decision, consider which one will show the most progress. If we start with the storage, the first two endpoints will be finished, and we'll see how they integrate together in an end-to-end test (or at least end-to-midway, because we won't be able to play). If we start with playing, we'll be playing on a new empty game at every guess, so testing will be difficult and flaky. Looks like storage it is, then.

If we were using some proven technology for data storage, for example, a SQL database, we would need some extra fields related to storage that the domain doesn't need, such as `created at`, `deleted at`, `versioning`, and so on. In that case, we would create a new `Game` structure, and adapters between the domain and the repository, just like we did for the API. That way, the schema of our database would be able to evolve independently from the domain or API.

Because we're aiming for the fastest storage option, we don't have any technology-related constraints. It means we can keep the domain structures.

8.4.1 In-memory database

There are loads of database options out there, and all of them are ideal for a limited set of situations. As we explained before, in-memory storage is ideal for no situation, but it's fast to write.

In our scenario, we'll keep a variable to store the games. All the operations we do on games rely on their ID, so a key-value storage is perfect. In Go, this takes the form of a `map`.

Let's create a package for the `map`. Again, do you want external modules to use your repository? Please say no. It would invalidate the whole point of the service and its API if clients went directly to the database. Any additional security or logic that you would add (sending events, leaderboards, etc.) would be immediately buggy.

8.4.2 Simplest repository

We've covered in previous chapters how to create an object that will work as a dependency. If we were using an external database, we would initialize a connection when our server starts and keep it as a dependency of the whole service. Here, we'll initialize the map instead and keep it in the same way.

Let's create the repository structure. It will hold methods such as Find and Update.

Listing 8.24   repository/memory.go: Declaring the structure

```
// GameRepository holds all the current games.
type GameRepository struct {
    storage map[session.GameID]session.Game      ◄─────┘ Uses domain types
}
```

Of course, this requires initialization, so we need a New() function. The code is shown in the following listing.

Listing 8.25   memory.go: New function for the repository

```
// New creates an empty game repository.
func New() *GameRepository {
    return &GameRepository{
        storage: make(map[session.GameID]session.Game),    ◄─────┘ Inits the map
    }
}
```

We could have a method Upsert for both creating and updating. But in our case, we know that some specific use cases create new games, and others are only working on existing ones, so we prefer to separate them. This allows us to validate that we're not trying to create the same entity twice or inserting a game where we've already been playing a few guesses. Use the following code to add a game to the storage.

Listing 8.26   memory.go: Adding a game to the storage

```
// Add inserts for the first time a game in memory.
func (gr *GameRepository) Add(game session.Game) error {
    _, ok := gr.storage[game.ID]
    if ok {
        return fmt.Errorf("gameID %s already exists",
            game.ID)
    }                                    ◄──┐ Can't add the
                                            │ same game twice
    gr.storage[game.ID] = game

    return nil
}
```

We'll come back to this error. If we want to check for it specifically in the calling code, it's currently difficult.

> **Side quest**
>
> You can write the `Find` and `Update` methods. The former needs to retrieve from the `map` and return some kind of error if nothing is there with the given ID. The latter should also prevent insertion and only accept overwriting an already existing value.
>
> You can also write unit tests on the four functions. Here, we would use `New` in the other three tests and consider the job done; there's no particular trick to it.

The package works, and it's tested. How do we use it, though?

8.4.3 Service-level dependency

We want the repository to be initialized on startup and passed to the service router as a dependency. Let's look back at what our `main` does:

```go
func main() {
    err := http.ListenAndServe(":8080", handlers.NewRouter())
    if err != nil {
        panic(err)
    }
}
```

We can easily add the initialization and pass the new variable to the router.

Listing 8.27 `main.go`: **Using the repository**

```go
func main() {
    db := repository.New()              ◄────┘ Inits the data storage

    err := http.ListenAndServe(
        ":8080", handlers.NewRouter(db))   ◄──── Passes the repository
    if err != nil {                              to the router
        panic(err)
    }
}
```

How does the router pass this to the handlers? Our `NewRouter` function doesn't call the handlers; it only gives the router a reference to them, so we can't simply add a parameter. What we can do instead is turn our `Handle` functions into anonymous functions that are created on startup.

In the following listing, we anonymize the `Handle` functions and wrap them instead in a `Handler` function that takes a repository as a parameter and returns the previous `http.HandleFunc`.

Listing 8.28 `newgame/handler.go`: **Using the repository**

```go
// Handler returns the handler for the game creation endpoint.
func Handler(db *repository.GameRepository) http.HandlerFunc {
    return func(
        w http.ResponseWriter, _ *http.Request) {    ◀──── Returns a HandlerFunc
        game, err := createGame(db)

        // ...
    }
}
```

The contents are the same so far. We can now update the router.

Listing 8.29 `router.go`: **Using the repository**

```go
// The provided router is ready to serve.
func NewRouter(db *repository.GameRepository) *http.ServeMux {
    r := http.NewServeMux()

    // Register each endpoint.
    r.HandleFunc(http.MethodPost+' "+api.NewGameRoute,        Passes the dependency
        newgame.Handler(db))    ◀────                         as a parameter
    r.HandleFunc(http.MethodGet+" "+api.GetStatusRoute,
        getstatus.Handler(db))
    r.HandleFunc(http.MethodPut+" "+api.GuessRoute, guess.Handler(db))

    return r
}
```

How do we test this? We can only pass a concrete repository to our `Handler` function. As soon as we use a real external database, we need to spin an instance and connect to it to run unit tests. That is absolutely not sustainable. Let's abstract it with an interface.

The `NewGame` endpoint only needs to add a game to the repository, nothing else. We can actually prevent it from doing anything else by defining a minimal interface.

Listing 8.30 `newgame/handler.go`: **Minimal interface**

```go
type gameAdder interface {                       gameAdder can
    Add(game session.Game) error    ◀────        only add a game.
}

// Handler returns the handler for the game creation endpoint.
func Handler(db gameAdder) http.HandlerFunc {
    return func(w http.ResponseWriter, _ *http.Request) {    Uses the mockable
        // ...                                               interface
    }
}
```

The router's `db` variable automatically implements this little interface, and now it becomes easy to create a stub with one single method for the unit test. Adapting the test requires only two changes.

Listing 8.31 `newgame/handler_test.go`: **Stubbing the repository**

```
func TestHandle(t *testing.T) {
    handleFunc := Handler(gameAdderStub{})    ◄──── Creates an anonymous
                                                    function
    req, err := ...
    // ...

    handleFunc(recorder, req)    ◄──── Calls it

    assert...
}

type gameAdderStub struct {    ◄──── Stubs the repository
    err error
}

func (g gameAdderStub) Add(_ session.Game) error {
    return g.err
}
```

You can adapt this logic to the other two endpoints. `GetStatus` only needs a `finder`, and `Guess` needs to call two methods.

Now before we rejoice, there is one thing: remember how our server accepts requests in different goroutines and treats them concurrently? Writing into a `map` isn't thread safe. This means that if two different routines write in the same `map`, we can't guarantee which one will win, if any. To fix this problem, we can use a concept we saw in the previous chapter: a mutex. The goal is to avoid concurrently accessing the `map` and to ensure the sanity of our server.

8.4.4 *Add a mutex to the repository*

The motivation is the same as in the previous chapter: we want to protect our repository—a `map`, here—from concurrent accesses. Let's keep it simple and use a `sync.Mutex` in the `Add()`, `Find()`, and `Update()` methods in `internal/repository/memory.go`.

> **NOTE** A mutex should be placed as closely as possible to a thread-unsafe variable. We theoretically could have a mutex on the server, preventing two requests from being handled at a time—but that would completely defeat the purpose of having a microservice. Imagine if your favorite website was only accessible to a single person at a time! On the other hand, if the storage solution was already thread safe—a database that, for instance, only accepted a single query at a time—we wouldn't need a mutex at all.

First, we need to add the mutex next to the resource we want to protect, the storage `map`, inside the `GameRepository` structure. The following listing provides the code.

Listing 8.32   `memory.go`: Adding `mutex` to `GameRepository`

```
// GameRepository holds all the current games.
type GameRepository struct {
    mutex      sync.Mutex                          ◀── Adds mutex to the storage
    storage    map[session.GameID]session.Game
}
```

Then, we're able to access the mutex from the receiver on each method. Here's the sample of code for the `Add` method.

Listing 8.33   `memory.go`: Calling the `Lock` and `Unlock` mutex on `Add()`

```
// Add inserts a game in memory the first time it is received.
func (gr *GameRepository) Add(game session.Game) error {
    log.Print("Adding a game...")

    // Lock the reading and the writing of the game.          Locks the mutex before
    gr.mutex.Lock()                                           executing any read or
    defer gr.mutex.Unlock()                            ◀──    write operation

    _, ok := gr.storage[game.ID]          Executes the unlocking at the end of
    if ok {                               the method in a defer statement
        return fmt.Errorf("%w (%s)", ErrConflictingID, game.ID)
    }

    gr.storage[game.ID] = game

    return nil
}
```

You can now update the other methods by yourself and run the tests. If the tests pass, your code is safely committed—let's play!

8.5 *Adapting the Gordle library*

From chapter 5, or from our repository, copy the `gordle` library. It's far more complex than what we need as it wraps the whole session. We need to refactor and simplify the library for our needs here. We know that we need the following use cases:

- Create and return a new Gordle game.
- Accept a guess and return the feedback.

We could choose to have the Gordle library be in charge of the number of attempts a player has, but we decided to have this logic in the session. Let's split the responsibilities, as shown in table 8.2.

Table 8.2 Package requirements

Package session's game	Package Gordle's game
■ Stores the number of attempts left	■ Creates a game using a corpus for its solution
■ Stores the list of attempts and feedbacks	■ Accepts a guess and computes the feedback
■ Plays a guess by calling Gordle	■ Allows feedback to tell whether a game is over

Now we need to separate the concerns of the `session` and `gordle` packages. The `gordle` library doesn't need an ID, but the `session` does. The library doesn't need the previous guesses, but it must tell the status of the game.

8.5.1 API of the library

Considering our previous decisions about the distribution of responsibilities, we want to be able to create a game and play. This is what we need to expose:

```
var g gordle.Game = gordle.NewGame(corpus)
var feedback gordle.Feedback = g.Play(guess)

var solution string = g.ShowAnswer()
var won bool = feedback.GameWon()
```

That should cover it. Add a `fmt.Stringer` on the feedback, and we're good. However, we do have a couple more design questions to answer:

- Who is responsible for telling us how many attempts are allowed and how many are left?
- Who is responsible for reading the corpus file and picking a random word from it?

This is open to discussion with a few options to choose from. As a first option, we could decide that the library takes the solution as a string parameter because it doesn't need anything else. As a second option, we could say that any use of the library requires this behavior, so we might as well expose it. As a third option, we could create a corpus-reading package, independent and testable.

In our case, because we copied most of the logic from a previous chapter, we chose the second option, which keeps the old code together until we prove that it should be refactored further. Therefore, we expose a `ReadCorpus` function that returns a list of strings, and this is what the `NewGame` function takes to randomly select a word. Note that `New` taking a single solution simplifies the tests because we don't have to go through randomization.

We didn't want to weigh this book down with lots of copy-pasted code from a previous chapter, so you can find the resulting simplified package in our repository or play around to see what you need. Have fun going through the exercise of reducing code yourself. For the sake of continuity and to make sure that we're working with the same code base, the final API of our package is shown in the following listing.

Listing 8.34 API of the package

```
> go doc internal/gordle

package gordle // import "learngo-pockets/httpgordle/internal/gordle"

const ErrInaccessibleCorpus =
    corpusError("corpus can't be opened")                          ◄── Reads the corpus
const ErrInvalidGuess = gameError("invalid guess length")          ◄─┐
func ReadCorpus(path string) ([]string, error)                     ◄─┤ The game
type Feedback []hint                                                  │ itself
type Game struct{ ... }                                               │
    func New(corpus []string) (*Game, error)                       ◄─┘
```

Reading the documentation shows that the third option, having a corpus reader somewhere else, would have made this API easier to understand. Feel free to refactor this way. If you're happy with the test coverage of the library, it's time to commit and use it.

8.5.2 *Usage in the endpoints*

At this point, we have everything we need to write the logic of the endpoints. We've already created a function to isolate that logic in each of the three endpoints, so we just need to fill this function up in each location.

The first thing to do is to keep a `gordle.Game` in our domain. If we add a field of this type to `session.Game`, we can use the field to play, as shown in the following listing. With this new type ready (and tests passing), we can complete the endpoints.

Listing 8.35 `session/game.go`: Using `gordle.Game` in the session

```
// Game contains the information about a game.
type Game struct {
    ID             GameID
    Gordle         gordle.Game      ◄──┐ Adds a new field
    AttemptsLeft   byte                │ for the game
    Guesses        []Guess
    Status         Status
}
```

NEWGAME

Here, we need to create a game, generate and save a random ID for the game, and then return the ID. Why random? Incremental IDs are a terrible security flaw, as anyone can create a game and play around to mess up with other people's games (note that authentication is discussed later in section 8.6.2).

We could use an integer. As we mentioned before, generating a random integer can be done quite fast with the `math/rand` package, with a rather poor randomization, or with better distribution but higher costs with the `crypto/rand` package.

There are other alternatives, such as universal unique identifier (UUID), for which Google's library is most generally used in Go, or universally unique lexicographically sortable identifier (ULID). We picked this last one, and we'll be using the generative library found at https://github.com/oklog/ulid. If you're using a relative path to the corpus, it needs to be defined relative to the compiled binary, not the file where it's defined, not necessarily main.go, and not the path of execution.

USING THE EMBED PACKAGE

Go's standard library comes with the very peculiar embed package. This package implements one very useful feature: it allows regular files' contents to be included in the source code of our program. To achieve this, we use a specific instruction sent to the compiler at compilation time called *directives*, or *pragmas*. These come in the form of a comment, starting something like //go:{something}. Directives are quite common to indicate specific parts of the code to code analysis tools such as linters. The syntax we need is the following:

```
//go:embed corpus/english.txt
var englishCorpus string
```

This englishCorpus variable needs to be defined outside of any function (placing it inside a function would be considered a regular comment by the compiler—and ignored). To use this, first, we need to import the embed package. However, as we're not going to use any constant, variable, type, or function from that package, your IDE might get rid of this line completely (wouldn't be unfair actually—after all, why import a package if we don't use it?).

Luckily, we can use a trick to force the import of a package by aliasing it to _ (underscore). This way, the package won't be dropped and will be available where we import it. Importing a package an _ is usually done when we need to call the init functions of some libraries. Here, it ensures that the embed package will properly load the contents of the file located at the path corpus/english.txt—this location is relative to the source .go file. We now have loaded the contents of the file into a variable.

Listing 8.36 newgame/handler.go: Endpoint logic

```
func createGame(db gameAdder) (session.Game, error) {
    corpus, err := gordle.ReadCorpus(          This path should come
        "corpus/english.txt")            ◄──┘  from the configuration.
    if err != nil {
        return session.Game{}, fmt.Errorf("unable to read corpus: %w", err)
    }

    game, err := gordle.New(corpus)
    if err != nil {
        return session.Game{},
            fmt.Errorf("failed to create a new gordle game")
    }
```

```
g := session.Game{
    ID:            session.GameID(
        ulid.Make().String()),         ◀———| Generates the ID
    Gordle:        *game,
    AttemptsLeft:  maxAttempts,         ◀———| Uses a constant
    Guesses:       []session.Guess{},
    Status:        session.StatusPlaying,
}
                                    |  Saves the game
err = db.Add(g)                   ◀——|  for future plays
if err != nil {
    return session.Game{}, fmt.Errorf("failed to save the new game")
}

    return g, nil
}
```

We chose to keep a constant for the maximum number of attempts, but if your corpus has words with different lengths, you can be more creative and derive this max number from the length of the word, the difficulty settings, the ELO of the player, or any other variable.

Here, we're reading the corpus every time the new game endpoint is called, which looks like a waste of resources. It would be ideal to load it on startup, deal with any error at this point (e.g., `File Not Found`), and fail to start if we have nothing. If the service can't access any list of words, it might as well not start at all.

Now that we have access to the solution, we can also update the API adapter to add the `WordLength`, and other fields that we may have left out so far. Additionally, this hardcoded path to the corpus will become a pain as soon as we start testing.

TEST THE NEWGAME HANDLER WITH REGULAR EXPRESSIONS

How do we test our handler? There's only one pitfall: randomization. We can't expect the output of this `createGame` function to be identical when it's called multiple times.

In this situation, it's important to determine what we want to test. We could use the trick of passing an ID generator interface as a parameter, providing a generator returning a fixed value in tests, and using a generator returning a ULID in real life. We can also agree that all we need to assert is that the ID is composed of that many alphanumeric characters; if so, we're happy. Whether it's our job to check if consecutive calls return different IDs is also arguable. We can trust that the library does it, but can we trust that we'll always call the library?

To validate that the ID is composed of that many alphanumeric characters, the trick is to use regular expressions. Look into the `regexp` package, and you'll find a lot of options.

When testing the handler itself, we can replace the ID with a known string, as shown in listing 8.37. For this, we isolate the generated ID in the JSON output and replace it using `strings.Replace`, which replaces a given number of instances of the old string with the new one (use `-1` as the last parameter to replace all occurrences).

Listing 8.37 `newgame/handler_test.go`: **Replacing the ID in JSON output**

```
// idFinderRegexp is a regular expression that will ensure the body
// contains an id field with a value that contains
// only letters (uppercase and/or lowercase) and/or digits.
idFinderRegexp := regexp.MustCompile(
    `.+"id":"([a-zA-Z0-9]+)".+`)                          ◄── Regexp to locate the ID

id := idFinderRegexp.FindStringSubmatch(body)             ◄── Finds match in the JSON body
if len(id) != 2 {                                          ◄── Checks the number
    t.Fatal("cannot find one id in the json output")          of occurrences
}
body = strings.Replace(body, id[1], "123456", 1)          ◄── Replaces the ID with
                                                                a known string
assert.JSONEq(t, testCase.wantBody, body)                 ◄── Compares the content
                                                                of a JSON easily
```

We need to look for `"id":"<somenumbersandletters>"` in the output body, so the regular expression we'll match against is `` `.+"id":"([a-zA-Z0-9]+)".+` ``. Let's break down this regular expression:

- `.+`—This indicates a list of one or more (+) of any (.) characters.
- `"id":"`—This is the very string composed of a double quotation mark, the letter i, the letter d, a double quotation mark, a colon, and a double quotation mark.
- `([a-zA-Z0-9]+)`—This is a captured block—that's what the parentheses represent. These parentheses aren't matched by the regular expression, which only matches one or more (+) of any letter or number (characters in the range from a to z, A to Z, or 0 to 9). The parentheses, however, capture what they matched, which will be returned by `FindStringSubmatch`.
- `".+`—This string starts with a double quotation mark, followed by one or more (+) of any (.) characters.

This string is enclosed in backticks `` ` ``, which is how we avoid having to escape double quotation marks in a Go string. The expected body contains the known string, so we can now use `assert.JSONEq` or some equivalent. If the ID doesn't match the expected format (alphanumerical characters), `FindStringSubmatch` won't find it and returns only one item: the full string. The test will fail.

Now, when we're testing the `create` function itself, we don't get an encoded body. We can use `FindStringIndex` instead, which finds the location of the leftmost match of the regular expression in a string. If the index is there, we're good. This is wrapped by `testify`'s `Regexp` function.

Listing 8.38 `newgame/handler_test.go`: **Validating ID with a regexp**

```
func Test_createGame(t *testing.T) {
    corpusPath = "testdata/corpus.txt"
```

```
g, err := createGame(gameCreatorStub{nil})
require.NoError(t, err)

assert.Regexp(t, "[A-Z0-9]+", g.ID)
assert.Equal(t, uint8(5), g.AttemptsLeft)
assert.Equal(t, 0, len(g.Guesses))
}
```

Declares a stub that
returns no error

Matches the ID
against a regexp

Validates other
fields ad lib

Regular expressions are extremely powerful but also very hard to understand when you don't know what you're looking at. Whenever you write one, don't expect the next maintainer (including yourself) to find it easy to parse: add a comment systematically to tell them what it's looking for. Check that your tests are passing and properly covering your code, and you can move on to the second endpoint.

GETSTATUS

Here, we only need to call the database and return the game. That's it. And, of course, deal with any errors. Ah. How do we deal with the errors? How do we know if the game wasn't found or if there was another unexpected error (e.g., connection error, in the situation of a real database)? We want to return a Status Not Found if the game doesn't exist and return an Internal Error otherwise. Fortunately, the repository exposes a specific error against which we can check.

Listing 8.39 `getstatus/handler.go`: Dealing with errors

```
game, err := db.Find(session.GameID(id))
if err != nil {
    if errors.Is(err, repository.ErrNotFound) {
        http.Error(w, "this game does not exist", http.StatusNotFound)
        return
    }

    log.Printf("cannot fetch game %s: %s", id, err)
    http.Error(w, "failed to fetch game", http.StatusInternalServerError)
    return
}
```

Checks in the repository
for the game

Checks against a
specific error

Note that here we choose not to bubble up the errors: the http.Error message doesn't contain the err value. This would expose the internals of our service to clients, which is rarely a good idea. The words sent back along with the error are hiding the true error's details, so we need to log it for debugging purposes.

GUESS

Finally, let's play our game! Here, we need to fetch the game, play the word, save the result, and return it.

POSSIBLE ERRORS

What can possibly go wrong? Problematic scenarios might include the game isn't found, the storage isn't responding, the proposed word isn't valid, and the game is over, either lost or won. One thing we didn't add yet was a sentinel error in the domain (the `session` package), to tell us that no, you can't play a game that you already won (or lost).

Let's first see what the function of achieving all the work must do. We'll omit the errors first, then think about each situation.

Listing 8.40 `guess/handler.go`: Endpoint logic

```go
func guess(id session.GameID, guess string, db gameGuesser)
    (session.Game, error) {
    game, err := db.Find(id)                       ◀──┘ Does the game exist?

    if game.AttemptsLeft == 0 ||                    ◀── Are attempts
        game.Status == session.StatusWon {               still allowed?
        return session.Game{}, session.ErrGameOver
    }

    feedback, err := game.Gordle.Play(guess)       ◀──┘ How does this guess fare?

    game.Guesses = append(game.Guesses, session.Guess{  ◀──┘ Records the play
        Word:     guess,
        Feedback: feedback.String(),
    })
                                              Nearing the end
    game.AttemptsLeft -= 1                  ◀──┘ of the game

    switch {                                ◀──┘ Updates the status
    case feedback.GameWon():
        game.Status = session.StatusWon
    case game.AttemptsLeft == 0:
        game.Status = session.StatusLost
    default:
        game.Status = session.StatusPlaying
    }

    err = db.Update(game)                   ◀──┐ Saves the game
                                                │ for the next round
    return game, nil
}
```

That's a long function. In each case, what should the error be?

When we look for the game, we can simply wrap the error with some context. We won't use much context here, but it's an example. This error will always be of type `repository.Error`, and this is where the `repository.ErrNotFound` can be returned:

```go
game, err := db.Find(id)
if err != nil {
    return session.Game{}, fmt.Errorf("unable to find game: %w", err)
}
```

We can also get an error while playing, and it will be a `gordle.Error`:

```
feedback, err := game.Gordle.Play(guess)
if err != nil {
    return session.Game{}, fmt.Errorf("unable to play move: %w", err)
}
```

Finally, we're calling the storage again:

```
err = db.Update(game)
if err != nil {
    return session.Game{}, fmt.Errorf("unable to save game: %w", err)
}
```

Because errors are values, we know what happened when we receive an error, and we can adapt the status code and message of the HTTP response.

Listing 8.41 `guess/handler.go`: Using `domain.Game`

```
game, err := guess(id, r, db)
if err != nil {
    switch {
    case errors.Is(err, repository.ErrNotFound):
        http.Error(w, err.Error(), http.StatusNotFound)
    case errors.Is(err, gordle.ErrInvalidGuess):
        http.Error(w, err.Error(), http.StatusBadRequest)
    case errors.Is(err, session.ErrGameOver):
        http.Error(w, err.Error(), http.StatusForbidden)
    default:
        http.Error(w, err.Error(), http.StatusInternalServerError)
    }
    return
}
```

Don't forget to test. There's no trick, but there are a lot of edge cases.

You have a functioning service! Congratulations. Do you want to write a frontend client now? Playing the game with curl only isn't user friendly. You can even write a CLI in Go that calls the service. Before we leave you, though, we need to consider a few warnings about the shortcuts we took.

8.6   *Security notions and improvements*

When writing a server, we need to keep in mind that the objective is to deploy the server somewhere so that it can serve requests. However, we don't always know how many users a single server will be in charge of or how many queries they'll send. When it comes to security, we have to bend our minds and think of all the "unhappy" paths. We need to identify what could possibly go wrong to prevent worst-case scenarios from happening. In this case, it's sometimes useful to imagine ourselves as people wanting to find flaws and break the system.

8.6.1 Limiting the number of requests served at a time

One of the most frequent attacks against a server is called a distributed denial of services (DDoS) attack—it's a process in which the goal is to overload the server with too many requests. This kind of attack doesn't extract any information from the server but causes the server to crash, which makes it unavailable for other users. This attack is usually performed by having lots of computers send thousands of requests to a server. Each request will cause the server to allocate memory to process the request—a parallel task (thread or goroutine), some stack allocation, and so on. Because servers have limited resources, at some point, a vast number of requests will cause these resources to be depleted, and the server won't be able to handle anything at all, at best.

As we've already seen, hitting an endpoint starts a goroutine that will serve our request. Fortunately, goroutines are light, and thousands can run in a single thread—but there's always a risk of being overloaded with requests. Some open source mux libraries offer throttling—limiting the number of simultaneous requests a mux can serve at a given time. This is one of the features that hasn't (yet) made its way into Go's standard library.

8.6.2 User authentication

We've mentioned that clients calling the service should be authenticated so that we can make sure a game created by one player will only be played by that one person. It can also help in limiting the number of requests per user and therefore the load on the service.

How do we authenticate a user? One very common protocol is Open Authorization (OAuth)—often written as the latest version of OAuth 2.0. It's used to authenticate a user via an authentication server. Typically, authenticating a user is the job of one service, which deals with all the security and provides a signed token. Our Gordle service then receives this token via an HTTP header, validates and decodes it, and then finds the user identifier in the token.

Depending on your needs, you can decide the level of authentication for the clients: you can require an identification for each player or authenticate each application connecting to your service. In the second option, a website and a mobile app would have different IDs and keys, and each would have a request rate limit, regardless of the number of players they serve.

Authentication and the security problems it solves could be the subject of a full chapter but it's not in the scope of our book. Read *OAuth2 in Action*, by Justin Richer and Antonio Sanso (Manning, 2017, www.manning.com/books/oauth-2-in-action), for more about authentication.

8.6.3 Logging

In this chapter, we used the native and very basic `log` package. This is a terrible idea in production: it mangles the log output in a concurrent environment, typically a service. There are lots of great logging libraries out there that protect your output and offer formatting options. Go 1.21 included a standard library structured logger in the form of the `slog` package—we recommend using it over the `log` package.

8.6.4   *Error formatting*

When we're returning an error, it's a simple string. Good practice teaches us that when an endpoint's output is formatted in JSON, the errors should also be formatted. Take this, for example:

```
{
  "error": "game over"
}
```

This way, your clients can use the same decoder whatever the status code of the response.

8.6.5   *Decode query parameters*

As we saw before, query parameters are used in APIs as optional parameters. They always come as pairs of a key and a value. They are used as filters to specify the resource to be created, updated, or deleted.

SYNTAX

Query parameters are appended after the path and separated from the path by a question mark. To use them, you put the key first, followed by an equal sign, and the associated value with which you want to filter. If we have multiple parameters, we add an ampersand sign between each pair. The whole list of pairs of `key=value` after the question mark forms the query string. The next subsection provides an example of this.

LET'S IMPLEMENT AN EXAMPLE

We want to add the possibility to choose the language in which we want to play Gordle. To do so, let's add the language as a query parameter. The URL to create the game will look like this:

```
http://localhost:8080/game?lang=en
```

In this example, the key is `lang`, and the value is `en`. First, we define the constant for the key, and we declare it next to the path parameter constant.

Listing 8.42   `internal/api/http.go`: Query parameter key as constant

```
const (
    // GameID is the name of the field that stores the game's identifier
    GameID = "id"
    // Lang is the language in which Gordle is played.
    Lang   = "lang"          ◀──────  Defines the key for
                                       the query parameter
    // ...
)
```

That was the interesting and easy part. We'll now see how to decode the query parameter from the request. All the query parameters are retrievable from the URL, thanks to the `url` library's `URL.Query()` method, which we can access from the `request.URL` field in our handlers. If you check the return type, you'll see that it's a `url.Values`, which exposes (among others) a `Get(key string)` string method:

```
> go doc url.Values
// Values maps a string key to a list of values.
// It is typically used for query parameters and form values.
// Unlike in the http.Header map, the keys in a Values map
// are case-sensitive.
type Values map[string][]string
...
```

So, let's use the `Get` method on the `Values` to retrieve the language in the file `internal/handlers/newgame/handler.go`.

> **Listing 8.43** `newgame/handler.go`: Reading the query parameter in handler

```
// Handler returns the handler for the game creation endpoint.
func Handler(db gameAdder) http.HandlerFunc {
    return func(w http.ResponseWriter, r *http.Request) {    ← Replaces blank operator with a param for the request
        lang := r.URL.Query().Get(api.Lang)    ← Retrieves the query parameter
        if len(lang) > 0 {
            // TODO create a game in the chosen language
            fmt.Println(lang)    ← You can print it to check that it's working by checking the server log.
        }
    }
```

Congratulations, you now know pretty much everything about REST APIs and how to decode all kinds of parameters!

Summary

- A web service is a program that continuously listens to a port and knows what to do with requests based on a set of handlers.
- We can use `http.NewServeMux()` to create a multiplexer that will route requests, based on the URL they were sent to, to specific handlers. Otherwise, use open source libraries.
- A handler's task is to fill an `http.ResponseWriter`. It should `Write` to it, and, sometimes, set headers with `WriteHeader`.
- The default status code set by `ResponseWriter.Write` is `http.StatusOK`. If we want to return a different code, we need to call `WriteHeader` before we start writing the contents of the response via `Write`.

- If an error happens in an endpoint, the handler shouldn't return this error. If you really want to know what's gone wrong, a log is the place where the error is last displayed.

- Some directory names have specific meanings in Go. Files inside `testdata/` won't be compiled by `go build` or `go run`. Files inside `internal/` won't be `import`-able by other modules. `vendor/` is a name that should be avoided for historical reasons.

- Types that we define for the API should only be used in the endpoint handlers. The rest of the time, we should be using types of our domain. Domain—or model—types shouldn't be visible from outside the service's module. Usually, they hide inside an `internal` directory.

- A repository, or repo, offers access to the data, which can be stored in a physical database, in memory, or in any form at all.

- It's always a good idea to check whether your code is thread safe. Write tests and make use of mutexes when necessary.

- The `embed` package can be used to load the contents of a file (or directory) at compilation time. This is useful, for instance, if you want to keep your SQL queries in `.sql` files, or when, as we did, you want to load a set of hardcoded values.

- Some, if not most, open source packages use semantic versioning. Go will natively use the latest v1.x.y version of a package if nothing is specified. To enforce using v4.m.n, you should explicitly use `"go get path/to/package/v4"` and use `import` `"path/to/package/v4"` in the `.go` files.

- Using regular expressions is a very powerful way to match patterns. You'll find yourself using them in various situations, including validating randomized values. As they can be quickly unreadable, don't forget to explain in a comment any regular expressions you write.

- A REST API, or RESTful API, is a set of constraints defining an interface between two systems. REST APIs communicate through HTTP and can exchange data through JSON, HTML, or even plain text.

- HTTP statuses are useful to communicate precisely what happened on the server side to the client. An HTTP status code is three digits from 1xx to 5xx, which could mean everything went well (`200`) or resources aren't found (the well-known `404`). Returning the proper code means that the client can better understand what happened. When in doubt, return `500`; when at a loss, return `418`.

- Wildcards can be used to represent path parameters in routes. Registering a handler function with the pattern `"/games/{id}"` will allow the handle to access the value of `id` with `request.PathValue("id")`.

- Several wildcards can be used in the same pattern: `"/users/{user_id}/games/{game_id}"` could be used to access a specific game for a specific user.

Concurrent maze solver

The oldest representation of a maze found by archaeologists, from Paleolithic times, was engraved in a piece of mammoth ivory. In Indo-European mythology, mazes are often associated with engineers, such as Daedalus in Greece. Mazes are also used as a symbol for the difficult path of a life toward a god figure in the O'odham tradition in North America, in India in the Chakra-vyuha style, or in Europe on the floors of medieval churches to represent the way to salvation.

Solving a maze has been an interesting engineering exercise for ages, including physically with an autonomous robotic mouse (see micromouse competitions, e.g., https://ukmars.org/contests/micromouse/) or virtually using graph theory. There are countless algorithms, each optimized for different constraints: Are there loops? Is the target inside the maze, like a treasure, or on another side, like a liberating way out? Are there curves or only right-angled corners? In the case of multiple possible paths, do we need the shortest, the fastest, or the one that goes through a collection of bonus stars?

In this chapter, we want to find the treasure in a maze, starting from an entrance position. Each intersection we meet raises a question: Which branch should we explore—to the left, to the right, or straight ahead? We'll answer that question by exploring all branches concurrently, spinning up goroutines each time we have an intersection. This project has the following requirements:

- Find the path through a maze that has no loops (there's only one path to reach any pixel).
- The maze is a PNG RGBA (Red Green Blue Alpha) image.
- The command-line tool should take an input image's path and write another image with the pixels from the entrance to the treasure highlighted.
- As a bonus, it should also generate a GIF image of the exploration process.

9.1   *Maze generation*

If we want to solve mazes, we need mazes to solve. Because we're developers, we decided to quickly code a maze generator as a side project.

A handful of recognized algorithms for maze generation is available online. By now, you should have enough understanding of the Go language to be able to code one yourself. Note that ours is available in the book's repository (https://mng.bz/YDlB), in a `builder` folder, for those most in a hurry. Here are a few important points for a maze generator.

A maze can be represented as a grid in which elements can be either walls or paths. Two special path elements can be found in the maze: the entrance and the treasure. The goal of the maze is to find a list of positions in the grid that links the entrance to the treasure. These positions need to be adjacent—teleportation isn't allowed in a maze. Figure 9.1 shows an example of a small maze with a treasure corresponding to an exit on the bottom edge.

But the treasure doesn't have to be on an edge. Figure 9.2 shows an example of a bigger maze with a treasure inside.

Because it's nice to have a preview of the maze, we decided to encode ours as an image. An image is a very convenient way of representing a two-dimensional (2D) grid because it has a fixed size. We can encode the information of

Figure 9.1   Example of a small maze with a treasure (exit) on the edge

Figure 9.2 Example of a maze with a treasure inside

whether a grid element is a wall, a path, an entrance, or a treasure by using color values. In the preceding examples, walls are painted black, while paths are painted white.

Because it's nice to have a preview of the maze, we decided to encode ours as an image. An image is a very convenient way of representing a 2D grid because it has a fixed size. We can encode the information of whether a grid element is a wall, a path, an entrance, or a treasure by using color values. In the preceding examples, walls are painted black, while paths are painted white.

9.1.1 *What is an image?*

In computer science, most 2D images are one of two kinds: vector images or bitmap images. Vector images are similar to mathematical entities—regardless of how much you zoom in, lines have no thickness, points don't look bigger on your screen, and so on. Scalable Vector Graphics (SVG) is a common format for vector images.

On the other hand, bitmap images, also called raster images, contain a 2D grid of picture elements. These picture elements (or pixels) each bear a color. When zooming in on a raster image, pixels are simply displayed larger. Common formats for raster images are Portable Network Graphics (PNG) and Joint Photographic Experts Group (JPEG). JPEG images offer lossy compression, which means they will usually require fewer bytes to store the information—but they might also modify the image while compressing it. The information encoded at the pixel positions is usually color, but sometimes, we use pixels for something else, such as a heat map or density (how MRI uses images to represent internal tissues) or for palettes, where each color has a specific meaning (e.g., a map of the world in which each country is represented with a different color).

Because we want to encode a 2D grid, a raster image format seems perfectly adequate. JPEG's lossy compression can result in a pixel's color being altered, and we want exact values to represent our walls, paths, entrance, and treasure. For this reason, we've decided to encode our image as a PNG.

Of course, Go has a package for image manipulation and also has a package for most common image formats:

```
> go doc image
package image // import "image"

[...]

type Image interface{ ... }
    func Decode(r io.Reader) (Image, string, error)

type Point struct{ ... }

type RGBA struct{ ... }
    func NewRGBA(r Rectangle) *RGBA

> go doc image.Point
type Point struct {
    X, Y int
}
    A Point is an X, Y coordinate pair. The axes increase right and down.
```

One of the types we see in the image package is the RGBAImage. This offers access to the RGBAAt(x, y) method, which allows us to retrieve the color of a pixel at a given position in the image.

9.1.2 *Maze constraints*

Remember the constraints we have on the initial version of the solver:

- The maze doesn't loop back to itself. There's exactly one path from the entrance to any given point of the maze.
- The generated image should be a PNG image using the RGBA color model.

When writing the maze generator, you can also add a complexity constraint on the length of the path from entrance to treasure to avoid straightforward answers. In our implementation, for example, that path—the solution—must have a length of at least the height of the image plus its width. We decided to use the following colors, but feel free to be more artistic and color-blind friendly:

- *Entrance*—Dark tone (deep blue)
- *Treasure*—Light tone (pink)
- *Wall*—Black
- *Path*—White

We now have a generated maze. Let's start solving it!

9.2   *Maze solver*

To solve the maze, we'll start by opening the maze image we generated, and we'll explore the possible paths, recording them at the same time. By the end, we'll have a first hacky version (it might be dirty, but at least it'll work), finishing when the treasure is found.

9.2.1 Setup

As usual, start by setting up your module and creating a `main.go` file at the root. Because this project is a simple command-line tool, we can have the `main.go` file at the root of the module and the rest in the `internal` folder. The first step to solving the maze will be to open it.

9.2.2 Loading the maze image

As we mentioned, we want the input PNG to be passed as an argument to the tool, with the output path:

```
> maze-solver maze_10x10.png solution.png
```

This means the first thing our `main()` will do is read these two arguments.

> **Listing 9.1 `main.go`: Reading the arguments**

```go
package main

import (
    "fmt"
    "log"
    "os"
)

func main() {
    if len(os.Args) != 3 {          // Checks the number of arguments
        usage()
    }

    inputFile := os.Args[1]         // The name of the program is found at index 0 before the arguments.
    outputFile := os.Args[2]

    log.Printf("Solving maze %q and saving it as %q", inputFile, outputFile)

}

// usage displays the usage of the binary and exits the program.
func usage() {
    _, _ = fmt.Fprintln(os.Stderr, "Usage: maze_solver input.png output.png")
    os.Exit(1)                      // Exits the program with error code 1
}
```

You can already run it and check various scenarios. We then open the first image that contains the maze. The errors that can happen at this point include there being no file at all or there being a non-PNG image. In each case, we want to print an explicit error.

The operation can be summarized in one sentence, so, of course, we put it in one function. It takes the string and returns an image of the `*image.RGBA` type. We want a pointer because, eventually, we'll want to modify the image when we write the path to the treasure. We write that function into a new file that will contain the file I/O operations:

```
func openMaze(imagePath string) (*image.RGBA, error)
```

Let's call our new function `openMaze`. It will check that the file exists, open it—don't forget to defer the call to `Close`—and decode the PNG. The last step is done by calling `Decode` from the `image/png` package, which takes an `io.Reader` and returns `image.Image`, which is an interface.

Now, unfortunately, the `image.Image` interface offers a single method to access a pixel's value—`At(x, y)`—which returns the `color.Color` of a pixel at the intersection of the x-th column and the y-th row. The `color.Color` returned by `At` from a regular `image.Image` needs to be converted to the RGBA color model to be usable. Instead of having to call `At(x, y).RGBA()` every time we want to access a pixel's value, we can use an `image.RGBA`—a type that offers a very convenient method `RGBAAt(x, y)`. For this, we'll simply try to type assert the `image.Image` we decoded from the file into an `image.RGBA` variable.

Go offers `image.RGBA`, but doesn't offer `image.RGB`. For this reason, it's simpler to consider RGBA images in this chapter, even though we only chose colors with 100% opacity. Create a file called `imagefile.go` next to `main.go`.

Listing 9.2   `imagefile.go`: Opening the maze image

```
package main

import (
    "fmt"
    "image"
    "image/png"
    "os"
)

// openMaze opens a RGBA png image from a path.
func openMaze(imagePath string) (*image.RGBA, error) {        // ◀── Checks that the file exists
    f, err := os.Open(imagePath)
    if err != nil {                                           // ◀── Opens the file
        return nil, fmt.Errorf("unable to open image %s: %w", imagePath, err)
    }
    defer f.Close()

    img, err := png.Decode(f)                                 // ◀── Tries decoding as a PNG
    if err != nil {
        return nil, fmt.Errorf("unable to load input image from %s: %w",
            imagePath, err)
    }

    rgbaImage, ok := img.(*image.RGBA)                         // ◀── Type asserts to *image.RGBA
```

```
        if !ok {
            return nil, fmt.Errorf(
                "expected RGBA image, got %T", img)     ◄───  %T prints the type
        }                                                     of a variable.

        return rgbaImage, nil
    }
```

We now have the image. Don't forget to call the function in your `main`, handle the error properly, and test manually what happens in different scenarios.

In the preceding code, there are two error cases that are easy to test automatically: unable to open the file and unable to load the PNG image. Testing whether the function is unable to type assert it as an RGBA image requires a PNG image that wasn't encoded as an RGBA image. We've provided such an image in our repository at https://mng.bz/KGJX. You should expect an output like this:

```
> go run . mazes/rgb.png solution.png
2023/10/16 18:26:28 INFO Solving maze "mazes/rgb.png" and saving it as
"solution.png"
ERROR: expected RGBA image, got *image.Paletted
exit status 1
```

Finally, we need to handle the `os.Open` error when we can't open a file that we're able to detect. This case is quite rare—on Unix, it requires execution rights on a directory and no read rights on a file in that directory. Still, it may happen, and we'll be happy to know if it does. Write a test, and then we can set up the solving part.

9.2.3 Add the solver

Solving the maze will be done by a dedicated object that carries a `Solve()` method and that can be constructed by giving it the image. Why? The object will be able (later) to hold settings such as the colors of the path, walls, entrance, treasure, and solution (the path from entrance to treasure). As you'll quickly see, it will also hold the channels for communication between the goroutines and the solution at the end. For now, let's keep it simple.

SOLVER STRUCTURE

The `Solver` is the heart of the tool and would benefit from living in a dedicated package: `internal/solver`. Remember—packages inside `internal` can't be used by anyone other than your module. Create a `solver.go` file in the `internal/solver` package.

> **Listing 9.3** `solver.go`: The `Solver` structure

```
package solver

import "image"

// Solver is capable of finding the path from the entrance to the treasure.
// The maze has to be a RGBA image.
```

```
type Solver struct {
    maze *image.RGBA
}
```

Before we go on, let's define the API of this object. It needs to solve the maze and write the solution image, as shown in the next listing. That's two operations, so that makes two exposed methods.

Listing 9.4 `solver.go`: **Solve API**

```
// Solve finds the path from the entrance to the treasure.
func (s *Solver) Solve() error {
    return nil
}
```

The `SaveSolution` method lives in `imagefile.go` because it's in the image manipulation scope. The code is given in the following listing.

Listing 9.5 `imagefile.go`: **Saving solution API**

```
// SaveSolution saves the image as a PNG file
// with the solution path highlighted.
func (s *Solver) SaveSolution(outputPath string) error {
    return nil
}
```

NEW FUNCTION

Actually, our implementation is highly tied to the image package. Why not delegate the opening of the PNG image to a `New` function? We'll need that function anyway.

Move the `imagefile.go` file containing the `openImage` function along with its test to the `solver` package, and then call the `openImage` function in a new function called `New`. Don't forget to replace the previous call to `openImage` with a call to `solver.New` in the `main` function. It takes the path as a parameter and returns a pointer to a `Solver` and an error, as shown in the following listing. Note that, in a file, we tend to write `New` functions and other such constructors after the structure definition.

Listing 9.6 `solver.go`: **New** `Solver`

```
// New builds a Solver by taking the path to the PNG maze, encoded in RGBA.
func New(imagePath string) (*Solver, error) {
    img, err := openMaze(imagePath)
    if err != nil {
        return nil, fmt.Errorf("cannot open maze image: %w", err)
    }

    return &Solver{maze: img}, nil
}
```

Your current tree should look like this:

```
> tree
.
├── go.mod
├── internal
│   └── solver
│       ├── imagefile.go
│       └── solver.go
└── main.go
```

At this point, you can even finish writing the `main` function by building your `Solver` and calling its public API in the proper order. Deal with the various errors in the way you prefer, but don't forget that command-line interface (CLI) tools are expected to return a status code 1 when there's an error via `os.Exit(1)`. If you have any doubts, look at the code in the folder at https://mng.bz/9Yxj.

Run the tests that you've written, commit, and have a cup of tea. The next section is the heart of the project.

9.3 | *Let's go exploring!*

In the previous section, we've loaded the maze image into memory. Our next objective is to find the path from entrance to treasure, but first we need to find the entrance.

9.3.1 *Finding the entrance*

The first step is quite straightforward, but of course we wouldn't be here if there were nothing to learn on the way. Having loaded the image in memory doesn't mean we can solve the maze immediately. First, we need to know how to explore it.

COLOR PALETTE

To encode information, the maze generator used pixels to store specific values at particular positions. In our maze, these values will represent the walls, paths, entrance, and treasure. We want to compare the colors of the pixels against these specific values. RGBA colors are expressed as structures in the `image/color` package, and structures can't be constants, which means our reference colors for the paths, walls, entrance, and treasure can't be constants. So how do we refer to them? We have a few solutions.

One way is to declare the colors as global variables in the `solver` package. Well, we don't like global variables because they can be modified by mistake and go undetected by any test, and then the whole behavior becomes completely unexplainable. It can be a good first step, but we prefer not to have it in production.

An interesting alternative is to create a `palette` structure to hold all the different values. You could load a palette from a configuration file when the maze solver is executed, but this is beyond the scope of our chapter. We don't need to expose the structure as long as the main package doesn't need to change the values. Create a file named palette.go in the internal/solver package.

> **Listing 9.7   palette.go: Declaring the list of colors**

```
// palette contains the colours of the different types of pixels in our maze.
type palette struct {
    wall        color.RGBA
    path        color.RGBA        The color of the possible paths
    entrance    color.RGBA
    treasure    color.RGBA        The pixel you're looking for
    solution    color.RGBA        Displays the solution
}
```

A palette structure populated with the values that we picked can be returned by a defaultPalette() function, as shown in listing 9.8, with the advantage over global variables that nothing can change the values a function will return. Unfortunately, it would create a new structure every time you need it, allocating precious memory that needs to be garbage collected. It can become costly as soon as we start exploring bigger mazes.

> **Listing 9.8   palette.go: Default colors function**

```
// defaultPalette returns the colour palette of our maze.
func defaultPalette() palette {
    return palette{
        wall:       color.RGBA{
            R: 0,   G: 0,   B: 0,   A: 255},        Black
        path:       color.RGBA{
            R: 255, G: 255, B: 255, A: 255},        White
        entrance: color.RGBA{
            R: 0,   G: 191, B: 255, A: 255},        Deep blue
        treasure: color.RGBA{
            R: 255, G: 0,   B: 123, A: 255},        Pink
        solution: color.RGBA{
            R: 225, G: 140, B: 0,   A: 255},        Orange
    }
}
```

What we did instead was to save these in the Solver structure as settings to solve the picture (see listing 9.9). It makes sense because another solver with another picture can use a different set of colors.

> **Listing 9.9   solver.go: Solver with palette**

```
type Solver struct {
    maze      *image.RGBA
    palette   palette
}
```

For the moment, you can simply set these colors to some default values in the New function of the solver package using the function we just defined, defaultPalette(). Now, let's follow the signs to find the entrance.

PIXEL DEFINITION

We'll be going through the maze by exploring pixels, identified by their coordinates on the 2D image. As we'll need to navigate in these 2D grids, let's use image.Point, provided by Go:

```go
type Point struct {
    X, Y int
}
```

One thing we can easily anticipate with a pixel is that we'll need to find its open neighbors: the pixels bearing the path color that are orthogonally connected to it. This will be easier if the pixel can give us the coordinates of its own neighbors. Because of how the maze is implemented, we don't want to include diagonally adjacent neighbors. Create a file named neighbours.go in the internal/solver package, and write the neighbours function.

Listing 9.10 neighbours.go: **Coordinates of a pixel**

```go
package solver

import "image"

// neighbours returns an array of the 4 neighbours of a pixel.
// Some returned positions may be outside the image.
func neighbours(p image.Point) [4]image.Point {
    return [...]image.Point{
        {p.X, p.Y + 1},      ◄──┐  One pixel down
        {p.X, p.Y - 1},      ◄──┐│ One pixel up
        {p.X + 1, p.Y},      ◄──┐││ One pixel to the right
        {p.X - 1, p.Y},      ◄──┘││ One pixel to the left
    }
}
```

NOTE In this function, we returned an array. Here, [...]image.Point is equivalent to [4]image.Point, which is an array (the length of the array is computed at compilation). Using an array is a minor optimization, as it will more likely be allocated on the stack than in the heap.

Nothing in this function guarantees that the neighbors are inside the image. For instance, two neighbors of the top-left corner at position (0, 0) are outside the image. We could add a safety net here, or we could require that none of the edges of the image should be explored.

An alternative is to consider how we'll use these neighbors. In our code later, we'll want to check whether they represent an explorable section of the maze, a wall, the treasure, or some other information that we code. For this, we'll have to look at the value returned, `RGBAAt(position)`, for each neighbor of a pixel. After checking its implementation, it's clear that `RGBAAt` returns a zero value when the position is outside the image. This means it's safe to have `neighbours` return points that wouldn't be within the bounds of our image.

Another thing that the API doesn't guarantee is the order of the neighbors. We could start from the top and go clockwise or be wild and just scramble them. This means the test is the perfect occasion to use the framework offered at https://github.com/stretchr/testify and its `assert.ElementsMatch` function.

FIND THE PIXEL OF THE ENTRANCE

Go back to the `solver.go` file, and create the function `findEntrance`. We'll have to scan the whole image to find one pixel that has the entrance color. To check each pixel's value, a common practice in image processing is to follow the row-major order with two nested loops: an outer loop that will iterate over the rows of the image, and an inner one that will iterate over the rows. This is similar to how some languages, such as English or Tifinagh, write text from the leftmost position to the rightmost, and then to the next line, from the leftmost again.

The reason for this specific pattern is that image formats tend to store pixel values in *scanline* format, where horizontally adjacent pixels of the image are stored in adjacent memory locations. This is understandable when we remember that most image format developers are English speakers.

Most of the time, our maze's first pixel will be at position (0, 0)—in the top-left corner. But if we're looking at a subsection of an image, our "top-left" corner might be at another position. Here, we can access our maze's bounds via the `Bounds()` method on the `image.RGBA` type. This returns two points that define the bounding box of our image: the `Min` and a `Max` fields.

Listing 9.11 `solver.go`: **Finding the entrance**

```go
// findEntrance returns the position of the maze entrance on the image.
func (s *Solver) findEntrance() (image.Point, error) {
    for row := s.maze.Bounds().Min.Y; row < s.maze.Bounds().Max.Y; row++ {
        for col := s.maze.Bounds().Min.X; col < s.maze.Bounds().Max.X; col++
        {
            if s.maze.RGBAAt(col, row) == s.palette.entrance {
                return image.Point{X: col, Y: row}, nil          ◄──── Returns as soon as
            }                                                           we find an entrance
        }
    }

    return image.Point{}, fmt.Errorf("entrance position not found")
}
```

Back in the `Solve` method, we can call this to know where to start, as shown in the following listing.

> **Listing 9.12** `solver.go`: **Call to** `findEntrance` **in** `Solve`

```
// Solve finds the path from the entrance to the treasure.
func (s *Solver) Solve() error {
    entrance, err := s.findEntrance()
    if err != nil {
        return fmt.Errorf("unable to find entrance: %w", err)
    }

    log.Printf("starting at %v", entrance))

    return nil
}
```

What if there's no entrance? Make sure to cover all kinds of situations in your tests. Maybe we want a maze to have a single entrance. If you have trouble writing tests, you can find our test cases in the file at https://mng.bz/jpMa, and all maze images used for the scenarios are located under `internal/solver/testdata` in the book's repository (https://mng.bz/GeMv). Figure 9.3 shows a maze for which the entrance has been identified.

Figure 9.3   Maze with entrance and next pixel

We've stepped into the maze at the entrance and explored one pixel. The next pixel(s) now need to be explored so that we can reach the treasure.

9.3.2 *Communicating new possible paths*

When solving a maze, there are lots of optimized algorithms available, but most offer an iterative approach—turn left at every corner, go to the location that is both nearest to the entrance and unexplored, and so on. Each time an intersection is met, a decision must be made: Should we start with the left side, then the right side, and then straight ahead? In this chapter, we answer this question with a question: Why not try all at the same time? This calls for parallel programming, which is implemented in Go with goroutines. Every time we find a branching in the path, we'll want to continue in one of the possible directions and start a goroutine with the other(s). Using goroutines means we can delegate the exploration of these other directions and focus on our current branch till we reach either the treasure or a dead end.

Using goroutines can increase the performance—making finding the solution faster—but this isn't guaranteed. Starting goroutines takes time, and communicating data with them adds on top of that. Usually, goroutines aren't necessary for very quick tasks. In our case, each goroutine has an undetermined scope: we don't know when it could end, so we might as well give the goroutine its chance. What's certain is that using goroutines increases CPU usage.

In figure 9.4, we're looking for the treasure (μ). Goroutine Daedalus (δ) starts in A5, then goes to B5, and needs to branch. A second goroutine, Theseus (θ), picks up at B6 while δ continues in B4, C4, and so on. As long as our maze contains no loop, Daedalus won't meet Theseus as they explore the maze, and this means Daedalus doesn't need to know about Theseus at all.

Figure 9.4   exploration by different goroutines

From there, both goroutines keep exploring and spinning new explorers. The exploration to reach the treasure could look like figure 9.5 (each goroutine's explored path is represented by a different Greek letter).

How does the δ goroutine communicate that a new exploration should be started from B6, and what should be in charge of listening to that notification? In other words, how do goroutines communicate? Via channels, of course.

Figure 9.5 Exploration representing a possible sequence of events

NOTE Communication between goroutines is the purpose of channels.

After finding the position of the entrance, our `Solve` function is in charge of initiating the exploration of our maze, starting from there. As soon as a new path should be explored, we want the solver to start the exploration of that branch. Each explorer will be in charge of notifying new branches to our solver with a channel, which will be listening to these notifications. We understand from this that we need two new methods on our solver—the first one will explore a path—we can call it `explore`—and the second one will be in charge of listening to branches—let's call it `listenToBranches`. Our solver initiates the exploration of the maze by sending a message to the channel that the `listenToBranches` method is listening.

The function `listenToBranches` reads the very first message and creates a goroutine, the one we called `Daedalus` (δ), for the path starting at A5. Figure 9.6 shows a diagram of the following events. `Daedalus` looks at the neighbors of A5: only B5 is eligible. The goroutine integrates B5 into its explored path and checks the neighbors of B5, finding that B4 and B6 are eligible candidates for exploration. Our exploring goroutine, `Daedalus`, sends the path to B6 to the channel and keeps exploring B4, C4, and so on. The listener of the channel reads the message sent by `Daedalus` and spins a new goroutine, `Theseus` (θ), which goes on to C6, C7, and so on, until it finds a dead end and finishes. Meanwhile, `Daedalus` has reached E3 and faces three new exploration paths. It (randomly) chooses to continue on its way (D3, E3, C3), and sends the paths leading to E2 and to E4 to the channel, and the listener has spun two new goroutines, λ and φ.

Of course, in this scenario, take the grammatical tenses with a dash of salt because depending on your architecture and the random reassignments decided by the CPU, the future, the present, and the past can vary from one run to the next. Implementing it will help us understand the details better.

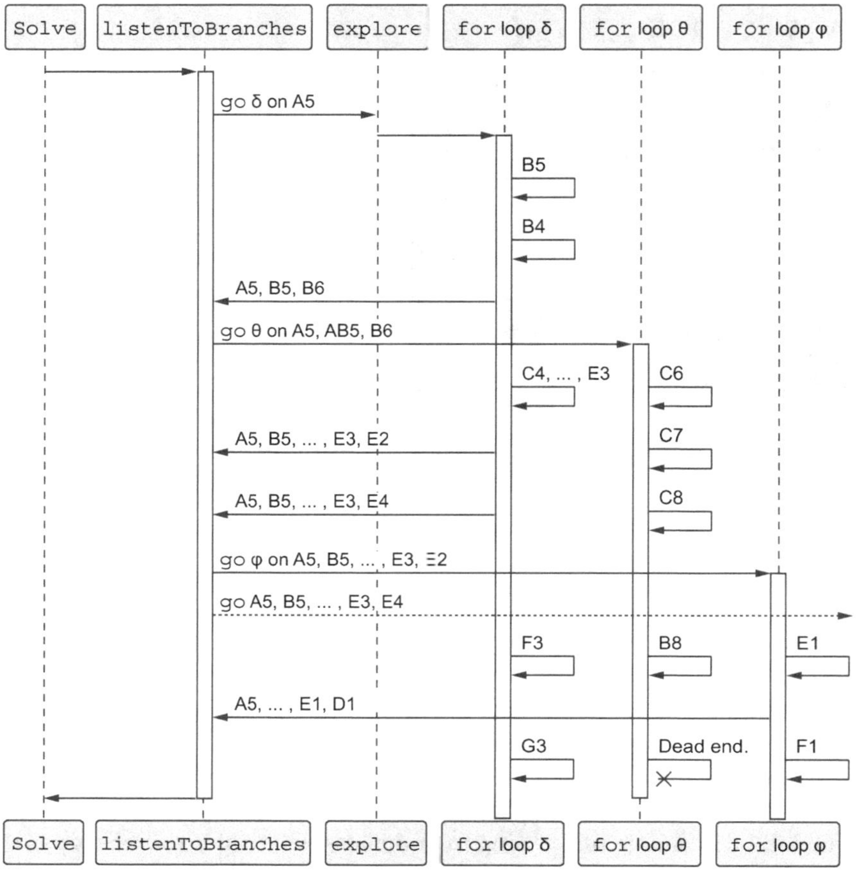

Figure 9.6   The sequence of events in `Solve`

For `Daedalus` to start an autonomous goroutine that will be able to explore the path from B6 onward, it needs to communicate just the path so far to `Theseus` and the goroutine that gets to the treasure. That's all. They need to know the path through pixels that have been explored to reach this point, which we can express as a linked list of `image.Point`, as shown in listing 9.13. Create an `internal/solver/path.go` file, and add the `path` structure.

Listing 9.13   `path.go`: Using a linked list to store the path so far

```
package solver

import "image"

// path represents a route from the entrance of the maze up to a position.
type path struct {
```

```
        previousStep  *path
        at            image.Point
}
```

Add a field to the `Solver` that is a channel whose messages are pointers to a `path`.

Listing 9.14 `solver.go`: Adding a channel to the `Solver` structure

```
type Solver struct {
    maze          *image.RGBA
    palette       palette
    pathsToExplore chan *path    ◄───┐  A channel that carries linked
}                                    │  lists of explored pixels
```

This is where goroutines will publish new paths to explore and where the `listenTo-Branches` method will listen to spin up new exploration goroutines. That method will be added in section 9.3.4, as common sense dictates you can't read from a channel into which nothing has been written yet (as long as the channel is open).

9.3.3 *Recording the explored path*

Considering that the aim of the program is to tell us how to go from one point to another, we need to know, whenever we explore a new pixel, how we got here. We can't drop pebbles behind us like Hop-o'-My-Thumb did in the French fairytale, but we can certainly make use of the computer's memory.

BEHAVIOR OF EACH GOROUTINE

Let's write the `explore` function, which takes a path as its parameter and explores it. This function will go on until it either finds a dead end or finds the treasure and will publish to the channel any branch it doesn't take. This function contains what each goroutine will do.

For a first version, if we find the treasure, let's only print a message and stop exploring with a `return`. We'll come back to that later.

We chose to put this function in a dedicated file `explore.go` in the `solver` package, as shown in listing 9.15. The function is important enough, and we'll regularly come back to debug it.

Listing 9.15 `explore.go`: Exploring one path

```
package solver

import (
    "image"
    "log"
)

// explore one path and publish to the s.pathsToExplore channel
// any branch we discover that we don't take.
```

```
func (s *Solver) explore(pathToBranch *path) {
    if pathToBranch == nil {
        // This is a safety net. It should be used, but when it's needed,
        // at least it's there.
        return
    }

    pos := pathToBranch.at          ◄──┤ This is the pixel we're at.

    for {
// We know we'll have up to 3 new neighbours to explore.  ◄──
        candidates := make([]image.Point, 0, 3)
        for _, n := range neighbours(pos) {          ◄──
            if pathToBranch.isPreviousStep(n){          ◄──
                // Let's not return to the previous position
                continue
            }
            // Look at the colour of this pixel.
            // RGBAAt returns a color.RGBA{} zero value if the pixel is
            // outside the bounds of the image.
            switch s.maze.RGBAAt(n.X, n.Y) {          ◄──
            case s.palette.treasure:
                log.Printf("Treasure found at %v!", n)
                return
            case s.palette.path:          ◄──
                candidates = append(candidates, n)
            }
        }

        if len(candidates) == 0 {
            log.Printf("I must have taken the wrong turn at position %v.",
                pos)
            return
        }

        // See below
    }
}

// isPreviousStep returns true if the given point is
// the previous position of the path.
func (p path) isPreviousStep(n image.Point) bool {
    return p.previousStep != nil && p.previousStep.at == n
}
```

Forever until we break out or find a dead end

Peeks in each direction for path pixels

This is where we came from.

Checks the color of the neighbor

This is a valid candidate.

Note that, so far, neighbors can only be wall, path, entrance, or treasure. Entrance has already been skipped because it was the previous pixel, and there's nothing we can do about a wall. This is why we only have two cases in the switch—and we didn't add an empty default case: we find either the treasure or another position to explore. Anything else isn't interesting. It's important to note that, as we look for eligible neighbors, we don't want to go back on our steps and return to the previous position. This could lead to an endless creation of goroutines and a crash of the program. We'll explore ways of preventing this in section 9.6.1.

Then, there are two cases to consider: either we have no next pixel to explore, in which case, it was a dead end, or we do have next pixels to explore, so we have to send messages to the listening goroutine. In the case of a dead end, we print a log message to understand what's going on, but there's nothing else to do anymore. We exit the loop, and the goroutine ends its execution.

BRANCHING OUT

If we do have one or more pixel candidates for exploration, we keep one for ourselves (in our case, the first, `candidates[0]`) and send the path to the others on the channel, as shown in the following listing. Then, we continue the exploration one step further.

> **Listing 9.16** `explore.go`: **Keep exploring**

```
for _, candidate := range candidates[1:] {          ◀──── Ignores
    branch := &path{previousStep: pathToBranch, at: candidate}      candidates[0]
    s.pathsToExplore <- branch          ◀──── Publishes the path
}                                              leading to the branch

pathToBranch = &path{
    previousStep: pathToBranch,
    at: candidates[0]}          ◀──── Continues exploring
pos = candidates[0]
```

This is a rather long function. We could refactor by extracting logical pieces of code. Loops are usually a good candidate because they can be summarized in one sentence, which is logically a unit. Let's take a look at our options:

- *Extract the inside of the big infinite loop.* For this option, there would be too many variables to return: the next position, the next "previous" position, a signal about whether to exit, and possibly an error.
- *Extract the first part, where we look for candidates.* This is where we chose to exit in the case of a success. It's possible, but not too easy.
- *Extract the second switch, where we look at the candidates.* In this situation, we also exit in the case of a dead end. We could pull out the publishing loop, but would the code really become easier to understand for three lines?

Let's keep it this way and see whether writing a test is overly complicated or not. As often, because we want to isolate the logic as much as possible, the test is a bit more complicated than the code itself and requires at least the same notions, so we'll keep it for just a bit later. Don't make it a habit, though.

9.3.4 *Waiting for unexplored paths and starting a goroutine*

As we explore, we need a function that listens to the channel and starts a new goroutine for each message in the channel. It doesn't need to be complex: for each message in the channel, call `explore`, as shown in listing 9.17.

The keyword in Go for listening to all the messages published to a channel is `range`, exactly like with `slices` or `maps`. Using `range` over a channel is blocking, meaning that this function will wait for a message to be published on the channel as long as close(s .pathsToExplore) wasn't called.

Listing 9.17 explore.go: Listening to the channel

```
// listenToBranches creates a new goroutine for each branch published in
// s.pathsToExplore.
func (s *Solver) listenToBranches() {
    for p := range s.pathsToExplore {
        go s.explore(p)
    }
}
```

This is a very short implementation; it can work but it has a catch with goroutines. We know when they start, but we don't know when they end. Here, we're not keeping track of the different goroutines (nor their amount), which means the program can end while some of them are still running and keep using memory and CPU. We need to fix this before our code is considered correct.

But let's first make our program work. The last thing we need to do to kick-start the exploration is to publish the first message. To start the first goroutine, the one we called Daedalus in our example, we only need to publish the entrance to the channel and start listening.

Let's come back to the Solve function. It knows the position of the entrance pixel, and we can publish that:

```
s.pathsToExplore <- &path{previousStep: nil, at: entrance}
```

Don't forget to call the listening function listenTobranches after that and try running the program. Do you get an error? You should. We now have this:

```
fatal error: all goroutines are asleep - deadlock!

goroutine 1 [chan send (nil chan)]:
learngo/09/maze/internal/solver.(*Solver).Solve(0x1400009c180)
```

We're trying to write to and read from a nil channel. Initialize the channel in the New function, and try again as follows:

```
pathsToExplore: make(chan *path),
```

We run into the same problem. We've chosen an unbuffered channel, and sending a message to it before reading from it will keep causing a fatal error.

NOTE   A send operation on an unbuffered channel blocks the sending goroutine until a corresponding receive on the same channel. At this point, the value is transmitted, and both goroutines may continue. For more on unbuffered channels, check out *The Go Programming Language* by Alan A. A. Donovan and Brian W. Kernighan (Addison-Wesley Professional, 2015).

We can't write to an unbuffered channel before we start reading from it. Instead, we can give a one-value buffer to the channel. One value is enough because after writing this value, our main goroutine will listen forever:

```
pathsToExplore: make(chan *point, 1),
```

Alternatively, if we had built an unbuffered channel with make(chan *point), the writing to that channel in the Solve function could have been done in a goroutine:

```
go func() { s.pathsToExplore <- &path{previousStep: nil, at: entrance} }()
```

As you can see, if you have logs everywhere, a size of 1 is enough to get to the solution of a small maze, but we still finish in a deadlock. As we said, the main goroutine listens forever, even when all subroutines have stopped publishing. Go notices that and ends the execution with a deadlock error after a little while. We need a way to tell the listening method to stop.

9.3.5 *Stop listening, we found it: Short version*

When one goroutine finds the treasure, it needs to save the path leading to it somewhere, and somehow tell all the other goroutines to stop looking, as well as tell the listener to stop listening. We'll start by implementing a quick version, so that we can get something pretty as soon as possible, see its limitations, and find a better solution.

We took a small shortcut a few pages ago, at the point where we found the treasure. At that point, we need to save the path of pixels somewhere that the SaveSolution function can find it. Most of the time, putting it inside the Solver is good enough, as shown in listing 9.18. Additionally, it can serve as a flag to tell different goroutines that the treasure has been found, and that they can stop looking for it.

Listing 9.18 `solver.go`: **Adding the solution**

```
type Solver struct {
    maze            *image.RGBA
    palette         palette
    pathsToExplore  chan *path

    solution *path              ◀─────┐ Saves the solution
}
```

In the explore function, writing to the field is done in just one line. Let's go back to the switch, as shown in the following listing.

Listing 9.19   `explore.go`: Saving the solution

```
case s.palette.treasure:
    s.solution = &path{previousStep: pathToBranch, at: n}
    log.Printf("Treasure found at %v!", n))
    return
```
◄─── Adds the treasure to the path

Wait—any goroutine could be writing to `s.solution`, so how do we avoid creating a race condition? Let's add a mutex to protect ourselves against this. The mutex is a new field of the `Solver` structure. The following listing shows how we use it in our case.

Listing 9.20   `explore.go`: Saving the solution with a mutex

```
case s.palette.treasure:
    s.mutex.Lock()
    defer s.mutex.Unlock()
    if s.solution == nil {
        s.solution = &path{previcusStep: pathToBranch, at: n}
        log.Printf("Treasure found at %v!", n))
    }
    return
```
◄─── It's OK to defer despite being in a loop because this case always returns.

Next, to tell other goroutines to stop, we'll use this `solution` field as a flag. Admittedly, this isn't a great solution, but it's fast. Because we'll need to check in several places whether the solution was found, we can write a function.

Listing 9.21   `explore.go`: Stop listening to new messages

```
func (s *Solver) listenToBranches() {
    for p := range s.pathsToExplore {
        go s.explore(p)
        if s.solutionFound() {
            return
        }
    }
}

// solutionFound returns whether the solution was found.
func (s *Solver) solutionFound() bool {
    s.mutex.Lock()
    defer s.mutex.Unlock()
    return s.solution != nil
}
```
◄─── Stops listening if the treasure is found

We have another infinite loop that could use a stop in the `explore` function. We can change the infinite loop so that it stops when the solution is found, as shown in the following listing.

Listing 9.22 `explore.go`: **Stop exploring a path**

```
func (s *Solver) explore(pathToBranch []image.Point) {
    //...

    for !s.solutionFound() {          ◄─────┐ While the solution
        candidates := ...                     │ hasn't been found
```

Let's run it. Has it stopped deadlocking? Depending on the complexity of our input maze, maybe yes, maybe no, because our solution is hacky. Before we fix it properly, it's time to start automating the test.

9.3.6 *Testing one goroutine's logic*

We can test this on an image that is only 4 pixels wide and 5 pixels high: we need a 2 x 3 grid plus some mandatory walls on three sides. The following test cases are shown in figure 9.7 from left to right:

- Only a path to the treasure
- A maze with one path leading to a dead end
- A maze with two branches
- A maze with a cross
- A maze with a treasure and a dead end

Figure 9.7   Maze test cases

If we send the first pixel as parameters, we can count the number of branches that have been published to the channel. For this, we'll create a `Solver`, but we won't listen to its channel. At the end of the run, each branch will have been published to the channel. We can check the number of messages inside a channel with the `len` built-in function, just as we would for `slices` or `maps`. Because we won't be listening to the channel, we need to build it with enough capacity to store all the messages that will be published there.

Create test file `explore_internal_test.go` and test function `TestSolver_explore`, as shown in listing 9.23. Feel free to copy these from the `internal/solver/testdata` folder in the book repository (https://mng.bz/zZqB).

Listing 9.23 `explore_internal_test.go`: Testing the `explore` function

```go
func TestSolver_explore(t *testing.T) {
    tests := map[string]struct {                    ◀──┐ Image of the test case
        inputImage string                              ◀┘
        wantSize   int                              ◀──┐ Expected number of
    }{                                                 │ branches published
        "cross": {
            inputImage: "testdata/explore_cross.png",
            wantSize:   2,
        },
        // ...
    }
    for name, tt := range tests {
        name, tt := name, tt

        t.Run(name, func(t *testing.T) {           ◀──┐ Runs all the test
            t.Parallel()                               │ cases in parallel

            maze, err := openMaze(tt.inputImage)    ◀──┐ Opening the file isn't
            require.NoError(t, err)                    │ what we're testing.

            s := &Solver{
                maze:          maze,                    ┌ Creates a channel with
                palette:       defaultPalette(),        │ capacity 3, as we expect a
                pathsToExplore: make(chan *path, 3),  ◀─┘ maximum of two messages
            }
                                                       ┌ Each of our tests has
            s.explore(&path{at: image.Point{0, 2}})  ◀─┘ the entrance at {0, 2}.

            assert.Equal(t,
                tt.wantSize, len(s.pathsToExplore))  ◀──┐ Checks the number of
        })                                              │ messages published
    }
}
```

Feel free to add more possibilities. You can also write a second test function for the cases where `len(s.pathsToExplore) > 0`, listen to all the messages, and check for the expected result. Be careful not to rely on the order of the neighbors sent by the `neighbours()` function because it's not guaranteed by the implementation. Currently, the behavior is to always continue exploring in this order of preference: above, below, right, and left. Imagine a future developer reordering the neighbors and breaking this seemingly unrelated test.

We aren't using `New` here as we want to control the size of the channel in the situation of our test because we're not reading from it. A standard `Solver` has an unbuffered channel; here, we want a buffer of three paths for all the potential candidates. We found the treasure, so now we need to show how to get there.

9.4 Show the result

We have a solution by now, printable on the terminal, but it's not exactly human friendly. The program takes a path in parameter for the output image, so writing it should present no particular traps. Don't forget, we want to show the path from the entrance to the treasure in orange.

Listing 9.24 `imagefile.go`: Saving the output image

```go
// SaveSolution saves the image as a PNG file with the solution path
// highlighted.
func (s *Solver) SaveSolution(outputPath string) (err error) {
    f, err := os.Create(outputPath)
    if err != nil {                                          // Creates the output file
        return fmt.Errorf("unable to create output image file at %s",
            outputPath)
    }
    defer func() {
        if closeErr := f.Close(); closeErr != nil {
            err = errors.Join(err, fmt.Errorf("unable to close file: %w",
                closeErr))
        }
    }()

    stepsFromTreasure := s.solution
    // Paint the path from last position (treasure) back to
    // first position (entrance).
    for stepsFromTreasure != nil {
        s.maze.Set(stepsFromTreasure.at.X, stepsFromTreasure.at.Y,
            s.palette.solution)
        stepsFromTreasure =
            stepsFromTreasure.previousStep          // Iterates over the linked
    }                                                //  list of pixels from
                                                     //  entrance to solution
    err = png.Encode(f, s.maze)                      // Encodes the image as PNG
    if err != nil {
        return fmt.Errorf("unable to write output image at %s: %w",
            outputPath, err)
    }

    return nil
}
```

There's a small piece of code that needs explaining here. We start by creating a file, which should always be followed by a defer f.Close(). However, Close() returns an error, and if we don't check the error, we lose it. So, how can we return both the error that could happen if the deferred call to Close() fails and any other error that Encode could return? If we take a close look at the signature of the method, we see that we named the output error. This allows us to override err in the deferred anonymous function and return an error that is both the error returned by Encode and the one returned by Close. Run the program on a small maze as follows:

```
> go run . mazes/maze50_50.png scl.png
2023/10/18 09:56:40 INFO Solving maze "mazes/maze50_50.png" and saving it as
"sol.png"
2023/10/18 09:56:40 INFO starting at (0,25)
2023/10/18 09:56:40 INFO Treasure found: (18,0)!
```

You should observe a new file in your project, `sol.png`, which looks somewhat like figure 9.8.

Now, try something bigger, and you'll find it still ends with a deadlock if your maze is complex enough. This happens because when one goroutine finds the solution and saves it in our `Solver` object, in the next nanoseconds, the listener stops listening to the channel, but some other explorers are still looping through their neighbors and publishing to that same channel. As soon as that channel has received as many messages as its capacity allows, writing to it causes a deadlock— and the program exits. In the next section, we'll fix this.

Figure 9.8 Example of a resolved maze that is 50 px wide

9.5   *Notify when the treasure is found*

We have a working solution that is flaky for two reasons: the most obvious one, a technical problem, is that we deadlock when we work on big enough mazes. The other and more urgent reason is a design problem; that is, we're not waiting on all of our goroutines before we end the program! Because our maze has only one solution, there's no reason for other goroutines to keep searching once we've found the treasure. Fixing the latter will solve the former: if the goroutines stop exploring, they'll stop publishing new paths to explore, the channel won't be full, and we won't have deadlocks any more.

9.5.1   *Keep track of all the goroutines*

The `listenToBranches` method, which is responsible for listening to the communication channel and starting goroutines, is the one that knows how many goroutines it started and how many are still running. This method should be keeping track of the goroutines and waiting for them to finish. The easiest way to keep track of goroutines is to use a `sync.WaitGroup`.

Add a wait group to the `listenToBranches` function. Every time a message is received, it should add one tracker to the wait group before spinning a new goroutine. That goroutine should then tell the wait group when it's work is done. We don't want to pollute the `explore` method with this logic or spread it across multiple functions, so we can make good use of an anonymous function to call both `explore` and `Done`.

Listing 9.25 `explore.go`: Stop listening to new messages

```
func (s *Solver) listenToBranches() {
    wg := sync.WaitGroup{}
```

```
    defer wg.Wait()                      ◄─── Don't leave until all
                                              goroutines are finished.
    for p := range s.pathsToExplore {
        wg.Add(1)                        ◄─── Tracks one more
        go func(path *path) {                 goroutine and starts it
            defer wg.Done()          ◄─────
            s.explore(path)                   Uses defer to make sure
        }(p)                         ◄─────── we don't finish early
        if s.solution != nil {
            return                        Protects the p variable
        }
    }
}
```

This way, we can be sure that the program will only end when all the goroutines are
finished. You might be wondering why we used an anonymous function with a parameter. The reason is both important and a bit complicated. All versions of Go, up to
1.22, suffer from the way `for` loops are handled: versions 1.21 and prior overwrite the
variable used to iterate—in our case, the `p` pointer. While this would be fine if we didn't
run concurrent activities in our loop's body, things are different here. Consider the
following piece of code:

```
for p := range s.pathsToExplore {
    wg.Add(1)
    go func() {
        defer wg.Done()
        s.explore(p)
    }()
}
```

This was equivalent to the following, as of Go 1.21:

```
var p *path
for {
    p = <-s.pathsToExplore
    wg.Add(1)
    go func() {
        defer wg.Done()
        s.explore(p)
    }()
}
```

Before Go 1.22, we had no guarantee that the value passed to the first call to explore is
the value we first read from the channel—it might have been overridden by the second
value by the time the code execution reaches `s.explore`. There are two common and
useful tricks to prevent that value from being overridden. The first one is the one we
presented earlier—by passing the pointer `p` as a parameter of our anonymous function
that starts the goroutine (rather than somewhere within the goroutine), we ensure
that it isn't overridden: the `for` loop can't read the next message from the channel as
long as the goroutine hasn't started.

The other common trick that is frequently used is to manually copy the iteration variable inside the loop. Most of the time, the name of the copy that is used is also the name of the iteration variable, which might seem strange:

```
for p := range s.pathsToExplore {
    p := p
    wg.Add(1)
    go func() {
        defer wg.Done()
        // use the local p
        s.explore(p)
    }()
    ...
```

We aren't simply replacing p by itself—here, we're sending the for loop variable to the shadow, and we make a safe copy of it that we can send to the goroutine. This trick is very commonly found when using test tables, in which we usually call t.Run() on a function that has a t.Parallel() in it.

We're now sure that our listenToBranches function won't return while some goroutines are still exploring, thanks to the call to Wait(). We don't want the explorers to reach dead ends (which they will, eventually). We also don't want them to start new goroutines at intersections—this would cost CPU and memory for no reason. It would be nice if we could kindly ask them to stop exploring as soon as we know the treasure was found.

9.5.2   *Send a quit signal*

We already have a stop-exploration condition in our explore function: the infinite for loop keeps exploring as long as the solution isn't found. But we don't like this check on solution: the field is used both to save a value and as a flag. This makes the code complex to understand and hard to refactor, and it introduces a data race. Thankfully, there's a better way to communicate between goroutines that the job is done—a channel, of course!

ADD A QUIT CHANNEL: THE SELECT KEYWORD

Let's replace the check of the solution value in the listenToBranches method. We'll be expecting the explorer that found the solution to send a message in a new channel. We want listenToBranches to read from that channel to know that it should stop launching exploration goroutines. However, our listenToBranches function is already listening to a channel, so how can it be listening to two at a time, if listening to one is blocking?

This is where the keyword select is useful in Go: it accepts several case statements (similarly to a switch), which can either be "read from a channel" or "write to a channel", and whichever is validated first gets to be executed while the others are skipped. If several case statements are eligible at the same time, Go will pick a random one.

However, most of the time, we aren't interested in only the first message received from a channel—we want to process all of them. For this, we can use the `for-select` combination, which allows us to listen to several channels at the same time. It can be seen as an extension of the `for msg := range myChannel` loop that we used to listen forever to one channel. In our case, we can replace the `for-range` loop with a `for-select` loop, which will have the same behavior:

```
for {
    select {
    case p := <-s.pathsToExplore:
        wg.Add(1)
        go func(p *path) {
            defer wg.Done()
            s.explore(p)
        }(p)
    }
}
```

`select` also accepts a `default` entry, which is mostly used when there's something other than the `select` in the infinite `for` loop.

Let's add a channel called `quit` to our `Solver` structure, which we'll use to inform `listenToBranches`, and later the explorer goroutines, that the solution was found and that it's time to stop. Because this channel won't carry any meaningful messages, we can declare it as a channel of empty structures: `chan struct{}`. Empty structures are a nice feature of Go, as they are extremely lightweight (they use 0 bytes) and quick to create or copy. We need to initialize the channel in the `New` function when creating a `Solver`:

```
quit: make(chan struct{})
```

We don't need a buffered channel, as we'll listen to it in the `listenToBranches` function. Let's see what this looks like in the following listing.

Listing 9.26 `explore.go`: **Stop listening to new messages**

```
func (s *Solver) listenToBranches() {
    wg := sync.WaitGroup{}
    defer wg.Wait()

    for {                                          Has anyone found
        select {                                   the treasure?
        case <-s.quit:              ◄──────┐
            log.Println("the treasure has been found, stopping worker")
            return
        case p := <-s.pathsToExplore:    ◄──┐ Keep exploring
            wg.Add(1)
            go func(p *path) {
                defer wg.Done()

                s.explore(p)
```

```
        } (p)
    }
  }
}
```

We're listening to the `quit` channel—but we need to write a message to this channel for it to be useful. Let's do this in the `explore` method, when we find the treasure.

Listing 9.27   `explore.go`: Notifying that the solution was found

```
func (s *Solver) explore(pathToBranch *path) {
    ...
    switch s.maze.RGBAAt(n.X, n.Y) {
    case s.palette.treasure:
        s.mutex.Lock()
        defer s.mutex.Unlock()
        if s.solution == nil {
            s.solution = &path{previousStep: pathToBranch, at: n}
            log.Printf("Treasure found at %v!", n)
            s.quit <- struct{}{}          ◄──┐
        }                                      │  Sends a message to notify
                                               │  that the treasure was found
    return
}
```

Let's run this on a few mazes to see if it works. Because we're working with goroutines, nothing is absolutely deterministic, but we did have errors on our side when running this. As soon as our goroutine listening to the new paths exits, we still have some goroutines trying to write in that channel, which is a blocking action. Some of our explorers will go into deadlock mode, trying to write to a channel that nothing reads. So far, we've just changed the way we reach the same problem, but there is hope.

To solve this, we need to make sure the explorers stop exploring as soon as the solution is found. We could read from the `quit` channel, but there's a small conundrum: we don't know how many explorers are still running at this moment. We would need to have one message per explorer goroutine if we want each explorer to quit when we find the treasure. This means we would need to broadcast a potentially huge number of messages in the `quit` channel to ensure every explorer receives its own.

But there's a more interesting way of solving this problem. We can `close` the `quit` channel. A closed channel can still be read from, but it can't be written to. A closed channel can't be reopened—it's a final action to take. The interesting part is that we can always read from a closed channel, and this will always return a value—either one that was previously written in there or the zero value of the type of messages the channel transmits if there are no written values left to read.

To know whether the value read from a channel was written there in the first place or if it's kindly returned because we're trying to read from a closed channel, we can use the second value returned by the `<-` operator:

```
msg, ok := <- myChannel
```

For our business, we don't care where the empty structure comes from because we only want to try and read from that `quit` channel. If we make sure nothing writes to this channel, the only moment when we could read from it will be when it's closed. And several goroutines can try to read from a closed channel without stealing each other's message, which means several goroutines can now know if it's time to stop working.

Let's replace the `s.quit <- struct{}{}` line with a `close(s.quit)`. This doesn't change the code in the `listenToBranches` method. Now, we need to figure out how to best use this `quit` channel when exploring.

Stop explorers

The `explore` method performs two tasks: advancing through the maze and notifying our listener of paths it doesn't explore. We want both of these tasks to be ended whenever the solution is found.

Let's start by thinking about what's happening with the `pathsToExplore` channel once the solution is found. When the `quit` channel is closed by an exploring goroutine, the `listenToBranches` function returns, which means nothing is listening to the `pathsToExplore` channel any longer, implying we can't write to that channel when the solution is found.

How do we make sure we only write there when allowed? We can't first check `quit` and then write to `pathsToExplore` because this would leave a tiny gap during which another explorer could close `quit`:

```
select {
case <-s.quit:
    log.Printf("I'm an unlucky branch, someone else found the treasure, I
give up at position %v.", pos)
    return
default:
    //A goroutine could close quit between the line above and the line below
    s.pathsToExplore <- branch
}
```

This solution isn't secure enough because of that gap. Instead, we want the same logic as we have in the `listenToBranches` method:

```
select {
case <-s.quit:
    log.Printf("I'm an unlucky branch, someone else found the treasure, I
give up at position %v.", pos)
    return
case s.pathsToExplore <- branch:
    //continue execution after the select block

}
```

In this piece of code, we first check whether `quit` is closed (it's the only case when we can read a message from it). If `quit` is closed, we return; otherwise, we publish our new branch.

It's important to note that the `select` statement in Go isn't order sensitive (unlike the `switch` statement, which prioritizes from the first to the last option). This means the order of the `case` statements of a `select` doesn't determine which one is selected first. Instead, if multiple `cases` are ready to proceed, Go will pick one at random. In our example, the `select` block ensures that we either detect the `quit` signal and stop exploring, or we send the new branch to the `pathsToExplore` channel, allowing the program to continue processing other candidates, as shown in the next listing. The `select` statement handles these cases efficiently without prioritizing one over another.

Listing 9.28   `explore.go`: Exploring only if the treasure isn't found

```
func (s *Solver) explore(pathToBranch *path) {
    // ...

    for _, candidate := range candidates[1:] {
        branch := &path{previousStep: pathToBranch, at: candidate}
        select {
        // s.quit returns a zero value only when the channel was closed
        case <-s.quit:
            log.Printf("I'm an unlucky branch, someone else found the
    treasure, I give up at position %v.", pos)
            return
        case s.pathsToExplore <- branch:
            // continue execution after the select block
        }
    }
}
```

Finally, we want to stop the exploring goroutines when the solution is found. We can do this as the first operation of our infinite loop in the explore method.

Listing 9.29   `explore.go`: First, checking if the solution was found

```
func (s *Solver) explore(pathToBranch *path) {
    for {
        // Let's first check whether we should quit.
        select {
        case <-s.quit:
            return              ◀—— Stops the exploring goroutine
        default:
            // Continue the exploration.
        }
```

It's a common pattern to dedicate a channel to communicate that everything should stop. Don't hesitate to have a look at the full method in `5_notify_treasure_` `found/5_2_send_quit_signal/explore.go` in this book's repository (https://mng .bz/KGpj).

You now have a working maze explorer, with a few known limitations. If you want to extend it, we have a few ideas for you.

9.6 *Visualization*

There are numerous ways to go further with this pocket project. One of the problems we haven't raised yet is mazes that contain loops. Imagine a maze containing the extract shown in figure 9.9.

The four X-marked spaces are paths, but they all go around a "pillar"—a piece of wall not connected to any other wall. At each intersection, a goroutine either stays close to the pillar or exits the room, but still creates a branch that explores around the room. This means that such a room would create an unlimited number of gorou-

Figure 9.9   Example of a maze with a pillar

tines, which is very harmful for our computers. We could ask for the user to provide a maze with no loops, but we could also try and handle it as part of the exploration.

Finally, we did solve the maze, but wouldn't it be nice if we could also show the intermediary steps? Here, we'll animate our progression through the maze and produce a nice GIF file of the exploration.

9.6.1 *Overcome the loop constraint*

We set ourselves a constraint in the beginning of this chapter that the maze should never have loops. If you see it as a graph, it's a tree, where each node only has one path leading to it.

If we remove that constraint, there can be multiple possible paths to the treasure. The goal of our chapter isn't to find the shortest path. To do that, we would need to keep track of the distance of each pixel to the entrance by giving it a weight, which could be achieved with increasing values of RGBA pixels. What we want to try instead in this section is just to find one of the solutions and avoid going through the same pixels multiple times.

STRATEGY

Because we don't want a goroutine to explore pixels that were previously explored—by either this goroutine or another one—we want to treat them as noncandidate neighbors of pixels being explored. For this, an easy trick is to mark them as `explored` as we explore them. First, define an `explored` value in the `palette` structure:

```
type palette struct {
    ...
    solution    color.RGBA
    explored    color.RGBA
}
```

Next, have our `defaultPalette` function return a value for this field (a different value than from the `palette.path`). Then, in the `explore` function, all we have to do is paint the pixel we're exploring, and voilà!

```go
func (s *Solver) explore(pathToBranch *path) {
    if pathToBranch == nil {
        // This is a safety net. It shouldn't be used,
        // but when it's needed, at least it's there.
        return
    }

    pos := pathToBranch.at

    for {
        s.maze.Set(pos.X, pos.Y, s.palette.explored)    ← Paints the current
        select {                                           pixel as explored
```

From now on, a pixel that was explored won't be eligible in our search for candidates because it won't be of the `s.palette.path` color. Now, let's run the program; you should see an image with the solution and the explored path colored, as shown in figure 9.10.

IMPLEMENTATION TRAPS

But wait—we're working with several goroutines, and we want each one to modify the contents of a pixel in our image—this is a door wide open for race conditions. Is this a problem in this scenario? One could argue that it isn't a problem in this case because whichever goroutine gets there first, the result will always be the same—each of the goroutines will write the same

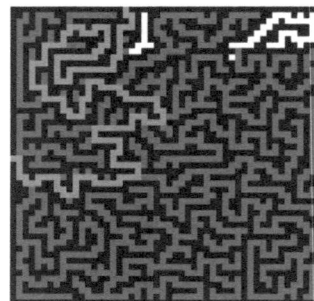

Figure 9.10   Example of a maze solved with the explored pixels colored

contents at that pixel. We're fine with any overwritten or partially written value. But this is totally wrong.

DEFINITION   Race conditions refers to undefined behavior. Avoid at all costs.

There's no such thing as a benign race condition. Even in the situation just mentioned, the same result won't occur because undefined behavior means that the memory could be corrupted somewhere else, or the code could accidentally trigger a bomb. We don't know. It's undefined. The compiler makes a lot of assumptions when turning our code into machine language, and one of these assumptions is that there's no data race.

9.6.2   *Animate the exploration*

We know our solution reaches the treasure. We have some logs that tell us which dead ends we managed to find. But this isn't very visual, and because this is a chapter about images, let's make it more fun!

The objective of this section is to generate a list of frames as we progress through the maze. Each frame should display the state of exploration at a given moment. We'll use another image format for this—a Graphics Interchange Format (GIF)—which can be used for animations (even though it wasn't the initial design). Without having to debate on the pronunciation of this format's name (at least until the audiobook version of this chapter), it's interesting to know that a GIF can contain more than a single raster frame. We can encode several frames within a single GIF file, and we can specify a duration for each of them to appear when the GIF file is displayed. These durations are expressed in hundredths of a second, as this is the closest to our screen's refresh rate a unit can be. Now that we've decided we want to show the state of the exploration, how do we do it?

ADDING FRAMES TO THE GIF

Well, first, we need to be able to keep track of the pixels we've explored so far, which is precisely what we did in section 9.5.1. Second, we need to add the frames—the image with its currently explored pixels—at specific moments of our exploration. Let's start by adding a new field to our `Solver` structure that is in charge of holding the GIF using the type from the standard library `image/gif`:

```
type Solver struct {
    ...
    animation        *gif.GIF
}
```

When do we want to take snapshots of our exploration? If we answer this question with a time unit—such as every millisecond—we might face different outputs depending on how fast the program runs on a computer. Otherwise, it could be worth considering that we want to display the status after 10 new pixels have been discovered. Although this would work, we'd face severe problems as our maze grows. Suppose our maze contains 40% of path pixels: on a 10 x 10 maze, there are about 40 path pixels to explore—which would make a 4-frame GIF. However, on a 1,000 x 1,000 maze, there would be about 400,000 pixels to explore, resulting in a 40,000-frame GIF. Such a file would, first, be very heavy, and second, if we gave each frame one hundredth of a second to be displayed, it would take more than 6 minutes, in the worst case, to display the exploration.

Instead, we can go with a different approach: let's decide that we want our final GIF to be 30 frames long if we explore the whole maze. That's an arbitrary number, but it will make for an animation that won't be too long. This means we need to print the state of exploration after (total explorable pixels) / (30 pixels) pixels were explored. We need to count all explorable pixels for our animation, so let's write a function for that in a new file, `animation.go`.

> **Listing 9.31** `animation.go`: **Counting all explorable pixels**

```
// countExplorablePixels scans the maze and counts the number
// of pixels that are not walls.
```

```
func (s *Solver) countExplorablePixels() int {          ┌─ The outer loop
    explorablePixels := 0                               │  is on rows.
    for row := 0; row < s.maze.Bounds().Dy(); row++ {  ◄─┘
        for col := 0; col < s.maze.Bounds().Dx(); col++ {  ◄──┐ The inner loop
            if s.maze.RGBAAt(col, row) != s.palette.wall {  ◄─┘ is on columns.
                explorablePixels++                      ┌─ Count path +
            }                                           │  treasure + entrance
        }
    }
    return explorablePixels
}
```

In section 9.6.1, we added an operation when we encountered a new unexplored pixel—we painted it. Here, we want to do something else when we meet a new pixel. This calls for refactoring these actions into a single method on the `Solver` structure that we can call `registerExploredPixel`. This function will paint explored pixels and, depending on how many were explored, will also add the frame to our animation. However, while painting a pixel with a color doesn't take too long, adding the frame to the animation will mean copying the whole image, which might take a long time. We don't want that copying to block any exploration process, which means we want the explorers to asynchronously send notifications that a new pixel is to be marked as registered. We wrote this method in a file named `animation.go`.

There are mostly two ways in Go to make asynchronous calls. The first one is to make the call in a goroutine:

```
go s.registerExploredPixel(pos)
```

This is a perfectly valid option, but we have to ask ourselves if race conditions could happen. Ultimately, this method will require the explicit use of a mutex. But what did we say about communication between goroutines? The answer leads to the second option, which we'll use here, to use a channel into which explorers send pixels they want registered. This approach means we'll have our `registerExploredPixel` receive pixels from a channel. There's no need for a mutex, as long as we process the pixels read from the channel one at a time. Let's add this channel to our `Solver` structure. Don't forget to initialize it in the `New` function:

```
type Solver struct {
    ...
    exploredPixels chan image.Point
    animation      *gif.GIF
}
```

The explorer's infinite `for` loop can be updated to either abort when the `quit` channel was closed because the solution was found or send a pixel for registration and continue with the exploration, as shown in the following listing.

Listing 9.32 `explore.go`: **Registering pixels as explored**

```go
func (s *Solver) explore(pathToBranch *path) {          ◄──┐  Replaces the previous
    ...                                                     │  default case
    for {
        // Let's first check whether we should quit.
        select {
        case <-s.quit:
            return
        case s.exploredPixels <- pos:                   ◄──┘
            // Continue the exploration.
        }
    }
    ...
}
```

Now we can write the function responsible for registering explored pixels, as shown in listing 9.33. To know how often we should write a new frame, we define `totalExpected-Frames` as the number of frames we want in the output GIF—let's say 30 max. We won't get exactly 30 because we won't be exploring every pixel. We then count the total number of explorable pixels and use the `for-select` pattern to keep going until we're told to quit.

Every time we receive the position of a newly explored pixel, we paint it, increment the counter of explored pixels, and paint a new frame if we reach the threshold.

Listing 9.33 `animation.go`: **Implementing** `registerExploredPixels`

```go
// registerExploredPixels registers positions as explored on the image,
// and, if we reach a threshold, adds the frame to the output GIF.
func (s *Solver) registerExploredPixels() {
    const totalExpectedFrames = 30
                                                              Checks how many
    explorablePixels := s.countExplorablePixels()   ◄──┘     pixels are explorable
    pixelsExplored := 0

    for {
        select {                   Checks whether we
        case <-s.quit:          ◄──┘ should quit first              Reads positions that
            return                                                  have been explored
        case pos := <-s.exploredPixels:                     ◄──┐
            s.maze.Set(pos.X, pos.Y, s.palette.explored)    ◄──┘ Paints explored pixels
            pixelsExplored++
            if pixelsExplored%(explorablePixels/totalExpectedFrames) == 0 {
                s.drawCurrentFrameToGIF()
            }
        }
    }
}
```

Let's now discuss the `drawCurrentFrameToGIF` method, what it does, and how we paint the frame. First, if we take a look at `go doc gif.GIF.Image`, we notice that the GIF structure uses a `slice` of paletted images. This is a compression algorithm by which each color used in the image is stored in a palette, and each pixel, instead of being encoded with the classic RGBA values, is encoded with the key of its color in the palette. Palettes usually have fewer pixels than the whole RGBA spectrum can offer, which sometimes leads to compression artifacts in resulting images.

Creating a paletted image is quite straightforward because Go has an `image/color/palette` package that only offers two palettes—`Plan9` and `WebSafe` (with a sweet mention to "early versions of Nestcape Navigator"). Here, the choice is yours. We also have to decide whether we want our GIF animation to be the same size as our initial maze or a fixed size. Using the same size as the input image is simpler, but it will make most GIFs too small or too large. Having a frame of a different size than our maze will require pixel interpolation, as we'll see in a few lines. For the purpose of this chapter, we'll go with a constant width of 500 pixels and height in the same ratio as the input image pixels for each frame:

```
const gifSize = 500
frame := image.NewPaletted(image.Rect(0, 0, gifSize, gifSize*s.maze.Bounds().
Dy()/s.maze.Bounds().Dx()), palette.Plan9)
```

Using the `image/color/palette` in our code will cause a conflict! We already have a type called `palette` in our package that defines what colors the walls and the paths should be. We can easily resolve this conflict by aliasing the import.

> **NOTE**   In Go, it's sometimes useful to alias an import. Here, we'll use `import plt "image/color/palette"`. When aliasing imports, it's best to use an alias that resembles the original package name to keep the code clear.

We've created an empty canvas, so let's draw the current state of the explored maze onto it. Unfortunately, Go's `image/draw` package doesn't allow for scaling images and therefore doesn't allow for any interpolation whatsoever. Instead, we'll have to use `golang.org/x/image/draw`, which is its more versatile version. This package offers a `golang.org/x/image/draw.Scaler` interface, which shrinks or expands a rectangle section of an input image to a rectangle section of an output image. `golang.org/x/image/draw` exposes three types that implement the `Scaler` interface: `NearestNeighbor`, `CatmullRom`, and `ApproxBiLinear`. For the purposes of this chapter, we'll stick to `NearestNeighbor`, as it's the one that won't blur our pixels' edges:

```
draw.NearestNeighbor.Scale(frame, frame.Rect, s.maze, s.maze.Bounds(),
draw.Over, nil)
```

Finally, we can add the frame to our GIF image. All three operations can be written into a single method called by `markPixelExplored`.

Listing 9.34   `animation.go`: Drawing the frame to the GIF

```
package solver

import (
```

```
        "image"
        plt "image/color/palette"                    ◀──┐  Aliases the import to avoid
                                                          │  conflict with the type palette
        "golang.org/x/image/draw"
)

// ...

// drawCurrentFrameToGIF adds the current state of the maze
// as a frame of the animation.
func (s *Solver) drawCurrentFrameToGIF() {
    const (
        // gifWidth is the width of the generated GIF.
        gifWidth = 500
        // frameDuration is the duration in hundredth of a second
        // of each frame.
        // 20 hundredths of a second per frame means 5 frames per second.
        frameDuration = 20
    )


    // Create a paletted frame that has the same ratio as the input image
    frame := image.NewPaletted(image.Rect(0, 0, gifSize,
        gifWidth*s.maze.Bounds().Dy()/s.maze.Bounds().Dx()), plt.Plan9)

    // Convert RGBA to paletted
    draw.NearestNeighbor.Scale(
        frame, frame.Rect, s.maze, s.maze.Bounds(), draw.Over, nil)

    s.animation.Image = append(s.animation.Image, frame)
    s.animation.Delay = append(s.animation.Delay, frameDuration)
}
```

We now have a single goroutine in charge of updating the values of the pixel of our image, which it does pixel by pixel, as they come through the channel. Let's not forget to start this `registerExploredPixels` method in `Solve`. We now have two "listening" goroutines we want to start—`listenToBranches` and `registerExploredPixels`. To launch both and synchronize after they've returned, we can use a `sync.WaitGroup`.

Listing 9.35 `solver.go`: Launching listeners in `Solve`

```
func (s *Solver) Solve() error {
    // ...
    log.Printf("starting at %v", entrance)

    s.pathsToExplore <- &path{previousStep: nil, at: entrance}

    wg := sync.WaitGroup{}
    wg.Add(2)
                                    ┌─  Solve won't return unless
    defer wg.Wait()            ◀──┘  both goroutines are done.
```

```
go func() {                    ┌─── One goroutine to
    defer wg.Done()        ◄───┘    register explored pixels
    // Launch the goroutine in charge of drawing the GIF image.
    s.registerExploredPixels()
}()
                               ┌─── One goroutine to
go func() {                ◄───┘    explore new branches
    defer wg.Done()
    // Listen for new paths to explore.
    // This only returns when the maze is solved.
    s.listenToBranches()
}()



    return nil
}
```

GENERATING THE GIF FILE

We've now added frames to our GIF. Each frame was copied, pixel by pixel, from the maze being explored.

Now, let's draw the GIF file. For this, we'll simply plug the call to a function writing the output animated image in our code when we know we're ready to print it. The current SaveSolution function is a good choice because it's already in charge of writing an output file. Let's call a new method in there to draw our final GIF.

Listing 9.36   `imagefile.go`: Generating the GIF file

```
func (s *Solver) SaveSolution(outputPath string) error {
    // ...
    gifPath := strings.Replace(outputPath, "png", "gif", -1)
    err = s.saveAnimation(gifPath)
    if err != nil {
        return fmt.Errorf(...)
    }

    return nil
}

// saveAnimation writes the gif file.
func (s *Solver) saveAnimation(gifPath string) error {
    outputImage, err := os.Create(gifPath)
    if err != nil {
        return fmt.Errorf(...)
    }

    defer func() {
        if closeErr := outputImage.Close(); closeErr != nil {
            // Return err and closeErr, in worst case scenario.
            err = errors.Join(err,
                fmt.Errorf("unable to close file: %w", closeErr))
```

```
        }
    }()

    log.Printf("animation contains %d frames\n", len(s.animation.Image))
    err = gif.EncodeAll(outputImage, s.animation)
    if err != nil {
        return fmt.Errorf("unable to encode gif: %w", err)
    }

    return nil
}
```

This code is very similar to that of the encoding of the PNG image. Now, let's run the program:

```
> go run . mazes/maze50_50.png solution.png
2023/10/18 11:42:57 INFO Solving maze "mazes/maze50_50.png" and saving it
as "solution.png"
2023/10/18 11:42:57 INFO starting at (0,25)
2023/10/18 11:43:00 INFO Treasure found: (18,0)!
2023/10/18 11:43:00 INFO the treasure has been found, worker going to sleep
2023/10/18 11:43:00 INFO animation contains 30 frames
```

This should generate the `solution.png` image, as well as a `solution.gif` file. Open this file to see how the maze was explored. Do you notice anything? The solution doesn't appear very clearly—if it's displayed at all—and the loop restarts immediately. It would be nice to make sure the solution is added to the list of frames and that this final frame is printed for a longer duration.

In section 9.4, we added the painting of the solution to the `SaveSolution` method. Now that we need to do something on the GIF, we might want a dedicated method for this and move the logic out of the code that writes files into the `Solver`. Let's write the final lines of code for this chapter. First, paint the pixels between the entrance and the solution in the image stored in the `Solver`, and then add a final frame (includes the painted solution pixels) to the GIF, as shown in the following listing. By setting a longer value, we ensure that the final frame will be displayed long enough to be admired.

Listing 9.37 `solver.go`: Finalizing exploration by saving the solution

```
func (s *Solver) Solve() error {
    // ...
    wg.Wait()

    s.writeLastFrame()

    return nil
}

// writeLastFrame writes the last frame of the gif,
// with the solution highlighted.
func (s *Solver) writeLastFrame() {
```

```
    stepsFromTreasure := s.solution                         Makes sure the
    // Paint the path from entrance to the treasure.        treasure is found
    for stepsFromTreasure != nil {
        s.maze.Set(stepsFromTreasure.at.X, stepsFromTreasure.at.Y,
            s.palette.solution)
        stepsFromTreasure = stepsFromTreasure.previousStep
    }
                                                      Draws the final frame of the
                                                      GIF with a longer duration
    const solutionFrameDuration = 300 // 3 seconds
    // Add the solution frame, with the coloured path, to the output gif.
    s.drawCurrentFrameToGIF()
    s.animation.Delay[len(s.animation.Delay)-1] = solutionFrameDuration
}
```

Rerun the program, and open the GIF. You can adjust the values of the frame durations or the number of frames to get the look and feel you really want. Unfortunately, we can't include the GIF in this book, but share yours with your friends!

Summary

- In computer science, the main type of 2D images are raster images and vector images.

- Vector images are used in fonts and logos, infographics, or icons. Vector images are very scalable—you can zoom in and not see any artifacts.

- The other half of the images we use are raster images—2D grids of pixels. Each pixel of an image has a color that can be expressed in the RGBA color model (but it might be encoded in another color model, such as the YCbCr, for JPEG images). The value of the color can be used to encode either physical information, such as the amount of light of red, green, and blue frequencies that is emitted by an object (as in the picture of a flower) or any numerical information (e.g., the density of population). In addition, a palette can be used to represent areas of the same category, such as in a map, where each country has its own color.

- The image/png package is used to Decode a file into an image.Image. This Image will frequently be type asserted to an RGBA or NRGBA. To encode an image, use the Encode function from the package you want to encode your image—available options are gif, jpeg, and png. Other formats require third-party libraries.

- Images usually have their pixel at position $(0, 0)$ in the upper left. However, some images might have $(0, 0)$ in any other corner. It all depends on the image format and the image metadata. Use what the image package returns to iterate over the pixels of an image.

- You can access a pixel's value in an image.Image with the .At() method. This returns a color.Color() that you have to convert to color.RGBA. When using an image.RGBA, you can use RGBAAt() instead, which will return a color.RGBA that can then be compared to known values.

- To write a pixel to an image.RGBA, use the Set(x, y, rgba) method.

- When scanning a whole image, use two nested loops—the outermost one iterating over the rows, and the innermost one iterating over the columns. This is beneficial performancewise for all scanline formats.

- When you can't have global constants, it's slightly cleaner to have a function that returns configuration values rather than using global variables. Avoid exposing global variables for safety reasons: other pieces of code might change them.

- Writing to an unbuffered channel that isn't read from is blocking. Either write to it in a goroutine, or use a buffered channel, whose size should be the maximum number of elements that will be written there before the reading starts.

- When starting goroutines in loops, make sure your loop variables are protected. The loop variables can be the messages you read from a channel, the keys or values of a `map` you iterate through, or the elements of a `slice`.

- There are three common ways of protecting iterators of a `for` loop when a goroutine is launched inside the loop:
  - Use a version of Go that guarantees that (currently, it's considered for Go 1.22).
  - Shadow the loop variable with another one in your loop (usually, we give the new variable the same name as the loop variable).
  - Launch your goroutine with an anonymous function that takes the loop variable as a parameter.

- The `select` keyword allows a piece of code to listen to several channels. Whenever a message is published in any of the channels, the code written in the `case` statement will be executed.

- If several `case` statements in a `select` are eligible, Go will pick a random one.

- It's common to have one of the `case` statements of a `select` be a return condition. This is especially true in servers, where the processing of an input request should be ended as soon as the request is canceled.

- The `for-select` infinite loop of listening pattern is very common. Usually, one of the cases of the `select` block will contain the condition to exit the loop.

Habits tracker
using gRPC

This chapter covers

- Writing a web service using Protobuf and generating the Go code of its gRPC definition
- Using the `Context` interface in Go
- Running the service with basic endpoints
- Testing with integration tests

As developers, we spend most of our work day in front of a screen, and spend leisure activity time there too. Unfortunately, the effects of a high number of hours watching these lit pixels—albeit sometimes positive for moral or psychological aspects—are mostly considered negative for eyesight, causing eye fatigue, dry eyes, or difficulty focusing. On the other hand, there are some activities that will alleviate these ophthalmic conditions—most of them include simply doing something other than watching a screen. Usually, recommendations go along the path of regularly taking a stroll, reading a book, or engaging in physical activity.

It's never easy to pick up a new habit, and no one has ever gone from never jogging to running a marathon. The goal is always achieved incrementally. But the important point is to track how much of these habits we can develop in a week, and maybe adjust objectives for the next week.

In this chapter, we'll write a service in charge of registering such habits. The user will be able to create habits, give them an expected frequency—a number of times per week they are expected to be experienced—and list them. We've already written an HTTP service, so this time we'll focus on another popular network remote procedure call protocol developed by Google: gRPC. This project has the following requirements:

- Create and delete a habit.
- List the created habits.
- Tick a created habit.
- Get the status of a habit.

Additional technical requirements include the following:

- gRPC service, with Protobuf input and output
- Run locally
- In-memory database initially

10.1 API definition

In the same vein as we did in chapter 8, we're going to create a web service to track personal habits, that is, a Go program that runs indefinitely, ready to listen to requests and respond to them. Requests are sent by clients, who need to know what to send and how to understand the response. Such a set of definitions is called an Application Programming Interface (API), which we've referred to here and there in this book. Here, the *clients* refer to users who want to track their habits. They will do it by calling the endpoints, such as `CreateHabit`, exposed on an API that we're going to build.

In this case, we want the communication between the clients and our service to use the gRPC framework, where messages are encoded using the Protocol Buffers (Protobuf) format and using the HTTP/2 network layer. Protocol Buffers are a programming language–independent description of how these messages are encoded.

Protocol Buffers (Protobuf)

Protobuf fields are used for serializing structured data. While this can also be achieved in many other ways (JSON, XML, YAML, etc.), Protobuf emphasizes two important points: versioning the serialized model and reducing any non-data information. Invented by Google in 2001 and released to the public in 2008, Protobuf is perfect for low-latency, high-speed applications, such as microservices. Protobuf is a way to describe communication between programs in a cross-language way. You can define what data is being sent via message definitions. You can also define endpoints for what is being communicated. For messages and service APIs, the endpoints are written in Protobuf files (text files with the `.proto` file extension, usually), which can then be compiled to generate clients for the programming language of your choice, as we'll explain later. Clients can be generated for many common languages, including Go.

> **(continued)**
>
> There are a few limitations, however: Protobuf messages aren't self-describing, so you need to know how to read them before you can access their contents. This also means we can't simply use regular tools such as curl to send messages to a gRPC endpoint. Testing will also be a bit trickier than with JSON APIs.

The first step in the development of a system, once we know the requirements, is generally to define the API, that is, how the system will be used. Any language can be used, as long as we know our users will use this language or that some tools can be used to generate adequate files to connect to our servers. In this section, we'll use Protobuf to declare our API. Our Protobuf files will be compiled into Go files that we can then use to implement our service. The final API will resemble the following listing, and throughout this chapter, we'll go through each step necessary to implement these endpoints.

Listing 10.1   Habits service API

```
// Habits is a service for registering and tracking habits.
type HabitsService interface {
    // CreateHabit is the endpoint that registers a habit.
    CreateHabit(CreateHabitRequest) (CreateHabitResponse, error)

    // ListHabits is the endpoint that returns all habits.
    ListHabits(ListHabitsRequest) (ListHabitsResponse, error)

    // TickHabit is the endpoint to tick a habit.
    TickHabit(TickHabitRequest) (TickHabitResponse, error)

    // GetHabitStatus is the endpoint to retrieve
    // the status of ticks of a habit.
    GetHabitStatus(GetHabitStatusRequest) (GetHabitStatusResponse, error);
}
```

10.1.1 *Protobuf declaration*

While this isn't a book about Protobuf, we need a few basics to define our API. Initialize your go module the usual way by creating a directory and running the following:

```
> go mod init learngo-pockets/habits
```

Even before creating a main.go or anything, create a folder at the root of the project, named api/proto, where we can store the Protobuf files that will have the .proto extension.

The service's job is to deal with habits, so create a file called habit.proto where we can define what a habit is. For the moment, we'll give it a name and a weekly frequency.

For example, if you want to practice Go five times a week, you want to be able to send something along these lines:

```
{"practice Go", 5}
```

HABIT ENTITY

Let's start with a minimal API definition of what a habit is. It has a name and a weekly frequency. We can write a Protobuf file with the entity.

Each `.proto` file starts with the version of the protocol, then defines a Protobuf package, and in our case, because we want to generate Go code, a `Go` package. Generated code will end up in the folder named after the package and situated inside the `go_package` module path. As usual, a piece of code will make things clearer.

Listing 10.2 `habit.proto`: **Headers of the proto file**

```
syntax = "proto3";          ◄─── Protobuf version

package habits;                         ◄─── Proto package name
option go_package = "learngo-pockets/habits/api";   ◄─┘ Go package path
```

Every structure in Protobuf is a *message*, and every field is given a number that will allow consumers to recognize it, as shown in listing 10.3. If we decide that the name is associated with 1, it will have to stay 1 forever, and future versions with different fields will still look for the name at index 1 to ensure backward compatibility.

Listing 10.3 `habit.proto`: **Defining the `Habit` message**

```
// Habit represents an objective one wants to complete
// a given number of times per week.
message Habit {                          ◄─── Defines a structure, or message
    // Name of the habit, cannot be empty
    string name = 1;                     ◄─── Field sequence starts at 1.
    // Frequency, expressed in times per week.
    int32 weekly_frequency = 2;
}
```

In a Protobuf message, each field must have a unique identifier. There's no point in leaving gaps, so just follow the incremental order. The syntax is to list each field with its type followed by its name and identifier. You can find more examples and lists of supported types here: https://protobuf.dev/programming-guides/proto3/.

Don't hesitate to be extremely verbose in your comments: this is what users will read to figure out how to use what you made, not the generated Go code. Comments in the `.proto` files will be carried over into the generated code.

SERVICE DEFINITION

Once we have this simple `Habit` object, we can declare a service to manipulate it. In another file, define a service that will use this message.

It's good practice, for version compatibility, to define a `Request` and a `Response`, even when they are empty or when they contain only one field: it makes changes smaller and avoids breaking the API. The gRPC `Habits` service is in charge of registering and tracking habits, as shown in the following listing. That is where we'll add, along the way, all the needed endpoints to track the habits.

Listing 10.4 `service.proto`: Defining the `Habits` service

```
syntax = "proto3";

package habits;
option go_package = "learngo-pockets/habits/api";      ◄────┤ Same headers

// Habits is a service for registering and tracking habits.
service Habits {                                        ◄─────┐
}                                                            ├ New service
```

FIRST ENDPOINT: CREATE

This service exposes nothing, as you can see. The first endpoint that we need is for creating a habit to track.

A generally accepted best practice when naming inputs and outputs of endpoints is to have a dedicated message (a structure with fields) for each of them, called `request` and `response`, or `input` and `output`, even when they are empty or contain only one field. Consider the difference between these two signatures:

```
func CreateHabit(Habit)
func CreateHabit(CreateHabitRequest) CreateHabitResponse
```

In the first case, we give a habit and expect nothing in return—simple. In the second case, we need to define two additional structures, and it's verbose and annoying. The first one will just contain a `Habit` field, and the other will be empty, so what's the point? The point is version intercompatibility. Let's say, in the next version, we want to add a user token to identify which user is creating the habit, and then return a habit identifier. In the more verbose case, we would just add a field in each structure, and if it isn't mandatory, any code written for the initial version will still work. In the first and straightforward case, however, we would break the whole API.

For this reason, the `CreateHabit` endpoint will use its `Request` and `Response`. You might wonder what happens in the case of errors: Why wouldn't they appear in the Protobuf API? The answer is that the gRPC compilation tool will be in charge of adding support for errors. This support differs from language to language—in Go, we can have several returned values, whereas in C++ or Java, the error needs to be returned differently, which means we don't write errors in the `.proto` file. Don't panic, though, the

Golang interface compiled from this Protobuf will allow us to return an error. We can add the endpoint to the service with one line and then define two new messages.

Listing 10.5 `service.proto: CreateHabit` **endpoint**

```
service Habits {
    // CreateHabit is the endpoint that registers a habit.
    rpc CreateHabit(
        CreateHabitRequest
    ) returns (CreateHabitResponse);
}
```

Don't forget the semicolon.

To use the `Habit` message in the response, we need to import the neighboring file, as shown in listing 10.6. We could write the request structure and the service definition in the same file—but knowing how to import a `.proto` file is useful.

Listing 10.6 `service.proto: Request and response`

```
import "habit.proto";

service Habits {
    ...
}

// CreateHabitRequest is the message sent to create a habit.
message CreateHabitRequest {
    // Name of the new habit. Cannot be empty.
    string name = 1;
    // Frequency of the new habit. Will default to once per week.
    optional int32 weekly_frequency = 2;
}

// CreateHabitResponse is the response of the create endpoint.
message CreateHabitResponse {
    Habit habit = 1;
}
```

Imports file using the relative path

Marks the field as optional

We're done. In a handful of lines, we have an API for the first step of the tracker, which is the creation of a habit. As you can see, there's no path and no verb: they are specific to HTTP. gRPC doesn't use them. Because we want to use it in Go, now is the time to generate the Go code.

10.1.2 Code generation

Generating code from Protobuf files is done using `protoc`, which is the Protobuf compiler. We'll also install two plugins: `protoc-gen-go` and `protoc-gen-go-grpc`. We'll cover the installation steps, but they are also provided at https://mng.bz/MDz7.

INSTALLATION STEPS

Depending on your system, installing `protoc` might be achievable simply through a package management tool such as Homebrew's `brew` (on Mac) or `apt` (on Linux). Unfortunately, there are a few more steps when installing it on Windows. Here are the commands you can run from a terminal:

```
> apt install -y protobuf-compiler #Linux
> brew install protobuf #Mac
```

Once `protoc` is installed, getting the Golang-specific dependencies is made easy by the fact that we can ask Go to do it:

```
> go install google.golang.org/protobuf/cmd/protoc-gen-go@latest
> go install google.golang.org/grpc/cmd/protoc-gen-go-grpc@latest
```

These two utilities are used to compile `.proto` files declaring messages and services into Golang files. They work as plugins for `protoc`, and they will be called if `protoc` detects we want to compile Golang files.

COMPILATION

The compilation command is pretty long. We'll try to decompose it step by step. In your favorite terminal, navigate to the root of the go module, and try the very minimal version:

```
> protoc api/proto/habit.proto
```

The compiler complains because it needs output directives regarding what language to generate the compiled files in and where. The `go_out` parameter will tell the compiler both the requested output language and the location for compiled files by specifying the target folder. By specifying this option, we also tell `protoc` to use the `protoc-gen-go` plugin:

```
> protoc --go_out=api/ api/proto/habit.proto
```

This generates a `Habit` structure, but it puts the structure in an impractical location: the whole module tree is created all over again:

```
> tree
.
├── api
│   ├── learngo-pockets
│   │   └── habits
│   │       └── api
│   │           └── habit.pb.go
│   └── proto
│       ├── habit.proto
│       └── service.proto
├── go.mod
└── go.sum
```

That's not what we want; we want the Go file to appear directly in the api folder. Fortunately, there's an option for that: `--go_opt=paths=source_relative`, as shown here:

```
> protoc --go_out=api/ --go_opt=paths=source_relative
    api/proto/habit.proto
```

Now the tree looks like what we want. The last step is to compile all the .proto files, not just habit.proto:

```
> protoc --go_out=api/ --go_opt=paths=source_relative api/proto/*.proto
```

It doesn't work. The compiler is taking each file separately and generating a Go file for it. When it reaches service.proto, it can't import Habit because we never told it where to look.

The -I option has the following documentation if you run protoc --help: "Specify the directory in which to search for imports. May be specified multiple times; directories will be searched in order. If not given, the current working directory is used." This is perfect for our needs:

```
> protoc -I=api/proto/ --go_out=api/ --go_opt=paths=source_relative
    api/proto/*.proto
```

Once you've run this command, your tree should look like this:

```
> tree
.
├── api
│   ├── habit.pb.go
│   ├── proto
│   │   ├── habit.proto
│   │   └── service.proto
│   └── service.pb.go
├── go.mod
└── go.sum
```

All the messages exist as Go structures, but not the service yet. We also need to generate the gRPC part.

The options are quite similar to the pure Go ones: go-grpc_out and go-grpc_opt. Passing these options on the command line will silently tell protoc to use the protoc -gen-go-grpc plugin:

```
> protoc -I=api/proto/ --go_out=api/ --go_opt=paths=source_relative
    --go-grpc_out=api/ --go-grpc_opt=paths=source_relative
    api/proto/*.proto
```

There's one final parameter that we must talk about when it comes to the Go gRPC compiler, and this has to do with forward compatibility. Suppose that we're happy with the current .proto API, that we use it to compile the Golang files, and that we implement the server interface with a structure of our own. Then, let's assume we want to add a new endpoint—we'll have to update the .proto file and regenerate the Golang files. As mentioned on the go-grpc repository, "It is a requirement that adding methods to a service can't break existing implementations of the service." So, how did they ensure this requirement is always met?

There are two options. The first one is to require that any implementation of the server embeds a type defined in the generated file. The other is to allow for the developers to not implement the required server interface. While this second option isn't recommended, it's still available by passing another parameter to the command line:

```
--go-grpc_opt=paths=source_relative,require_unimplemented_servers=false
```

In the rest of this chapter, we'll use files that were generated without this final option, and we'll remind you to embed the type when creating the server type.

AUTOMATED GENERATION

Remember to put this massive command in a place where you and future maintainers will find it, typically in a Makefile or as part of a script. You might wonder why we wouldn't place this in a generate.go file containing only a //go:generate directive (writing this is a nice trick to keep up our sleeve). The reason is that we were lazy in our command line and used a * to send all the .proto files to protoc. Unfortunately, while shells understand the string *.proto as every file with a proto expansion, go generate doesn't, which prevents us from using the same command line directly in a //go:generate directive. However, if you have access to bash or sh, or any other shell you fancy, you can tell go generate to run a command in a shell with the following syntax (don't forget the double quotation marks around the command that you really want to run):

```
//go:generate bash -c "protoc -I=api/proto/ {...} api/proto/*.proto"
```

We provided an example of a generate.go (a common name for files that only contain //go:generate directives) file that contains a similar command. We slightly adapted it because we placed it directly into the api directory. It's up to you to decide whether you want a target in your Makefile or if you'd rather call go generate to produce these files.

Make sure to document it, like everything that isn't considered general knowledge in the industry. Your tree should now look something like this:

```
> tree
.
├── api
│   ├── proto
│   │   ├── habit.proto
│   │   └── service.proto
```

```
|    ├── generate.go
|    ├── habit.pb.go
|    ├── service_grpc.pb.go
|    └── service.pb.go
├── go.mod
└── go.sum
```

Ready to start coding in Go? Let's get to it.

10.2 Empty service

Now that we have an API exposing the create-habit endpoint for our user, we can write the code and make it run. We'll first create an empty service, make it run, and then add the endpoints. After that will come the data layer, and, finally, integration tests, and we'll be ready to start again with more functionalities.

10.2.1 Creating a small logger

A logger is often the first package that is written in a module, as it will likely be used by every other package. But loggers can sometimes be problematic—they'll write to whatever output we tell them to write to. Sometimes, this causes problems, for instance: Should the log messages always be printed when testing? And to what output? In this section, we'll implement a small logger that will make it easier for us to both run and test our code with logs.

Notice that the `testing.T` structure already implements a `(t *T) Logf(format string, args ...any)` method that will only print what we called it with when the current test fails. To be able to use a logger in our code and in our tests, let's write a small logger that will only expose one method—the same as exposed by `testing.T`, as shown in the following listing. This way, we'll be able to create loggers in our code and inject the `t` test variable in tests as the test logger. This will prevent output jamming.

Listing 10.7 `log/log.go`: Defining a small logger

```go
package log

import (
    "io"
    "log"
    "sync"
)

// A Logger that can log messages
type Logger struct {
    mutex  sync.Mutex            ◀─────  We don't know if writing to
    logger *log.Logger                   the output is concurrency
}                                         safe, so we enforce it.

// New returns a logger.
func New(output io.Writer) *Logger {
    return &Logger{
```

```
        logger: log.New(output, "", log.Ldate|log.Ltime),
    }
}
```

Adds some niceties to
the default log package

```
// Logf sends a message to the log if the severity is high enough.
func (l *Logger) Logf(format string, args ...any) {
    l.mutex.Lock()
    defer l.mutex.Unlock()
    l.logger.Printf(format, args...)
}
```

Now that we have our basic logger, we can start implementing the server package. We'll
need this logger in each of our packages.

10.2.2 *Server structure*

First, we create a structure that will be our server. It wouldn't make sense if our server
structure were to stay empty for long; it will soon contain a repository for data retention.

In a new folder named `internal/server`, create a `server.go` file, and add the struct
with a `New` function. As we'll want to use a logger, let's declare a one-method interface
that we'll use as our logger.

Listing 10.8   `server.go`: Defining the web service

```
// Server is the implementation of the gRPC server.
type Server struct {
    lgr Logger
}
```

Uses the local interface

```
// New returns a Server that can ListenAndServe.
func New(lgr Logger) *Server {
    return &Server{
        lgr: lgr,
    }
}
```

Injects the logger
dependency

```
type Logger interface {
    Logf(format string, args ...any)
}
```

Next, we need to add a `ListenAndServe` method on the `Server`, so that it can start
listening to and serving new requests sent on a given port. Ports are virtual "doors"
through which messages transfer, either internally or with the rest of the world, so that
only one application can listen to a given port on the same machine. Ports are identified with their port number—80 is used by HTTP, 443 by HTTPS, and so on. When
listening to a specific port, either use one that is assigned by a standard, such as 80 for
HTTP, or use a port number between 1024 and 49151 for internal usage.

A gRPC server, just like the HTTP server we saw in chapter 8, is first and foremost a
good listener. We give it a port to listen to, and start it with a call to `Serve`. This call will
only return when the server shuts down.

But a gRPC server is a bit more than a HTTP server—it must implement the desired gRPC API. For this, we start by creating a barren server using the `grpc` package, and we then attach our implementation to that server by registering it with the generated `RegisterHabitsServer` function of the `api` package, as shown in the next listing. Registering a server associates a specific service implementation to a generic gRPC server.

Listing 10.9 `server.go`: **Listening to a given port**

```
import (
    ...
    "google.golang.org/grpc"

    "learngo-pockets/habits/api"
)

// ListenAndServe starts listening to the port and serving requests.
func (s *Server) ListenAndServe(port int) error {
    const addr = "127.0.0.1"

    listener, err := net.Listen("tcp",
        net.JoinHostPort(addr, strconv.Itoa(port)))        ◀── Uses the given port with TCP
    if err != nil {
        return fmt.Errorf("unable to listen to tcp port %d: %w", port, err)
    }
    grpcServer := grpc.NewServer()                          ◀── Creates a standard gRPC server
    api.RegisterHabitsServer(grpcServer, s)                 ◀── Registers our methods in it

    s.lgr.Logf("starting server on port %d\n", port)

    err = grpcServer.Serve(listener)                        ◀── Starts listening
    if err != nil {
        return fmt.Errorf("error while listening: %w", err)
    }

    // Stop or GracefulStop was called, no reason to be alarmed.
    return nil
}
```

There are better ways of starting the server to support graceful shutdown. We'll improve this later in the chapter. Additionally, if you want to allocate a free port randomly, you can use port `0`. The documentation of `net.Listen` explains which networks are supported.

Wait—this doesn't compile. We can't register a `HabitService` that doesn't know how to create a habit. As you can see, `api.RegisterHabitsServer` takes as a second parameter anything that implements the `HabitServer` interface, which was generated from our Protobuf service. We just need to implement that one method.

When trying to compile or run, we also faced an error mentioning that our `Server` type can't be registered as a `HabitsServer` because it doesn't implement a method named `mustEmbedUnimplementedHabitsServer`. This is a reminder that when we generated the Go files from the .proto files, we used the recommended way, which requires embedding a structure, as the non-implemented method's name suggests. So, let's embed the required type:

```
// Server is the implementation of the gRPC server.
type Server struct {
    api.UnimplementedHabitsServer
    lgr Logger
}
```

Composition and embedding

Both the composition and embedding concepts extend the notion of a structure, but in a different way. While composition, which in Go is achieved by listing named fields of a structure, represents a "has-a" relationship between two types, embedding corresponds to an "is-a" relationship.

In our case, our server is an `UnimplementedHabitsServer`, so it has an implementation for that required method. You can read more on the Go dev blog (https://go.dev/doc/effective_go#embedding).

As we know that this method will require tests and probably side functions, we can already put it in a create.go file in the server package. The signature of this function was generated by the protoc toolchain; we can't alter it. In the following listing, there's a mysterious first parameter, which we'll dive into later in section 10.3.

Listing 10.10   create.go: Implement the HabitServer interface

```
// CreateHabit is the endpoint that registers a habit.
func (s *Server) CreateHabit(
    _ context.Context,                        Ignores the
    request *api.CreateHabitRequest           context for now
) (*api.CreateHabitResponse, error) {
    s.lgr.Logf("CreateHabit request received: %s", request)

    return &api.CreateHabitResponse{
        Habit: &api.Habit{},                  For now, returns
    }, nil                                    an empty response
}
```

This should be enough for now. We'll come back to it very quickly. Our endpoint's scaffolding is implemented—our whole gRPC layer is implemented. It's now time to spin up the service.

10.2.3 Creating and running the server

We can call these New and ListenAndServe functions in main. As this is a web service, we prefer to put the main.go file in a cmd/habits-server folder, decluttering the root of the module. On some operating systems, such as Windows, `go run dir/main.go` will cause an executable file called `dir.exe` to be generated and executed, so placing the `main.go` file in an aptly named directory is important in that regard.

The `main` function creates a new instance of our server and calls `ListenAndServe`, which only returns if there's an error. Because we need to inject a logger into our server instance, we can create it in the `main` function and pass it via `server.New`. We can use that logger in the main function too. The following listing shows how we create a new server in our `main` package and run it.

Listing 10.11 `main.go`: **Running it**

```
package main

import
    "fmt"
    "os"

    "learngo-pockets/habits/internal/server"
    "learngo-pockets/habits/log"
)

const port = 28710                    Declares a port in
                                      range 1024–49151

func main() {
    lgr := log.New(os.Stdout)         Sets the new
                                      logger output

    srv := server.New(lgr)            Creates a new server

    err := srv.ListenAndServe(port)          Runs the server
    if err != nil {
        lgr.Logf("Error while running the server: %s", err.Error())
        os.Exit(1)
    }                                 Exits with an error code
}
```

There's basically no logic inside the `main` function. This means that our service will be easier to test because all the logic is in isolated packages. Run it as follows:

```
> go run cmd/habits-server/main.go
```

It does absolutely nothing, but it runs, which is wonderful! Add a few logs in `Listen-AndServe` to make sure.

10.3 *First endpoint: Create*

We have a running gRPC server that implements the desired API. We might want to go a step beyond and have our endpoint do something other than print a pretty message. This is, after all, chapter 10.

Before we start coding, let's do a bit of thinking. The compiled code, generated from the Protobuf files, has defined a `Habit` structure. Should we reuse that structure or define a new one? The answer is quite straightforward here: it's always best to not leak protocol definitions into the core business code because it will create problems when we start to add support for other protocols, such as XML or JSON. These data definitions that are used only for describing protocols are called data transfer objects (DTOs). Instead, our core business code, often called "domain" or "model," should have types for every entity that needs to be handled internally. Let's look at a clean target architecture in figure 10.1.

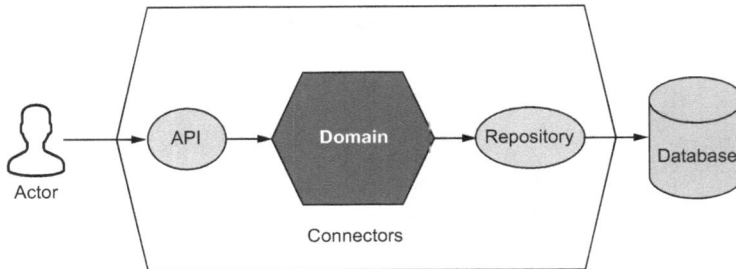

Figure 10.1   **Architectural diagram with domain and connectors**

For the same reasons that we saw in chapter 8, the Go structures representing the transferable data, here the generated code, must be capable of evolving independently from the rest of the code.

10.3.1 *Business layer*

In chapter 8, we created a `session` package with our logic. Create an `internal/habit` folder where we can define our domain `Habit` and the types that it needs, as shown in listing 10.12. We want to keep the data that was received as input but also remember when the habit was created and give it an ID to find it again. These fields aren't part of the input message—we're able to add them here because we're not reusing the API structure.

```
// ID is the identifier of the Habit.
type ID string

// Name is a short string that represents the name of a Habit.
type Name string

// WeeklyFrequency is the number of times a Habit should happen every week.
type WeeklyFrequency uint

// Habit to track.
type Habit struct {
```

```
ID              ID
Name            Name
WeeklyFrequency WeeklyFrequency        Fields internal
CreationTime    time.Time             to the domain
}
```

It's always good to create a specific type for each of the fields in our main entity, even though the usage might seem more verbose: functions and methods will take typed arguments that will serve as documentation and make the API clearer. For example, if a function takes the name and the ID, and both are strings, it's quite easy to mix them up. On the other hand, if one is explicitly an ID and the other explicitly a name, casting the name into an ID type should raise a red flag to the developer writing the call.

REQUIREMENT: CREATE A HABIT

If we look at the requirements, the first thing we need to do is create a `Habit`. We defined some optional values in the Protobuf documentation, meaning that we must complete the fields if needed. First, we must determine if input validation is the job of the API layer or the domain layer. Both solutions make sense for different reasons. We decided that if some new feature needs to create a habit inside our service, it will call the domain directly, and we want this `NewHabit` to always return a valid entity. We can't rely on the API layer to always send what the domain needs.

> **TIP** If you're in a situation where validation on the API layer makes more sense, there are a few libraries out there, such as the package validator at https://github.com/go-playground/validator, that can do it for you with a few tags.

What if the input is invalid? Just like HTTP, gRPC uses different status codes, as shown in table 10.1, to make sense of the response defined by the RPC API. These codes are included in the error that is returned alongside the response, by the endpoint.

Table 10.1   A few gRPC status codes

Code	Number	Description
OK	0	This isn't an error; it's returned on success.
INVALID_ARGUMENT	3	The client specified an invalid argument.
NOT_FOUND	5	Some requested entity (e.g., file or directory) wasn't found.
PERMISSION_DENIED	7	The caller doesn't have permission to execute the specified operation.
UNIMPLEMENTED	12	The operation isn't implemented or isn't supported/enabled in this service.
INTERNAL	13	An unspecified error occurred while processing the request.

These are only a few; the rest, with deeper explanations, can be found in the official documentation. You can run `go doc google.golang.org/grpc/codes` to get the list.

Well, that's not exactly true because go doc limits its output, which causes only the first few codes to be printed. To get the whole list, run the following:

```
> go doc --all google.golang.org/grpc/codes
```

With these codes in mind, we know that any invalid input will return a code 3 (INVALID_ ARGUMENT). The business layer certainly shouldn't be in charge of returning such a code 3. Returning this code is the role of the API layer—the domain layer isn't even aware that we're implementing a gRPC server—and it needs to know what happened inside the domain layer. This is the perfect occasion to use a typed error.

VALIDATE WITH TYPED ERROR

Let's start with the validateAndComplete function in a new create.go file dedicated to this business logic, as shown in listing 10.13. It must check that the name isn't empty, set the frequency to 1 if empty, and also fill up the two internal fields. Arguably, it could be two functions: validate and complete.

Listing 10.13   `internal/habit/create.go`: **Validate/complete entity**

```
// validateAndCompleteHabit fills the habit with values that we want in
// our database.
// Returns InvalidInputError.                            ← Tells readers what to
func validateAndCompleteHabit(h Habit) (Habit, error) {     expect from your function
    // name cannot be empty
    h.Name = Name(strings.TrimSpace(string(h.Name)))    ← A row of spaces
    if h.Name == "" {                                      is invalid too.
        return Habit{}, InvalidInputError{               ← Returns a
            field: "name", reason: "cannot be empty"}      structured error
    }

    if h.WeeklyFrequency == 0 {
        h.WeeklyFrequency = 1                            ← Defaults to 1
    }

    if h.ID == "" {
        h.ID = ID(uuid.NewString())                      ← A new unique ID
    }

    if h.CreationTime.Equal(time.Time{}) {
        h.CreationTime = time.Now()
    }

    return h, nil
}
```

We now need to define this typed error, in a new errors.go file in the habit package.

Listing 10.14   `errors.go`: **Typed error for invalid input**

```
// InvalidInputError is returned when user-input data is invalid.
type InvalidInputError struct {
```

```
    field  string
    reason string
}
```
← **A short description of why the provided value is invalid**

```
// Error implements error.
func (e InvalidInputError) Error() string {
    return fmt.Sprintf("invalid input in field %s: %s", e.field, e.reason)
}
```

We could expose the given value of the field too: it's very useful when we get an error to know what the server actually got, as it differs from what we think we sent more often than we care to admit. But this error will be logged and copied around, and malevolent users could send in gigabytes of data and crash our system. There are some ways to avoid this (limiting the size of requests, truncating logs, etc.), but for now, let's just avoid logging the field.

TESTING THE VALIDATION

We can already write an easy unit test for this `validateAndComplete` function. There's no need to mock any dependency—what a pleasure!

When writing this test, we found out that each test case had very different assertions, so we chose to write a named function for each. You can write several independent `TestXxx` functions or group them inside a single one with an explicit name.

Listing 10.15 `create_internal_test.go`: Testing `completeHabit`

```go
func Test_validateAndFillDetails(t *testing.T) {
    t.Parallel()

    t.Run("Full", testValidateAndFillDetailsFull)
    t.Run("Partial", testValidateAndFillDetailsPartial)
    t.Run("SpaceName", testValidateAndFillDetailsSpaceName)
}
```

The first function, `testValidateAndFillDetailsFull`, checks that if the habit is complete, nothing is changed:

```go
func testValidateAndFillDetailsFull(t *testing.T) {
    t.Parallel()

    h := Habit{/* all fields are filled */}

    got, err := validateAndCompleteHabit(h)
    require.NoError(t, err)
    assert.Equal(t, h, got)
}
```

The second function checks that if the habit is incomplete, ID and creation time are filled up, and the rest didn't change. Each run of the test will give us different values, so we're only certain that these fields are at least using the NotEmpty function. If you want to be more thorough, you can check that the ID follows a given format using regular expressions and that the time is within the past second or so:

```
func testValidateAndFillDetailsPartial(t *testing.T) {
    t.Parallel()

    h := Habit{/* only Name and Freq */}

    got, err := validateAndCompleteHabit(h)
    require.NoError(t, err)
    assert.Equal(t, h.Name, got.Name)
    assert.Equal(t, h.WeeklyFrequency, got.WeeklyFrequency)
    assert.NotEmpty(t, got.ID)
    assert.NotEmpty(t, got.CreationTime)
}
```

Then, we check the name. If we send only spaces, we should get an InvalidInput-Error. At this point in the development, the exact content of the error might still change, so we just focus on the type:

```
func testValidateAndFillDetailsSpaceName(t *testing.T) {
    t.Parallel()

    h := Habit{Name:"    "}

    _, err := validateAndCompleteHabit(h)
    assert.ErrorAs(t, err, &InvalidInputError{})
}
```

That's good. Run the test to make sure you're happy about your coverage.

Now, let's call the endpoint. The Create function in the business (or domain) layer will fill the habit and be ready to save it to a data storage.

Listing 10.16   create.go: Business function to create a habit

```
// Create validates the Habit, saves it and returns it.
func Create(_ context.Context, h Habit) (Habit, error) {
    h, err := validateAndFillDetails(h)
    if err != nil {
        return err          ◄──┐ Wraps it if you want
    }                          └ some context

    // Need to add the habit to data storage...

    return h, nil
}
```

You can already write a closed-box test for this one, or at least the structure for the test. We added a context as the first parameter, but we've ignored it until now. Why? The answer to this is quite simple, and we'll explain it fully in section 10.6. For now, let's provide a `context.Context` variable, which, in Go, is almost always called `ctx`.

10.3.2 *API layer*

Now that we've implemented the validation in the domain layer, let's move back to the server package and update the `CreateHabit` method on the server structure, as shown in listing 10.17. This is the gRPC layer, where we transform an API-specific signature into domain objects, call the domain function, and transform the response back into API-specific types.

Listing 10.17 `create.go`: **API layer**

```
// CreateHabit is the endpoint that registers a habit.
func (s *Server) CreateHabit(ctx context.Context,
    request *api.CreateHabitRequest) (*api.CreateHabitResponse, error) {
    var freq uint
    if request.WeeklyFrequency != nil {          ◄─── Initializes with
        freq = uint(*request.WeeklyFrequency)          default value 0
    }

    h := habit.Habit{
        Name:            habit.Name(request.Name),
        WeeklyFrequency: habit.WeeklyFrequency(freq),
    }

    createdHabit, err := habit.Create(ctx, h)
    if err != nil {
        ...
    }

    s.lgr.Logf("Habit %s successfully registered", createdHabit.ID)

    return &api.CreateHabitResponse{
        Habit: &api.Habit{
            Id:              string(createdHabit.ID),
            Name:            string(createdHabit.Name),
            WeeklyFrequency: int32(createdHabit.WeeklyFrequency),
        },
    }, nil          ◄─── Doesn't return {...}, status.Error(codes.OK,
}                        "everything went fine")
```

If we want the default value of a habit's frequency to be `1`, why are we setting the `freq` to `0` (by using Go's default value) when it's absent? We decided that this default value was a business requirement and not an API definition. It's arguable and can only be decided on a case-by-case basis. Imagine what you expect if you call the domain method with an empty frequency from somewhere other than the API layer, and act accordingly.

How do we manage the error returned by the domain layer? We made sure that if the error is caused by a bad input, it will have a specific type. We can use `errors.As` to cast it into the `InvalidInputError` type and check whether we should return a code `3`. To be perfectly honest, we could use errors.Is instead because we're not using any field or method specific to the type InvalidInputError, but we chose to show you how As can be used.

But what if we receive something that isn't an InvalidInputError? After all, our future implementation of the endpoint logic might have to face database calls, which could cause errors that wouldn't be due to an input message validation.

A rule of thumb to remember when implementing a gRPC endpoint is that every return statement should either return a nil error or an error built from the status. Error function (or Errorf). The status package is a neighbor of the codes package: google.golang.org/grpc/status. When in doubt about which error code we should return, the default choice is codes.Internal, as shown in the following listing.

> **Listing 10.18   create.go: Error management**

```
got, err := habit.Create(ctx, h)
if err != nil {
    var invalidErr habit.InvalidInputError
    if errors.As(err, &invalidErr) {
        return nil, status.Error(codes.InvalidArgument, invalidErr.Error())
    }
    // other error
    return nil, status.Errorf(codes.Internal, "cannot save habit %v: %s",
        h, err.Error())
}
```

When a service ends up having several endpoints, checking the error and outputting the appropriate status code can be factored in a single function, toAPIErrorf(err error, format string, args ...any). Feel free to implement it when the need arises.

Now it's time to test our server manually. The tool we used in chapter 8 to call our service, curl, only does HTTP calls, but it has a cousin, grpcurl, which does the same job. There are alternative options to grpcurl—many providing a GUI, but this one is the one we find most convenient. If you fancy a nice GUI, Postman supports gRPC and has been able to send Protobuf messages to servers since version 10.

First, start your server with go run cmd/main.go. Next, you can install grpcurl with the following command:

```
> go install github.com/fullstorydev/grpcurl/cmd/grpcurl@latest
```

Now, we can start using the tool to send requests to our server. There's a major difference between curl and grpcurl: the format of the message was, for curl, a regular JSON document, whereas for grpcurl, we need to provide a valid Protobuf entity. If you remember the beginning of this chapter, Protocol Buffers have indexed fields, which means the message we'll send via grpcurl will need to be properly written, with its fields in the correct positions. There are two options for us here—we can either provide the Protobuf definition to `grpcurl` or have it ask for that definition from the server. The second option is called *reflection*, and we won't be using it here. Reflection adds a small overhead to our server—something that usually we don't want to ship to production.

To tell `grpcurl` how to structure our query (and understand the response), we simply pass it the `.proto` files with the `-proto` parameter—we'll give it the `service.proto` file, as this is where the definition of the endpoints lie. Because some of the files include other files, we need to specify the root from which they refer via the `-import-path` parameter. Finally, we need to tell which endpoint we want to aim at. This is passed as the final parameter of the request in the form of `{package}.{service}/{endpoint}`. Here's the command line that we're able to run:

```
> grpcurl \
    -import-path /.../learngo-pockets/habits/api/proto/ \   ← Absolute path to the proto directory
    -proto service.proto \                                  ← File declaring the service
    -plaintext -d '{"name":"clean the kitchen"}' \          ← Provides the request in JSON format
    localhost:28710 \                                       ← Host and port where the server runs
    habits.Habits/CreateHabit                               ← Target endpoint
```

If everything went fine, you should receive a response from the server (formatted in JSON). Does it contain an ID field? Is the weekly frequency set? Did you also try with an "invalid" name for the habit?

Check the server's output—it should be logging a message every time a request is received. If your tests are conclusive, it's time to do a bit more than logging in our endpoint!

10.3.3 *Data retention*

The service tells its clients that it can create habits, but it doesn't store them. We need to fix that. There are several options for data retention—the most common one being using a database. Appendix G shows how to connect to a database.

REPOSITORY PACKAGE

For the first version, we can use the same kind of in-memory repository that we used for games in chapter 8 in a package called `internal/repository`. It has the same drawbacks of being unscalable and likely soon unstable, but it gives us something quickly, so it's OK for a proof of concept.

Write a `Repository` structure with a `New` function that builds it and initializes its `map` of data. Similar to the `New` function of the `server` package, we want to inject a `Logger` in here too. For now, we'll need one `Create` method on the `Repository` type, but soon we'll want to add `List`, which will return all the contents of our database.

If you've followed us through nine chapters, you should be able to create the package; expose the right functions, structures, and methods; and of course cover them with some tests. Don't forget to add a mutex to lock the data when reading and writing on the repository storage:

```
> go doc
package repository // import "learngo-pockets/habits/internal/repository"

Package repository accesses the habits data.

type Error string
type Logger {...}
type HabitRepository struct{ ... }
    func New(lgr Logger) *HabitRepository

> go doc HabitRepository
package repository // import "."

type HabitRepository struct {
        // Has unexported fields.
}
    HabitRepository holds all the current habits.

func New(lgr Logger) *HabitRepository
func (hr *HabitRepository) Create(_ context.Context, habit habit.Habit) error
func (hr *HabitRepository) ListAll(_ context.Context) ([]habit.Habit, error)
```

By having a `context.Context` parameter in each of our methods, we anticipated that when we replace this with a real database, we'll need a `context` to stop looking for data when a client interrupts the call. If you need it, remember that an example of the code can be found in the book's repository (https://mng.bz/nRj2).

DEPENDENCY INJECTION

We didn't really test this `repository` package. The main reason here is that all we do in this package is write to a `map` and list all values of a `map`. We can add the call to `Add` inside the domain function.

We've implemented the API-to-domain connection in the server package, but we lack the right-hand calls. For that, we need the server to have an instance of the `Repository` connector, and we need the domain's `Create` function to expect a small interface with `Add` in it.

Let's first inject a repository dependency to the server, as shown in listing 10.19. But why don't we simply call `repository.New()` in the server, rather than doing it in the `main` function? As we'll see, this makes tests a lot simpler than having to rely on a hardcoded implementation of that dependency. This is one of Go's best usages of its lightweight interfaces. We're using an interface here so that tests for the server can use mocks.

```go
// Server is the implementation of the grpc server.
type Server struct {
    db  Repository
    lgr Logger
}

type Repository interface {                                    Use the smallest possible
    Add(ctx context.Context, habit habit.Habit) error          interface we need.
    FindAll(ctx context.Context) ([]habit.Habit, error)
}

// New returns a Server that can Listen.
func New(repo Repository, lgr Logger) *Server {
    return &Server{
        db:  repo,
        lgr: lgr,
    }
}
```

First, Update the `main` function to comply with this new signature of `New`. We need to pass an entity that implements the interface, such as the output of `repository` `.New(...)`.

Second, the `Create` endpoint on the domain needs to take an interface as parameter (see listing 10.20) for stubbing and mocking purposes as well as to reduce the scope of problems. By using an interface with only the `Add` method, we ensure that `Create` can't use any other future method and mess with the logic. Imagine you observe in your logs that calls to `FindEverything` are messing with the performance of the service. You know by seeing this interface that the culprit isn't `Create`, and you can move on.

```go
type habitCreator interface {
    Add(ctx context.Context, habit Habit) error
}

// Create adds a habit into the DB.
func Create(ctx context.Context, db habitCreator, h Habit) (Habit, error) {
    h, err := validateAndCompleteHabit(h)
    if err != nil {
        return Habit{}, err
    }

    err = db.Add(ctx, h)
    if err != nil {
        return Habit{}, fmt.Errorf("cannot save habit: %w", err)
    }

    return h, nil
}
```

Can you see in the logs that your call goes all the way to the database? Let's write a couple of tests to ensure we properly catch the errors. For this, we'll start with a simple stub, as we did in chapter 6, to implement the `habitCreator` interface.

But how can we update the tests of `Create` to make sure that `Add` is properly called? That's what we're going to see in the next section.

10.4 Unit testing with generated mocks

In the preceding chapters, you've seen how to write your own stubs when the interface is small enough and the logic is simple. There are a few libraries out there capable of taking an interface and generating mocks for you.

> **DEFINITION** Stubbing and mocking are two very common ways of making use of an interface for tests. While *stubbing* consists of writing a structure that implements the interface and returns hardcoded values, to test the behavior of your code when the stubbed dependencies returns this or that, *mocking* adds a check of how many times each dependency was called and if it was done with the correct parameters.

10.4.1 Generate mocks

The best known libraries are `mockgen`, `mockify`, and `minimock`. They are based on different design decisions, so feel free to pick your favorite. In our example, we chose `minimock` because it provides mocked functions with typed parameters. Install `minimock` with the following:

```
> go install github.com/gojuno/minimock/v3/cmd/minimock@latest
```

Because the mocks are generated, this is a perfect occasion to use the `go:generate` syntax. Pick an interface, for example, `habitCreator`, and add the following line right before the interface's declaration:

```
//go:generate minimock -i habitCreator -s "_mock.go" -o "mocks"
type habitCreator interface {
    ...
```

We're asking `minimock` to generate a mock for the interface (`-i`) `habitCreator` in a file with a specific suffix (`-s`) and in a specific output folder (`-o`). You need to create that folder before you can continue: from the root of the module, it will be `internal/habit/mocks`. In your favorite terminal, navigate to the `habit` package and run the following:

```
> go generate .
```

Alternatively, you can navigate to the root of the module and run all the generate commands in the project with

```
> go generate ./...
```

You can see that a new file has appeared in the `mocks` folder. Check the contents with
go doc:

```
> go doc internal/habit/mocks
package mocks // import "learngo-pockets/habits/internal/habit/mocks"

type HabitCreatorMock struct{ ... }
    func NewHabitCreatorMock(t minimock.Tester) *HabitCreatorMock
type HabitCreatorMockAddExpectation struct{ ... }
type HabitCreatorMockAddParams struct{ ... }
type HabitCreatorMockAddResults struct{ ... }
```

10.4.2 *Use the mocks*

The closed-box test for `Create` doesn't compile anymore, so let's fix it. First, there are
two imports that we need to add. One is pretty obvious, but the second calls for a little
explanation:

```
import (
    // ...
    "learngo-pockets/habits/internal/habit/mocks"
    "github.com/gojuno/minimock/v3"
)
```

The first import is here to access the mocks we just generated. The second, on the
other hand, is about the `minimock` library.

If you pay extremely close attention, you'll realize that the second import's path ends
with `/v3`. Are we really importing a package named `v3`? This would be a very strange
name for a package.

Versioning modules in Go

Sometimes, a module needs to go through heavy changes that make the new version
incompatible with the previous one. Interrupting the backward compatibility of a module requires a version change. When this happens, the `go.mod` file should be updated
to reflect the version: the first line of minimock's `go.mod` is `module github.com/`
`gojuno/minimock/v3`.

Users who want to use `minimock` (or any other versioned module) have to remember
to specify the version they want to use in the import path, right after the name of the
module, for instance: `import "github.com/jackc/pgx/v5"` and `import "github`
`.com/jackc/pgx/v5/pgxpool"`. When using functions or types defined in these
packages, ignore the "/v5" part: `pgx.Connect(...)` or `pgxpool.New(...)`.

We need to use the `minimock` library because the generated code doens't contain
enough tools. In fact, the generated `mocks` package exposes a `NewHabitCreator(...)`

function, which returns the type we want—HabitCreatorMock, an implementation of the habitCreator interface. But this function's parameter is of type *minimock .Controller. Don't worry, there's no other package to import.

Next, we can now define a function that builds a mock for each of the test cases. It takes a controller and returns a mocked instance of the required interface, habit-Creator, as shown in listing 10.21. The test case structure will hold a new field whose type is a function—to be honest, if you look at the test with error cases that we have in the book's repository (https://mng.bz/8OYz), you'll see that it would be far easier to read if we had written it as two separate functions, but we wanted to show you how functions can make your life better as fields of a test case struct.

The controller is created at the start of the test, and it can be shared by all the test cases. In addition, if your version of minimock is recent enough (v3.3.0), it automatically registers a check at the end of the test to ensure each expected call was met with an actual call. In the nominal test case, or happy flow, the mock should take the input habit, previously declared as a variable called h, and return no error.

Listing 10.21   create_test.go: Adding a mock function to each test case

```
tests := map[string]struct {
    db            func(
        *minimock.Controller) *mocks.HabitCreatorMock
    expectedErr error
}{
    "nominal": {
        db: func(ctl *minimock.Controller) *mocks.HabitCreatorMock {
            db := mocks.NewHabitCreatorMock(ctl)
            db.AddMock.Expect(ctx, h).Return(nil)      ◄── Registers the
            return db                                       expected call
        },
        expectedErr: nil,
    },
}
```

Finally, we can plug this into the TestCreate function.

Listing 10.22   create_test.go: Using the mock when testing

```
t.Run(name, func(t *testing.T) {
    t.Parallel()

    ctrl := minimock.NewController(t)
    defer ctrl.Finish()          ◄── Versions >= 3.3.0 of minimock
                                     no longer require this line.
    db := tt.db(ctrl)

    got, err := habit.Create(ctx, db, h)
    assert.ErrorIs(t, err, tt.expectedErr)
    if tt.expectedErr == nil {
```

```
        assert.Equal(t, h.Name, got.Name)
    }

}
```

The code runs and succeeds. You can commit to make sure you don't forget this state, before playing around with the mocks. For example, what happens if you comment out the call to `Add`? Your test should tell you.

You can also read the documentation of the `mocks` package and how the `minimock` tool can best be used to define your favorite style. There's one more way of testing that is perfect for this kind of CRUD (create, read, update, and delete) service: integration testing.

10.5 Integration testing

Whereas unit tests focus on one function, integration tests will check the behavior of the entire service with scenarios. Here are example scenarios for our service:

- *Scenario 1: Add and list*
  a Add a habit: walk in the forest three times a week
  b Add a habit: water the plants twice a week
  c List the habits: check the two habits that we get
  d Add a habit: read a book five times a week
  e List the habits: check the three habits that we get
- *Scenario 2: Add and delete*
  a Add a habit: walk in the forest three times a week
  b List the habits: check the one habit that we got
  c Add a habit: no name, expected error with code 3
  d Add a habit: water the plants twice a week
  e List the habits: check the two habits that we got
  f Remove the first habit
  g List the habits: check that we still have the second

And there can be many more scenarios, of course. Some people will intertwine this with API testing; others will separate testing the flows from testing the gRPC response for each endpoint's error cases. To test an entire flow, we need to be able to list the habits that we saved. Then, we'll write the first scenario.

10.5.1 List habits

Adding an endpoint requires a few additions, but it should be quick enough. Follow these steps:

1 Update the Protobuf file with a `ListHabits` endpoint, as shown in listing 10.23. This way, you can already publish the interface for the rest of your team to use and mock.

Listing 10.23   `service.proto`: Adding the list endpoint

```
// Habits is a service for registering and tracking habits.
service Habits {
  // CreateHabit is the endpoint that registers a habit.
  rpc CreateHabit(CreateHabitRequest) returns (CreateHabitResponse);

  // ListHabits is the endpoint that returns all habits.
  rpc ListHabits(ListHabitsRequest) returns (ListHabitsResponse);
}

// ListHabitsRequest is the request to list all the habits saved.
message ListHabitsRequest {
}
```
This request has no parameter.

```
// ListHabitsResponse is the response with all the saved habits.
message ListHabitsResponse {
  repeated Habit habits = 1;
}
```
This is how arrays are represented in Protobuf.

From there you can regenerate the corresponding Go files with the following:

```
> go generate ./...
```

2 Add the logic in the domain layer, following the pattern of `internal/habit/`
   `create.go`, as shown in listing 10.24. Don't forget to use a tiny interface for the
   database, generate a mock for it, and test thoroughly. Note that it isn't always necessary to have a mock framework to test. An alternative to using a simple function
   replacing the database behavior is to have a structure holding the output content
   you want to mock and have the database call returning it.

Listing 10.24   `list_test.go`: Testing list without `minimock`

```
// MockList is a mock for FindAll method response.
type MockList struct {
    Items []habit.Habit
    Err    error
}
```
The database call output to mock: list of habits and the error

```
// FindAll is a mock which returns the passed list of items and error.
func (list Mocklist) FindAll(context.Context) ([]habit.Habit, error)
{
    return list.Items, list.Err
}

func TestListHabits(t *testing.T) {
    // TODO: Write the needed content for the tests cases

        "empty": {
            db:            MockList{
                Items: nil, Err: nil},
            expectedErr:    nil,
```
Fills the expected output from the database call to the FindAll method

```
                    expectedHabits: nil,
            },
            "2 items": {
                    db:             MockList{Items: habits, Err: nil},
                    expectedErr:    nil,
                    expectedHabits: habits,
            },
            "error case": {
                    db:             MockList{Items: nil, Err: dbErr},
                    expectedErr:    dbErr,
                    expectedHabits: nil,
            },
    }

    for name, tc := range tests {
        name, tc := name, tc

        t.Run(name, func(t *testing.T) {
            t.Parallel()

            got, err := habit.ListHabits(
                context.Background(), tc.db)         ◁─┐ Calls the mocked
            assert.ErrorIs(t, err, tc.expectedErr)       database interface
            assert.ElementsMatch(t, tc.expectedHabits, got)
        })
    }
}
```

3 If you don't have one already, write the repository function that lists all the saved habits, as shown in the next listing. The repository should return a deterministic list of habits, sorted using a specific criterion, such as the creation date of the habits.

Listing 10.25 `memory.go`: Deterministic output of habits

```
// FindAll returns all habits sorted by creation time.
func (hr *HabitRepository) FindAll(
    _ context.Context) ([]habit.Habit, error) {
    log.Infof("Listing habits, sorted by creation time...")

    // Lock the reading and the writing of the habits.
    hr.mutex.Lock()
    defer hr.mutex.Unlock()

    habits := make([]habit.Habit, 0)
    for _, h := range hr.habits {                  Inline implementation
        habits = append(habits, h)                 of sorting habits by
    }                                              creation time

    // Ensure the output is deterministic by sorting the habits.
    sort.Slice(habits, func(i, j int) bool {       ◁─
        return habits[i].CreationTime.Before(habits[j].CreationTime)
    })

    return habits, nil
}
```

4 Add the `ListHabits` method to the service, following the pattern of `internal/server/create.go`. Isolate the transformation of the generated structure into the domain structure in a separate function, and unit test it too. We decided that a repository containing no habits shouldn't be a problem and return an error, but feel free to make a different choice here. In addition, think about determinism: If the repository contains two elements, should they always be returned in the same order by the endpoint? Determinism is very important, and we can only recommend enforcing it wherever possible. Testing deterministic endpoints is a lot simpler than testing nondeterministic endpoints!

5 Test manually with `grpcurl` or a similar tool.

Now that you trust that this new endpoint works the way you expect, we can write an integration test.

10.5.2   *Integration with go test*

We want to write a test that will go through every layer of the service, all the way to the network outside of it. Considering that our database is currently a hacky in-memory thing, there's no point in mocking it, but when we finally use a real database system, it will be necessary to either mock it or run an instance locally. This test will run the service for real and call it as any client would.

RUN A SERVICE

First, create a test file as `internal/server/integration_test.go`, and add a `Test-Integration` function in the file, as shown in listing 10.26. There are several places an integration test file can be stored, but because we're testing the API of the server, we placed the file close to it.

First, we create a gRPC server instance and register it—something similar to what we already have in the `main` function. Second, we create a listener, and by giving an empty string as the address parameter, we ask it to find a free port on the host and use it. Third, we run that server in a parallel thread so that the rest of the test can keep running and calls can be made to it. Of course, we need the server to stop at the end of the test, whenever that is.

If we need to write any utility functions, we can start their implementation with `t.Helper()`. This will tell the Go test suite to ignore this layer when an error is surfaced.

Listing 10.26   `integration_test.go`: Starting the service

```
func TestIntegration(t *testing.T) {
    grpcServ := newServer(t)
    listener, err := net.Listen("tcp", "")
    require.NoError(t, err)

    wg := sync.WaitGroup{}
    wg.Add(1)
    go func() {
        defer wg.Done()
```

```
            err = grpcServ.Serve(listener)
            require.NoError(t, err)
    }()
    defer func() {
        // terminate the GRPC server
        grpcServ.Stop()
        // when that is done, and no error were caught, we can end this test
        wg.Wait()
    }()
}
```

> Using a WaitGroup ensures the goroutine has checked for any error returned by the Serve method.

```
func newServer(t *testing.T) *grpc.Server {
    t.Helper()
    s := server.New(repository.New(t), t)

    grpcServer := grpc.NewServer(
        grpc.UnaryInterceptor(timerInterceptor(s.lgr)))
    api.RegisterHabitsServer(grpcServer, s)
    reflection.Register(grpcServer)

    return grpcServer
}
```

> Skips this func when printing test details

> t has a Logf method, so it implements server.Logger and repository.Logger.

The server is running, so a client can enter the scene. We'll take care of that next.

CREATE A CLIENT

A client must know which address to send its requests to and the shape of the server (what the endpoints are). We create a function to build that new client, and it takes the address as a parameter, as shown in listing 10.27.

Note that we need to pass some credentials to connect to the server. The grpc library kindly offers a function that generates credentials that disable Transport Layer Security (TLS). While this is usually a security breach, we're running our server in a very restricted environment, and we can accept not having to pass credentials. Depending on which network the request will be sent through, you might have to use credentials, or you might be able to use the insecure package to generate some for you.

> Listing 10.27 `integration_test.go`: **Creating a client**

```
func TestIntegration(t *testing.T) {
    ...
    // create client
    habitsCli, err := newClient(t, listener.Addr().String())
    require.NoError(t, err)
}

func newClient(t *testing.T, serverAddress string) (api.HabitsClient, error){
    t.Helper()
    creds := grpc.WithTransportCredentials(
        insecure.NewCredentials()
    )
    conn, err := grpc.Dial(serverAddress, creds)
```

> Insecure means "no TLS."

```
    if err != nil {
        return nil, err
    }

    return api.NewHabitsClient(conn), nil
}
```

The scene is set. Let's start the scenario.

RUN SCENARIO

As we're only testing two endpoints, we can create a function for the happy path for each of them. Then, we create an error path function for `CreateHabit` because `ListHabits` never returns a business error.

Listing 10.28 shows an example with the endpoint listing habits, which is the trickier of the pair, as it returns generated IDs whose value will change at every run. So, we overwrite the `Id` field after checking that it has been filled.

Listing 10.28   `integration_test.go`: Function to list a `Habit`

```go
func listHabitsMatches(
    t *testing.T, habitsCli api.HabitsClient, expected []*api.Habit) {
    list, err := habitsCli.ListHabits(
        context.Background(), &api.ListHabitsRequest{})
    require.NoError(t, err)


    for i := range list.Habits {
        assert.NotEqual(t, "", list.Habits[i].Id)    ◄─── This field's value was
        list.Habits[i].Id = ""                              randomly generated.
    }                                                       We only want to ensure
    assert.Equal(t, list.Habits, expected)    ◄───         that it's not empty.
}
                                              Use ElementsMatch for
                                              nondeterministic endpoints, and
                                              use Equal for deterministic ones.
```

Consider the option of basing your integration test on a struct that holds the client as a field and can hold methods that wrap calls to the client to make your test easier to read. We decided to use functions only, but all of them will start with the same two arguments, which can become very verbose—usually a cue for refactoring. With this kind of helper functions, the scenario can look fairly readable.

Listing 10.29   `integration_test.go`: Scenario in the code

```go
// add 2 habits
addHabit(t, habitsCli, nil, "walk in the forest")
addHabit(t, habitsCli, ptr(3), "read a few pages")
addHabitWithError(t, habitsCli, 5, "         ", codes.InvalidArgument)

// check that the 2 habits are present
listHabitsMatches(t, habitsCli, []*api.Habit{...})
```

```
// ...

func ptr(i int32) *int32 {
    return &i
}

func addHabit(t *testing.T, habitsCli api.HabitsClient,
    freq *int32, name string) {
    _, err := habitsCli.CreateHabit(context.Background(),
        &api.CreateHabitRequest{
            Name:            name,
            WeeklyFrequency: freq,
        })
    require.NoError(t, err)
}
```

Make sure you isolate your different scenarios so that they can run in parallel—you can even run that many instances of the server in parallel, one for each integration scenario. You can also use this opportunity to play with concurrency and call Add a large number of times concurrently to check for performance.

USING TEST.SHORT TO ONLY RUN LIGHTWEIGHT TESTS

So far, our test resembles any other unit test that we've written, except that it's called an integration test. Sometimes, these integration tests can be quite intense because they go through lots of features and cases, they include some benchmarks, or they run some load or performance tests. These tests usually take quite some time, and it isn't advised to include them in continuous integration (CI) toolchains, as they might slow down the delivery process. For instance, it could be a requirement to have "light" tests run on pull requests but "heavy" tests run on tagging and image building. The go test ./... command accepts a -short flag. Setting this flag in the command line will change the output of the testing.Short() function, which we can invoke in any test. Let's start our TestIntegration with a check on that flag:

```
func TestIntegration(t *testing.T) {
    // Skip this test when running lightweight suites
    if testing.Short() {
        t.Skip()
    }

    grpcServ := newServer(t)
```

Now, let's take a look at the output of go test -v ./.... Using the -v flag makes the output verbose and lists each test function called. The output should contain Test-Integration as follows:

```
> go test -v ./...
...
ok      learngo-pockets/habits/internal/habit    1.004s
=== RUN   TestIntegration
```

```
              create.go:17: Create request received: name:"walk in the forest"
...
--- PASS: TestIntegration (0.00s)
...
```

Let's try the same, but this time with the short flag: `go test -v -short ./...`. This time, the output should explicitly indicate that `TestIntegration` was skipped:

```
> go test -v -short ./...
...
ok      learngo-pockets/habits/internal/habit    1.004s
=== RUN   TestIntegration
    integration_test.go:23:
--- SKIP: TestIntegration (0.00s)
...
```

We now have a way of running only the lightweight tests in our CI pipelines. When running a more expensive or consuming one, check for that `-short` flag. Its presence should be an indicator that we want a quick result.

So far, we've been using our own in-memory database, which we trust. If that database were to be unavailable, we'd have serious problems in our server because the server and the database are part of the same program. But most of the time, the database is a remote entity, one that could behave erratically due to network problems, external load, or lots of other pesky bugs. Even worse, what if our own query crashes that database? We already handle the case when the database returns an error, but what if it doesn't answer our query? How long should we wait before realizing something is wrong?

10.6   *Getting the best out of the context*

When relying on remote services, a good practice is usually to allow the callee to provide a response within a specific time frame. There are two ways of expressing a time limit—either by providing a timeout, just like *Mission Impossible*'s "This message will self-destruct in 5 seconds," or by providing a deadline, "You have until Friday, 11 A.M." The choice of which one to use depends on the activity being performed, but the former is more common than the latter when it comes to calls to remote network entities.

10.6.1   *What is a context?*

Earlier in the chapter, we mentioned but didn't define what a `Context` really is; it's now time to run `go doc context.Context` to find out. As we can read there, the purpose of a `Context` is to carry around deadlines, cancellation signals, and values across API boundaries. The documentation also tells us that a `Context` is an interface with the following methods:

- `Value(key any) any`
- `Deadline() (deadline time.Time, ok bool)`

- `Done() <-chan struct{}`
- `Err() error`

Before we go any further, it's important to note that even though `context.Context` is an interface, it's one of the few that you should never need to implement.

The `Value` method available on a `Context` is here to implement the "carrying values across API boundaries" requirement. While a `Context` can be seen as key-value storage, we highly recommend you don't think of it that way. If you place important values inside `Context`, then it's not clearly visible anymore what input different functions require. It's better to only stick to sending noncritical data, such as monitoring identifiers or requesting identifiers in the `Context`. Business values shouldn't be passed via the `Context`. If you're thinking of this as an option, we recommend going for an alternative. We'll see an example in section 10.6.3 of how to use the `Context`'s storage feature.

The `Deadline` method returns whether and when a `Context`'s deadline is set. The deadline is the time when the `Context` will start saying it's reached its expiration date to whomever might ask.

The `Done` method returns a channel that will be closed when the `Context` has reached its end. Calling `Done()` is simpler than comparing `Deadline()` with `time.Now()`, so this is usually done.

Finally, the `Err` method returns an error describing why the channel returned by `Done` is closed, or `nil` if it isn't closed yet. Now, let's take a look at how to create `Context`s.

10.6.2 Create a context

Golang's `context` package offers several functions that allow for the creation of a `Context`. They are mostly divided into two categories: those that create a child `Context` from a parent one, and those that spring a `Context` out of the blue.

This latter set contains only `context.Background()` and `context.TODO()`. We recommend always creating your application's `Context` in your `main` function and then passing it around to any dependency that might need it. Create it with the `Background` method, and try to avoid calling `TODO`. Overall, your application should have a single parent `Context`.

Now that we've got a `Context`, we can create children. They can come in a variety of shapes, but the main difference lies in how we want to set their `Deadline` property. We can call `WithDeadline` to provide a specific timestamp at which time the child will be canceled, or `WithTimeout` if we want to specify how long a `Context` should "live." The second option is by far the most common when it comes to making calls to remote services.

Most of the time, however, a function will receive a `Context` as one of its parameters. There's a silent convention to always provide the `Context` as the first parameter of a call to a function—and, just as we usually name the errors `err`, we similarly very often call our `Context`s `ctx`. When a function receives a `Context`, it shouldn't try to create a new one with `Background()` or `TODO()`. In our gRPC generated code, we can observe that the endpoints' signatures all start with an incoming `Context`—that's the one we should be using.

While it might seem repetitive to always have to pass the `Context` as a parameter, we strongly encourage you to resist the urge to use composition to save a `Context` into a variable.

10.6.3 *Using a context*

In which scenario should we create a child `Context`, though? Why not provide the parent `Context`? After all, it might have a deadline itself. The answer relates to good practices in coding and controlling with precision every call that is made across your network. If a service needs to call two other services to answer a request, we want to know which of these two is taking an awfully long time to return a response, if any. To achieve this, each remote call must be using its own `Context` with its own deadline. Depending on your application, a timeout value can range between 10 ms and some days. Don't be too strict, and be sure to take into account network latency.

Let's consider an example with our database and say we want to ensure that the repository call in our `Create` endpoint doesn't take too long. In listing 10.30, we show how to do this by creating a `Context` with a timeout of 100 ms, before we call our repository.

Listing 10.30   `create.go`: Adding a context around the db call

```go
// Create adds a habit into the DB.
func Create(ctx context.Context, db habitCreator, h Habit) (Habit, error) {
    h, err := validateAndCompleteHabit(h)
    if err != nil {
        return Habit{}, err
    }

    dbCtx, cancel := context.WithTimeout(
        ctx, 100*time.Millisecond)
    defer cancel()
    err = db.Add(dbCtx, h)
    if err != nil {
        return Habit{}, fmt.Errorf("cannot save habit: %w", err)
    }

    return h, nil
}
```

Annotations:
- Always reuse the parent context.
- Makes sure we clean up after ourselves
- Don't forget to use the new context.

If we run this, everything works fine, but it's not tested, and we should test it. It's even worse than not tested—it actually breaks our existing tests! If you remember, we're using mocks, and mocks are very strict about what they expect. Our tests didn't worry too much about the `Context`—after all, we didn't fiddle with it so far. But now, the `Context` used to call `Add` in the `Create` endpoint isn't the `Background` one any more. We should update the test, but to provide the exact same `Context`, we need to know exactly when the deadline is to be able to expect it properly.

Many mocking libraries face this problem at some point. `Minimock` has decided to expose a `minimock.AnyContext` variable that will match any `context.Context` variable. Some other mocking libraries go a step beyond and propose a `mock.Anything` variable that can be used as a wildcard for any input parameter. We only need to use the `Context`, so we'll limit ourselves to this option.

Listing 10.31 `create_test.go`: **Mocking the child** `context`

```
func TestCreate(t *testing.T) {
    // ...
    "nominal": {
        db: func(ctl *minimock.Controller) *mocks.HabitCreatorMock {
            db := mocks.NewHabitCreatorMock(ctl)
            db.AddMock.Expect(minimock.AnyContext, h).
                Return(nil)
            return db
        },
        expectedErr: nil,
    },
    "error case": {
        db: func(ctl *minimock.Controller) *mocks.HabitCreatorMock {
            db := mocks.NewHabitCreatorMock(ctl)
            db.AddMock.Expect(minimock.AnyContext, h).
                Return(dbErr)
            return db
        },
        expectedErr: dbErr,
    },
```

Replace the ctx with the minimock variable.

While this fixes the current tests, it doesn't test the current feature of having a timeout on our database call. For this, we'll need to improve our mock.

As you now know, a `Context` is something that can reach its deadline, and, when this happens, the channel returned by `Done()` is closed, which means reading from this channel starts returning a zero value instead of being a blocking call. This is how applications check for a canceled/expired timeout. The following piece of code is present in various forms in most libraries that handle timeouts:

```
select {
// Read from channel used by backend to communicate response
case response := <-responseChan:
    return response, nil
// Check for deadline
case <-ctx.Done():
    return nil, ctx.Err()
}
```

In this `select`, whichever happens first causes the function to return—either we received a response, or the deadline was met. The line `case <- ctx.Done():` appears more than 60 times in the standard library alone, and it's always followed by returning the cause of the deadline via `ctx.Err()`.

Go 1.23 introduced functions that create a `Context` and that can cancel it with a "cause," that is, a specific error. For instance, we now have a `context .WithTimeoutCause(parent Context, timeout time.Duration, cause error)` function. Calling `ctx.Err()` on these is quite ambiguous: Do we expect the `context .DeadlineExceeded` error to be returned, or do we expect the `cause` error we provided to `WithTimeoutCause`? To answer this, Go 1.23 provided a new function : `context .Cause(ctx context.Context)`. If no cause was set, this returns the usual error causing the `Context` to be canceled; however, if a cause was provided, that cause is returned by this function. Overall, we recommend using `context.Cause(ctx)` over `ctx.Err()`.

Let's add a test that implements this logic. For this, we can't use `Expect`, as this immediately returns the specified values. Instead, we'll have to overwrite the behavior of the `Add` method, which `minimock` allows with the `Set` method.

Listing 10.32   `create_test.go`: Testing the timeout

```go
func TestCreate(t *testing.T) {
    // ...
    "db timeout": {
        db: func(ctl *minimock.Controller) *mocks.HabitCreatorMock {
            db := mocks.NewHabitCreatorMock(ctl)
            db.AddMock.Set(
                func(ctx context.Context, habit habit.Habit) error {
                    select {
                    // This tick is longer than a database call
                    case <-time.Tick(2 * time.Second):
                        return nil
                    case <-ctx.Done():
                        return ctx.Err()
                    }
                })
            return db
        },
        expectedErr: context.DeadlineExceeded,
    },
},
```

This error is returned when a context reaches its deadline.

So, as we've seen, `Context`s can be used to detect unexpectedly long remote calls. Some functions allow you to register key-value pairs inside a `Context`, but we recommend keeping that option as a last resort. The main reason is that a `context.Context` is only an interface that allows for the retrieval of values via a `Value` method, which means each network protocol might implement their own version of a `context.Context`. These versions will usually expose a way of adding a key-value pair into the `Context`. To achieve this purpose, the standard `context` package offers `subCtx := context.With- Value(ctx, key, value)`. Instead, let's resume our habits server, and implement the final endpoint—one that allows us to keep track of what we do on a weekly basis.

10.7   *Track your habits*

Congratulations, at this point of the chapter, you know all the basics about gRPC in Go! This next section is a guided exercise where you'll prove your autonomy and test your aggregated knowledge. If you struggle with anything here, you can find all the code in the repository (https://mng.bz/EaBd).

First, let's quickly reset the final goal of this pocket project and define what tracking a habit means. We can create a list of habits with a target of weekly frequency, tick a habit when we achieve it, and retrieve the current status so that we can plan the rest of the week. You'll be able to answer questions like these: Am I done for the week? Should I block a time slot to go for a walk? To do this, we'll build the following scenario:

1 Create several habits.
2 List the created habits.
3 Tick the habits that you achieve.
4 Get the status of the habits.

We're missing the bricks to fulfill steps 3 and 4, so let's go for the implementation. On the API, we'll need two new endpoints: `TickHabit` and `GetHabitStatus`.

10.7.1 *Tick a habit*

Let's define a new endpoint `TickHabit` on the Protobuf side with its associated request and response, as shown in the following listing. Don't forget to regenerate the Go library!

Listing 10.33 `service.proto`: `TickHabit` **definition**

```
    // TickHabit is the endpoint to tick a habit.
    rpc TickHabit(TickHabitRequest) returns (TickHabitResponse);
...

// TickHabitRequest holds the identifier of a habit to tick it.
message TickHabitRequest {
    // The identifier of the habit we want to tick.
    string habit_id = 1;
}

// TickHabitRequest is the response to TickHabit endpoint.
// Currently empty but open to grow.
message TickHabitResponse {          ◄─── Nothing yet, but having a message
}                                         makes it easier to evolve
```

Then, add the implementation on the server with the following signature:

```
TickHabit(ctx context.Context, request *api.TickHabitRequest)
    (*api.TickHabitResponse, error)
```

Because ticks and habits are different concepts, we store them in different tables in a SQL database. In our memory implementation, we'll store the ticks in a structure of their own, next to the habits. If we develop a UI, this will allow us to retrieve only the list of habits or the full status of a habit for a week.

10.7.2 *Store ticks per week*

This is the same logic that we used previously for the habits in memory; the only tricky part is the data definition. We want to store all the ticks for each habit grouped by week, so we can get a weekly status. The built-in Go library package provides a very useful method named `ISOWeek()` that returns the ISO 8601 year and week number in which that time occurs. Running `go doc time.ISOWeek` returns the following:

```
func (t Time) ISOWeek() (year, week int)
```

We'll use `ISOWeek` in our code. Let's create a new package called `isoweek` and a new file where we'll define an `ISO8601` structure holding a `Year` and a `Week`.

Listing 10.34 `isoweek/isoweek.go`: `ISO8681` **structure**

```
package isoweek

// ISO8601 holds the number of the week and the year.
type ISO8601 struct {
    Year int
    Week int
}
```

It's now easy to define the data storage type in `Repository`. To retrieve the status of a habit for the current week, our storage will store a `map` for each habit ID of the `isoweek` with its associated events, which are timestamps:

```
storage map[habit.ID]map[isoweek.ISO8681][]time.Time
```

For more readability, we chose to have a custom type called `ticksPerWeek`, which is a `map` holding all the timestamps per ISO week. It will now be very easy to retrieve the status of a habit at the current time. If you want to extend the project, you can even have an endpoint retrieve the status for a given week or date. Let's add a new type of storage to `HabitRepository` and rename `db` into `habits` to be more explicit.

Listing 10.35 `repository/memory.go`: `ticks` **storage**

```
// ticksPerWeek holds all the timestamps for a given week number.
type ticksPerWeek map[isoweek.ISO8601][]time.Time

// HabitRepository holds all the current habits.
type HabitRepository struct {
    habits map[habit.ID]habit.Habit          ◀── Refactors db field into habits
    ticks  map[habit.ID]ticksPerWeek         ◀── Adds a new storage for ticks
}
```

Do you feel confident in creating the needed methods? Let's not anticipate and create only the Add for the moment. All the logic of ISO8601 computation is done in a dedicated function, so if we pass it directly as a parameter, it will be easy to reuse over the other endpoints and tests:

```
AddTick(_ context.Context, id habit.ID, t time.Time) error
```

Don't forget to verify whether the habit and the ISOWeek exist in the storage before inserting a new tick. As shown in the following listing, the full implementation of Tick on the domain side should now be ready!

Listing 10.36 habit/tick.go: Tick implementation

```go
package habit

import (
    "context"
    "fmt"
    "time"
)

//go:generate minimock -i habitFinder -s "_mock.go" -o "mocks"
type habitFinder interface {
    Find(ctx context.Context, id ID) (Habit, error)
}

//go:generate minimock -i tickAdder -s "_mock.go" -o "mocks"
type tickAdder interface {
    AddTick(ctx context.Context, id ID, t time.Time) error
}

// Tick inserts a new tick for a habit.
func Tick(ctx context.Context, habitDB habitFinder, tickDB tickAdder, id ID,
    t time.Time) error {
    // Check if the habit exists.
    _, err := habitDB.Find(ctx, id)           // Checks that the habit
    if err != nil {                            // exists in the repository
        return fmt.Errorf("cannot find habit %q: %w", id, err)
    }

    // AddTick adds a new tick for the habit.
    err = tickDB.AddTick(ctx, id, t)
    if err != nil {
        return fmt.Errorf("cannot insert tick for habit %q: %w", id, err)
    }

    return nil
}
```

We now just have to call it on the server side and transform the request and the response. Because we need to provide a timestamp when the habit was ticked, we could have it passed by either the caller or the gRPC endpoint. If the value is set in the server layer rather than read from the request, we need to remember that the server and the client might be in different time zones and that the "current day" is only a relative notion. Wait! What happens if someone tries to tick a habit that doesn't exist?

10.7.3 *Handle corner cases*

If the habit doesn't exist in the habits repository, we don't want to have inconsistent data and store a new tick for an unknown habit. Let's create a `Find` method on the habit repository:

```
Find(ctx context.Context, id habit.ID) (habit.Habit, error)
```

A good practice is to create a custom error that is checked on the server side to return the proper gRPC code. Here, we chose to switch on the domain error and convert in `codes.NotFound`, for example, if the habit doesn't exist in the database:

```
err := habit.Tick(ctx, s.db, s.db, habit.ID(request.HabitId), time.Now())
if err != nil {
    switch {
    case errors.Is(err, r.ErrNotFound):
        return nil, status.Errorf(codes.NotFound,
            "couldn't find habit %q in repository", request.HabitId)
    default:
        return nil, status.Errorf(codes.Internal,
            "cannot tick habit %q: %s", request.HabitId, err.Error())
    }
}
```

You can test the endpoint manually using `grpcurl` on a created habit, for instance, one with an ID of 98ab1bbe-41d5-4ed3-8f33-e4f7bec448c8:

```
> grpcurl \
-import-path api/proto/ \
-proto service.proto \
-plaintext -d '{"habit_id":"98ab1bbe-41d5-4ed3-8f33-e4f7bec448c8"}' \
localhost:28710 \
habits.Habits/TickHabit
```

Upon inspection, no errors have been returned. Our interest now lies in determining the frequency of calls made to the tick endpoint for a given habit. Let's retrieve this information next.

10.7.4 *Get habit status*

The last task entails retrieving the count of habit ticks for a given week. This requires both the habit ID and a timestamp to specify the desired week. We'll implement an endpoint capable of accepting the ID and timestamp parameters, which will then furnish habit details alongside the tick count. The Potobuf definition looks like the following listing.

Listing 10.37 `api/proto/service.go`: `GetHabitStatus` **definition**

```
    // GetHabitStatus is the endpoint to retrieve the status of
    //ticks of a habit.
    rpc GetHabitStatus(
        GetHabitStatusRequest
    ) returns (GetHabitStatusResponse);

// GetHabitStatusRequest is the request to GetHabitStatus endpoint.
message GetHabitStatusRequest {
    // The identifier of the habit we want to retrieve.
    string habit_id = 1;

    // The time for which we want to retrieve the status of a habit.
    optional google.protobuf.Timestamp timestamp = 2;
}

// GetHabitStatusResponse is the response to retrieving the status of a
// habit.
message GetHabitStatusResponse {
    // All the information of a habit.
    Habit habit = 1;
    // The number of times the habit has been ticked for a given week.
    int32 ticks_count = 2;
}
```

At this point, you should be well equipped to do the remainder of the steps:

1. Create a method on the server side.
2. Isolate the logic on the domain.
3. Retrieve the data on the repository side.
4. Plug all the calls.
5. Don't forget to test!

If you test with `grpcurl`, you should get something like this:

```
> grpcurl \
-import-path api/proto/ \
-proto service.proto \
-plaintext -d '{"habit_id":"98ab1bbe-41d5-4ed3-8f33-e4f7bec448c8"}' \
localhost:28710 \
habits.Habits/GetHabitStatus

{
  "habit": {
    "id": "98ab1bbe-41d5-4ed3-8f33-e4f7bec448c8",
    "name": "read a few pages",
    "weeklyFrequency": 3
  },
  "ticksCount": 2
}
```

10.7.5 Add a timestamp

Until we pick up the habit of remembering to tick the habits we complete, it would be helpful to have the option to dive into the past to tick a habit we forgot to update. To do so, we can extend the two last endpoints by adding a timestamp to the requests.

In Protobuf, you can import different types that will be nicely serialized in the programming language you choose. You can always refer to the full list of well-known types in the Protocol Buffers documentation (https://mng.bz/avXz). The expected format is an RFC3339 date string such as 2024-01-25T10:05:08+00:00. Let's import the timestamp type by adding this line in the top imports of our `service.proto` file:

```
import "google/protobuf/timestamp.proto";
```

The following listing shows an example of how to add the timestamp as a new field `GetHabitStatusRequest`, using the Protobuf `Timestamp` type. By default, a field is optional in Protobuf version 3 (meaning a message without that field will be considered valid), and the usage of the `required` keyword has been discontinued (meaning a message without that field will be considered invalid).

> **Listing 10.38   `api/proto/service.go`: Importing the timestamp**

```
message GetHabitStatusRequest {
    string habit_id = 1;
    google.protobuf.Timestamp time = 2;
}
```

Sometimes, dealing with time as a parameter is a bit tricky—the server and the client might be in different time zones, which makes 8:30 A.M. unclear, for example. We recommend always using the server as the truth when asking what time it is. For now, we'll keep this field here, as it will be useful for tests. Update the two endpoints, and test your code!

10.7.6 Habit tracker in action

We're now able to play with the habit tracker, so let's play a full scenario where we add habits, tick them, retrieve their status, tick them again with a timestamp, and retrieve their status for the given date. You can do it manually by using `grpcurl` in your terminal, or you can update the integration test. Let's first see the `grpcurl` commands and compare the responses:

  1 Create this habit: "Write some Go code."
    Request:

```
> grpcurl \
-import-path api/proto/ \
-proto service.proto \
-plaintext -d '{"name":"Write some Go code", "weekly_frequency":3}' \
```

```
localhost:28710 \
habits.Habits/CreateHabit
```

Response:

```
{
  "habit": {
    "id": "94c573f1-df03-45ec-97fc-8b8fc9943472",
    "name": "Write some Go code",
    "weeklyFrequency": 3
  }
}
```

2 Create this habit: "Read a few pages."

Request:

```
> grpcurl \
-import-path api/proto/ \
-proto service.proto \
-plaintext -d '{"name":"Read a few pages", "weekly_frequency":5}' \
localhost:28710 \
habits.Habits/CreateHabit
```

Response:

```
{
  "habit": {
    "id": "96b72dce-7a2e-43ce-9091-0f9fc447b8a1",
    "name": "Read a few pages",
    "weeklyFrequency": 5
  }
}
```

3 Retrieve the list of habits.

Request:

```
> grpcurl \
-import-path api/proto/ \
-proto service.proto \
-plaintext -d '{}' \
localhost:28710 \
habits.Habits/ListHabits
```

Response:

```
{
  "habits": [
    {
      "id": "94c573f1-df03-45ec-97fc-8b8fc9943472",
      "name": "Write some Go code",
```

```
        "weeklyFrequency": 3
      },
      {
        "id": "96b72dce-7a2e-43ce-9091-0f9fc447b8a1",
        "name": "Read a few pages",
        "weeklyFrequency": 5
      }
    ]
}
```

4   Tick the "Write some Go code" habit without a timestamp because you just did it.
    Request:

```
> grpcurl \
-import-path api/proto/ \
-proto service.proto \
-plaintext -d '{"habit_id":"94c573f1-df03-45ec-97fc-8b8fc9943472"}' \
localhost:28710 \
habits.Habits/TickHabit
```

Response:

```
{

}
```

5   Get the status of the "Write some Go code" habit for the current week.
    Request:

```
> grpcurl \
-import-path api/proto/ \
-proto service.proto \
-plaintext -d '{"habit_id":"94c573f1-df03-45ec-97fc-8b8fc9943472"}' \
localhost:28710 \
habits.Habits/GetHabitStatus
```

Response:

```
{
  "habit": {
    "id": "94c573f1-df03-45ec-97fc-8b8fc9943472",
    "name": "Write some Go code",
    "weeklyFrequency": 3
  },
  "ticksCount": 1
}
```

6   Tick the "Read a few pages" habit without a timestamp because you're doing it.
    Request:

```
> grpcurl \
-import-path api/proto/ \
-proto service.proto \
-plaintext -d '{"habit_id":"96b72dce-7a2e-43ce-9091-0f9fc447b8a1"}' \
localhost:28710 \
habits.Habits/TickHabit
```

Response:

```
{

}
```

7 Get the status of the "Read a few pages" habit for the current week.
Request:

```
> grpcurl \
-import-path api/proto/ \
-proto service.proto \
-plaintext -d '{"habit_id":"96b72dce-7a2e-43ce-9091-0f9fc447b8a1"}' \
localhost:28710 \
habits.Habits/GetHabitStatus
```

Response:

```
{
  "habit": {
    "id": "96b72dce-7a2e-43ce-9091-0f9fc447b8a1",
    "name": "Read a few pages",
    "weeklyFrequency": 5
  },
  "ticksCount": 1
}
```

8 Tick the "Read a few pages" habit with a timestamp in the previous week.
Request:

```
grpcurl \
-import-path api/proto/ \
-proto service.proto \
-plaintext -d '{"habit_id":"96b72dce-7a2e-43ce-9091-0f9fc447b8a1",
  "timestamp": "2024-01-24T20:24:06+00:00"}' \
localhost:28710 \
habits.Habits/TickHabit
```

Response:

```
{

}
```

9 Get the status of the "Read a few pages" habit during the previous week.

Request:

```
grpcurl \
-import-path api/proto/ \
-proto service.proto \
-plaintext -d '{"habit_id":"96b72dce-7a2e-43ce-9091-0f9fc447b8a1",
 "timestamp": "2024-01-24T20:24:06+00:00"}' \
localhost:28710 \
habits.Habits/GetHabitStatus
```

Response:

```
{
  "habit": {
    "id": "96b72dce-7a2e-43ce-9091-0f9fc447b8a1",
    "name": "Read a few pages",
    "weeklyFrequency": 5
  },
  "ticksCount": 1
}
```

Launching the commands manually can be a bit annoying and repetitive, so let's automate this and update the integration test, as shown in listing 10.39. First, we can write helper functions as we did previously to tick a habit and to verify that the habit status matches when calling `GetHabitStatus`. These functions will both make the call to the API and validate the returned values.

Listing 10.39   `integration_test.go:` `TickHabit` **and** `GetStatus` **calls**

```
func tickHabit(t *testing.T, habitsCli api.HabitsClient, id string) {
    _, err := habitsCli.TickHabit(context.Background(), &api.
     TickHabitRequest{
        HabitId: id,
    })                                   Fails if TickHabit
    require.NoError(t, err)          ◀── returns an error
}

func getHabitStatusMatches(t *testing.T, habitsCli api.HabitsClient,
    id string, expected *api.GetHabitStatusResponse) {
    h, err := habitsCli.GetHabitStatus(context.Background(),
        &api.GetHabitStatusRequest{HabitId: id})
    require.NoError(t, err)
                                            Verifies the content of the
    assert.Equal(t, expected.Habit, h.Habit)    ◀── GetHabitStatus response
    assert.Equal(t, expected.TicksCount, h.TicksCount)
}
```

The generated ID is needed to call `TickHabit` and `GetHabitStatus` endpoints. We can retrieve the ID from the `addHabit` helper method, as shown in the following listing.

Listing 10.40 `integration_test.go:` Updating `addHabit` to retrieve the ID

```
func addHabit(t *testing.T, habitsCli api.HabitsClient,
    freq *int32,
    name string) string {
    resp, err := habitsCli.CreateHabit(context.Background(),
        &api.CreateHabitRequest{
        Name:            name,
        WeeklyFrequency: freq,
    })
    require.NoError(t, err)

    return resp.Habit.Id
}
```

We need to update the signature to return the ID and to update the main test function.

Retrieves the response from the endpoint

Returns the habit ID

With the following listing, you can now add the calls to the main test function by calling the two helpers `tickHabit` and `getHabitStatusMatches`, shown earlier in listing 10.39.

Listing 10.41 `integration_test.go:` Calling `tickHabit`/verify statuses

```
func addHabit(t *testing.T, habitsCli api.HabitsClient, freq *int32,
    name string) string {
    // add 2 ticks for Walk habit
    tickHabit(t, habitsCli, idWalk)
    tickHabit(t, habitsCli, idWalk)

    // add 1 tick for Read habit
    tickHabit(t, habitsCli, idRead)

    // check that the right number of ticks are present
    getHabitStatusMatches(t, habitsCli, idWalk, &api.GetHabitStatusResponse{
        Habit: &api.Habit{
            Id:              idWalk,
            Name:            "walk in the forest",
            WeeklyFrequency: 1,
        },
        TicksCount: 2,
    })

    getHabitStatusMatches(t, habitsCli, idRead, &api.GetHabitStatusResponse{
        Habit: &api.Habit{
            Id:              idRead,
            Name:            "read a few pages",
            WeeklyFrequency: 3,
        },
        TicksCount: 1,
    })
    ...
```

Congratulations! You've built a solid habit tracker backend that can be reused easily for a frontend application. You can commit and enjoy your new project!

Summary

- The `go generate` command is a Go tool that enables you to generate programs from the source code. The compiler scans comments with the specific syntax `//go:generate` and executes the command that follows on the rest of the line.

- gRPC is a framework to connect services, devices, applications, and more. It's a powerful and efficient framework for transporting lightweight messages in Protobuf format.

- The Protocol Buffers framework (Protobuf) provides serialization for structured data while guaranteeing high performance. It comes with its own syntax composed of Protobuf messages and services written in `.proto` files.

- Protobuf messages are language neutral. Thanks to the Protobuf compiler (`protoc`), you can generate interfaces and structures in many programming languages (Go, Java, C++, etc.).

- Communication between gRPC clients and servers is standardized thanks to status codes defined by the RPC API. A status is composed of an integer code and a string message. While designing the API, you should pick the most appropriate return code for your use case (you can always refer to the documentation at https://mng.bz/gapl).

- `grpcurl` is an open source command-line interface (CLI) tool that enables you to communicate with gRPC servers easily. It's basically like curl but for gRPC. This human-friendly CLI allows you to define JSON requests instead of unreadable bytes. It's very useful when you need to test services manually.

- Declare small interfaces close to their use. It comes in handy when testing to mock your dependencies instead of counting on hardcoded behaviors.

- Dependency injection is a technique to give all the needed objects to a function instead of creating or building them internally. Note that it's useful to mock the dependencies when testing the function.

- While testing, there are different ways of simulating dependency behaviors, and mock tools are great for describing expected results. The main well-known mock tools are `mockgen` (comes with Go), `mockify`, and `minimock`, which we used in this chapter.

- The standard `context` library provides the `Context` type and its associated methods to carry information along requests and responses. For example, when a user sends a request, you can store its identity in the `Context` and retrieve it later in the chain of functions. It's safe to use methods such as `WithCancel` or `WithDeadline` across multiple goroutines.

- A program should create only one `Context` and provide it to its functions. Most of the time, the `Context` will be coming from an external caller. Creating children for a `Context` is perfectly fine and encouraged.

- Always pass a `context.Context` as the first parameter of a function, even if you're not using it (you can use the blank identifier in this rare case).

- A `Context` is necessary any time we make a remote call across the network, whichever protocol or framework is being used. Setting a deadline for the remote call is a good safety net; otherwise, your application calls might be hanging forever.

- To check if a `Context` has expired, try reading from `<- ctx.Done()`. This will return something when the `Context` is no longer usable. To know why a `Context` is over, check its error with `ctx.Err()` or, even better, with `context.Cause(ctx)`.

- Don't use a `context.Context` as a key-value storage inside an application.

- Mocking functions that use a `Context` is sometimes tricky, especially if the function being tested creates a `context` of its own. To solve this, many libraries offering mocks expose a variable that can be used as a wildcard for the `Context`.

- Generated mocks are programmed to behave as specified. If they receive a call for a precise set of parameters, they will return the specified values. However, it's sometimes necessary to override this default behavior of always returning something, especially when testing the behavior when a deadline is reached.

- Using `testing.Short()` allows us to know if the `-short` flag was passed on the `go test` command line. Long or expensive tests should be skipped altogether when this flag is set, by using `t.Skip()`.

- Dealing with "current time" is tricky because asking what time it is provides different results based on the time zone of the person being asked. As a result, we recommend checking for current time on the server side, rather than expecting the client to provide that value.

11
HTML templating with a gRPC client

This chapter covers

- Creating a gRPC client
- Using templates in Go to fill an HTML page
- Calling an existing backend

When you have data that you want to show, there are two main questions to answer: What should you show, and how should you show it? While answering the first question is part of understanding the problem, knowing how to present the results, and making them clear, is often a requirement to make the solution meaningful. As computer scientists, we deal with huge amounts of data, most of which is mundane to the people who live next door, the other school parents, or the person in front of us at the grocery store. In chapter 5, we explained how using icons made the game Wordle (and our game Gordle) more entertaining than a display of mere numbers. Being able to clearly give a picture of the raw data is so important that the Golang developers introduced the `text/template` package to support this in the first version of the language. The goal of this package and of its sibling `http/template` is to generate enriched text output based on the contents of some data. Most of the time, the data needs to be nicely formatted—add a tab here, insert a new line there, or add this or that tag—and we'll explain why other Golang tools aren't better at this task than templates.

Templating has been intensively used by tools such as Helm to factor YAML deployment configuration files and make them more generic. In this chapter, we'll use Go's template packages to provide a nice UI on top of our habits tracker that we wrote in the previous chapter. For this, we'll interact with a web server that displays an HTML page containing all the important information about our habits. Let's face it—grpcurl is useful, but having buttons will be a much better user experience—even if it's only for tests! This project has the following requirements:

- The user must be able to access an HTTP server via a web browser.
- The web page exposes the current habits in a visually pleasing way.
- The web page allows the user to tick a habit for this week and to create new habits.
- The HTTP server communicates with our gRPC habits service.
- The HTTP server returns an HTML document containing the habits.

NOTE This chapter relies on the code from chapter 10. If you skipped it, you can use the code from the book's repository.

11.1 *Your basic HTTP server*

Let's begin by examining figure 11.1 to gain a comprehensive understanding of our objectives for this chapter. Currently, we've implemented the gRPC habits service and the storage logic. Next, we need an HTTP server to convert our content into an esthetically pleasing HTML page, which will be served to our users' web browsers.

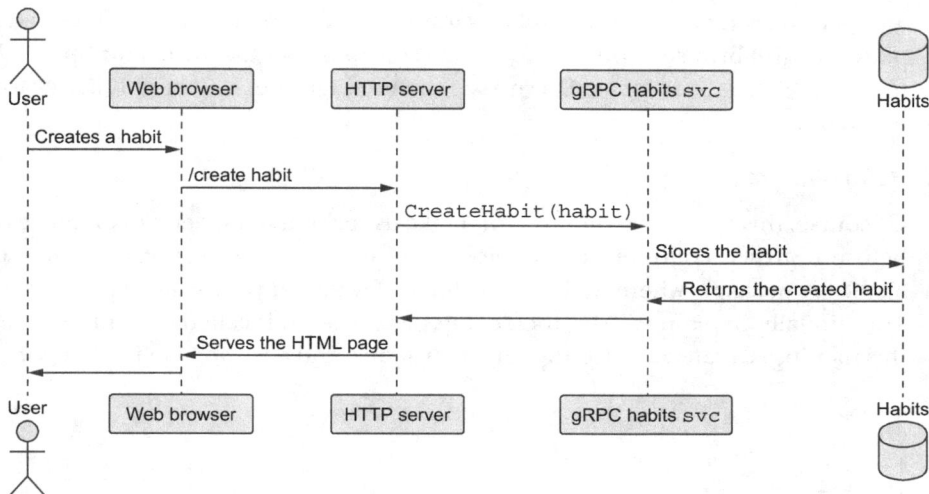

Figure 11.1   A unified modeling language diagram of the global architecture

In this first part, we want to run a server that returns some HTML to a web browser. First, let's run a server that returns something, just to check that it works. This is like a `hello, world` on HTTP, at the root path of the service, namely, `localhost:8083/`. Pick the port you like—usually 8080 and above is a good range during development. This server will be the bridge, receiving HTTP requests from the web page the user is browsing, and sending adequate Protobuf messages to the gRPC server on the other side.

In chapter 8, you saw the basics of an HTTP server, but let's recap. Create your module in a new folder, run `go mod init learngo-pockets/templates` or any other module name, and create a `main.go` in the `cmd/httpserver` folder. Writing this server can be done in a handful of lines.

Listing 11.1   Minimal HTTP server

```go
func main() {
    http.HandleFunc("/",
        func(w http.ResponseWriter, r *http.Request) {       // Defines a handler
            io.WriteString(w, "ሰላም፡ሰዎች።")                     // function for the
    })                                                        // root ("/") path
                                                              // The contents of the page

    err := http.ListenAndServe(":8083", nil)
    if err != nil {
        fmt.Fprintln(os.Stderr, "Error while serving: " + err.Error())
    }
}
                                                              // Starts the HTTP
                                                              // server on port 8083
```

Run it, open a browser, and visit `localhost:8083`. When displaying this page, a request is sent by the browser to local port 8083. There, it's received by our server, which sends the following response: "ሰላም፡ሰዎች።" (Amharic for "Hello, world."—and, no, the comma and period aren't the "," and "." characters here). This request is then received and displayed by the browser. You can `go run cmd/httpserver/main.go` and open a browser to `http://localhost:8083`. Do you see the message? Let's make this better for future maintainers.

11.1.1 Hello plain text

Of course, this flat code structure won't take us very far, so we need to organize the code before it grows. Following our choices from chapter 8, we can create an `internal/handlers` package, where we'll put the logic of what happens when a path is requested. Traditionally, in plain HTML, the default page to show is called the index, so let's keep this naming. Create a file for the server structure and a file for the index logic:

```
> tree
.
├── cmd
│   └── httpserver
│       └── main.go
├── go.mod
```

```
├── go.sum
└── internal
      └── handlers
             ├── index.go
             └── server.go
```

MAIN FUNCTION

First, let's update the `main` function to create a new server, listen, and serve requests using the router, as shown in listing 11.2. We'll implement the server next. As you notice, listening to a port and serving doesn't change from our previous straightforward implementation, except for the router parameter: we want all the routes to be managed by the server that we'll write next.

Listing 11.2 `main.go`: Using the server's router

```go
const port = 8083

func main() {
    srv := handlers.New()              ◄──┘ Creates the server
                                            but doesn't compile
    addr := fmt.Sprintf(":%d", port)
    // TODO: Log a message: we are listening

    err := http.ListenAndServe(addr, srv.Router())   ◄────┘ Listens on port 8083
    if err != nil {
        panic(err)
    }
}
```

Unhappy compilers make unhappy developers, so let's implement this server.

SERVER STRUCTURE

As usual, we want the server to be a struct holding its dependencies, so we can put it under test with the relevant mocks. Before we add the gRPC client as a dependency, the first function that this structure needs must build a router, linking to its different endpoints. We saw in chapter 8 why we picked the standard library as our routing library, rather than `go-chi`, `fiber`, or `gorilla`. Let's do it again here. Write the `Server` struct with this one field, and add a `New()` function to build it, taking no parameters yet.

Listing 11.3 `server.go`: Server struct

```go
// Server serves all the HTML routes on this service.
type Server struct {}                          ◄──┘ Defines an empty struct

func New() *Server...          ◄──┘ Implements New

// Router returns an HTTP handler that listens to all the proper paths.
```

```
func (s *Server) Router() http.Handler {
    r := http.NewServeMux()                              ◀──────  Creates the server

    // Register each endpoint.
    r.HandleFunc(http.MethodGet+" "+"/", s.index)        ◀──────  Registers the handler
                                                                  "s.index" to the route
    return r                                                      "/" for the verb GET
}
```

Each page, endpoint, or path will be processed by a method on our `Server` structure. Now we need to implement the `index` method, which tackles the root of the server.

INDEX PAGE

What logic will run whenever a client navigates to the index page? From the preceding code listing, our server knows that it must call the `index` method, which needs to return a status code and some page content.

As you can see in the documentation, the `HandleFunc` function declares an HTTP route with the eponymous verb and directs the request to the second parameter, which is an `http.HandlerFunc`. This means we need to create the method `index` with a specific signature, defined in the documentation as follows:

```
// The HandlerFunc type is an adapter to allow the use of
// ordinary functions as HTTP handlers.
// [...]
type HandlerFunc func(ResponseWriter, *Request)
```

Write the `index` method with this signature in a dedicated file, for example, `index.go`:

```
// index serves the root page of the app.
func (*Server) index(w http.ResponseWriter, r *http.Request) {}
```

The only operation that this function needs to do is to output some HTML on the `w` variable. Should we use `fmt.Fprint` or `io.WriteString`? When writing a string to a writer, two main options are available: `io.WriteString(w, ...)` or the family of `fmt.Fprint(w, ...)`. If what needs to be printed is a hardcoded string, `WriteString` is perfect. However, as soon as you need to add information to the string and make it more dynamic, using the `fmt` package becomes a necessity. Now that this is cleared up, let's output our `Hello, World` again and see if it works after refactoring.

Listing 11.4   `index.go`: Handler for the index page

```
// index serves the root page of the app.
func (_ *Server) index(w http.ResponseWriter, _ *http.Request) {
    io.WriteString(w, "ሰላም፣ዓለም።")
}
```

Run the server, refresh the page at `localhost :8083`, and see what happens. Figure 11.2 shows the first page.

It's cute, but we're boldly ignoring a potential error returned by `WriteString`! If an error occurs, the first thing to do is log it. Using `fmt .Println` will help in development but not in production or during tests where the logs will get

የሰላም፡ሰዎች፡፡

Figure 11.2   A first page—not yet HTML

mangled in the test output. Let's delay the answer to this till the end of this section.

NOTE When there are errors writing the HTML response, as soon as we call `Write` using the response writer, the HTML headers are set, and we can't change them anymore by using `Error`. The only remaining option is to log the error.

The log is for developers who will have to debug the problem, but we also need to tell the client what happened:

```
_, err := io.WriteString(w, "የሰላም፡ሰዎች፡፡")
if err != nil {
    // TODO: Log a message.
    fmt.Println("Error while rendering: " + err.Error())
}
```

With this, the user's browser can know how to interpret the response.

RESPONSEWRITER'S DEFAULT BEHAVIOR

Why aren't we explicitly returning a status when everything is correct? If you look at the `WriteString` documentation, it states that in our case, "`[Writer.Write]` is called exactly once." Click along in the documentation, and you'll find out that `http.ResponseWriter` has a lot of useful behaviors to make your life easier: "If `[ResponseWriter.WriteHeader]` hasn't yet been called, `Write` calls `WriteHeader(http .StatusOK)` before writing the data. Additionally it deals with the `Content-Type` and `Content-Length` headers in the majority of situations." Of course, we always get over the edge of that "majority" case when least expected, so keep it in mind when your hotfix suddenly breaks everything.

> **HTML basics**
>
> This book isn't about frontend technologies, and none of these authors would dare claim any expertise in the area. What we're good at, though, is reading documentation (and looking up things on the internet). The W3C, responsible for the web's norms, states the following:
>
> - All HTML documents must start with a document type declaration: `<!DOCTYPE html>`.

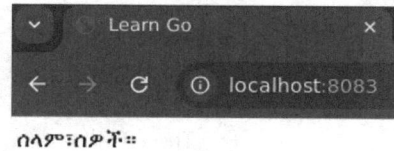

(continued)
- The HTML document itself begins with `<html>` and ends with `</html>`.
- The visible part of the HTML document is between `<body>` and `</body>`.
- The HTML `<head>` element is a container for the following elements: `<title>`, `<style>`, `<meta>`, `<link>`, `<script>`, and `<base>`.

We can replace the `hello, world` with some HTML code.

Listing 11.5   `index.go`: HTML for the index page

```
_, err := io.WriteString(w, `          ◄──────  Uses backquotes to
<!DOCTYPE html>                                 escape double quotes
<html lang="en">
<head>
    <title>Learn Go</title>        ◄──────  A title for the browser's tab
</head>
<body>
    <h1>YAY</h1>                    ◄──────  The main title of the page
    <p>Way to go!</p>               ◄──────  Message to display
</body>
</html>
`)
```

Run it and enjoy the experience of the first days of the web, when people were writing HTML by hand. Figure 11.3 shows the page as it will appear in a browser.

Looking good, but we still have a TODO that needs some attention.

USE A PROPER LOGGER

We now need to add a proper logger to the server. Let's reuse a logger similar to what we used in chapter 10: a type `Logger` in charge of

YAY

Way to go!

Figure 11.3   The page in a browser

writing to a specified output. This type only exposes one method, `Logf`. This logger will be a dependency of the server, where we'll declare it as an interface to help with tests.

Listing 11.6   `log.go`: Implementing a lightweight logger

```
// Logger is a lightweight logger.
type Logger struct {
    lgr    *log.Logger        ◄──────  Our logger uses the log
}                                       package internally.

// New returns a logger that prints to the specified output.
func New(w io.Writer) *Logger {
```

```
        return &Logger{lgr: log.New(
            w, "", log.Ldate|log.Ltime)}        ◀────  Adds some default
}                                                      formatting parameters

// Logf formats the message and sends it to the output.
func (l *Logger) Logf(format string, args ...any) {
    l.lgr.Printf(format, args...)
}
```

Now, we can add a logger dependency in our server. For this, we don't want to rely on the `log.Logger` type, as this will make testing our code painful. When we test the `server` package, we don't also want to be affected by code in the `log` package. Instead, we can declare the local interface that we expect the logger to implement.

> **TIP** "Accept interfaces, return types" is a little axiom that should help you design the signatures for your functions and methods. You can always define a minimal interface for a parameter. For the return type, there's usually no reason to return an interface, unless you specifically want to return something generic.

Our choice, in the `log/logger.go` file, was driven by what the `testing.T` structure already implements—a method called `Logf`, as shown in the following listing. This will allow us to use a `testing.T` in our tests instead of creating a `Logger` variable.

Listing 11.7 `server.go`: **Receiving a logger**

```
type Logger interface {
    Logf(format string, args ...any)       ◀────  Defines a local interface
}

type Server struct {
    lgr     Logger          ◀────  Stores the logger
}                                  in the server struct

func New(lgr Logger) *Server {     ◀────  Receives an
    return &Server{lgr: lgr}              injected logger
}
```

Finally, all we have left to do is update the `main` function, where we can now build the logger, and inject it into our server when creating it. We'll now be able to log what's going on in the backend when we tick a habit or perform any other action. The server's `os.Stdout` won't be sent to the client and will remain "internally" on the server's premises for developers to investigate.

UNIT TESTING HTML

For the moment, the index outputs a static HTML document. We want to manage our future habits with a nice UI. To make sure it stays nice, let's set up testing using the `httptest` package.

First, we check that everything went well, and we get a `200 OK` response when we call `index`. We can use the popular `github.com/stretchr/testify/assert` and `github.com/stretchr/testify/require` packages here.

As we saw in chapter 8, we need a response recorder from the `httptest` package to test the output of an HTTP request.

Listing 11.8   `index_test.go`: Checking the status code

```
func TestServer_index(t *testing.T) {
    rr := httptest.NewRecorder()        ◄──┘ Creates a response recorder

    s := New(t)                          ◄──   The testing.T structure
    s.index(rr, nil)                     ◄──   implements our Logger interface.

    assert.Equal(t, http.StatusOK,       ◄──   Calls the handler for the path "/"
        rr.Result().StatusCode)          ◄──
}                                              Checks the status code
```

To check the contents of the response, we can have a real HTML file with the expected output as our reference. It's a test fixture, so it should go in a `testdata` folder:

```
expect, err := os.ReadFile("testdata/index.html")
```

In tests, such files are referred to as *golden files*. They contain the absolute truth of what the generated contents should be. It's sometimes customary to give them a `.golden` suffix.

If you use a simple equality between the two strings, you may be surprised by differences caused by the tabs and carriage returns—differences that your test really shouldn't care about. If you happen to add a tab somewhere for legibility, why should it break your test?

Usually, comparing the entire output is a bad idea: any change would break your test for bad reasons. In the test case shown in the following listing, every whitespace needs to be exactly right.

Listing 11.9   `index_test.go`: Checking the contents with strict equality

```
expect, err := os.ReadFile("testdata/index.html")
require.NoError(t, err)

assert.Equal(t, string(expect), rr.Body.String())     ◄──┘ Strict string comparison
```

There are better and more convoluted ways to test HTML by thinking about what exactly we're testing: we're not testing Go's `io.WriteString` function or `html` package. Frontend frameworks have thought about this thoroughly. For now, we'll stick to a golden file. We'll find quick ways to make this version work for our purpose in a satisfying way.

Run the test. You can also write an error test, to check what happens when Write-
String blunders (and try to come up with a scenario when it would blunder).

We have some HTML output, and we've automated the test to check for changes.
Don't worry, we're never going to write HTML in a .go file again (torture is illegal since
the Geneva convention in 1987). That's where templates come in to save the day.

11.1.2 Templates: Display a variable

While the format library (fmt) does a great job of getting the exact format we want for
a variable, it reaches its limits when we have many variables that we want to print on different lines. Suppose you wanted to display a menu in a restaurant. Each menu entry
would have a name, maybe a reference number (helpful for both staff and customers), a list of ingredients, a list of allergens, maybe a suitability for vegetarians and veg-
ans, and a price. You could use fmt.Sprintf for this, but the odds of your command
line exceeding 80 characters are extremely high. Another option is to use a strings
.Builder, which is a slightly better choice but still a painful one. Imagine how difficult
and complex it would be if you also want to add a translation to another language or
add a calorie count somewhere.

When you tangle large portions of static text with some dynamic values, templates
are a valid alternative. As we'll see in this chapter, templates provide a representation of
the structured output in a very clear way—one that doesn't involve counting commas
when you call Sprintf to identify which value is printed for the fourth %s of the line of
code.

Go comes with two libraries for templates—the text/template and the html/
template. They both have the same interface; the only difference is that the HTML
implementation automatically escapes HTML-sensitive characters such as &, <, or é.
It also makes the generated text safe against code injections—preventing a text value
such as "</html>" from ending the page being rendered by the browser or, worse, a
mischievous JavaScript piece of code from being executed.

Choosing between these two libraries should always be driven by feature requirements. In this chapter, because we want to render an HTML document, we'll be using
the HTML templates. Unless you need to escape some characters, which is common in
XML-based languages such as HTML, using the standard text/template should cover
all your needs. Similarly, using templates to generate any format relying on tags (e.g.,
JSON) or structure (e.g., YAML or CSV) should raise two questions: Is it safe to blindly
trust the user's input? What is the worst that can happen if the template receives a "bad"
value?

Go's templates bind a piece of code and a model. The model comes in the shape of
text, usually loaded from another file, but a short template can sometimes be defined as
a variable of type string. Here, we'll mostly use templates from external files.

A template, after being loaded from a source and parsed (to check its syntax and
grammar), will be executed on various data to produce an output. Templates in Go
are based on the notion of an *action*. The template engine will apply each action in the

template when it executes the template. Actions, in templates, are encapsulated by double curly braces: {{...}}.

Actions can be thought of as the companion to the %v argument in fmt.Printf calls. An action serves as a placeholder where we want a value to be printed. In the template, everything that isn't part of an action will be printed as such, whereas actions will be executed to whichever values they received. We therefore need to provide values to the actions in our template by using the dot . operator (a period character). Now that we've had enough background, let's start writing our very first template!

HTML TEMPLATE

There are a few steps we still need to go through before we can make full use of templates in Go, but we can at least start now to clean our code and extract the HTML code into a real HTML file with the .html file extension. This file will contain our template. Your IDE will be happier and way more useful there because it can at least help with formatting and spotting mistakes in the markup, provided it recognizes the file format from its extension. We'll resume the setup of our HTTP server right after this first example.

The first task here is to pass a variable to the template and see how it renders. Let's take the number of habits as an example. Move the HTML string into an index.html file, and change it using the action {{.}}—the default action is to print the current variable, as shown in the following listing. This is exactly the same as calling %v in the middle of a rather complex string.

Listing 11.10 index.html: Outputting a variable

```
<!DOCTYPE html>
<html lang="en">
<head>
    <title>Learn Go</title>
</head>
<body>
<h1>Habits</h1>
<p>You have {{.}} habits to follow.</p>          ◄─── Prints a variable between
</body>                                                "have" and "habits"
</html>
```

SPACES

Writing {{.}} isn't very clear. Instead, we can write {{ . }} with spaces to increase readability. These two are strictly identical; some people prefer having spaces, while some don't. You can even use any of {{.}}, {{ . }}, {{ .}}, or {{. }} if you want. The output will be the same. Clarity, readability, and consistency are paramount here.

However, sometimes we have to add a piece of text right after the value printed from the template. Suppose we need to print a value that is a percentage. It makes sense to display it as 17.5%, with no space, rather than 17.5 %. We can use a template, and it would look like {{.}}% or {{ . }}%. In both cases, it might be difficult to see the

% symbol. For this reason, templates support a feature for removing previous/next space characters. Adding a minus sign (-) on any side of the template will remove any whitespaces (newline, tab, nonbreakable space, or regular space—but, strangely enough, not an em space or an en space). When using the - in the template, remember to stick it to the curly bracket and to keep it separated from the body of the action with a space: don't write {{-.}}, but instead {{- .}}. In addition, keep in mind that - drops all whitespaces, not just those that happened to be printed right before the {{ characters (or right after the }} ones): this includes tabs and newlines that might have been written purposely. For instance, the following pairs produce the same outputs:

- {{ . -}} % and {{.}}%
- ${{ . }} and $ {{- .}}
- [{{- . -}}] and [{{.}}], and [{{- .}}] and other variations

Now that we've written our first template, we need Go to read it and fill it up. That trailing "s" in "habits to follow" in listing 11.10 will be taken care of later (it shouldn't be there when you have only one habit).

TEMPLATING IN GO

First, Go needs to read this file into a variable. We could use a file reader, but considering that the file isn't changing from one run to the next, the best tool for this is the go:embed tag:

```
//go:embed index.html
var indexPage string
```

This syntax means that, on compilation, the contents of the index.html file should be put into this variable. We can only use embed on a global variable. To understand this, the compiler requires that the embed package be imported, but because we're not explicitly calling any of its functions or types, we need to "silently" import it using the underscore import:

```
package server

import (
  _ "embed" // Allows us to load files
  ...
)

//go:embed index.html // Load the file contents to the indexPage variable.
var indexPage string
```

If you like, you can change your unit test to use this instead of a file reader for the expected value. We can now create the template using template.New and give it a name. Then, we can Parse it from the contents of the file. The New function takes the name that we want to give our template, while Parse takes a string containing the full template. The reason templates need names will become clear by the end of this chapter, but long story short, templates can call other templates by their registered name:

```
template.New("index").Parse(indexPage)
```

Finally, we're ready to execute our template over a value. We can do this with the method `Execute`, which returns an error.

Listing 11.11   `index.go`: Outputting a variable

```
func (s *Server) index(w http.ResponseWriter, r *http.Request) {
    tpl, err := template.New("index").Parse(indexPage)
    if err != nil {...}

    err = tpl.Execute(w, 5)          ◄──┐  Provides a number
    if err != nil {...}                 │  of habits, such as 5
}
```

Make sure you return an internal error and log the reason it happens. You can test the error path by providing a badly formatted template (e.g., omit a curly brace). Figure 11.4 shows the result of listing 11.11.

Update the test output, the documentation, and everything necessary to make your code future-proof. Next, we'll call the backend service because who wants a web page that never displays live data?

Habits

You have 5 habits to follow.

Figure 11.4   Result with a variable in a browser

11.1.3   Add a gRPC client

Our HTTP server currently isn't connected to anything. To return "real" data, we need to connect it to a habits server. In a different terminal, run the `Habits` service from chapter 10. Define the port where that service listens on your machine, and write it down because you'll need it very soon. In our example, we'll use port `8084`. You can use the integration test or a `grpcurl` list of commands to add some dummy habits to that service's database.

Keeping our good habit of separating concerns, let's see what packages we'll need in the HTTP server:

- `habit`—This is our core data layer, where we define the data structures that can be passed between packages.
- `client`—The anticorruption layer isolates the gRPC structures required to speak with the backend from the rest of the code and makes the calls simpler.
- `handler`—This is where the server listens to some routes and responds in HTML.

All of these are internal, inside the `internal` folder, and the `main` function will inject one into the next to get its fully functioning server. The first package, `habit`, is easy to start if we look at the same package in the gRPC service and remove what we don't need. Listing 11.12 shows the `Habit` structure that we defined in the previous chapter; in this case, only the creation time, which isn't exposed through the API, can be discarded. What we want to expose instead is the number of times the habit was ticked this week.

Listing 11.12 `habit.go`: Defining the data object

```
// ID is the identifier of the Habit.
type ID string                             ◀——— Defines clear types

// Name is a short string that represents the name of a Habit.
type Name string

// TickCount defines a number of ticks.
type TickCount uint

// Habit to track.
type Habit struct {
    ID              ID
    Name            Name
    WeeklyFrequency TickCount
    Ticks           TickCount      ◀——— Adds the ticks count
}
```

With this building block, it's possible to pass habits around between packages in our server without any of these packages' specificities leaking between them.

BACKEND CLIENT STRUCTURE

As a reminder, the client that was generated from the Protobuf definitions in the previous chapter has the following interface:

```
type HabitsClient interface {
    CreateHabit(context.Context,
        *CreateHabitRequest,
        ...grpc.CallOption) (*CreateHabitResponse, error)
    ListHabits(context.Context,
        *ListHabitsRequest,
        ...grpc.CallOption) (*ListHabitsResponse, error)
    TickHabit(context.Context,
        *TickHabitRequest,
        ...grpc.CallOption) (*TickHabitResponse, error)
    GetHabitStatus(context.Context,
        *GetHabitStatusRequest,
        ...grpc.CallOption) (*GetHabitStatusResponse, error)

}
```

We want to be able to mock it for testing purposes. This means we'll take an interface as a parameter of the `client` package's `New` function. As it happens, the interface was already generated, so why not use it? We'll be using all of these methods anyway by the end of the chapter. If we only needed a subset of methods, we would simply declare a local interface in our `client` package. Next, you'll see how to import the interface that was generated in chapter 10 into this module.

ADDING A DEPENDENCY ON A LOCAL PACKAGE

When creating a module with `go mod init <module_name>`, there are two common practices. The first popular option, mostly used for command-line applications, is to simply give the module a name, which is what we've been doing in this book: the first line of our `go.mod` file for this chapter is `learngo-pockets/templates`. The other choice is to use the full domain name of the module, for instance, `k8s.io/kubernetes` or `github.com/grafana/grafana`. This option is mostly used for libraries, or modules that are intended to be shared, but it can very much be used for applications too, as these examples show.

Now, we're faced with a problem—because our module for chapter 10 wasn't published and exposed, how can we access its files from the module of this chapter? How do we access the generated gRPC server definition, the one that lives in the `learngo-pockets/habits` module?

If we try to add a dependency to it using the standard command, we get an error:

```
> go get learngo-pockets/habits
go: learngo-pockets/habits@v0.0.0-00010101000000-000000000000:
malformed module path "learngo-pockets/habits": missing dot in
first path element
```

As you can see, Go expects a `.` in the name of the module we're trying to import—the separator between the host name and the top-level domain name. We could try and import a local file by using the relative path to the `.go` file, such as `import "../habits/api"`. However, this also won't end happily, as trying to solve the imports afterward will result in an error:

```
> go mod tidy
        ../habits/api/: "../habits/api" is relative, but relative import
paths are not supported in module mode
```

So, to solve this conundrum, we can use `go mod edit -replace` to override the version or the path of a module. This has two main uses: when we want to specify which version/tag/branch of the library is to be used, or when we want to refer to a local implementation. The syntax is as follows:

```
> go mod edit -replace=old_module=new_module
```

For example, if we wanted to use a local clone of `github.com/stretchr/testify` that we stored at `../stretchr/testify` (could also be an absolute path), we would use the following:

```
> go mod edit -replace=github.com/stretchr/testify=../stretchr/testify
```

To specify the version/branch/tag to use, simply add @ and the reference:

```
> go mod edit -replace=github.com/moby/moby=github.com/moby/moby@dev
```

In our case, we want to use a version of the module that is stored locally in a different path. We need to provide the path to the module (not the package), which, in the case of our implementation, is the following:

```
> go mod edit -replace=learngo-pockets/habits=../10-habits/7_track
```

If you haven't implemented chapter 10, you can clone it from our repository and then run the command with the appropriate path.

Now, if we take a look at the go.mod file, it should have a line (usually at the end) showing the effect of the replace command: replace learngo-pockets/habits => ../10-habits/7_track. Great! We can now import the api package of the learngo -pockets/habits module—Go should now be able to import the local package. However, remember that this adds a dependency to a local file, so sharing this with colleagues will very likely cause trouble. For this reason, it's almost always a better option to publish modules prefixed by a domain name (e.g., github.com), from where they can be retrieved by the Go toolchain.

IMPLEMENTING THE gRPC CLIENT

Now that we can access the definition of the backend service, let's create a new client structure in the internal/client package with one field: the gRPC client that we want to hide from the rest of the service.

Listing 11.13 client.go: **A wrapping client**

```
// HabitsClient is a wrapper around the gRPC client.
type HabitsClient struct {
    cli api.HabitsClient          ◄─────┐  gRPC client
}

func New(cli api.HabitsClient) *HabitsClient {     ┌  Builds by taking the
    return &HabitsClient{cli: cli}       ◄─────┘  client as parameter
}
```

We want our HTML document to list all registered habits and their statuses, as well as offer the possibility to tick a habit with a click. This isn't a single feature, and we need to start somewhere. It makes sense to start by retrieving all the habits registered, as we'll then be able to use their ID to perform other actions.

We want this client to retrieve the registered habits, so we'll add a ListHabits method on it, as shown in listing 11.14. Using the hexagonal approach, which recommends clustering code into independent packages, the types generated by the proto toolchain shouldn't be exposed outside this client package, as its API must only rely on the local habit package for domain type definitions.

Listing 11.14   `list.go`: Client can list the habits

```
// ListHabits lists the habits available.
func (hc *HabitsClient) ListHabits(ctx context.Context,          Provides a timestamp
    t time.Time) ([]habit.Habit, error) {                        for the tick count
    resp, err := hc.cli.ListHabits(ctx,
        &api.ListHabitsRequest{})              Calls the backend
    if err != nil {...}

    list := make([]habit.Habit, len(resp.Habits))
    for i, h := range resp.Habits {
        list[i] = habit.Habit{                  Converts from gRPC
            ID: //...                           to the domain type
        }
    }
    return list, nil
}
```

We also need to know for each habit how many times it has been ticked during the week of the timestamp. To express times, use the `timestamppb` package for Protobuf-compatible timestamps. Add the dependency with `go get`:

```
> go get google.golang.org/protobuf/types/known/timestamppb
```

The number of ticks for that week is available, but only on a per-habit basis: it's the `GetHabitStatus` endpoint. That means we need another call inside the loop.

Listing 11.15   `list.go`: Getting the number of ticks

```
import "google.golang.org/protobuf/types/known/timestamppb"

...

for i, h := range resp.Habits {
    status, err := hc.cli.GetHabitStatus(ctx,          Gets each habit's status
        &api.GetHabitStatusRequest{
        HabitId:    h.Id,
        Timestamp: timestamppb.New(t),
    })
    if err != nil {...}

    list[i] = habit.Habit{
        ID: //...
        Ticks: habit.TickCount(status.TicksCount),
    }
}
```

Now would be a good moment to wonder whether a `ListHabits` endpoint that already returns the ticks as part of the gRPC API of the backend is appropriate or if a bulk `GetHabitStatuses` that gets the statuses of a whole list of habits in one call would be better. The rationale behind our design is that optimizing too soon often leads to optimizing in the wrong places. Donald Knuth, author of *The Art of Computer Programming*, said the following:

> We should forget about small efficiencies, say about 97% of the time: premature optimization is the root of all evil. Yet we should not pass up our opportunities in that critical 3%.

Users will rarely have loads of habits that would generate hundreds of similar calls; if they do, maybe paginating is a better idea than adding complexity to the backend service. If you run this code in production, and your monitoring tools show that a lot of your resources are spent fetching statuses and hampering the performance of your application, then one of the two options is worth exploring.

Here, we could add an extra layer of logic to cover timeouts when contacting the backend service. Because this isn't the purpose of this chapter—and because it's already been covered in chapter 10, we'll blindly trust that our connection to the backend is reliable. Just don't do this in a production environment!

There are only three paths for testing: success, error while fetching the list, and error while fetching the statuses. Let's write these test functions—one with a mock that returns some data, and two where the mock returns an error. Again, we'll be using `minimock` to generate the mocks, as we did in chapter 5.

Note the use of `minimock`'s `Expect` when we only expect one call, and the slightly more verbose `Set` when we need multiple responses depending on the input.

Listing 11.16 `list_test.go`: **Testing the happy path**

```go
package client_test

//go:generate minimock -i                                    Generates a mock
  learngo-pockets/habits/api.HabitsClient -s "_mock.go"       from the external
                                                              interface

func TestListHabits(t *testing.T) {
    mockClient := mocks.NewHabitsClientMock(t)       Creates a mock instance

    mockClient.ListHabitsMock.Expect(                Mocks the call that
        minimock.AnyContext,                         returns some habits
        &api.ListHabitsRequest{}).
    Return(&api.ListHabitsResponse{                  Any context is valid in this situation.
        Habits: // ...,
    }, nil)                                          Mocks the call for get status
    mockClient.GetHabitStatusMock.Set(getHabitMock)

                                                     Instantiates the client
    habitsClient := client.New(mockClient)
    habits, err := habitsClient.ListHabits(context.Background())

    require.Nil(t, err)                Checks that everything went well
    expectedHabits := //...
    assert.Equal(t, expectedHabits, habits)
```

```
}

func getHabitMock(_ context.Context,
    in *api.GetHabitStatusRequest,
    ...grpc.CallOption) (*api.GetHabitStatusResponse, error) {
    if in.HabitId == "ID1" {
        return &api.GetHabitStatusResponse{TicksCount: 3}, nil
    }
    // ...
    return nil, fmt.Errorf("unexpected ID")
}
```

Because this tests the behavior of the client's exposed function, it makes sense to not write it as an internal test. For this reason, the package for this test file is `client_test`. This test file needs to import the package containing the implementation, `learngo` `-pockets/templates/internal/client`. In the following listing, let's have a go at testing the error path, where we don't need to mock the `GetStatus` call at all.

Listing 11.17 `list_test.go`: Testing when listing returns an error

```
func TestListHabits_error(t *testing.T) {
    sentinelErr := fmt.Errorf("list habits error")    ◄──┐ Defines the
                                                          │ expected error
    mockClient := mocks.NewHabitsClientMock(t)
    mockClient.ListHabitsMock.Expect(minimock.AnyContext,    ◄──┐ Instantiates the
        &api.ListHabitsRequest{}).Return(nil, sentinelErr)     │ client with the
                                                               │ error-sending mock
    habitsClient := client.New(mockClient)
    habits, err := habitsClient.ListHabits(context.Background())

    require.ErrorIs(t, err, sentinelErr)    ◄──┐ Asserts that we
    assert.Nil(t, habits)                       │ get the error
}
```

Finally, the third test covers the case where one of the calls to `GetStatus` fails. The mock for `ListHabits` returns some good data, but the mock for the second status returns an error. While some mock tools allow calling an equivalent of `Expect(EndpointName, ExpectedParameters)` several times per endpoint, `minimock` doesn't. Instead, we need to override the behavior of the mock. For this, we use the `Set` method and provide it with our fake implementation that we can adapt to the calls we'll make.

Listing 11.18 `list_test.go`: Testing when `get status` returns an error

```
func TestListHabits_statuserror(t *testing.T) {
    now := time.Now()
    mockClient := mocks.NewHabitsClientMock(t)
    habitsClient := client.New(mockClient)

    mockResponse := &api.ListHabitsResponse{
```

```
        Habits: []*api.Habit{
            {Id: "ID1", Name: ...},
            {Id: "ID2", Name: ...},
        },
    }

    sentinelErr := status.Error(codes.Internal, "not after 10PM")
    mockClient.ListHabitsMock.
        Expect(minimock.AnyContext, &api.ListHabitsRequest{}).
        Return(mockResponse, nil)     ◄──┐ Sets the output of
                                          │ the call to ListHabits
    mockClient.GetHabitStatusMock.Set(
        func(ctx context.Context,
            in *api.GetHabitStatusRequest,
            opts ...grpc.CallOption) (
            *api.GetHabitStatusResponse, error) {
            switch {
            case in.HabitId == "ID1":
                return &api.GetHabitStatusResponse{}, nil  ◄──┐ The first GetStatus
            case in.HabitId == "ID2":                          │ succeeds.
                return nil, sentinelErr   ◄──┐ The second GetStatus fails.
            default:
                return nil, fmt.Errorf("unexpected call")
            }
        })

    habits, err := habitsClient.ListHabits(context.Background(), now)

    require.ErrorIs(t, err, sentinelErr)    ◄──┐ The overall response
    assert.Nil(t, habits)                       │ is an error.
}
```

We've now a tested client's `ListHabits` logic. To use it, we need the `main` function to build the dependencies required by our server.

DEPENDENCY INJECTION

On one side, we're writing an HTTP server. On the other side, we're using a gRPC client to retrieve habits. The layer in charge of instantiating these two and plugging them together is the `main` function, which will inject the dependencies in the layers below it as needed. The `server` package shouldn't use the API generated by the `proto` tools. Instead, it should use its own small interface of what a `habit` client is—that's generally the approach in Go.

The `main` function will need to create a gRPC client and feed it to the HTTP server as shown in listing 11.19. For this, we'll instantiate the gRPC client as we did in the integration tests section of chapter 10. Usually, the remote dependency's address won't be `localhost:8084` (unless you're very lucky). It should be possible to inject the other service's address via a configuration file, a Kubernetes configuration map, a Docker network setting, or whatever the platform uses.

Listing 11.19 `main.go`: Building the client

```
func main() {
    cli, err := newClient("localhost:8084")       ◄─── Includes the backend
    if err != nil {                                     service's port
        log.Fatalf(...)           ◄─── No point in going
    }                                  any further

    srv := handlers.New(cli)
    //...
}

// newClient creates a client to the habits service.
func newClient(serverAddress string) (*client.HabitsClient, error) {
    creds := grpc.WithTransportCredentials(insecure.NewCredentials())
    conn, err := grpc.Dial(serverAddress, creds)  ◄───
    if err != nil {                                     A lot of dial options are
        return nil, err                                 available; check go doc
    }                                                   grpc.DialOption for a list.

    grpCli := api.NewHabitsClient(conn)

    return client.New(grpCli), nil
}
```

The HTTP server needs to know what to do with this new parameter. Let's update the
code of the `New` function in the `server` package, and define the small easy-to-mock
interface we'll use from the server's point of view, as shown in listing 11.20. Thanks
to our interface, it should now be clear that the HTTP server is totally unaware that
retrieving habits requires a gRPC client under the hood.

Listing 11.20 `server.go`: Using the client dependency

```
// HabitsClient is the dependency towards the Habits client.
//go:generate minimock -s "_mock.go" -o "mocks"    ◄───
type HabitsClient interface {                           Mocks the
    ListHabits(ctx context.Context) ([]habit.Habit, error)  dependency for tests
}

// Server serves all the HTML routes on this service.
type Server struct {
    client HabitsClient      ◄─── Adds a field in the
    lgr    Logger                 server struct
}

// New builds a new server.
func New(cli HabitsClient, lgr Logger) *Server {   ◄─── Requires the dependency
    return &Server{
        client: cli,
        lgr: lgr,
    }
}
```

```
// Router returns an HTTP handler that listens to all the proper paths.
func (s *Server) Router() http.Handler {...}
```

Finally, let's return to the `index` method. It now has access to the backend client via its receiver s and can call it to get the habits. Hopefully, everything will go smoothly when the HTTP server calls the gRPC server, but in case of an error, we should display some pretty 5xx (internal server errors) message to the client, as shown in the following listing. A Retry button would be cool, but let's keep it simple and assume that people know how to refresh a page.

Listing 11.21 index.go: **In case of an error**

```
// index serves the root page of the app.                    Uses the
func (s *Server) index(w http.ResponseWriter, r *http.Request) {    request
    habits, err := s.client.ListHabits(r.Context())             context
    if err != nil {
        s.lgr.Logf("error! %s", err.Error())              Logs the error
        http.Error(w, "Error while fetching data",
            http.StatusInternalServerError)               Returns an obfuscated
        return                                             error, as we haven't
    }                                                      called Write on w yet
    ...
```

Of course, we could be more specific and check inside the client package of the RPC return code that we get, turn it into a named error, and there check for this error. At the moment, there's no situation where a different code returned by the backend service would mean anything but `Internal Problems`, so this piece of code will do the work.

Habits

You have 2 habit(s) to follow.

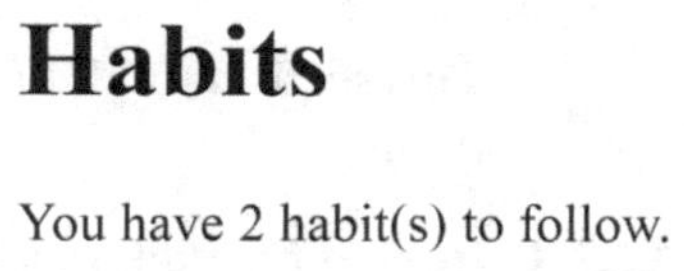

Figure 11.5 Browser result with a variable

If, for example, you decide to add some authentication on the `habits` server, then returning a `401` instead when relevant can make sense.

Replace the hardcoded value 5 in the call to `Execute` on our template with `len(habits)`. Figure 11.5 shows the result.

We have an extra "s" in the generated page at "habits" and no details on our habits themselves. It's time to provide some visibility and play with lists. Let's crack open the power of templates!

11.2 Basic template operations

You've seen how to insert one variable inside the HTML template. In this section, we'll go through operations such as accessing fields and expressing conditions with templates. We'll see how we can display the details of a `slice` of habits. Templates in Go are engines that update a string's contents using values. The following listing shows an example of using a template.

Listing 11.22 `index.html`: **Unordered list in the template**

```
package main

import (
    "fmt"
    "text/template"
    "os"
)

func main() {
    tmpl := `{{ range . }}{{.}}, {{end}}`
    t, err := template.New("my_template").Parse(tmpl)
    if err != nil {
        fmt.Fprintln(os.Stderr, err)
        return
    }

    values := []string{"a", "b", "c"}
    err = t.Execute(os.Stdout, values)
    if err != nil {
        fmt.Fprintln(os.Stderr, err)
        return
    }
}
```

Imports text/template or html/template depending on the overall goal

Defines the template

Parses the definition into a usable template

Applies the template on a string and writes it somewhere

This section will help you understand templates and explain how to start working with them.

11.2.1 *Iterate through a slice*

Templates can do a bit more than just print a variable, as they also have control flow statements. To iterate through a list of values, templates support the `range` action. Remember that in our current setup, the habits `slice` is the variable that we pass to our template execution, which means it's represented by the dot `.` as in the following:

```
{{ range $index, $value := . }} <some html> {{ end }}
```

Don't forget that the `{{ end }}` (or `{{end}}`) is the equivalent of Go's closing curly bracket in a `for` loop. The input value can be a `slice`, `map`, `channel`, `array`, or anything that Go knows how to `range` over. Using `$index` and `$value` creates variables that are usable in the scope of the `{{range}}`...`{{end}}` block. The action to print the index, for instance, is `{{ $index }}`.

Alternatively, if you're not using the `index` variable in the template, you can use `{{ range . }}` ... `{{ end }}`, and the value of the dot variable inside the action will iterate through the values of the `slice`. This might be counterintuitive, as when we only iterate over a `slice` or `map` in Go with the `for x := range values` syntax, x is either the index in the `slice` or a key of the `map`. With `{{ range . }}`, we iterate through elements of the `slice` or values of the `map`. Let's see it in action first with just a `slice` of your favorite numbers.

If we want to show a list of `index : number` as a list of items in a web page, our source HTML won't differ much from the syntax described previously. Let's add the following snippet in the `<body>` section of our `index.html` document.

Listing 11.23 `index.html`: **Unordered list in the template**

```
<ul>
    {{ range $index, $value := . }}
    <li>{{ $index }} : {{ $value }}</li>     ◄──┐ Loops over some data
    {{ end }}
</ul>
```

We're using the more verbose version because we want to show the `index` variable. Then, we just pass the `slice` to the template.

Listing 11.24 `index.go`: **Outputting a** `slice`

```
values := []int{47, 52, 88, 18}

err = tpl.Execute(w, values)     ◄──┐ Passes the slice as
if err != nil {...}                  parameter to the template
```

The result will look a bit stark, but in a very few lines, we have a working demo. Figure 11.6 shows the result in a browser.

Now that we've checked the `{{range}} {{end}}` with a `slice` of integers, let's return to our habits, and try to print the list of one habit's registered objectives.

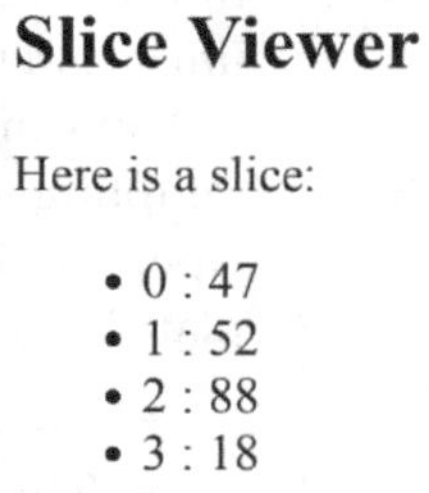

11.2.2 Accessing fields

We want to display the name and weekly target frequency for each habit. In an unordered list (`ul`), each list item (`li`) could display the name in bold (`b`) and the number of times a week, as shown in figure 11.7. Some say that bold shouldn't be a tag but should be a styling property, and we should replace this with a `span`, but let's keep it old school for the sake of clarity. After all, this chapter is about Go's templates, not HTML syntax.

The static HTML code for this example looks straightforward:

```
<ul>
  <li>
    <b>Knit</b> - 5 times a week
  </li>
</ul>
```

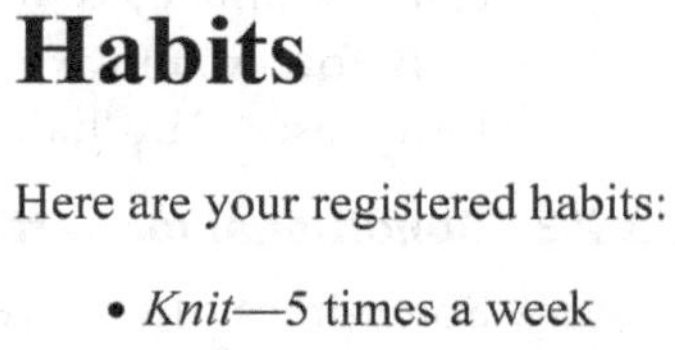

Slice Viewer

Here is a slice:

- 0 : 47
- 1 : 52
- 2 : 88
- 3 : 18

Figure 11.6 Browser result with a slice of ints

Habits

Here are your registered habits:

- *Knit*—5 times a week

Figure 11.7 Browser result with a list of habits

To get this result, our template is already ranging over the habits. We're using the shorthand version where . represents the `slice` of habits in {{range .}}, and, inside this range, the dot . is the habit currently being iterated over (see listing 11.25). To access the fields of this specific habit, just append the name of the field after the symbol. It absolutely needs to be exposed! This means that the template and the codebase are heavily intertwined. Changing the name of a field or making it unexposed will result in it no longer being printed.

Listing 11.25 `index.html`: **Accessing fields**

```
<ul>
    {{- range .}}              ◄───── This dot is the slice.
    <li>
        <b>{{ .Name }}</b> - {{ .WeeklyFrequency }}   ◄──── Thes dots are the current
 time(s) a week                                              element. We access the
    </li>                                                    habit's Name and
    {{- end}}                                                WeeklyFrequency.
</ul>
```

Give the `slice` of habits to the template for execution, and you can run it:

```
err = tpl.Execute(w, habits)
```

Do you see all of them? Does your test break? Are you struggling with the whitespaces in the test? Remember that using {{- or -}} can help reduce the whitespaces, new lines, and tabs.

You can already play around and show different fields of the habits. While it's very tempting to try and get the output of a method (after all, aren't they exposed from a type, just like fields?), a fair warning is recommended here: calling methods in a template is possible with two main requirements:

- The method must be niladic (receive no arguments)
- The method must return one value (or two, if the second one is an error). In this case, the (first) returned value will be printed.

If the method ticks the box, it's possible to call it in the template with no parentheses: {{ .Method }}. It's even possible, as suggested by the official documentation, to chain the calls, something we don't recommend doing at all, for clarity: {{ .Field1 .Method1.Field2.Method2 }}. Please don't do this. Instead, use a function or a dedicated template, as we'll see later.

Before we move on to more functionalities for our users, let's see how we can fix the lowercase "s" in "habit(s)" that currently requires parentheses.

11.2.3 *Conditional formatting*

Sometimes, there are panels that you want to show on certain conditions. The good news is you can use an `if` pattern inside the templates. There are a handful of keywords for this, just like in Go:

```
{{ if <condition> }}
{{ else if <condition> }}
{{ else }}
{{ end }}
```

The end keyword is the same that we use to close the scope of a range statement.

The conditions are a bit different: they use a pattern where the comparing operation comes first, and the operands come next. Comparison operators are strict: lt stands for "(strictly) less than," and gte stands for "greater than or equal to." You can find more Go templates conditions in table 11.1.

Table 11.1 Conditions

Go code	Go template
if h (Boolean)	{{ if . }}
if h != 0 (any numeric type, including rune)	{{ if . }}
if h != "" (string)	{{ if . }}
if len(h) != 0 (slice, map, array, string, *not* channel)	{{ if . }}
if h != nil (interface, uninitialized slice, map, channel, pointer)	{{ if . }}
if h < 3 (numerical value)	{{ if lt . 3 }}
if h == "pockets"	{{ if eq . "pockets" }}
if h >= -8	{{ if gte . -8 }}
if h != 4	{{ if ne . 4 }}
if s.X < 40 && !s.End	{{ if and (lt s.X 40) (not .End) }}

With the {{if}} action, using a singular form for the number of times a week becomes possible. Note the use of - to remove extra spaces:

```
{{ .WeeklyFrequency }} time{{ if gt .WeeklyFrequency 1 -}} s {{- end }} a week
```

You can even use pretty words like once or twice:

```
{{ if eq .WeeklyFrequency 1 }} once {{ else if eq .WeeklyFrequency 2 }}
twice {{ else }} {{ .WeeklyFrequency }} times {{ end }} a week
```

The result isn't necessarily easier to read for the end user (ask a UX designer), but it works: you can see it in figure 11.8. This kind of complex logic can be extracted into a function, as we'll see in section 11.5.2.

We can now display a web page containing the real data living in our database. However, all we can do so far is access it for reading—as a user, it would be quite frustrating to not be able to register some of these activities! Before we move on to our next step, don't forget to test. If the mocked call to the `Habits` service already provides some data, you only need to update the test output. Make sure you also have error cases covered.

Commit your code. It's time to tell the system when some of this to-do list gets done.

11.3 Send a tick to the server

Having a to-do list is a good way to get things out of your mind and onto paper, but ticking the boxes is the only way to make sure the day feels

Habits

Here are your registered habits:

- *Knit*—2 out of 5 <u>Tick!</u>
- *Call mom*—1 out of 1 <u>Tick!</u>
- *Code*—0 out of 3 <u>Tick!</u>

Figure 11.8   The list of habits with their associated frequencies per week

productive. Cognitive research suggests that keeping a "Done" list is healthy for people who highly value productivity, as it provides a sense of accomplishment. It's better for your brain than keeping a list in view of what you still haven't tackled after all this time.

11.3.1 What page should we display?

In this chapter, we decided to have all the logic happen server-side, as opposed to inside the browser. This means that to send information or a command to the server (e.g., "tick habit with ID 987 now"), the only action we can ask the user's browser to take is to go to another page. An alternative is to use JavaScript to execute requests to the HTTP server.

Because the "HT" in HTML stands for Hypertext, we can use this ancient magic where a piece of text can help navigate to another page. The goal here is to implement an HTTP endpoint that ticks a habit, given its ID. The target URL is `/tick/{habitID}`. Let's first add such a link in each of the habits in our list.

Listing 11.26   `index.html`: Adding a link to tick each habit

```
<li>
...
    <a href="/tick/{{ .ID }}">Tick!</a>          ◄─┐ The HTTP link
</li>
```

If you click it, the browser will redirect to this link and try to GET the page. As this is an action, we should probably use a POST verb. We'll do this in the next section. In the meanwhile, we'll use a GET here, as shown in listing 11.27. Let's add this route to our service, to avoid the classic 404. As we've seen in previous chapters, the standard `html` library understands a path parameter as a string inside curly brackets.

Listing 11.27   `server.go`: Registering the tick endpoint route

```
func (s *Server) Router() http.Handler {
    // ...
    r.HandleFunc(http.MethodGet+" "+"/tick/{habitID}",   ◄─┐ Registers the route with the URL parameter habitID
```

```
        s.tick)
    return r
}
```

Now we need to implement this new `tick` method on the server. The signature is imposed: the `http` package requires it to implement an `http.HandlerFunc`. First, the endpoint needs to parse the identifier from the request's URL using the `http` `.Request`'s `PathValue` method. Second, we can call the client—let's keep this bit for last. Write this endpoint in a new file, `tick.go`.

Listing 11.28 `tick.go`: **Ticking a habit**

```
// tick adds a tick to the given habit.
func (s *Server) tick(w http.ResponseWriter, r *http.Request) {
    const (
        habitIDPathValue = "habitID"
    )
    id := r.PathValue(habitIDPathValue)        ◀─── Uses the name of the
    if id == "" {                                    url parameter
        http.Error(w, "missing the id of the habit", http.StatusNotFound)
        return
    }


    // TODO call the gRPC client
}
```

Next, we need to provide some feedback to the user. We could write something like "Well done, click here to return to the main page," but we don't want to worsen any possible carpal tunnel syndrome by asking for more clicks. An alternative is to display the index discreetly, after the backend's `Tick` endpoint has been called:

```
s.index(w, r)
```

Doing so would work, so you can try it. The user navigates to `/tick/ID` and sees the index again, but with the new data. But if the user refreshes the page, there will be another tick marked, which is counterintuitive.

Fortunately, we're not the first developers to need a redirect after sending some command to a server. The HTTP status `303`, delicately described as `See Other`, seems to have been made for us:

```
http.Redirect(w, r, "/", http.StatusSeeOther)
```

This tells the browser to go back to the previous page, which, in our case, was the index. Here, you can see the point of using a constant for the main page's path: redirecting to the constant called `indexPath` will make your code clearer than the mysterious `"/"` in the preceding example.

We can already test this part: reading the `habitID`. You'll need, as usual, a `Response-Recorder`. You also need to provide our request with the URL parameter by setting the value with the `SetPathValue` method. Let's write some tests in `handlers/tick_test.go`.

Listing 11.29   `tick_test.go`: **Testing with URL parameters**

```go
func TestServer_Tick(t *testing.T) {
    rr := httptest.NewRecorder()

    req := httptest.NewRequest(              // Creates the request
        http.MethodGet, "/tick/", nil)       //   as usual
    req.SetPathValue("habitID", "1234")      // Provides the
                                             //   URL parameter
    s := New(nil, t)

    s.tick(rr, req)

    assert.Equal(t,
        http.StatusSeeOther, rr.Result().StatusCode)    // Validates the status
    assert.Contains(t, rr.Body.String(), `<a href="/">`) //   and redirection
}
```

In this test, we're not testing the full flow, but providing a request with some already prepared data. This might look like a cheat, but this is a unit test, and we don't want to test the `PathValue` logic and what happens before the `tick` method is called. If we really wanted to test the entire logic, then an integration test is necessary, where we would run the service and call it like any client would do. We chose to stay within the scope of a unit test. This endpoint is nice but it doesn't do its job yet, so we need to call the gRPC client.

11.3.2 *Send tick to the backend*

Finally, we need to connect the client to the backend `Habits` server. Using the same pattern as `ListHabits` does, write a `TickHabit` method on the `HabitsClient`. The method takes a `context.Context` and a habit ID, and it can return an error. It hides the call to the gRPC client. Because the backend's response for `TickHabit` is empty, we can keep only the returned error, if any.

The backend's request, however, requires a timestamp for when the habit was ticked. How are we telling the client which week we want? Let's first hardcode the current date in the next listing, and come back later (in section 11.5.1) to add a parameter.

Listing 11.30   `tick_test.go`: **Testing with URL parameters**

```go
// TickHabit adds a tick now.
func (hc *HabitsClient) TickHabit(ctx context.Context, id habit.ID) error {
    req := api.TickHabitRequest{
        HabitId:   string(id),
        Timestamp: timestamppb.Now(),        // A Protobuf-compatible version
                                             //   of the current timestamp
```

```
    }

    _, err := hc.cli.TickHabit(ctx, &req)        ◀——┘ Calls the Habits service
    return err
}
```

As you can see, if the API changes and the backend server starts returning something useful in the response, this is the layer that will decide how to handle it and whether to expose it. Before we can use this new method, we need to update our `HabitsClient` interface server-side, as shown in listing 11.31. Our server's dependency to the client layer only exposes a single method—`ListHabits`. Let's add the new `TickHabit` there and regenerate the mocks. Finally, call this client inside the `tick` method in the server layer, write a test with a pretty mock, run it, and enjoy. We can now display the habits we registered, and we can click our page to record the progress.

> **Listing 11.31 `server.go`: Adding the `TickHabit` method in the interface**

```
//go:generate minimock -s "_mock.go" -o "mocks"
type HabitsClient interface {
    ListHabits(ctx context.Context, t time.Time) ([]habit.Habit, error)
    TickHabit(ctx context.Context, id habit.ID) error
}
```

Add the client's mock to your unit test, and check that it does receive the proper `Habit` ID. Running the server and clicking on the Tick! link should now update the counter. While this is great, we can improve on the user experience by adding visual feedback, improving on the data already displayed.

11.3.3 Adding colors

HTML has a best friend that grants it pretty colors: Cascading Style Sheets, commonly referred to as CSS. They are called *cascading* because properties of the containers are inherited from their parent container. To cut the frontend theory short, we can add a class to any HTML tag and apply some styling to it. This won't add much to the code of the list items (or any other container), but it will change the way they are rendered in the browser window.

> **TIP** We recommend *CSS in Depth* (Manning, 2024, www.manning.com/books/css-in-depth-second-edition) by Keith J. Grant if you want to learn more about CSS.

Let's create a CSS class called `done` for habits whose number of ticks have reached the targeted weekly frequency, and let's add a class attribute to the list items. To compare if the goal has been met, we'll use an `{{ if ... }}` template, comparing the tick count to the objective.

Note that if you code more than the target of three times a week, it still counts as completed; basically, any number of times greater or equal to the target works:

```
<li class="{{ if gte .Ticks .WeeklyFrequency }}done{{end}}">
```

Actually, this logic should be in Go, as it will be much easier to test: a `Habit` variable should be able to tell whether it's completed or not. Write that method (remember, it needs to be exposed for the template to access it), write a test for it, and you can add an `IsDone` method on our `habit`, as shown in listing 11.32, and call this new method in the template instead of using the preceding line of code:

```
<li class="{{ if .IsDone }}done{{end}}">
```

Listing 11.32 `habit.go`: Exposing whether a habit was completed

```go
// IsDone returns whether a habit has been fully completed.
func (h *Habit) IsDone() bool {
    return h.Ticks >= h.WeeklyFrequency
}
```

Add the following styling code inside the `<head>` tag to show the difference (we're keeping the styling very minimal, not indicating how CSS should be written):

```html
<head>
...
<style>
 .done {
    color: white;
    background-color: darkgreen;
 }
</style>
...
</head>
```

Feel free to change the colors to make them colorblind friendly and to match your own taste. Restart the server, and check the result: Does ticking a habit enough times to reach the objective change its appearance? Update the test, and make sure it runs smoothly and covers all the relevant cases.

11.4 Use a form to create a habit

In software development, we always try to ship little increments to the users, so that we can align the product with their needs. More concretely, adding small changes to a product also allows it to be deployed early and generate revenue as soon as possible. When making an idea happen, be it a full product or a single feature, we start by looking for the minimal viable product, eliminating as many features as possible, and then iterating on the users' feedback. We've already pushed the feature of ticking a habit at a specific date to a later time, but there's one feature without which we can't ship our product: creating a habit.

11.4.1 HTML form

To create a habit, we need to retrieve some values from the user, such as the habit's name or its frequency. For this, we'll ask the user to fill in a form, and provide a way of "sending" the habit to the server to have it created. HTML has the `form` tag for sending data to a server. Among the different attributes `form` can take, we'll focus on `action`, which determines the path where the data should be sent, and `method`, which determines the verb that will be used:

```
<form action="/create" method="post">
```

We want to create a habit, so `POST /create` seems pretty straightforward. If we were also dealing with other kinds of entities, it would be polite to prefix the path with the word `habits`, but let's keep it simple.

A `form` element can itself contain several other elements, each of them with a specific purpose. For our needs, we'll only use three of them: the `input`, the `label` to parse input values, and a `button`, in charge of making the call to the server.

From a server's perspective, we only need each field to be attached to a name that will help us discriminate between them. That's where the `input` tag is used—it's an empty field in which the user can write data. From a user's perspective, though, we need to display some text to tell the user what data we expect in our different inputs, and that's the role of the `label`. A `label`'s `for` attribute needs to correspond to the `input`'s `id`.

Some programs, such as readers for people with visual impairments, use labels extensively. You can read more about the Web Accessibility Initiative (WAI) on the W3C website. Finally, a `button` will send the form's data to the server when clicked. The following listing shows the contents of our form.

> **Listing 11.33** `index.html`: Form to create a habit

```
<form action="/create" method="post">
    <label for="habitName">Objective:</label>      ← Matches the for attribute of the habitName label to the habitName input's id value
    <input type="text" id="habitName" name="habitName">

    <label for="habitFrequency">Weekly frequency:</label>   ←
    <input type="number" id="habitFrequency" name="habitFrequency">

    <button>Create</button>                 Matches the for attribute of the habitFrequency label to the habitFrequency input's id value
</form>
```

Check the result in your browser and add some pretty styling if you like. Figure 11.9 shows the result, and as you can see, we didn't style it.

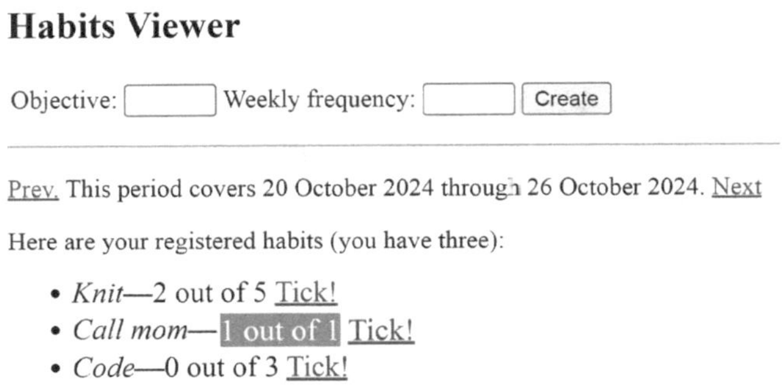

Habits Viewer

Objective: [   ] Weekly frequency: [   ] [Create]

Prev. This period covers 20 October 2024 through 26 October 2024. Next

Here are your registered habits (you have three):

- *Knit*—2 out of 5 Tick!
- *Call mom*—1 out of 1 Tick!
- *Code*—0 out of 3 Tick!

Figure 11.9   Browser result with a form

11.4.2 *Read a form's values*

We defined the /create route where the data is sent when the button is clicked, so now let's listen to it on the server's end. To implement the whole chain of calls, we'll need to add a call to the backend's CreateHabit endpoint. Let's start with the internal/client/create.go. The implementation should be straightforward: we receive a habit's definition, we convert it to its Protobuf representation, and we call the backend's endpoint. Test it with a mocked gRPC client using the same strategy as we used with TickHabit.

Then, we need to add a handler similar to tick on the server. The data is accessible via the FormValue method on http.Request, which only returns strings. Use the strconv package to parse the target frequency as an integer.

Listing 11.34   create.go: Parsing form values

```
// create takes a JSON request and creates a Habit from it,
// then redirects to index.
func (s *Server) create(w http.ResponseWriter, r *http.Request) {
    habitName := r.FormValue("habitName")          ◄──┐  Reads a string
    weeklyFreq, err := strconv.Atci(               ◄──┐
        r.FormValue("habitFrequency"))                │  Reads an int
    if err != nil {...}

    // call client

    // redirect to index                           ◄──┐  Creating a new habit
    http.Redirect(w, r, "/", http.StatusSeeOther)       should refresh the page.
}
```

Finally, we need to update the router to register the new POST endpoint:

```
r.Post("/create", s.create)
```

Who should validate the fields of the new habit? Should it be the role of the HTTP server—after all, an early check would save time on useless calls. Should it only be the responsibility of the backend—doesn't the backend know what a "valid name for a habit" should be? We decided to not have this logic in the frontend. However, this shows we need a safety net here to protect the backend against nasty attacks. For instance, we could make sure the weekly frequency is meaningful—maybe something between 1 and 100. Similarly, the habit's name should be a string of between 1 and 200 runes in length.

For now, if the user inputs invalid data, we don't really have a way of sending the user a pop-up explaining what went wrong. We'll continue logging to os.Stdout from the server. This chapter is about templates, so let's explore what extra possibilities they offer.

11.5 More template niceties

We've seen the most common tags that can be found in templates and how to use them. There are also a handful of other ways of using templates in Golang.

11.5.1 Passing more than one object to the template

The list of habits isn't the only data we want to pass to the template upon execution. The product, so to speak, is designed to be based on weeks, yet we don't display the date and can't navigate through the previous or future weeks.

Let's see how we can display the week's start and end dates. The constraint here is that we have one template document (our HTML page), and we'd like to pass it several values, instead of solely the current list of habits. Let's first decide what we want to display, and then look at a way to achieve it.

FORMATTED WEEK TYPE

Passing a timestamp directly to the template and having it printed in the web page wouldn't be very user friendly. Instead, we want to display something like "Week from June 30 to July 6." For a simpler code, we'll make the week start on a Sunday. The reason for this is that the time.Weekday's zero value is time.Sunday—using a Monday or a Saturday (the other usual first days of the week), a Friday (in the Maldives), or any other day would require a little arithmetic.

We can create a type built from a timestamp and expose two methods: Start and End of the week containing this timestamp, as shown in the following listing. This type can live in the internal/habit package with all our business types (for the moment just the one: Habit).

Listing 11.35 week.go: API

```
// FormattedWeek defines the start and end of a week, and formats them.
// Start to end will be from Sunday 00:00 to Saturday 23:59,
// rounded to the minute.
type FormattedWeek struct {}          ◀─┐ Exposed type      Builds from a
                                                            provided timestamp
// NewFormattedWeek builds an immutable week from one moment inside it.
func NewFormattedWeek(include time.Time) FormattedWeek     ◀─
```

```
// Start returns the formatted first day of the week.
func (w FormattedWeek) Start() string
```
◄——— **Methods that return only a string can be called in the template.**

```
// End returns the formatted last day of the week.
func (w FormattedWeek) End() string
```
◄———

We have two options here: keep the provided timestamp and compute the start and end when they are needed, or compute the start and end in the `NewFormattedWeek` function and return them when they are needed. The latter forces us to create an immutable type, which is always a good idea when dealing with value objects, as is the case here.

Let's compute the timestamps of the start and end of week when we build the `FormattedWeek` instance and keep them as fields. From the time included in the week, we get the start of the day (same date, midnight), and then subtract the index of the day in the week (Sunday is 0, Monday is 1, etc.). To subtract a day, we use the method `AddDate`. This method allows us to add and/or subtract years, months, and days to a `time.Time`. The method covers all use cases that would be painful to write manually, such as leap years or winter/summer time changes. It's good to keep in mind that adding a month is implemented as adding 31 days. As a result, adding 1 month to January 31, in ordinary years, returns March 3 (31 days after January 31), which might be surprising. `AddDate` is very useful because it can be used to travel both in the future and in the past, as it allows a negative number of years, months, or days as its parameters:

```
start := startOfDay(include).AddDate(0, 0, -int(include.Weekday()))
```

From there, add seven days and remove 1 minute to get the end of the week. If we don't remove at least 1 ms, the end falls on Sunday morning next week, and formatting that date won't give us the proper day. We chose to remove a full minute to ease our job when debugging and testing; we could remove a full day as long as we don't need to display the time at all, only the date. This also covers the uncommon problem of leap seconds. To remove a minute, we'll use `Add`. Why are we using two different methods, `Add` and `AddDate`, to do the same operation? The answer is that their scope isn't really the same—`Add` should be used for durations shorter than a day, and `AddDate` should be used for anything beyond that. The following listing shows how to use the `NewFormattedWeek` function.

Listing 11.36   `week.go`: New formatted week

```
// FormattedWeek defines ...
type FormattedWeek struct {
    start, end time.Time          ◄——— Keeps the computed
}                                       timestamps

// NewFormattedWeek builds ...
func NewFormattedWeek(include time.Time, layout string) FormattedWeek {
    start := startOfDay(include).
```

```
        AddDate(0, 0, -int(include.Weekday()))
    return FormattedWeek{
        start:  start,
        end:    start.AddDate(0, 0, 7).
            Add(-1 * time.Minute),
        layout: layout,
    }
}
```

◄── **Computes the start of the week that includes the parameter**

◄── **Computes the end of the week**

```
// startOfDay returns the same date as given, at midnight.
func startOfDay(t time.Time) time.Time {
    year, month, day := t.Date()
    return time.Date(year, month, day, 0, 0, 0, 0, t.Location())
}
```

Typically, logic needs to be strongly unit tested, with test cases that go over months and over years; input times on Sundays, Mondays, and Saturdays; non-UTC time zones, during daylight saving time changes; and so on.

Finally, we need a way to format these two timestamps in a human-readable way. The time package has a function for this—it takes a formatting string as a parameter, for example, "02 January 2006". It has to be in that format for Go to understand it.

We could hardcode this string as a constant of the package, but is it really the habit package's job to decide how things should be displayed? Ideally, we would pass that parameter to the Start and End methods. Because we first want to see how a function can be called via the templates without the complexity of a parameter, we decided that the week would be formatted (hence the name of our structure), and the layout would be passed to NewFormattedWeek and kept as a field. It makes the methods' implementation quite straightforward.

Listing 11.37 Start and End methods

```
// Start returns the formatted first day of the week.
func (w FormattedWeek) Start() string {
    return w.start.Format(w.layout)
}
```

◄── **Formats the time using the layout field**

```
// End returns the formatted last day of the week.
func (w FormattedWeek) End() string {
    return w.end.Format(w.layout)
}
```

All that is left to do is to update NewFormattedWeek accordingly.

Side quest 11.1

Set Monday or Saturday as the first day of the week, and update the tests accordingly. You can find our solution (we chose Monday because we're from Europe) in the book's repository under a different build tag (https://mng.bz/OBzR).

MULTIPLE TEMPLATE ARGUMENTS

Back in the index page, build the week that you want to pass to the template execution:

```
week := habit.NewWeek(time.Now(), "02 January 2006")
```

The Execute method on the template can only take one parameter, and we already need to send the habits—how can we pass more values, such as this timestamp? One option is to create a clutter of a local struct, containing lists of habits and dates, but that can become wordy to use. A simple map can do the job instead, as shown in the following listing. The template will receive the map as the dot and can access its values by using the keys as if there were fields.

Listing 11.38 index.go: **Passing more data**

```
err = tpl.Execute(w, map[string]interface{}{
    "Habits": habits,
    "Date":   week,                            ◀──┐  The template can
})                                                │  access .Habits.
if err != nil {...}
```

Add a line in the HTML to show the date. In Go, a function is similar to a field:

```
<p>This period covers {{.Date.Start}} -> {{.Date.End}}.</p>
```

You might notice that this line only deals with the Date field. If this were Go code, we could have a function accepting a Date and returning the start and end, and we would have factored this. While it's possible to declare variables in templates to help with readability, we don't recommend it. Their scope is too loose. Instead, we can restrict the template's visibility to only the .Date field using the with action:

```
{{with .Date}}<p>This period covers {{.Start}} -> {{.End}}.</p>{{end}}
```

This syntax sets the "local value" of the dot to .Date while inside the {{ with }} ... {{ end }}. Of course, we renamed the slice of habits from . to .Habits when we passed multiple arguments to our template, so this needs to be reflected in the {{range}} section. We can even wrap the whole block in a condition, so that when the slice is empty, the list isn't displayed at all.

Listing 11.39 index.go: **Hiding an empty list**

```
{{- if .Habits }}
<!-- titles and nice displays -->        ◀──┐  Using the - will discard
    <ul>                                     │  this empty line from the
        {{- range .Habits }}                 │  generated document.
        <li>
            ...
        </li>
```

```
        {{- end }}
    </ul>
{{- end }}
```

Update your tests, and add a test case where the `slice` is empty. Figure 11.10 shows the result in the browser.

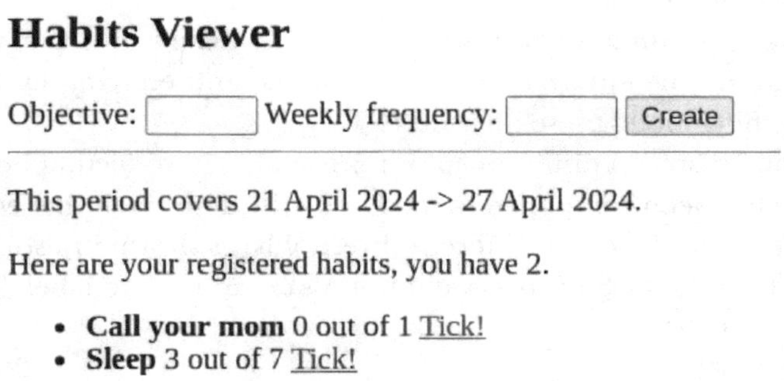

Habits Viewer

Objective: [   ] Weekly frequency: [   ] [Create]

This period covers 21 April 2024 -> 27 April 2024.

Here are your registered habits, you have 2.

- **Call your mom** 0 out of 1 <u>Tick!</u>
- **Sleep** 3 out of 7 <u>Tick!</u>

Figure 11.10   Browser result with the week details

Do you see why the test can't possibly be stable in the current situation? We're still using `time.Now()` as the input for our week. Next week, the test will be broken.

> **Side quest 11.2**
>
> Now that we know the status of our habits for the current date, it would be nice to check the previous weeks and anticipate the next ones. Try it at home by following these steps:
>
> 1 Add links for navigation in the HTML, and implement `Previous` and `Next` on the formatted week:
>
> ```
> <a href="/?week={{ .Date.Previous }}">Prev.</a>
> ```
>
> 2 Pass the time as a query parameter to the index, defaulting to `time.Now()` if it's absent. Remember, the difference between path and query parameters is that the former is mandatory, whereas the latter is not. Use `r.URL.Query().Get("week")` to retrieve a value from the URL query.
>
> 3 Update the client call to include a timestamp of the habits we want to retrieve.
>
> 4 Add a query parameter to the unit test request, and update the output.
>
> 5 Should it be possible to tick something in the past? You decide. How should that be shown in the UI? Does the redirection after a tick still work, or does it go back to the current week? How can you fix this?
>
> 6 Should it be possible to navigate to the future? Does it make sense? How can you block the navigation to future weeks? Hiding the Next button isn't enough: What if the user passes a future timestamp as a query parameter?

11.5.2 *Calling functions*

As we've already seen, the template engine can access values, but it can do a lot more than that. In fact, we can run functions from the templates. From a certain angle, some actions, such as range and if, could be considered as functions in {{ range . }} and {{ if . }}, and we've already met {{ len . }}. In Go, you can write your own functions and call them in the template.

REGISTERING NEW FUNCTIONS IN THE TEMPLATE

Currently, we only show the number of times a habit was ticked. But this isn't fun enough. A web page should be entertaining, full of colors, and enticing its visitor to return. Let's add something along these lines here.

For instance, we could display a different color for each habit, reflecting how much of the weekly objective has been completed so far. Let's write a function that computes the progression and returns a label for different thresholds, as shown in listing 11.40. We can then use this label as a CSS class—we'll use a string for the label. This will replace the previous done class.

Listing 11.40 `index.go:` **Label for progression**

```
func statusCSSClass(habit *habit.Habit) string {
    prog := float32(habit.Ticks) /
        float32(habit.WeeklyFrequency)       ◄─── Computes the
    switch {                                       progression
    case prog == 0:
        return "not_started"
    case prog < 0.5:
        return "started"
    case prog < 1:
        return "good_progress"
    default:
        return "completed"          ◄─── One or more if there are
    }                                    more ticks than the target
}
```

To call this function from the template, the function needs to be registered in the template by calling the Funcs method when we create the template, as shown in listing 11.41. The Funcs method accepts a map of functions, where the keys are the names of these functions as they'll appear in the template {{ myFunc . }} (and the values are the Go functions to be called).

Listing 11.41 `index.html:` **Providing the function to the template**

```
tpl, err := template.New("index").
    Funcs(template.FuncMap{
        "statusCSSClass": statusCSSClass,   ◄─── Maps the template's function
    }).                                          name to a Go function
    Parse(indexPage)
if err != nil {...}
```

In the template, you can now use the identifier of the function, and give it the habit as an argument. Inside the {{ range . }} loop, the current habit is identified by a dot, which means we can retrieve the CSS class as shown in the following listing.

```
<style>
    li.habit.completed {                    ◄────  Declares the styles in
        background: #afa;                          the <header> section
    }
    li.habit.good_progress {
        background: #ffa;
    }
    ...
</style>
...
<ul>
    {{- range .Habits }}
    <li class="habit {{ statusCSSClass . }}">   ◄──┐ Calls the function
    <b>{{.Name}}</b>
```

Run it. What do you think? Feel free to change the colors, of course. Don't forget to complete the CSS to support all the different labels. Write a test for the function, and then update the test for `index`.

PIPELINES

Templates in Go enable you to use pipelines. They should be used when the output of a function has to be used as the input of the next. Unix users will recognize the syntax as it's exactly the same: {{ func1 . | func2 }} produces the same result as calling `func2` on the output of `func1(.)`, which we usually write as `func2(func1(.))`. There's no limit to the number of | used in a pipeline.

Let's consider an example outside the scope of this chapter: suppose we need to print the hostnames that appear in a list of URLs. We also want to normalize this output—we want all hostnames to be lowercase. First, we'll need a function (in Golang) to extract the hostname from the URL. We can do this with the `net/url` package.

```
func extractDomainName(rawURL string) string {
    u, err := url.Parse(rawURL)
    if err != nil {
        return ""          ◄────  Errors sent to the template
    }                             won't really be used.

    return u.Hostname()
}
```

Now, we can register this function in the template we would use for this side project. Because we'll also need to lowercase the whole string, let's also register that. But why not call `strings.ToLower` directly in `extractDomainNames` instead of dealing with the hassle of registering two functions? The following listing shows how we would build the template.

Listing 11.44   Registering all the functions using the pipeline

```
tmpl, err := template.New("domains").
    Funcs(template.FuncMap{
        "lower": strings.ToLower,
        "extractDomainNames": extractDomainNames}).
    Parse("{{range .}}{{extractDomainNames . | lower | println}}{{end }}")
```

Here, we added an extra `println` to have every hostname printed on its own line (the default action is to print with no empty line). Calling this on the `slice`

```
[]string{"http://google.com", "https://www.wikipedia.fr", "http://UN.org"}
```

produces the following:

```
google.com
wikipedia.fr
un.org
```

When it comes to pipelines, it's equivalent to write `{{ . | len }}` and `{{ len . }}` as both will print the length of the value. The difference here is to put some emphasis on the value on which we operate, rather than on the function we use. Both syntaxes are valid and lead to the same result. As the developer, you'll decide which one corresponds to your situation.

11.5.3 *Using define to declare functions*

Go's templates offer the last action we'll be looking at in this chapter: writing functions as template actions instead of providing them from Go via `Funcs()`. One of the implications of this feature is that if a program is in charge of loading the template and executing it, we could update the behavior of the program by simply updating the template file it loads. This is dangerous on many levels (you need to keep track of the template currently being used, you need to make sure the template is always correct, etc.), but sometimes it's an interesting feature to have.

Let's take a look at our HTML template: we currently iterate through the habits with `{{- range .Habits }}`, and there are five lines before we reach the associated `{{- end }}` statement. In these five lines, the only thing we achieve is to turn a structure into a pretty list item. This is something a function could do, which would clarify the code a bit.

Here, we'll define a new template whose role is to format a habit into its HTML representation. Let's start by defining a new template in an HTML file. We could define it in the same file as our whole page, but we'd have to place it somewhere where it wouldn't make the HTML skeleton scream. Instead, we'll simply write it to another file, as shown in listing 11.45. Actually, because we're starting to have more than one file for our template, let's move our `index.html` to a new folder, `internal/handlers/templates`. That's where we can create the new template file in charge of converting the habit to an HTML item: `habititem.html`.

The syntax to define a template is relatively short: we use the `{{ define "template-Name" }} ... {{ end }}` action. We'll simply move the contents of the `{{ range }}` loop from `index.html` into this file.

Listing 11.45 `habititem.html`: **Declaring a template in another file**

```
{{- define "habitItem"}}
        <li class="habit {{ statusCSSClass . }}">
            <b>{{.Name}}</b>
            <span class="{{ if ge .Ticks .WeeklyFrequency -}} done
{{- end -}} "> {{- progress . }}</span>
            <a href="/tick/{{ .ID }}">Tick!</a>
        </li>
{{- end }}
```

At this point, a few notes on formatting are required. As you can see, both `{{- define }}` and `{{- end}}` start with the `-` to ignore previous spaces, with the `\n` preceding them. But we could also instead remove the `\n` after them, and use `{{ define -}}` and `{{ end -}}` (or even use the `-` on each side). Unfortunately, there's a side effect to that: `-` removes all subsequent space characters, including any indentation. While this wouldn't break the generated HTML document's rendering, it would make its source code look broken. And this is the other important point of this file: its contents must be properly indented. Go doesn't provide a function in its templates for this, but Helm—a tool that heavily relies on Go templates to work with YAML files—does, and we frequently see an action end with `| indent 4 }}` in Helm files.

We now have to update the `index.html` file to call the new template: simply replace the section we copied with the action `{{ template "habitItem" . }}`. This will call the other template with the value of the dot, which, at that time, is iterating through the habits. Sometimes, the call to another template via `{{ template "habitItem" }}` will omit the dot—it's the default parameter. We decided to keep it:

```
{{- range .Habits }}
    {{- template "habitItem" . }}
{{- end }}
```

Again, we decided to indent the action for clarity—but you'll notice that the indentation before the call to `"habitItem"` will be discarded by the `-` in the `{{- define` piece of code.

Now that we've moved our file to a new folder, however, we need to adapt how we load it. We didn't write anything like `import habititem.html` in the `index.html` file, so how can it refer to a template in a different file? We used to `embed` the template file, but now, should we embed several files? What would a good limit be before we end up embedding a nonsensically long list of files? We don't want to decide for you, but we think that anything beyond one is already a lot, and, for that matter, we won't embed each file. Instead, because we've placed both our template files into a single directory, we can embed all the contents of that directory! This will load them in memory at compilation time. Let's look at the changes in `index.go` that this brings.

> **Listing 11.46 `index.html`: Embedding the contents of a directory**

```
//go:embed templates/*.html              ◄──────    Indexes all the files in the templates
var templates embed.FS                              directory with an .html extension

...
tpl, err := template.New("index").Funcs(template.FuncMap{
    "statusCSSClass": statusCSSClass,
    "progress":       progress,                      Parses all the files with an .html
}).ParseFS(templates, "templates/*.html")    ◄───┘  extension in the templates directory
```

It's important to limit the scope of which files are embedded. There's no point in preloading an image or any file that doesn't pertain to the rendering of the index page here. If we try running our program, we now face an error:

```
Error in index: template: "index" is an incomplete or empty template
```

We registered two files in our template engine. Which one should be used when we execute the template? We need to be explicit, and ask for a specific template to be run. Because we've loaded files, the only way to point at one template in particular is to use the filename. The `ParseFS` function already registers the files by their base name. Instead of calling `Execute`, we'll call `ExecuteTemplate`, which takes the extra argument of the base name of the template file we want to execute:

```
err = tpl.ExecuteTemplate(w, "index.html", map[string]interface{}{
    "Habits": habits,
    "Date":   week,
})
```

> **NOTE** We mentioned earlier that `New` registers templates using the name provided, when we use `Parse`. For this reason, we could have called `tpl.Execute-Template(w, "index")` from the beginning with the same effect. But when there's only one template available, and it's been loaded with `Parse`, there's no ambiguity, and Go can determine what to do on its own.

Oh, in case you wonder—yes, it's possible to have a template's definition call itself. Please, just don't, for everyone's sake. If you really need recursion, try and do it in a piece of code, generating data ready to be displayed rather than computing it on the fly while displaying it.

That's it! We were able to define the equivalent of a function, which allowed us to factor our HTML document template and isolate the logic relative to a habit. If we had opened the template files with os.Open instead of using //go:embed, we would access whatever contents are present in the files every time the endpoint is called, which could lead to a lot of malicious scenarios.

Let's imagine another feature: we want users to be able to pick their favorite color for the interface. Somehow, we've stored that the current user likes dark mode after 10 P.M., and wants a light blue that they picked for daylight. We could simply give a class to the body and arrange the CSS so that colors correspond to either day or night. But if each user has their own preferences, it becomes interesting to use a template to generate the CSS on the fly. In a real production project, overriding in the HTML is probably better than generating the whole thing, but let's have fun.

For this, we'll create a new file, which will contain a new template. We can first try with just one variable.

Listing 11.47   `styles.css`: A text template

```
html {
    background-color: {{.Background}};       ◀——————  Passes the background color
    color: {{.Foreground}};
}
```

The corresponding handler would look like what we had at the start of the chapter, except for a few details and one major change: we're not creating HTML anymore, so we need to use the more basic text/template package. The main difference is that the first escapes a lot of different characters, and the second does not. We don't want our background color to be hijacked by the dangerous value </html>.

Additionally, to tell the browser that this piece of text is to be used as a style sheet, we need to explicitly state the content type. Let's write this new file in the internal/handlers/templates directory, alongside the other .html template files.

Listing 11.48   `styles.go`: Applies the CSS

```
import (
    _ "embed"
    "text/template"       ◀——————  Uses text templates
    ...
)

//go:embed templates/styles.css
var stylesPage string

func (s *Server) styles(w http.ResponseWriter, r *http.Request) {
    tpl, err := template.New("styles").Parse(stylesPage)
    if err != nil {...}

    w.Header().Add("Content-Type", "text/css")       ◀——————  Explicitly states the content type
```

```
    err = tpl.Execute(w, map[string]interface{}{
        "Background":"DarkSlateGray",
        "Foreground":"LightGray"})          ◄─────┐ Applies colors
    if err != nil {...}
}
```

Expose the endpoint, link the CSS inside the `<head>` tag of your index, and run it. Don't forget to test it as well.

You can go further by replacing the color string in the preceding code with a full palette that you pull from a database. The path to your main stylesheet becomes `styles .css?mode=dark`, for example. Or the color scheme can be linked to the user's preferences, the time zone (don't do this, VPNs make the user's time zone unreliable), or how far in the past we're browsing. You can even generate random colors and border styles. This is when giving a free rein to backend developers to pick designs becomes unmanageable..

Of course you can also generate deployment files in the same way, or, why not, Go code as well—Go code that generates Go code that generates . . . you get the picture.

Summary

- Golden files are used in tests to compare the expected contents of a call to the real output.

- Use `go mod edit -replace=old[@version]=new[@version]` to replace or override where Go fetches the module. This is common when using branches of libraries or when you want to use a local version on your computer.

- Templates are used to replace `fmt.Sprintf` or `strings.Builder`. They should be used when the blob of text that needs to be printed would make the two other options very cumbersome.

- Templates can be created using `text/template` or `html/template`. The main difference is that the HTML implementation protects the values printed against any HTML injection.

- It's best to write templates in different files than source code and to load their contents using `embed`.

- The `//go:embed` directive can be used to access (read-only) files as an `embed .FS`, a filesystem. This is quite useful when you need to load everything inside a directory.

- Load a template with `New()`, and provide a name, followed by `Parse`.

- Templates are based on actions, which appear between curly braces `{{ ... }}`.

- Templates use the current variable, called the dot, and represented by a period.

- `{{ . }}` is equivalent to Go's `fmt.Sprintf("%v", var)`.

- `{{.}}` and `{{ . }}` are equivalent.

- `{{- . }}` removes the space before the curly braces, while `{{ . -}}` removes the space after them.

- Templates and the codebase are heavily coupled—the template string needs to know the names of fields and methods that structures expose.
- Templates can access exposed fields of structures with `{{ .Field }}`.
- Templates can access methods, but we don't recommend it with `{{ .Method }}`. Only methods that return a printable value (with or without an error) can be called from a template.
- Unexposed fields and unexposed methods can't be accessed by templates.
- To iterate through a `slice`, `array`, `map`, or channel, use `{{range $index, $value := .}} ... {{end}}`.
- Alternatively, use `{{ range . }} ... {{end}}`; inside that range, the value of `.` will iterate through the values of the `slice`, `array`, channel, and `map` (values), not the index/keys.
- Use `{{ if <cond> }} ... {{ else if <cond> }} ... {{ else }} ... {{end}}` to express conditional behaviors. You can use Boolean operators (`and`, `or`, etc.) and numeric comparisons (`lt`, `lte`, `gt`, `gte`, `ne`, `eq`).
- Use `{{with .Date}} <section where we use only .Date subfields> {{end}}` to limit the length of accessors used: `.Date.Start` becomes `.Start` here.
- It's possible to register your own functions and make them available in the template: use the `Funcs` method when creating it.
- Pipelines can be used in templates to sequence actions. The pipeline character is the pipe `|`. Using a pipeline takes the output of the action on its left for the input of the action on its right.
- `{{ define "name" }} ... {{ end }}` can be used to declare the equivalent of functions. To call these functions, use `{{ template "name" . }}`.
- When several templates are available, be explicit about which one should be executed. Templates that were loaded from a filesystem are indexed on the base name of the files that were loaded. When several template definitions are loaded, use `ExecuteTemplate` instead of simply `Execute`, and provide the name of the root template.

12
Go for other architectures

This chapter covers

- Exploring WebAssembly and TinyGo
- Developing and integrating Go, JavaScript, and HTML via WebAssembly
- Compiling, testing, and debugging WebAssembly applications
- Investigating TinyGo's unique features
- Flashing a microcontroller using TinyGo

Congratulations on the progress you've made and the knowledge you've gained throughout this journey. We hope you found it fulfilling! Consider this chapter an added bonus where we explore two technologies revolving around Go: WebAssembly (Wasm) and TinyGo. Both are ways of writing and compiling code for small processors, such as those found in web browsers or microcontrollers used in robotics and the Internet of Things (IoT)—environments where memory and CPU resources are limited.

Your projects so far have been running on your machine, but most of the time, we have to write programs that will end up running on machines other than our own.

Those machines might be different from ours regarding available resources, operating system, CPU architecture, or the networks they're connected to. Go can help us build executables for specific environments. As an example, we'll start by exploring Wasm.

Finally, it's interesting to note that a `hello, world` Go executable weighs around 1.9 MB (your mileage may vary, but this is what we observed). It won't even fit on a floppy disk! Why is it so heavy, and can we make it smaller? We'll address these questions in the second part of this chapter, where we'll consider running applications on a board with limited resources.

12.1 Getting started with Wasm

In the first part of this chapter, we explore how to work with WebAssembly (Wasm), how to compile using TinyGo, and some initial differences from standard Go. Figure 12.1 describes how Wasm works: you write code in Go, it's compiled in bytecode, and then it's executed by a Wasm interpreter, which will run on the client side. In our case, the Wasm interpreter will be loaded from a generic JavaScript library.

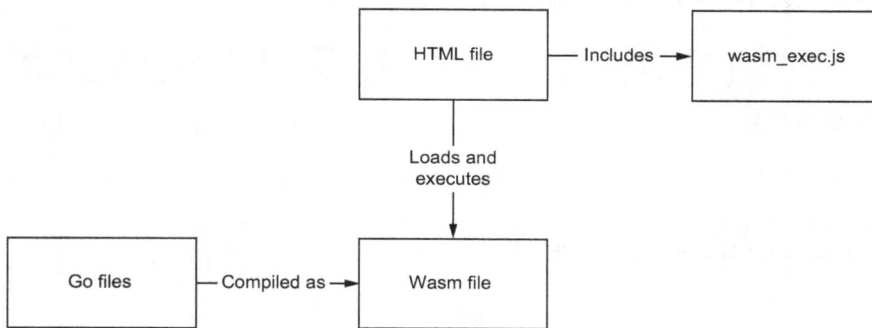

Figure 12.1   From Go code to Wasm executed by JavaScript

Wasm and its benefits

If you were alive in the 1990s, you experienced the 56k modem and its cryptic sound, the birth of GIF, and the appearance of the first static HTML websites. In the meantime, big companies developed a new programming language called JavaScript to add interactivity to websites and build web applications.

Nevertheless, JavaScript has its challenges and limitations. It's an interpreted language that can slow resource-consuming websites and applications, meaning performance is one of its main problems. JavaScript is also not cross-platform compatible. While most modern web browsers support JavaScript, differences in implementation and interpretation can lead to inconsistencies and compatibility problems across various platforms and devices.

(continued)

Wasm was created to cope with these limitations by providing a low-level, high-performance, and language-agnostic compilation target for web applications. Life as a developer is made better as we can write our applications in our favorite languages—Go, Rust, Python, or C++—and compile them into modules that can be executed in web browsers with near-native speeds and improved cross-platform compatibility.

12.1.1 *Some practice with Hello Wasm*

Let's start with a simple `hello, world` using Go and compile it using Wasm. For now, we'll use a flat-file organization, having every file in the same place to make things simpler. In the next section, we'll arrange files in a more usual fashion. In this section, we just want to use Go to write a message into a web browser console.

Here is our Hello, WASM! program's code. The steps are the same as for writing a Go program that would be compiled the usual way. Start by running `go mod init` in a new directory, and then create the `main.go`.

Listing 12.1   `main.go`: Hello, WASM!

```
package main

import "fmt"

func main() {
    fmt.Println("Hello, WASM!")
}
```

To compile it, we'll use the following command:

```
> GOOS=js GOARCH=wasm go build -o main.wasm
```

Developers working with Windows can use the following lines:

```
> set GOOS=js
> set GOARCH=wasm
> go build -o main.wasm
```

Let's decompose these commands: `GOOS=js` means that the operating system we're using is JavaScript. The second argument is the architecture `GOARCH=wasm`, which enables the compiler to convert your code into a binary depending on the platform you're running on. By default, these two environment variables will use the values of the environment of your machine—`linux`, `windows`, or `darwin` (for macOS)—for `GOOS`, and what your processor is for `GOARCH`. Note that you can list all the supported distributions using the following:

```
> go tool dist list
```

Most of the time, these variables on your machine are set to the corresponding architecture Linux, Windows, or Darwin. But let's go back to our principal command: the output of the `go build` is `main.wasm`. We'd like to execute this program, but because Wasm requires a runtime environment, we're going to need some help. There are some standalone tools that can run compiled Wasm files, such as Wasmtime (https:// wasmtime.dev/) or Wasmer (https://wasmer.io/). However, there is another way of running our file: a modern browser. A browser can run JavaScript, and JavaScript can load Wasm. Even better, Go can help us with this implementation! We only have two more quick steps before we can see our message.

INCLUDE THE JAVASCRIPT SUPPORT FILE

You need to copy a JavaScript file from your Go installation. This JavaScript file is always the same for all Wasm projects, which is why it's already provided. It's in charge of spinning up the environment in which the Wasm code will be executed. We can run the following generic command to copy the file to the project's directory. Note that during Go 1.23, there were discussions on whether the file should be under /misc/ or under /lib/, so check in both

```
> cp "$(go env GOROOT)/misc/wasm/wasm_exec.js" .
```

and

```
> cp "$(go env GOROOT)/lib/wasm/wasm_exec.js" .
```

to be sure. Windows users should use the `COPY` command via the `wasm_exec.js` file path. That's it. You can include this line in your `Makefile` if you're using one, when building the assembly file. As long as this file is loaded by an HTML page, the page can execute Wasm code. So, let's load this page and our program inside an HTML page.

WRAP IT ALL UP WITH THE HTML FILE

We now have a compiled Wasm file on one side and a JavaScript file that can execute it on the other side. The glue that binds them will be an HTML file loading them both. The goal is to open the HTML file in a browser and delegate all the JavaScript execution to that application.

Let's create an `index.html` file in the same directory as `main.go`, `wasm_exec.js`, and `main.wasm`. For now, we want a very simple HTML page with basic content:

```html
<body>My first HTML page</body>
```

The location of scripts is debatable—some place them at the end of the body, so they won't be loaded before the document, and others place them in the header because they're not part of the body. Adding scripts in the `head` makes loading the whole page longer (as more bytes need to be downloaded). Adding scripts in the `body` makes them require the whole page to be downloaded before they can be executed. In our examples, we decided to have them at the end after the <body> section. Let's first add the wasm_exec.js there.

> **Listing 12.2 index.html: HTML file loading wasm_exec.js**

```
<!DOCTYPE html>
<html>
    ...
    <body>
        ...
    </body>
    <script src="wasm_exec.js"></script>    ◀——— Loads the script
</html>
```

We now have a file that can execute Wasm code, but we still need to feed it our own compiled file. We'll do this in another <script> section, as shown in the following listing. This time, we need to use some JavaScript to load it.

> **Listing 12.3 index.html: Loading the main.wasm file**

```
<script src="wasm_exec.js"></script>
<script>
  const helloWASM = new Go();                         ◀——— Creates a new helloWASM constant
  WebAssembly.instantiateStreaming(fetch("main.wasm"),
    helloWASM.importObject).then((result) => {        ◀——— Fetches the compiled file main.wasm
    helloWASM.run(result.instance);
  });
</script>
```

A lot of things are going on here. We won't detail the JavaScript calls, but here's the big picture:

- helloWASM is the communication layer between the Go runtime (written in the .wasm file) and the JavaScript/browser environment. That's how we can run Go via Wasm in JavaScript.
- We load the contents of main.wasm into this instance. We pass a path relative to the index.html file's location.
- Then, we execute the program with run.

WARNING In our example, the Wasm file is loaded by the HTML page. It needs to be available locally, which means our code artifact (the .wasm file) can be read by anyone when they load the page. From the compiled file, they could extract symbols such as passwords and authentication tokens, or simply retro-engineer the code. Code obfuscation can be used to make this harder, but it won't protect against it. Keep in mind that it's always best to control the environment where your code is executed anyway.

Open the `index.html` file in a browser, and, lo and behold, you'll see . . . nothing. The page only contains "My first HTML page." Where did our "Hello, WASM!" message go? What happened?

The main problem here is that our program writes to `os.Stdout`—that's the default behavior of `fmt.Println`. But the HTML page doesn't display the standard output. Instead, that output is sent to our browser's console.

If you open the developer tools or inspect the page (usually by pressing F12), you should be able to access the console of your browser. There, you should be greeted by a heartwarming "Hello, WASM!" message, as shown in figure 12.2.

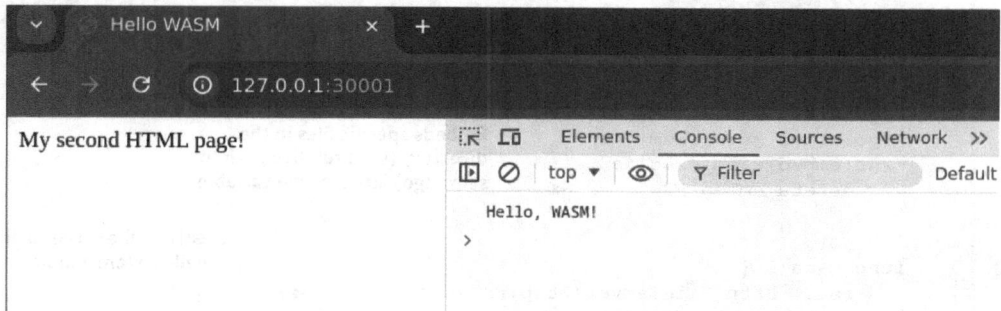

Figure 12.2 The console page shows what Wasm sends to `stdout`.

NOTE You might face problems with cross-origin resource sharing (CORS). We did have problems with Google Chrome and Edge, but not with Firefox. CORS is a security tool, so don't disable it—if you don't get the error message, maybe you have specific security parameters. You can avoid this by serving these files on a server.

12.1.2 *Write a file server*

When we open the URL `file://.../index.html`, we're using the file protocol. Using HTTP instead, via a file server, is a better way of accessing the files using the browser because it mimics the production environment. Writing a simple implementation of such a server in Go is a matter of a few lines, so let's create a new `server.go` file in the same directory, as shown in listing 12.4. This file will contain a `main` function.

Several main functions in the same package

A Go package can only contain functions with unique names. There are two major exceptions. The first one is the `init` function. A package can have multiple initializers, and a single file can have several `init` functions. However, if you end up doing

(continued)

this, you should definitely provide strong justification via comments. There's no guarantee of which one will be called first (don't assume alphabetical order of filenames or earliness within a file).

The second exception, and it's a big one, is for the `main` function. While a single file can't have multiple `main` functions, having multiple files containing `main` functions forces us to tell the `go run` or `go build` commands where to find the entrypoint of our program by passing its file to the command line: `go build server.go`.

Listing 12.4   `server.go`: HTTP file server

```
package main

//go:embed index.html
//go:embed main.wasm                    Embeds specific files in the
//go:embed wasm_exec.js                 directory (uses relative path to
var assets embed.FS                     server.go) into a single variable

                                                Creates a file server using
                                                the filesystem handle
func main() {
    fs := http.FileServer(http.FS(assets))
    http.Handle("/", fs)
                                        Prepares serving
                                        requests on the path /
    log.Print("Listening on 127.0.0.1:30001...")
    err := http.ListenAndServe("127.0.0.1:30001", nil)
                                                Starts listening
    if err != nil {
        fmt.Println("Failed to start server", err)
        return
    }
}
```

We can now start this server by running `go run server.go`. This time, accessing `http://127.0.0.1:30001` in a browser doesn't show any errors in the console; instead, we should see our `Hello, WASM!` Using an explicit `127.0.0.1` address avoids the Windows firewall pop-up, which can get annoying over time. This approach works perfectly fine on Linux and macOS.

There are two different `main` functions in the same package. This isn't a great idea, as the Go tool won't know which to use. We'll avoid this in the next section.

We've managed to interact with the data the user receives, but wouldn't it be a bit nicer if we could update the contents of our page from within our Go code, instead of only sending messages to the console?

12.2   *Multiplication quiz project*

Now that we know how to execute Go code inside an HTML page, let's make a fun project out of it! And to be honest, what's more fun than math? Well, at least, simple math, such as multiplication of two numbers between 1 and 10. If you have children around you, tell them you're creating a game for them. Surely, this will thrill them!

In this section, we'll build an HTTP page that displays a multiplication problem and requires the user to enter the correct result. Of course, we could write this code in Java-Script, but our goal is to practice manipulating the Document Object Model (DOM) that exists in the HTML document from within the Go layer. We want to fill the contents of the page from the Go side.

The requirements for our project are as follows:

- Create an HTML file that asks for a random multiplication problem and that can read the user's answer.
- If the file is correct, a new multiplication problem is offered; otherwise, the user gets to submit a new value.

If you were to code this tiny game in real life, JavaScript is of course enough. Wasm has better uses, typically high-computation programs such as 3D rendering or large data manipulation, that would need to happen offline on the client side. The first steps, as usual, are to create a new directory and run `go mod init` inside.

12.2.1 *Displaying random numbers on the HTML page*

In this section, we want to create an HTML document that contains data populated by the Go layer. Let's start by creating a page that displays a button, which, when clicked, displays a new multiplication problem. To help with file organization, we'll write everything loaded by the client into an `assets` directory. The Go file (in this example, we'll only have one) will be at the root of the module.

Because we want to load a Wasm file in our page, we can start by copying the support file here again, using the same command as earlier:

```
> cp "$(go env GOROOT)/misc/wasm/wasm_exec.js" .
```

Next, we can start by writing the "skeleton," that is, the HTML file. We'll write place-holders where the operands should be written by our Go code.

Listing 12.5 `index.html`: **Multiplication content**

```
<!DOCTYPE html>
<html lang="en">
<head>
    <meta charset="UTF-8">
    <meta name="viewport" content="width=device-width, initial-scale=1.0">
    <title>Multiplication Table Practice</title>
</head>

<body>
<h1>Multiplication Table Practice</h1>
```

```
<button>Generate new exercise</button>          ◀——  Button generating
<div>                                                  the operands
    <span id="operand1"></span>      ◀————————
    <span>x</span>                                Placeholder for
    <span id="operand2"></span>      ◀————————   the left operand
    <span>=</span>
</div>                                            Placeholder for
                                                  the right operand
</body>
</html>
```

You can easily adapt the `server.go` file from the previous section and see what the page looks like. Feel free to style it to your liking.

Of course, when you click the button, nothing happens. We now have to write code that fills the content of the spans.

The Go standard library provides a `syscall/js` package. However, this package is flagged as experimental, which means the Go team may need to make backward-incompatible changes there, due to Wasm, JavaScript, or browser changes. We'll assume that the most common functionalities are stable enough to be used. Keep an eye out in release notes for changes to this package.

The `js` package can interact with the DOM, setting and reading fields, and even more, such as registering functions, as we'll see. Let's write the first step of our Go program using the `js` package to retrieve the whole DOM and set the operands.

The `main.go` file we create will serve as a library, so we dedicate a package to it in `wasm/multiply`, as shown in listing 12.6. If another tool is needed in the page or website, it can live in another package under `wasm`. We'll explain right after how to compile this file—it's possible that your IDE gets confused by the `js` package.

Listing 12.6 `main.go`: Filling the operands

```
package main

import (
    "math/rand/v2"      ◀——  Only available since Go 1.22.
    "syscall/js"             Use math/rand otherwise.
)
                                              Generates two
                                              random numbers
func main() {
    operand1 := rand.IntN(11)
    operand2 := rand.IntN(11)
    document := js.Global().Get("document")   ◀——  Retrieves the DOM

    document.Call("getElementById', "operand1").Set("innerHTML", operand1)
    document.Call("getElementById', "operand2").Set("innerHTML", operand2)
}
                                              Updates the DOM
```

We can update the contents of the DOM because we previously had set IDs over the spans. The `Call` method allows the execution of a JavaScript function (in this case, getElementById), and Set updates the property of the object with the new value. Here, we override the innerHTML property—the value of the field. Let's compile the code:

```
> GOOS=js GOARCH=wasm go build -o multiply.wasm wasm/multiply/main.go
```

Because this .wasm file is a compiled output, we recommend not integrating it in your version control system (i.e., add it to your .gitignore). We can now integrate the Wasm into our index.html page.

Listing 12.7   index.html: **Loading the** multiplications.wasm **file**

```html
<script src="wasm_exec.js"></script>
<script>
    const multiply = new Go();
    WebAssembly.instantiateStreaming(           Loads the
        fetch('multiplications.wasm'),          compiled Wasm file
    multiply.importObject).then((result) => {
        multiply.run(result.instance);          Runs the Wasm
    });                                         program
</script>
```

By now, the list of files that we've created for this project should look something like this:

```
> tree
.
├── go.mod
├── index.html
├── main.go
├── multiplication.wasm
└── wasm
    └── multiply
        └── main.go
```

This should be enough to get our first version running in a browser. Depending on which one you use and how it's configured, CORS might raise an error when trying to run Wasm. In this case, simply implement an HTTP file server on top of the assets directory, as we described in section 12.1.2 (you can even use //go:embed * instead of explicitly listing each file to load).

Refreshing the page should produce a new multiplication problem to solve because every refresh runs the Wasm program anew. Our next step is to fill the values when the button is pressed.

Before we do this, let's do a small refactoring: the Go program needs to keep the two generated numbers for later, to validate the player's input. This can be done via a simple struct, as shown in the following listing. From there, we can add the button's action.

```go
type multiplication struct {
    opLeft, opRight int                      ◀─────┐  Uses a struct
}

func main() {
    m := &multiplication{}
    m.opLeft = rand.IntN(11)
    m.opRight = rand.IntN(11)

    document := js.Global().Get("document")

    document.Call("getElementById", "operand1").Set("innerHTML", m.opLeft)
    document.Call("getElementById", "operand2").Set("innerHTML", m.opRight)
}
```

12.2.2 *Registering functions in Go*

Our `multiplications.wasm` file must result from the compilation of a program, and running it will result in execution of the `main` function. If we want our HTML page to be able to generate numbers at will, we'll have to change our program and make it run as a library—exposing an API that allows for calls from the HTML page and is always available.

EXPOSE AN API TO THE JAVASCRIPT LAYER

We've already seen how to use `Set` to update the `innerHTML` value of an element in our DOM. This method can also be used to register functions in Go for the JavaScript layer. Registering functions at the root of the DOM makes them available throughout the whole document. For example, the following registers a function called `generate`:

```go
js.Global().Set("generate", js.FuncOf(generate))
```

The first parameter of `Set` is the name under which it will be visible from the JavaScript section, and the second should be a variable of type `js.Func`, which is a rather cryptic entity. The good news is we won't create any `js.Func`s manually, as we can use the `js.FuncOf` function. The signature of `js.FuncOf` needs a little bit of clarification:

```go
func FuncOf(fn func(this Value, args []Value) any) Func
```

The first argument it receives, `this`, is the current DOM element from where the call was made. The second argument is a list of values from the JavaScript layer. Finally, the return value can be anything. However, it's good to know that there is no nice error handling here—if our `fn` returns an error, the `js` package will cause a `panic`. As a side note, it's worth noting that calling `FuncOf` too many times will result in a leak—it's sometimes necessary to manually call `.Release()` on our `Func`.

Let's add the registration of this function to our program, as shown in listing 12.9. We'll need a function that updates the operands and that matches the signature expected by `js.FuncOf`, and we'll need to register it by calling `Set` on the DOM.

Listing 12.9 `main.go`: Exposing a Go function to JavaScript

```go
func main() {
    m := &multiplication{}
    js.Global().Set("generate", js.FuncOf(m.generate))          // Register for JavaScript
}

func (m *multiplication) generate(_ js.Value, _ []js.Value) any {
    m.opLeft = rand.IntN(11)
    m.opRight = rand.IntN(11)

    document := js.Global().Get("document")

    document.Call("getElementById", "operand1").Set("innerHTML", m.opLeft)
    document.Call("getElementById", "operand2").Set("innerHTML", m.opRight)

    return nil
}
```

Brilliant! We can now call `generate()` in a `<script>...</script>` section of the HTML page to reach this piece of code.

Listing 12.10 `index.html`: Running Wasm and calling the registered function

```html
<script>
    const multiply = new Go();
    WebAssembly.instantiateStreaming(fetch('multiplications.wasm'),
        multiply.importObject).then((result) => {
            multiply.run(result.instance);          // Runs the program
            generate();          // Calls the registered function
    });
</script>
```

Is it really that simple? Well, if you give it a try, the page should appear without any numbers. When trying to understand what's going on with a web page, a good place to start investigations is the developer's console, where we saw the standard output being written in the first section. There, we can see the following error message:

```
Uncaught (in promise) Error: Go program has already exited
    _resume wasm_exec.js:543
    _makeFuncWrapper wasm_exec.js:556
    <anonymous> (index):13
```

Line 13 of the `index.html` file is our call to `generate()`. The reason for this error is that the Go program that had registered this function has exited by the time we call generate(). We need a way to have it hang around and be available as long as our web page is opened.

DON'T EXIT THE MAIN GO PROGRAM

The idiomatic way to have a program run forever in Go is to read from an empty channel. Any kind of channel will do, but there's no point in making any preallocation, so let's use an unbuffered channel of empty structs. This will have a minimal memory effect:

```
c := make(chan struct{})
<- c
```

As long as nothing is sent to the channel c of this example, the second line will block, as nothing can be read from it. We can use this trick in our program to have it never return. We can even write this syntax in a single line: `<-make(chan struct{})`. Alternatively, we can also use `select {}` to similarly block forever. Don't forget to comment on such lines of code.

Let's add this to our Go program, as shown in the next listing. We want this piece of logic in the `main` function, after having registered any functions to JavaScript.

Listing 12.11 `main.go`: Hanging forever

```
func main() {
    m := &multiplication{}
    js.Global().Set("generate", js.FuncOf(m.generate))

    # Wait forever
    <-make(chan struct{})        ◄──────┘ Or select {}
}
```

Compile the Wasm file, and reload the page in your browser. The call to generate() in the `<script>` section should now generate two numbers and fill them in the placeholders. We're almost there—we still have to refresh (Ctrl-R, F5, Cmd-R) the page to get numbers—we want to click the button.

PLUG THE CALL TO THE BUTTON

Now that the function is registered, it can be used from anywhere on the page. All we have to do is call it when the button is pressed:

```
<button onclick="generate()">Generate new exercise</button>
```

Reloading the page should be enough here—we didn't change the Go code, which means there's no point in recompiling. We still need the call to generate() in the loading script; otherwise, loading the page wouldn't populate the operands.

Congratulations! We now know how to update the DOM from the Go code, and we know how to expose a Go function to our JavaScript layer. As developers, although we understand the inestimable value of writing a function that produces random numbers, we should also be interested in whether a user's input is correct or not.

SCOPE OF OUR NEW FUNCTION

Calling `Set` on `js.Global()` means our `generate` function will be available everywhere—sometimes not the best practice. Instead, we might want to restrict it to a specific JavaScript object or JavaScript namespace. This can be achieved with the following steps.

Listing 12.12 `main.go`: **Exposing a function in a specific namespace**

```
multiply := js.Global().Get("Object").New()          ◄──── Creates a new
multiply.Set("generate", js.FuncOf(m.generate))      ◄──── JavaScript object
js.Global().Set("multiplyApp", multiply)             ◄────
```
Creates a new JavaScript object

Registers the function in that object's scope

Registers the object in the global scope

Finally, we can now call our function:

```
<button onclick="multiplyApp.generate()" ...>.
```

Determining whether your functions should be exposed in the global namespace or in more specific ones will be driven by the size of your JavaScript application. In our case, it's small, and it's OK to have everything in the global namespace. Now, let's jump into the last part of this section—reading a value that the user typed in a field.

12.2.3 *Reading an input from the page*

A math quiz isn't really a quiz if it doesn't allow the player to enter answers to the questions. We should fix this first on our HTML page. Then, we'll see how to check if the answer is correct, and, finally, we'll notify the user of when they aced the question, or return to `index.html` to allow for second thoughts.

ADDING A NEW FIELD FOR THE USER'S ANSWER

To enter their response, the user needs a place to input their response. The code for this is shown in the following listing.

Listing 12.13 `index.html`: **Adding an empty field for the user's answer**

```
...
<span>=</span>

    <form
        onsubmit="validate(providedAnswer.value)"          ◄──── Input from a user should
        class="inline-form"                                       be enclosed in a form.
    >
        <label for="providedAnswer"></label>               ◄──── Labels are mandatory
                                                                  for each input.
```

```
<input
    type="number"
    id="providedAnswer" autofocus
>           <button class="submit" type="submit">Submit answer</button>
</form>
```
→ Empty cell where the user
can type any number

. . .

This adds a field and a button. The `type` attribute of the `input` is `number`, which provides a limitation to what kind of values can be entered here. Our next step will be to do something when the button is pressed. Here, again, we'll be registering a new function—`validate()`. Let's update our `main.go` code, create the `validate` function, and register it in `main`, as shown in the following listing. This function must have the same signature as required by `js.FuncOf`.

Listing 12.14   main.go: Registering the validate() function

```
func main() {
    m := &multiplication{}
    js.Global().Set("generate", js.FuncOf(m.generate))
    js.Global().Set("validate", js.FuncOf(m.validate))     ◀── Registers validate
    <-make(chan struct{})                                      at the DOM level
}

...
func (m *multiplication) validate(
    this js.Value, args []js.Value) any {     ◀── This signature is
    return nil                                    forced by js.FuncOf
}
```

Now that the skeleton is ready, let's flesh it out. What should we write inside `validate()`?

READING THE USER'S ANSWER

In HTML, forms (e.g., our `input` element) allow for their content to be retrieved via the `value` attribute. As a result, we could get the user's guess with

```
dom.Call("getElementById", "providedAnser").Get("value")
```

The other option is to have the HTML page pass the value to the `validate` function. This is achieved when declaring the button:

```
<button onClick="validate(providedAnswer.value)">Validate</button>
```

If we use this option, we can now read the value in the `args []js.Value` parameter of our Go `validate` function, as shown next. It will be the first element in the `slice`.

Listing 12.15   main.go: Retrieving operands

```
func (m *multiplication) validate(this js.Value, args []js.Value) any {
    if len(args) == 0 {
```

```
        return nil
    }

    document := js.Global().Get("document")

    guess := args[0].String()
    numGuess, err := strconv.Atoi(guess)
    if err != nil {
        // Handle error
        return nil
    }
    ...
}
```

> **NOTE** As we can see, we can either read the DOM by passing its values as parameters of the JavaScript function, or we can access it from the Go layer. As Go developers, we prefer to handle everything from within our Go code. If you have experience in JavaScript, you might prefer to do a few steps there (e.g., checking that values are valid numbers). Here, we wanted to show that both options are available.

Our user can write anything in an `input` field—numbers, but also letters, emojis, or cake recipes. While setting the type of the input field to `number` limits the set of runes that can be entered in this field—and this is why we didn't go with a `text` type in the first place—a value such as - (minus character), +, e (for exponent, in a scientific notation) can be input. We should be able to tell our user that something is wrong if we can't parse their input as a number.

So, how do we let the user know they've not entered a valid answer? Because we're working with the HTML page, we could send a log to the console—but the odds of the user checking it are low. We could display a message in our HTML page or highlight something in red. But we find it more interactive to send a pop-up, so let's do this! On your side, feel free to update the DOM with your favorite notification method.

To create a pop-up, the `js` package offers the `Call("alert", msg)`. From Go, we're running a JavaScript function—`alert`—which opens the pop-up and prints the message. Let's handle our error this way here:

```
if err != nil {
    js.Global().Call("alert", fmt.Sprintf("not a number: %q", guess))
    return nil
}
```

Now is a good moment to try this in your browser. Using `alert` is great for debugging and testing, but the user experience of having a pop-up every time isn't great. Are non-numbers triggering a pop-up? Are numbers going through fine? Great! The final piece of code is to check that the answer is mathematically correct.

Giving feedback

We can compare the input with the multiplication result and simply send an `alert` via JavaScript. The code for this is given in the following listing.

Listing 12.16   `main.go`: Validating the user's input

Ask a new question when they get it right.

```
if m.opLeft * m.opRight == numGuess {
    js.Global().Call("alert", "Bravo! Here's a new exercise.")
    m.generate(this, args)
} else {
    js.Global().Call("alert",
        "Try again... "+guess+" is not the correct answer.")
}
```

Amazing! We can now check that we know our multiplication tables. After a few manual tests, you'll notice something is slightly annoying: after clicking the `Validate` button, the input field still contains our value, regardless of whether it was correct (for the previous operation) or not. A simple way to clear the input field when the user clicks `Validate` is to set the value to an empty string. We can safely do this in a defer of the `validate` function.

Listing 12.17   `main.go`: Resetting the input field

```
func (m *multiplication) validate(this js.Value, args []js.Value) any {
    document := js.Global().Get("document")

    defer func() {
        // Reset the contents of the input field
        // after the user clicked Validate
        document.Call("getElementById", "providedAnswer").Set("value", "")
    }()
    ...
}
```

That's it! We've now created an HTML document, controlled by Go, which interactively updates the DOM and retrieves values from it. We were able to communicate through pop-ups with our user to let them know of their computational excellence.

Testing and debugging

Our app is running in a web browser. It relies on a DOM but doesn't have any control over it. Therefore, the app isn't responsible for the DOM, meaning we don't need to test that part. In Go, we need to test the code that generates numbers and validates them against a result. That's not a very interesting test, though. Considering that our library does nothing interesting, we would rather depend on the HTML layer to test it in an end-to-end test.

> **Side quest 12.1**
>
> We now want to show the score every time the user gives an answer. The score should display the number of correct guesses and the total number of guesses. There's no limit to a session, and refreshing the page should reset the session. How can we adapt our program to display these numbers?

12.3 *TinyGo*

Now that we've explored using Go and Wasm, let's move to on to discuss TinyGo, another powerful compiler that also supports Wasm and excels in targeting microcontrollers. These tiny computers, embedded in countless devices since the 1970s, have revolutionized electronics. With TinyGo, we can deploy Go code on these microcontrollers and other resource-constrained devices, unlocking new possibilities for Go developers. Let's finish this book with the most entertaining and exciting aspect of Go you've ever seen. Get ready for a wild ride in TinyCity!

TinyGo is a Go compiler that produces small executables. It's source compatible with Go, allowing you to write Go code and compile it with TinyGo without making changes to the code. However, because TinyGo has a smaller standard library focused on the needs of embedded and IoT devices, not all Go features are supported by TinyGo. This means that you may need to make modifications to your code if you want to use advanced features such as networking or cryptography.

TinyGo requires its own installation, which is detailed here: https://tinygo.org/getting-started/install/. Most of the time, using TinyGo is driven by the thrill of experimenting with small hardware, such as LEDs, temperature sensors, or photoreceptors. You'd be amazed at the creativity of enthusiasts!

If you don't have a microcontroller board, don't worry. TinyGo has a playground at https://play.tinygo.org/, which emulates plugging in virtual LEDs into your virtual microcontroller (compiled using TinyGo and Wasm). The best part is that you don't have to add resistors everywhere on the playground, which is required in a real-world environment. For the rest of this section, we'll be using that environment, using an Arduino Nano 33 IoT. If you have or want to use another microcontroller, the only difference will arise when we deploy the executable there—called *flashing*—as you'll soon see.

TinyGo addresses the main problem of microcontrollers—very limited amounts of CPU and memory, which is used for both storage and execution. We'll show you how in the following subsections.

12.3.1 *Building a simple TinyGo application*

Now that we know what TinyGo is used for, let's practice! Here's our goal: we're the architects of TinyCity, and the city council has asked us to take care of the traffic light in front of the train station. We want to allow for pedestrians to cross the street and for car traffic to flow smoothly. There's no intersection in front of the train station. Figure 12.3 represents the situation.

Figure 12.3   Traffic lights for cars and pedestrians, consisting of three possible lights (red, amber, green) for cars, and two possible lights (red, green) for pedestrians. A similar implementation is on the other side of the road.

Our task is now to implement this system here. The project requirements are as follows:

- The pedestrian light must be red when the cars' light is green or amber.
- TinyCity traffic lights must follow the Vienna Convention on Road Signs and Signals.
- The pedestrians can ask for the traffic lights to turn red by pressing a button.
- When the traffic lights go red, the pedestrians are allowed to cross and their light turns green.
- The system must regularly allow for pedestrians to cross, even if they can't reach the button.
- After a little while, the lights should return to green for the cars.

Because the signals are mirrored, we can focus on implementing one side of the road for now.

BLINKING LIGHT

Let's start a new project in a new directory and initialize it with `go mod init tinycity`. The next step is to write a few lines of code in the `main` function. In this first section, we'll use the built-in LED of the Arduino Nano 33 IoT and make it blink. Most microcontrollers have an LED, usually used to signal that they're properly receiving voltage. This LED doesn't require any plugging in to the power input or to the ground—these connections already exist within the microcontroller.

How do we access this LED? The answer is both short and complex: via the `machine` package.

> ### TinyGo packages
>
> The `machine` package isn't the only one that differs between Go and TinyGo. This means programs written for TinyGo can't be compiled with Go—but most programs written for Go can be compiled with TinyGo.
>
> Other packages that differ, as you'll see, include `net`, `reflect`, and `runtime`.

The goal of the `machine` package is to expose pin mappings for each possible microcontroller. Pins are the little legs of the microcontroller—each of them has a specific name, as described by their manufacturer. Let's take a look at the first lines of the `machine/board_arduino_nano33.go` file, as provided by TinyGo, in the following listing. The first line of this file is a build tag.

Listing 12.18 `board_arduino_nano33.go`: **Exposed pins**

```
//go:build arduino_nano33          ◄─── Build tag for
                                        Arduino Nano 33 IoT

// This contains the pin mappings for the Arduino Nano33 IoT board.
...
const (
    D13 Pin = PA17          ◄─── Exposing PA17 as D13
    LED = D13          ◄─── LED is an alias to D13,
)                             which is the pin PA17.
...
```

BUILD TAGS

Build tags, also called *build constraints*, are used to expose a file for specific environments only. If we don't provide the tag to the Go (or TinyGo) command-line tool, files with build tags will be ignored, as if they were absent. A build tag must be the first line of a file and must be in the syntax of `//go:build {tag}`.

To provide a build tag in the command line, we use `-tags={comma,separated,tags}`. We can provide more than one tag when calling `test`, `run`, and `build`.

The most common use of build tags is when we want to include specific files for specific architectures or filesystems. For instance, many files in Go's `os` package need to adapt to the environment they're running on—`linux`, `windows`—or even the architecture, such as `amd64` or `arm`.

To use the contents of this file when we compile it, remember that we need to provide the tag `arduino_nano33`. Let's write a simple `main` function using this file, as shown in the next listing. Here, all we're interested in is having the LED of the Arduino Nano 33 IoT blink. This example is taken straight from the TinyGo documentation.

Listing 12.19 `main.go`: Blinking the Arduino LED

```
package main

import (                          Imports "machine"
    "machine"                     as any other package
    "time"
)

func main() {                     Controls the LED of
    led := machine.LED            the microcontroller
    led.Configure(
        machine.PinConfig{Mode: machine.PinOutput})   Initializes the LED
    for {
        led.High()                Sets state to on
        time.Sleep(time.Second/2)

        led.Low()                 Sets state to off
        time.Sleep(time.Second/2)
    }
}
```

Let's see what happened there. The first line to notice is the import of the `machine` package: its path is the same as if it were an SDK package. TinyGo knows how to load packages from both Go's SDK and its own packages. Packages provided by TinyGo always supersede those provided by Go.

The second piece of code that might raise questions is the `Configure` call. After all, we've declared an `led` variable, so you may wonder why we need to configure anything. This call tells our program that this isn't just a regular pin—it's a pin used as output. Output pins can be set to `High` and `Low`. This will send current through the pin or block it. Later in this chapter, we'll see how to use a `machine.PinInput`.

Finally, you'll have noticed that the program runs an infinite `for` loop. Indeed, we want our LED to blink forever. Now that we have code and a compiler, let's make our program run on our microcontroller.

FLASHING A VIRTUAL MICROCONTROLLER

Deploying a program to a microcontroller is called *flashing*. We can flash a virtual microcontroller on TinyGo's playground (https://play.tinygo.org). Over there, all we have to do is select the microcontroller we want to use, paste our code, and click the Flash button. The Arduino Nano 33 IoT's orange LED appears in the bottom-left area, just below the USB port. Can you see it blink on the playground? Try changing the microcontroller to a Phytec reel board and flashing our code again. This time, there should be no blinking, as the `machine.LED` isn't defined for that platform.

We'll see how to flash a real microcontroller in a few moments. For now, let's return to TinyCity and implement the basic light signals.

TRAFFIC LIGHTS

The Arduino Nano 33 IoT offers more than its internal LED as we can connect components to its other pins. There are lots of different components that can be plugged to our microcontroller, but for now, we'll stick to external LEDs. In our case, we need three LEDs for the traffic lights (a red one, an amber one, and a green one) and two LEDs for the pedestrian crossing (a red one and a green one). These LEDs will be connected to our microcontrollers via its pins, with each pin controlling one LED. Because LEDs are output components, they should be attached to an output pin. If we look in the `board_arduino_nano33.go` file, we see that pins RX0, TX1, and D2–D13 are described as GPIO pins, that is, general purpose input/output pins. This is the type we want for LEDs and other outputting devices. Some devices are in charge of sending data to the microcontroller, for instance, temperature or keyboard inputs. These components should be connected to analog pins, which are A0–A7, in our case. Always check the pin configuration of the microcontroller before plugging anything to it. And, remember, in real life, LEDs are very sensitive components that need a resistor to protect them. Don't simply connect LEDs to something that will send power directly to them.

For detailed information about the board, refer to the official documentation available at Arduino (https://mng.bz/eygz). This resource provides comprehensive details on the microprocessor's characteristics, peripheral descriptions, mechanical specifications, and—most importantly—pin descriptions. Figure 12.4 presents an excerpt from the Connector Pinouts section of the datasheet, which clearly indicates the function of each pin, whether it's digital, analog, a power supply, or ground, along with additional relevant details. We strongly recommend consulting this schematic when configuring your pins.

Figure 12.5 illustrates a schematic of the electrical system we aim to build. On the left side of the diagram is the Arduino Nano 33 IoT board to which the various components are connected. On the right, we have the pedestrian lights, represented by two LEDs (green and red), each with a 10 kΩ resistor, as well as the car lights, represented by three LEDs (green, amber, and red), each with its corresponding resistor. The schematic also includes a push button for pedestrians, which we'll discuss later in the chapter. This button is a simple on/off switch, accompanied by a resistor similar to those used with the LEDs.

Now, let's write some code that controls how the LEDs are lit. We'll need to declare variables for each LED. Because we can pack them into car-controlling LEDs and pedestrian-controlling LEDs, we can start by defining two structures: `carLight` and `walkLight`.

Listing 12.20 `main.go`: **Types wrapping the lights**

```
// carLight controls the traffic lights for cars.
type carLight struct {
```

```
    red    machine.Pin
    amber machine.Pin
    green machine.Pin
}

// walkLight controls the lights for pedestrians.
type walkLight struct {
    red    machine.Pin
    green machine.Pin
}
```

ARDUINO
NANO 33 IoT

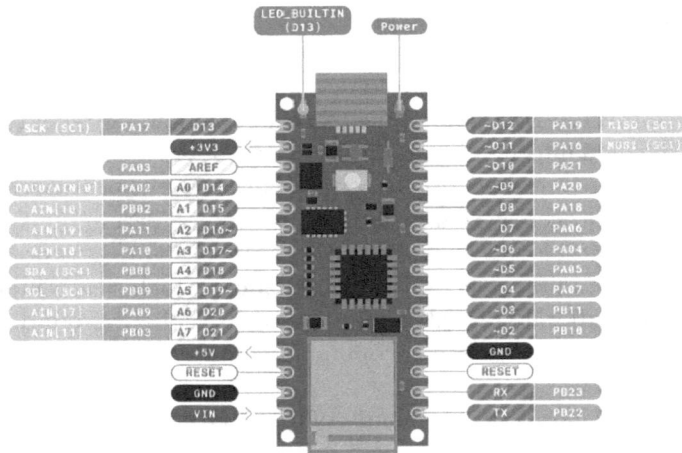

Pinout

Figure 12.4   Schema of the Arduino Nano 33 IoT's pinouts extracted from the datasheet. (Illustration from adruino.cc, licensed under the Creative Commons Attribution-ShareAlike 4.0 International License. To view a copy of this license, visit http://creativecommons.org/licenses/by-sa/4.0/ or send a letter to Creative Commons, PO Box 1866, Mountain View, CA 94042, USA.)

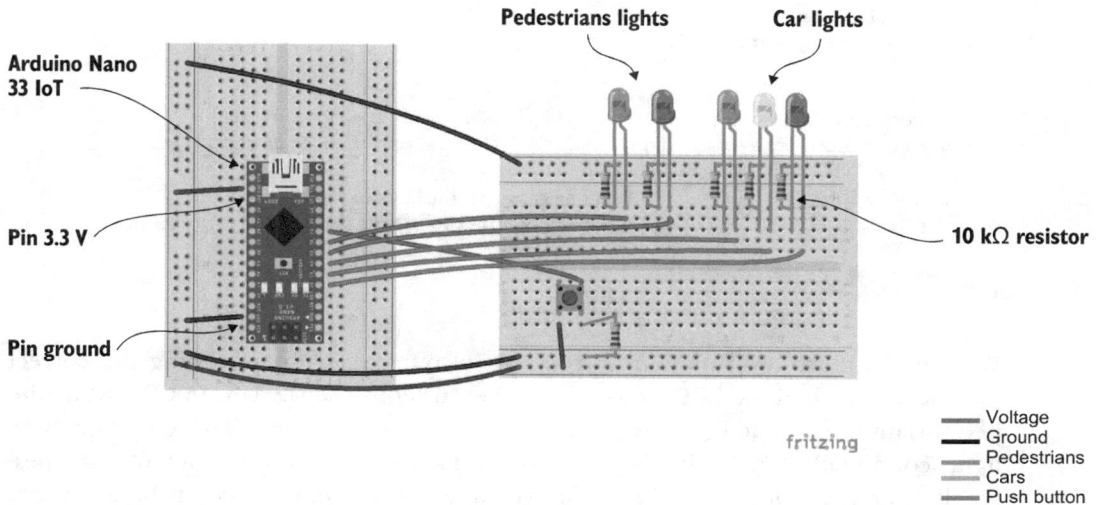

Figure 12.5   Electrical schema of the traffic lights for cars and pedestrians

Remember when we had the controller's LED blink, in the previous section, that we also had to call `Configure` to be able to switch it on and off? Well, external LEDs are similar—they need to be configured as `OutputPins`. So, let's write functions that return usable sets of traffic lights for each of these two types. As we'll be plugging our LEDs to various pins, we should provide these pins as parameters of these constructors, as shown in the following listing. Because there's no default state for LEDs, we can set them in these constructors.

Listing 12.21　`main.go`: **Initializing lights**

```go
func newCarLight(redPin, amberPin, greenPin machine.Pin) *carLight {
    c := &carLight{
        red:   redPin,
        amber: amberPin,
        green: greenPin,
    }
    c.red.Configure(machine.PinConfig{Mode: machine.PinOutput})
    c.amber.Configure(machine.PinConfig{Mode: machine.PinOutput})
    c.green.Configure(machine.PinConfig{Mode: machine.PinOutput})

    c.red.High()
    c.amber.Low()            Don't forget to set the LEDs to High
    c.green.Low()            or Low right after configuring them.

    return c
}

func newWalkLight(redPin, greenPin machine.Pin) *walkLight {
    w := &walkLight{
```

```
        red:    redPin,
        green:  greenPin,
    }

    w.red.Configure(machine.PinConfig{Mode: machine.PinOutput})
    w.green.Configure(machine.PinConfig{Mode: machine.PinOutput})

    w.red.High()
    w.green.Low()

    return w
}
```

Don't forget to set the LEDs to High or Low right after configuring them.

We can call these two functions at the start of our `main()` by providing the correct pins we've attached the LEDs to—let's say the car lights use D2, D3, and D4, while the pedestrians use D5 and D6. The rest of the code of our program will be to update these lights continually. We'll write a `Go` function and a `Stop` function for each of our types. Finally, our `main` function will loop forever, alternating every 5 seconds between cars being allowed to cross and pedestrians being allowed to cross.

In our implementation, we follow the Vienna Conventions on Road Signs and Signals mentioned earlier, as shown in listing 12.22. Not every country follows them—for instance, in some countries, the cars' red light immediately goes to a cars' green light, without having a red + amber pause.

Listing 12.22   `main.go`: Full implementation

```
func main() {
    car := newCarLight(
        machine.D2, machine.D3, machine.D4)
    walk := newWalkLight(machine.D5, machine.D6)

    for {
        walk.Stop()
        car.Go()
        time.Sleep(time.Second * 5)

        car.Stop()
        walk.Go()
        time.Sleep(time.Second * 5)
    }
}

// Stop lights on the red signal for cars.
func (c *carLight) Stop() {
    c.green.Low()
    c.amber.High()
    time.Sleep(time.Second)
    c.amber.Low()
    c.red.High()
}

// Go lights on the green signal for cars.
```

Initializes the LED pins for car and pedestrian

Cars go for 5 seconds and then pedestrians.

```go
func (c *carLight) Go() {
    c.red.High()
    c.amber.High()
    time.Sleep(time.Second)
    c.red.Low()
    c.amber.Low()
    c.green.High()
}
```

Make sure Red and Amber LEDs are both on before it turns off

```go
// Stop lights on the red signal for pedestrians.
func (w *walkLight) Stop() {
    // Blink the green signal a few times before turning red.
    for i := 0; i < 5; i++ {
        w.green.Low()
        time.Sleep(time.Millisecond * 300)
        w.green.High()
        time.Sleep(time.Millisecond * 300)
    }
    w.green.Low()
    w.red.High()
}

// Go lights on the green signal for pedestrians.
func (w *walkLight) Go() {
    w.red.Low()
    w.green.High()
}
```

We're now ready to test this. We can use TinyGo's playground to do so. On the bottom-right corner of it's web page, you can switch between Terminal, Properties, and Add. The Add option is how we can connect virtual components to our controller.

LEDs are polarized—they have an anode and a cathode. The anode should be receiving current through a resistor, while the cathode should be connected to the ground. Connecting the LED the other way around could damage it. Let's add a red LED to our playground and connect its anode to the D2 pin (the fifth from the top right). We can then add all other required LEDs for our program to run: an amber one connected to D3, a green one connected to D4, and, for pedestrians, a red one on D5 and a green one on D6. These values are those we set in the main() function. Don't forget to connect the cathodes to the ground (GND), which, on the Arduino Nano 33 IoT, is right next to the D2 pin. After plugging everything in, your schema should look something like figure 12.6, showing the car lights at the top and the pedestrian lights at the bottom.

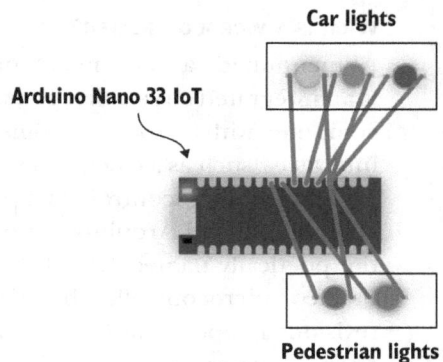

Figure 12.6 Electrical schema from the TinyGo playground using an Arduino Nano 33 IoT

At the bottom of the figure, two LEDs indicate whether pedestrians can cross. These LEDs are connected to pins D5 and D6 (and to GND). At the top, three LEDs indicate whether cars can go. These LEDs are connected to pins D2, D3, and D5 (and to GND).

> ### Side quest 12.2
> Because every call to `cars.Go()` has to be performed with a `walks.Stop()` and vice versa, it makes sense to combine these two into a single function. Create a new struct, `crossing`, that contains a `carLight` and a `walkLight`, and implement a `Switch()` method on the struct.

We show our prototype to the mayor, and they're happy with our work. The intervals we set for this demo are a bit too short for a real-life implementation—pedestrians barely have time to cross the street, and only a handful of cars can go before the light goes red again. Demonstrating with longer periods isn't practical—but the mayor reminds us that pedestrians should always be able to interrupt incoming traffic when they press the button.

PEDESTRIAN BUTTON

We want to add a button to allow for pedestrians to cross the street at will. A button is a new type of component that *sends* a signal to our microcontroller. Such components can be attached to either a digital pin or an analogue pin. The choice will depend on what kind of signal the component sends. If the signal is binary (on/off), which is the case for our button, a digital pin does the job. An analogue pin should be used for "continuous" signals—a thermometer, a microphone, a light sensor, an input device such as a mouse, and so on.

Let's add a button to our program and connect it to the next digital port available (D7). For this, we'll have to configure our variable to a value other than `machine .PinOutput`. To find out what other values are available, we'll have to dive into TinyGo's configuration files.

WHAT IS A MICROCONTROLLER?

As mentioned earlier, a microcontroller, such as our friend the Arduino Nano 33 IoT, is an integrated circuit that contains several components. It can be seen as a very small computer, with a processor, some memory, ports (the pins of the controller), and other interfaces, such as a clock or a power management module.

Because microcontrollers are mass produced, they usually are built with the same components. All Arduino Nano 33 IoT microcontrollers have the same processor—the poetically named *SAMD21 Cortex®-M0+ 32bit low power ARM MCU*. All Raspberry Pi Pico microcontroller boards come with an RP2040 processing chip. However, revisions happen: the Raspberry Pi 3B initially featured the BCM2837A0 integrated circuit, but was improved to BCM2837B0. These dependencies are tracked in TinyGo's configuration files. In particular, the `targets` directory of TinyGo's installation contains files that describe how a microcontroller uses this or that chip. Because we're using an Arduino Nano 33 IoT in our example, let's take a look at the file named `targets/arduino-nano33.json`.

Listing 12.23 `targets/arduino-nano33.json`: **Target specifications**

Imports this dependency when targeting Arduino Nano 33 IoT

List of build tags automatically passed when targeting Arduino Nano 33 IoT

```
{
    "inherits": ["atsamd21g18a"],
    "build-tags": ["arduino_nano33"],
    "flash-command": "bossac -i -e -w -v -R -U --port={port}
        --offset=0x2000 {bin}",
    "serial-port": ["acm:2341:8057", "acm:2341:0057"],
    "flash-1200-bps-reset": "true"
}
```

These lines can be ignored for now—they define how to flash the microcontroller.

The first line indicates that, when targeting the `arduino-nano33` file (without the extension), the file `atsamd21g18a.json` will also be used. That file defines the architecture of the microcontroller and imports the `cortex-m0plus.json` file, which describes the CPU chip.

All the steps of this import chain add build tags that TinyGo will automatically add to the command line. Instead of running

```
> tinygo build --tags=cortex-m0plus,atsamd21g18a,sam,arduino_nano33 main.go
```

we can run

```
> tinygo build --target=arduino-nano33 main.go
```

and TinyGo will, by itself, resolve the architectural tree of dependencies, providing every necessary build tag.

Now that we know this, we should look for a `machine/machine_XXX.go` file that has a build tag provided by our dependency tree. In our case, it's `machine_atsamd21.go`. In that tag, we can (finally) see that the available `PinMode` constants include `PinOutput`, which we've already used; `PinInput`; `PinInputPullup`; `PinInputPulldown`; and a few others. So, which one should we use for our button?

They each serve a different purpose, and it all boils down to what kind of information a digital pin input can produce. The first thing to understand is that, as digital input components, we can read the state they are in by calling `Get() bool`. This method will tell us if the input is in state High or Low. A button can be in either of two states—`pressed` or `not-pressed`. `PinInputPullup`'s `Get` will return `true` if the button isn't pressed (it's up), and `PinInputPulldown`'s `Get` will return `true` if the button is pressed (it's down). `PinInput`, itself, isn't very useful with buttons—it behaves like `PinInputPullup`. Instead, `PinInput` should be used when connecting the pin to the digital output of some other component. In our case, we'll use `PinInputPulldown`, but we recommend that you read the datasheet for the component you're adding as it might behave differently, requiring that you adapt the code.

Using the code base of our previous exercise, we can add a button to our `crossing` structure. We already know we want to be able, at any point, to interrupt car traffic and give priority to pedestrians. We want to always listen to users pressing the button. For this, we can start a goroutine that will permanently listen to the button's state, and notify our main program when the cars' light should go red.

Listing 12.24   `main.go`: Updating the crossing structure for the button

```go
func main() {
    car := newCarLight(machine.D2, machine.D3, machine.D4)
    walk := newWalkLight(machine.D5, machine.D6)
    button := machine.D7
    c := newCrossing(car, walk, button)
        ...
}

type crossing struct {
    cars          *carLight
    walks         *walkLight
    button        *machine.Pin
    pedestriansGo bool
    buttonPressed chan struct{}
}

func newCrossing(
    cars *carLight, walks *walkLight, button machine.Pin,
) *crossing {
    button.Configure(machine.PinConfig{
        Mode: machine.PinInputPullup})        ◄────┐  Configures the button
                                                   │  to be a PinInputPullup
    return &crossing{
        cars:          cars,
        walks:         walks,
        button:        &button,                          Channel used to communicate
        buttonPressed: make(chan struct{}, 1),  ◄────┐   to the main goroutine that
    }                                                │   the button is pressed
}
```

Now, all that is left to do is to listen to pedestrians pressing the button. We'll achieve this by starting a goroutine in the `main` function and using the channel when necessary.

Listing 12.25   `main.go`: Listening to pedestrians pressing the button

```go
func main() {
    car := newCarLight(machine.D2, machine.D3, machine.D4)
    walk := newWalkLight(machine.D5, machine.D6)
```

```
button := machine.D7
c := newCrossing(car, walk, button)

go c.listenButton()

for {
    c.Switch()
    select {
    case <-c.buttonPressed:
    case <-time.After(time.Second * 5):
    }
}
}

func (c *crossing) listenButton() {
    for {
        if !c.pedestriansGo && !c.button.Get() {
            c.buttonPressed <- struct{}{}
        }
        time.Sleep(time.Millisecond * 100)
    }
}
```

The button being pressed (!Get()) when cars are going is the trigger. Depending on the component, you might want to remove "!."

To test your code, you can modify your electrical schematic in the TinyGo playground, as shown in figure 12.7, by adding the push button component. Connect the button to the power supply and the D7 pin. Then, copy your code into the playground and observe the traffic lights in action.

We show our prototype to the mayor, who is delighted with the outcome. We can now provide safety to the citizens of TinyCity. However, all we have so far is a piece of code that runs in an online simulator. We must deploy our solution to reap the rewards of our success.

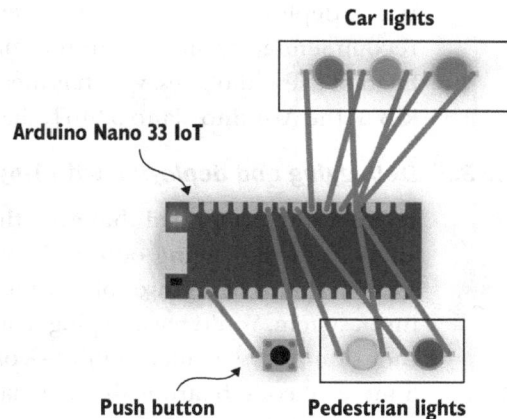

Figure 12.7 Electrical schema from the TinyGo playground with the push button

12.3.2 Differences with Go

The goal of TinyGo is to provide smaller executables so that they can be shipped on small environments. However, as we saw in the introduction to this chapter, even a hello, world program, after Go's compilation, can be relatively heavy. An Arduino Nano 33 IoT has 256 kiB of memory, and it would require more than 8 kiB to load a single hello, world program. So, how can TinyGo manage to produce that small of a binary, as opposed to its big brother Go?

First, TinyGo uses low-level virtual machine (LLVM), which is a compiler-optimizer. The optimization is about removing unused code when compiling, and it produces executables for specific architectures.

Second, a few packages of the Go's SDK have been re-implemented. The most notable ones are the `reflect` and the `runtime` packages. One of the effects is that TinyGo has a limited garbage controller that's not as powerful as Go's but is also a lot less resource intensive.

One way to obtain small executables with Go is to use the Go toolbox. When generating an executable with `go build` or running our code directly with `go run`, we can pass linking options via the `link` tool. To get a list of supported linking flags, we can run `go tool link`. Among those returned by this command are two of the most useful: `-w` and `-s`. Using these flags produces a lighter executable that will behave the same—at least while on the happy path. Here's how to pass these options while building (it's the same for running). Don't forget the quotation marks, as they are passed as the value of the `ldflags` flag:

```
> go build -ldflags "-w -s" main.go
```

When deploying to microcontrollers, because the execution environment is tiny, it's recommended to not create too many goroutines. Usually, a goroutine has an overhead of a few kilobytes, which is meaningless on our modern machines, but on the 256 kiB of the Arduino Nano 33 IoT, that's already more than 1%.

12.3.3 Debugging and deploying with TinyGo

So far, we've pretended that everything was fine in the world and that we didn't need any logs or debugging output. However, microcontrollers, albeit being akin to small PCs, lack a lot of features of our modern computers. First, they don't natively have an input system. You'd have to plug in a mouse or keyboard to interact with them. Second, they don't have a video output—some might, the bigger ones, but most of them are a mere silicone board with a few dashes of metal that connect the important components—hardly enough to mine some bitcoin or play a game of Gordle.

HOW DO WE DEBUG?

So, now you know you need to debug in TinyGo. There are several debugging options available, but ultimately, the best debugging technique for you will depend on your specific needs and the development environment you're using. Here are some options to consider:

- *Use print statements and listen to the USB port.* This is a simple way to debug your code and identify problems. You can output data from your microcontroller to your computer using print statements, which can help you identify errors and problems in your code. However, this method is limited and may not be suitable for more complex debugging scenarios.

- *Use the Delve debugger.* TinyGo supports the Delve debugger, which allows you to interactively step through your code and inspect variables. This can be a powerful tool for debugging problems related to logic and flow control.
- *Use the TinyGo debugger (based on the GNU Debugger [GDB]).* This is a useful option when a serial port isn't available—for example, if there is a bug before the port initialization. The TinyGo debugger allows you to print a stack trace, even in a panic, which can be useful for debugging problems related to memory management or performance. For more on this debugger, see the documentation (https://tinygo.org/docs/guides/debugging/).
- *Connect a debug probe.* Depending on the board you're using, you may have a debug probe already included; they are typically found on evaluation boards. If not, you can plug in an external debug probe for Arduino boards, for example. This allows you to connect your microcontroller to a debugger and inspect variables and memory in real time.

LET'S DEPLOY

Now that our code is tested in the emulator, it's time to ship it to our (real) microcontroller. TinyGo helps with this task, but we'll need to help as well. The first step is to connect our microcontroller to the computer where the code is available. Microcontrollers usually have a USB port.

The second step is to identify to which port of our computer our microcontroller is connected. Here, as we'll be using the host's operating system, we'll face three (main) scenarios, all of which are made simpler by having only one USB port in use on your computer:

- On Linux, run `ls /dev/ttyUSB* /dev/ttyACM*`, which should return `/dev/ttyUSB0`, for instance.
- On macOS, run `ls /dev/tty.*`, which should return `/dev/tty.usbmodemABC`, for instance.
- On Windows, go to the Device Manager, and explore the Ports (COM & LPT) section. One of them should be used by the USB connection, for instance, `COM3`.

Once the port has been identified, run the flashing command:

```
> tinygo flash -target=arduino-nano33 -port=/dev/ttyUSB0
```

As we've seen previously, we don't need to pass build tags—they're already handled by the TinyGo `target` option. If the microcontroller has an LED (internally), it should blink while the flashing is performed. Once this is achieved, your microcontroller is now running your program!

Flashing means the default program that the microcontroller will run will be the one you just shipped. You can unplug your microcontroller and power it elsewhere, and it will rerun the program. TinyCitizens will be thrilled to finally cross the street to go to the station!

Summary

- Wasm is assembly for the web, that is, compiled code that can run in a browser.
- Go can compile code to a Wasm executable.
- You can load the Wasm executable in an HTML page using JavaScript.
- You can register Go functions for JavaScript using the `js` package.
- The `js` package is used to interact with the DOM.
- TinyGo is a Go compiler that produces small executables. It's source compatible with Go, allowing you to write Go code and compile it with TinyGo without making changes to the code.
- TinyGo has a specific library called `machine` that exposes pin mappings for the supported microcontrollers.
- TinyGo has fewer standard libraries implemented than Go, and some are quite different in their behavior (`runtime`, `reflect`).
- LEDs are a binary output that should be connected to GPIO pins. Usually, digital pins serve this purpose, rather than analog pins (used for input).
- Input should be connected to a digital pin if it's binary (on/off, 0/1) and to an analogue pin if it measures continuous data, such as a temperature sensor.
- Always refer to the datasheet of a component before plugging it in.
- You have several methods to debug with TinyGo, but it provides its own debugger based on the GNU Debugger (GDB).
- Build tags, or build constraints, are comments that are written at the beginning of a file. They have to follow the syntax of `//go:build {tag}`.
- A build tag can require the absence of a tag by negating it: `//go:build !windows`.
- Several build tags can be used at the same time—in this case, we use Boolean operators to specify which tags should be present or absent: `//go:build (darwin || dragonfly || freebsd || (linux && !android) || netbsd || openbsd) && cgo`.
- To compile or run a program using the build tags, the command line should include these values in the `-tags` parameter: `go build -tags=amd64 main.go`.
- Linking flags can be passed while building or running. They can help reduce the size of the generated executable: `go build -ldflags "-w -s" main.go`. Using these flags comes at the expense of losing some debug information in case something goes terribly wrong.

appendix A
Installation steps

Any compiled language needs, first and foremost, a compiler. The Go toolchain was initially written in C. Since Go 1.3, it's written directly in Go, following the principle of *eating your own dog food*. As everything is open source, you can at any time suggest improvements or look into the standard library's source code for how other developers write their Go.

A.1 Install

Start by visiting the Go website for a simple explanation (did we tell you that Go aims for simplicity?) of how to download the installer and run it on Linux, Mac, or Windows. Follow the installation steps (https://go.dev/doc/install), and don't forget to add go to your path.

There is no good reason to pick old versions. Just for the record, we're writing this book using Go 1.23.

A.2 Check

As mentioned in the online installation guide, you can check the version of Go that you're using and also verify that Go is properly installed by running the command shown in the following listing in any directory.

Listing A.1 Checking the installation in your console

```
> go version
go version go1.23.3 darwin/arm64
```

A.3   Go's environment variables

Under the hood, Go uses several variables without being explicit about it. In this section, we'll look closely at two of these variables: GOROOT and GOPATH.

If you've just installed Go, these variables won't be set in your sessions. If you're questioning why Go uses them if they're not set, the answer is that Go is able to use default values for these variables.

A.3.1   The go env command

The go command can access environment variables, just like any program. However, Go comes with an extra layer of variables that aren't visible to you from a terminal. These variables can be listed with the go env command. go env will return all the Go environment variables it can access. Typically, you'll paste the output of this command along with any question you post online or when you open a bug.

Alternatively, we can pass it a list of the variables we want to retrieve, which limits the output. Listing A.2 shows an example of the results of this command. Don't worry if your output differs from this—after all, we don't share the same environment.

Listing A.2   Example go env output

```
> go env -json GOBIN GOENV GOROOT GOPATH CGO_ENABLED
{
    "GOBIN": "",
    "GOENV": "/home/user/.config/go/env",
    "GOPATH": "/home/user/go",
    "GOROOT": "/usr/local/go",
    "CGO_ENABLED": "1",
}
```

We won't go through the long list of variables displayed by go env, as most are beyond the scope of this book. For instance, the variables toward the end of the list are related to cgo, the utility that allows integration of C code within Go code.

The values returned by go env here are the default values, which are based on your machine's architecture and your Go installation directory. We hardly ever need to modify any of these values, but, for your knowledge, they can be overridden with regular environment variables.

Listing A.3   Environment variable's value read outside of Go

```
# On Linux:
> CGO_ENABLED=0 go env -json CGO_ENABLED
{
    "CGO_ENABLED": "0",
}

# On Windows:
C:\> set "CGO_ENABLED=0" & go env -json CGO_ENABLED
```

They can also be written in Go's configuration file (which is pointed to by the GOENV variable) with the go env -w VARIABLE=VALUE command.

Listing A.4   Environment variable's value retrieved with go env

```
# On Linux:
> go env -w GOBIN=/home/user/bin
> go env GOBIN
{
    "GOBIN": "/home/user/bin",
}
# On Windows
C:\> go env -w GOBIN=%LOCALAPPDATA%
```

A.3.2   The GOBIN variable

The GOBIN variable contains the path of a directory in which Go will download any tools you install with go install url@version. This is the standard way of retrieving utilities in Go (more on this in section A.5.1):

```
> go install golang.org/x/tools/cmd/godoc@latest
```

A.3.3   The GOPATH variable

The GOPATH variable contains a list of paths to directories in which Go will resolve its dependencies. Earlier versions of Go used a decentralized approach; that is, if two projects require the same dependency, that dependency is downloaded twice and stored in the burdensome vendors directory of each project. This is no longer the case: now, when a dependency is needed, it's stored locally, and your projects will use the local version rather than re-download that dependency.

Make sure your workspace is contained in the GOPATH list of directories. If you're working in ${HOME}/go, you'll be fine. Otherwise, you can use the command shown in the following listing. Windows users should use a semicolon to add an extra path.

Listing A.5   Adding a directory to your go **path: Unix-based system**

```
# On Linux
> go env -w GOPATH=${GOPATH}:/path/to/workspace
# On Windows
C:\> go env -w "GOPATH=%GOPATH%;C:\path\to\workspace"
```

A.3.4   The GOROOT variable

The GOROOT variable points to the directory containing the Go installation. We recommend not changing the GOROOT tree because installing a new version of Go would mean discarding any of your changes there. Similarly, it's not ideal to have any other Go environment variables pointing to somewhere within the GOROOT.

As part of your installation, you made sure the path ${GOROOT}/bin was included in your PATH environment variable—that's how we can run go. This directory contains another executable—gofmt—which is in charge of formatting code.

A.4   *Hello!*

The hello, world instructions are detailed on Go's website, but here is a short version. You'll find, at the very beginning of the first project, in chapter 2, explanations regarding each line of the typical hello, world.

Create a hello folder in your work folder (it can be anywhere on your computer) with a file named hello.go. Paste the code from the following listing into your file.

Listing A.6   hello.go

```
package main

import "fmt"

func main() {
    fmt.Println("Hello, World!")
}
```

To manage dependencies and versions in Go, we use modules. In this hello directory, run the following command to create your first module, naming this module hello:

```
> go mod init hello
```

A go.mod file appears that contains the path to your module and your Go version.

Then, run your code in the same folder, as shown in the following listing, and wave at your screen: your machine is trying to communicate! Funny how quickly we personify our computer friends.

Listing A.7   Running a Go file

```
> go run hello.go
Hello, World!
```

A.5   *Installing new dependencies*

When developing new functionalities, we like to build on the work of others. Go has two different tools to retrieve existing work, each with its specific objective: go install and go get. They work in a very similar way, but they are used in different contexts.

Both commands accept the name of a repository and will retrieve its contents at a specific version. The main difference is that go get only retrieves Go files from that repository, whereas go install also compiles the retrieved package into an executable. Which one you use will depend on what you need: Do you want the sources or the executable? go get will install the sources—something we do when using new libraries—and go install will be used when installing new tools (formatters, linters, profilers, etc.).

The go install command is rather recent, and some public repositories will still list go get as the method to install their binaries. If you follow that path, you'll be faced with a message suggesting using go install—in these cases, use the second option of go install as described next.

A.5.1   *go install*

If you need to retrieve a binary written in Go, use go install. It will fetch the sources and compile them locally for your machine's architecture. There are three different ways of calling the go install tool, as shown in listing A.8.

The first option lets you retrieve a specific version of a repository. This is very useful when writing automation tools, and you want a constant and deterministic flow.

The second option is very similar and retrieves the code at the latest version of the repository using its main (or master) branch. This is the most common way of using go install manually.

The last option uses the contents of your project's go.mod file to find which version to download and install. This will only work if you're running the command from within a Go project.

Listing A.8   go install **examples**

```
# Install a specific version.
> go install golang.org/x/tools/cmd/godoc@v0.1.12

# Install the highest available version.
> go install golang.org/x/tools/cmd/godoc@latest

# Install the highest available version for your project.
> go install golang.org/x/tools/cmd/godoc
missing go.sum entry for module providing package golang.org/x/tools/cmd/
     godoc; to add:
        go mod download golang.org/x/tools
```

A.5.2   *go get*

If you need sources that your own code depends on, go get will update your module file (see listing A.9) and download the sources into ${GOPATH}/pkg/mod. You can then look into them to understand what the code does. Like go install, the go get command can be used with different behaviors.

The first option you have is to run go get on a URL, without specifying a version or anything. This will retrieve the contents of that dependency and its own dependencies to your go.mod file—you're telling Go you need that repository in your project.

The second option is to retrieve the code by explicitly giving the name of a tag, branch, or commit. This is extremely useful when working on two projects at the same time, or when working with a project that hasn't been merged into `main` yet. This option will register that new package into your `go.mod` file, at the desired version. Listing A.9 shows various examples of `go get` usage.

Listing A.9 `go get` **examples**

```
# Retrieve the experimental slices package using the version defined in
the go.mod file.
> go get golang.org/x/exp/slices
# Retrieve the experimental slices package, latest commit on branch master.
> go get golang.org/x/exp/slices@master
# Retrieve the experimental slices package at a specific commit or tag.
> go get golang.org/x/exp/slices@c99f07
```

A.6   *Code editors*

Go is supported by more and more code editors. As always, the best tool is the one you know how to use. The official Go website, as we write this, lists three editors:

- *GoLand, by JetBrains*—JetBrains has a long list of editors for various languages, the most famous being IntelliJ for Java. You can install GoLand as a standalone editor or add the Go plugin to any other editor in the list.
- *Visual Studio Code, by Microsoft*—This editor has a Go extension.
- *vim-go*—This editor is great if you already know Vim.

A quick search around the web will give you instructions to add Go support to your usual tool, if it's not already there, for example, check the list here: https://go.dev/wiki/IDEsAndTextEditorPlugins.

Go is now installed on your machine, and you can start using it and following the book's instructions. Your terminal now knows how to greet you in English using Go as well.

appendix B
Formatting cheat sheet

Go offers several *verbs* that are passed to printing functions to format Go values. In this appendix, we present the most known verbs and special values that can be passed to these functions. You can refer to these tables throughout the book. The results for each of the following entries were generated by `fmt.Printf("{Verb}", value)`.

Table B.1   Default

Verb	Output for `fmt.Printf("{Verb}", []int64{0, 1})`	Description
%v	[0 1]	Default format
%#v	[]int64{0, 1}	Go-syntax format
%T	[]int64	Type of the value

Table B.2   Integers

Verb	Output for `fmt.Printf("{Verb}", 15)`	Description
%d	15	Base 10
%+d	+15	Always show the sign

Table B.2   Integers (*continued*)

Verb	Output for fmt.Printf("{Verb}", 15)	Description
%4d	␣␣15	Pad to 4 characters with spaces, right justified
%-4d	15␣␣	Pad to 4 characters with spaces, left justified
%04d	0015	Pad to 4 characters with prefixing zeros
%b	1111	Base 2 (binary)
%o	17	Base 8 (octal)
%x	f	Base 16, lowercase
%X	F	Base 16, uppercase
%#x	0xf	Base 16 with leading 0x

Table B.3   Floats

Verb	Output for fmt.Printf("{Verb}", 123.456)	Description
%e	1.234560e+02	Scientific notation
%f	123.456000	Decimal point, no exponent. The default precision is 6.
%.2f	123.46	Default width, precision 2 digits after the decimal point
%8.2f	␣␣123.46	Width 8 chars, precision 2 digits after the decimal point. Default padding character is space.
%08.2f	00123.46	Width 8 chars, precision 2 digits after the decimal point. Left padding with specified character (here, 0).
%g	123.456	Exponent when needed, necessary digits only

Table B.4   Characters

Verb	Output for fmt.Printf("{Verb}", 'A')	Description
%c	A	Character
%q	'A'	Quoted character
%U	U+0041	Unicode
%#U	U+0041 'A'	Unicode with character

Table B.5   Strings or byte `slices`

Verb	Result for `"gophers"`	Description
`%s`	gophers	Plain string
`%8s`	␣␣gophers	Width 8, right justified
`%-8s`	gophers␣␣	Width 8, left justified
`%q`	"gophers"	Quoted string
`%x`	676f7068657273	Hex dump of byte value
`% x`	67 6f 70 68 65 72 73	Hex dump with spaces

Table B.6   Booleans

Verb	Output for `fmt.Printf("{Verb}", true)`	Description
`%t`	true	Equivalent to `%v` but only for Booleans

Table B.7   Pointers

Verb	Output for `fmt.Printf("{Verb}", new(int))`	Description
`%p`	0xc0000b2000	Base 16 notation with leading 0x

Table B.8   Special values

Verb	Description
`\a`	U+0007 alert or bell
`\b`	U+0008 backspace
`\\`	U+005c backslash
`\t`	U+0009 horizontal tab
`\n`	U+000A line feed or newline
`\f`	U+000C form feed
`\r`	U+000D carriage return
`\v`	U+000b vertical tab
`%%`	The % character: `fmt.Printf("%05.2f%%", math.Pi)` prints 03.14%

All Unicode values can be encoded with backslash escapes and can be used in string literals. There are four different formats:

- \x followed by exactly two hexadecimal digits: \x64
- \ followed by exactly three octal digits: \144
- \u followed by exactly four hexadecimal digits: \u0064
- \U followed by exactly eight hexadecimal digits: \U00000064

The escapes \u and \U represent Unicode code points. Here's an example of a Unicode value embedded in a string:

```
fmt.Println("Thy bosom is endear\u00e8d with all hearts")
```

appendix C
Zero values

C.1 What is a zero value?

Sometimes while coding, you'll need to use a variable without assigning a value. For example, a variable should be declared before a condition to exist outside of it:

```
var counter int
if readline(&buf) {
    counter += 1
}
fmt.Println(counter)
```

In this case, the variable `counter` is declared without an explicit initial value, meaning `counter` is given its zero value by default, which, for an integer, is `0`. Note that the initialization to zero value is done recursively either for a `slice`, a `map`, or a structure: each element or field will be set to its zero value according to its type.

C.2 The zero values of any types

Most zero values are intuitive, but a few are worth keeping in mind. Those that you should absolutely remember are listed here:

- Booleans have a zero value of `false`.
- `slice`s and `map`s have a zero value equal to the `nil` entity.

Table C.1 shows examples from the simplest to the more complex types with their zero values. Feel free to come back to this table throughout the book.

Table C.1   Zero values of any types

Variable declaration	Observed zero value
`var r rune`	`r == 0`
`var f float32`	`f == 0.`
`var b bool`	`b == false`
`var i []int`	`i == nil`[1]
`var a [2]complex64`	`a == [2]complex64{0+0i, 0+0i}`
`var m map[string]int`	`m == nil`[1]

`type person struct {`
`  age int`
`  name string`
`}`
`var p person`
	p has been allocated in memory; it can't be `nil` (`nil` is also not of type `person`).
	`p.age == 0`
	`p.name == ""`

`var i *int`	`i == nil`

`type Doer interface {`
`  Do()`
`}`
`var d Doer`
	`d == nil`

`var c chan string`	`c == nil`
`type translate func(string) string` `var t translate`	`t == nil`

[1] The maps and `slices` should be defined with the `make()` function. If not, they take the zero value of `nil`, as described here.

There are a few things to know about `slices` and `maps` that can come in handy at any time. We'll cover those in the next section.

C.3   *Slices and maps specificities*

`Slices` and `maps` have some specificities that should be noticed when manipulating zero values and `nil` entries.

The `len` function can be called on `nil` `slices` or `maps`, and it returns the value `0`. In most cases, checking the length is better than checking if the structure is `nil`. Let's look at an example in the following listing.

Listing C.1   Checking the length of a `slice`

```
func main() {
    data := []string{}
```

```
    fmt.Println(data == nil)
    fmt.Println(len(data))
    fmt.Println(data[0])
}
======
false
0
panic: runtime error: index out of range [0] with length 0
```

As you can see in this example, declaring an empty `slice` doesn't return a `nil slice`. To be able to check any of its elements, we should always check the length of a `slice`.

However, one thing we can do with uninitialized `slices` is append entries to them. This won't cause any panic error and will simply return a non-`nil` `slice` with the new elements, if there were any.

Listing C.2 Appending to a `nil slice`

```
func main() {
    var data []string
    fmt.Println(data == nil)
    data = append(data, "hello")
    fmt.Println(data)
}
======
true
[hello]
```

`maps` follow the same logic (see listing C.3): when declaring one without initializing it, the `map` will be `nil`. The important information is that you can't write data in such a `map`.

Listing C.3 Trying to add elements in a `nil map`

```
func main() {
    var m map[string]int
    m["hello"] = 37
}
======
panic: assignment to entry in nil map
```

However, accessing items in a `nil map` will return the zero value of this item (it's obviously not present), as shown in listing C.4. This is useful information because you sometimes receive a `map` from a library. It's safe to check for keys in the `map`, but it's even safer to check for its length first.

Listing C.4 Trying to read elements from a `nil map`

```
func main() {
    var m map[string]int
    count, found := m["hello"]
```

```
    fmt.Printf("found: %v; count: %d\n", found, count)
}
======
found: false; count: 0
```

C.4   *Benefiting from zero values*

Suppose we want to count the number of different words in a text and keep track of the number of times they occur. One simple way of achieving this goal is to use a map, as shown in the following listing, where the keys are the different words, and the values are their current count, as we iterate through the list of words.

Listing C.4   A structure to count different words in a text

```
wordCount := make(map[string]int)
```

When accessing an entry absent from this map—a word we haven't seen so far—the returned value at the index of the new word will be the zero value of the integer type: 0. This is extremely convenient, as it means we can consider words that haven't been seen so far as words that have been seen zero times. Recording an occurrence of a word doesn't need any extra effort if the word has or hasn't been registered before: we simply add 1 to the counter.

Listing C.5   Counting different words in a text

```
import (
    "fmt"
    "strings"
)

func countWords(s string) {
    wordCounter := make(map[string]int)
    for _, word := range strings.Fields(s) {
        wordCounter[word]++
    }

    // print results
    for word, count := range wordCounter {
        fmt.Printf("We recorded the word %q %d time(s).\n", word, count)
    }
}

func main() {
    countWords("to be or not to be")
}
======
We recorded the word "or" 1 time(s).
We recorded the word "not" 1 time(s).
We recorded the word "to" 2 time(s).
We recorded the word "be" 2 time(s).
```

appendix D
Benchmarking

One of the great tools Go offers is a benchmarking command. Writing benchmarks to compare the allocation of memory and the execution time is extremely simple—it's very similar to writing a test over a function.

We'll use the type B, defined in the testing package (you'll never guess what B stands for). The type B has one exposed field and an integer N, which counts the number of iterations the benchmark has executed. When running benchmarks, this field has an initial value that will allow at least a certain number of iterations to ensure that we have a steady result—no need to try and set it manually. Test benchmarking functions follow a convention very similar to test functions: their name must start with Benchmark.

In section 5.2.1 of chapter 5, we explained that using concatenation to build long strings isn't a good idea, and you should use a builder. Don't take our word for it; measure it yourself!

We're building a string that represents the feedback type, which is a slice of statuses. The following listing shows the necessary code.

> **Listing D.1** `status_internal_test.go`: **Examples of benchmarks**

```
// Benchmark the string concatenation with only one value in feedback
func BenchmarkStringConcat1(b *testing.B) {
    fb := feedback{absentCharacter}
```

```
for n := 0; n < b.N; n++ {                      The value b.N is already set
    _ = fb.StringConcat()                       by the environment.
}
}
```

Side quest

Instead of having a `feedback` of one status (i.e., an `absentCharacter`), write benchmark functions that will test longer feedbacks. Because Gordle will mostly be used
with words of five characters, that's probably the length we want to benchmark.

As mentioned earlier, the benchmark can be run using our friend the `go test` tool,
with specific options. To run benchmarks (just as we had for tests) for all files in subdirectories, we pass the `-bench=.` option, and, if we want to display details of memory operations, we can add `-benchmem`. Running benchmarks will, however, also run
the tests. If we want to avoid that and run only the benchmarks, we can add an extra
parameter to the command line, an indication to help Go find our tests by their name:
a regular expression. We cover this topic a bit more extensively in chapter 8, section
8.5.2, but for now, we'll use the (very) loose `^$`, which matches all benchmark test functions. The following listing shows the command line to run this test and provides the
benchmark results (as run on our computer—your mileage may vary).

Listing D.2   Result of the benchmarks

```
> go test ./... -run=^$ -bench=. -benchmem

goos: darwin
goarch: arm64
pkg: learngo-pockets/gordle
BenchmarkStringConcat1-10    174882942    6.850 ns/op      0 B/op    0 allocs/op
BenchmarkStringConcat2-10     15633693   74.28 ns/op      24 B/op    2 allocs/op
BenchmarkStringConcat3-10      8609542   137.1 ns/op      56 B/op    4 allocs/op
BenchmarkStringConcat4-10      5873654   201.1 ns/op     104 B/op    6 allocs/op
BenchmarkStringConcat5-10      4455464   275.2 ns/op     160 B/op    8 allocs/op

BenchmarkStringBuilder1-10    71407350   16.69 ns/op       8 B/op    1 allocs/op
BenchmarkStringBuilder2-10    30721999   38.28 ns/op      24 B/op    2 allocs/op
BenchmarkStringBuilder3-10    27036134   45.64 ns/op      24 B/op    2 allocs/op
BenchmarkStringBuilder4-10    17278303   70.44 ns/op      56 B/op    3 allocs/op
BenchmarkStringBuilder5-10    16189770   73.27 ns/op      56 B/op    3 allocs/op
PASS
ok      learngo-pockets/gordle   13.762s
```

The output of this command can be a bit scary at first. After all, we only wrote a five-
line test! When we take a look, we can see several lines and several columns. Each line
corresponds to a function that was benchmarked by the Go tool when it found it in our

code (respecting our earlier loose regular expression). The columns represent metrics that were observed by the test tool during the execution of the benchmark, as follows:

- The first column is the name of the function, with a suffix indicating the number of processors on the machine.
- The second column indicates the number of loops that were executed (the b.N value, if you remember).
- The third column indicates the amount of time (usually in nanoseconds) each operation took.
- The fourth column indicates the number of bytes allocated per operation.
- The final column indicates the number of memory allocations per operation.

Some quick math should show that the benchmark tool gave roughly the same amount of execution time to each line (the second column multiplied by the third column). The benchmark results are interesting as they are pretty simple to read.

String concatenation is three to four times slower than using the string builder when we need to append five times. Using the a + b string concatenation makes a number of memory allocations proportional to the number of strings to concatenate (which makes sense because strings are immutable), and these operations cost more and more memory every time. On the other hand, the memory allocations of the string builder are scarcer and lighter. This benchmark confirms we definitely should be using the strings.Builder to generate feedback.

appendix E
Passing by value
or by reference

We constantly use functions in our code, and, most of the time, they have parameters. Let's imagine we're writing code for the bowling alley that opened last week. We need to print the scores on the screen after a player's turn. We write the function shown in the following listing.

Listing E.1   Showing a player's score

```
type Player struct {
    name   string
    score int
}

// ShowScore displays the player's score
func ShowScore(p Player) {
    fmt.Printf("Player %q has %d points!\n", p.name, p.score)
}
```

This does the job, so we're happy. However, we notice that the function updating the score doesn't seem to work.

Listing E.2   Updating the player's score

```
func AddPoints(p Player, points int) {
    p.score += points
}
```

After writing a simple test, we realize that the player's score after calling `AddPoints` didn't change! The main reason behind this lies with Go's handling of parameters in functions known as *passing parameters by value* and *passing parameters by reference*.

E.1   Go passes everything by value

Even though the name of this appendix suggests there are different behaviors in Go, this isn't true. If there's one thing to remember from reading this appendix, it's that every call to a function in Go copies every parameter. But all hope isn't lost for our player's score, as we'll see in this section. The trick lies in understanding what "copying" implies. First, let's dive into what this means and how we can reach our goal of updating variables through function and method calls.

E.1.1   Copying parameters on the stack

When we call a function, its parameters are copied on the stack, ready for the new function to use. While this is pretty simple to understand for literal types such as integers or strings, let's look at what that means when using structures.

Listing E.3 `bowling.go`: Address of a variable inside a function

```go
type Player struct {
    Name  string
    Score int
}

func main() {
    angavu := Player{"Angavu", 250}
    fmt.Printf("in main: %p\n", &angavu)       // Prints the address of the angavu variable
    ShowScore(angavu)
}
                                               // Prints the address of the player parameter
func ShowScore(player Player) {
    fmt.Printf("Player %q has %d points!\n", player.name, p.score)
    fmt.Printf("in showScore: %p\n", &player)
}
```

When running this small program, we get the output in the following listing.

Listing E.4 `bowling.go`: Output

```
> go run bowling.go
in main: 0x00000a8018
Player "Angavu" has 250 points!
in showScore: 0x00000a8030
```

The addresses themselves will change at every run. The important point is that they are different because we're dealing with two `Player` structures. One structure was created in the `main` function, and one was created and pushed on the stack when we called the `showScore` function.

Calling a function makes a copy of every parameter you pass to it—always. When copying the `Player` structure, every field—`Name` and `Score`—was copied. In our previous example, because it was copied, the object that `AddPoints` receives to work with isn't the one that exists in the `main` function. This explains why we can't simply pass the object player to the `AddPoints` function. Let's see how we can use this feature to our advantage.

E.1.2   Using pointers

Pointers are a special type of variable, as they only represent the memory address of an entity, not the entity itself. A pointer can be considered a structure comprising a pair of values (see listing E.5): an address in the memory (where the data is) and the definition of the data (is it an `int` or a `Player`?).

Listing E.5   Simplified version of pointers

```
type pointer struct {
    address          uint64
    representedValue reflect.Type
}
```

Let's now copy a pointer and look at what happens inside (see listing E.6). For this, we have to use two packages. The first package appears on the `reflect` line in the previous listing. This package allows us to determine the type of variables.

The second package we'll use is the dreaded `unsafe`. This package is extremely well named with the following official description:

> *Package* `unsafe` *contains operations that step around the type safety of Go programs. Packages that import* `unsafe` *may be non-portable and aren't protected by the Go 1 compatibility guidelines.*

We'll make minimal use of `unsafe` here and only use it to convert a variable's address in memory into a `uint64`. There are other ways of doing so, but in the end, we're not supposed to do it, and the language makes that clear.

Listing E.6   `pointer.go`: Copying a pointer

```
func main() {
    dom := Player{"Dom", 43}
    domAddr := uint64(uintptr(unsafe.Pointer(&dom)))    ◄──┐ Converts the address
    domPtr := pointer{domAddr, reflect.TypeOf(dom)}        │ to an uint64
    domPointerCopied := ptr
    fmt.Printf("parent: at %p -- pointing to 0x%x\n",
        &domPtr, domPtr.address)
    fmt.Printf("copied: at %p -- pointing to 0x%x\n",
        &domPointerCopied, domPointerCopied.address)
    fmt.Printf("Dom: at %p -- %p\n",
```

```
        &dom.name, &dom.score)                     Prints the address of each field
}                                                  of the Player structure
```

Running this small program will result in the output shown in the following listing.

Listing E.7 A copied pointer points to the same address

```
> go run pointer.go
parent: at 0xc000010048 -- pointing to 0xc000010030
copied: at 0xc000010078 -- pointing to 0xc000010030
Dom: at 0xc000010030 -- 0xc000010040
```

As we can see, the first `at` value is different as it's the address of the variables `ptr` and `copiedPtr` where they are stored in memory. Because these are two different variables, they live in different places, which is expected. The second value of each line, the `pointing to` value, is the address of the pointed `Player`. We can see they are the same, meaning we managed to keep access to player Dom, even after copying it. Get excited because this means we can use pointers to share objects between functions.

Let's pass a pointer parameter in `AddScore`, as shown in listing E.8. In Go, you can get the address of a variable by using the `&` operator (called *reference*). The `*` operator is used to get the value pointed by a pointer (called the *pointee*), which is called *dereferencing*. The same `*` symbol is used.

Listing E.8 `bowling.go`: Calling `addScore` with a pointer to a player

```
func ShowScore(p Player) {
    fmt.Printf("Player %q has %d points!\n", p.name, p.score)
}

func main() {                                The & operator is used to get
    mia := &Player{"Mia", 42}                a pointer to the variable.
    ShowScore(*mia)
    AddScore(mia, 8)                         The * operator is used to get the
    ShowScore(*mia)                          value pointed by the pointer.
}

func AddScore(p *Player, score int) {        The * represents that p is a
    p.score += score                         pointer to the type Player.
}
```

We now get the expected result, as shown in the following listing, and can rejoice!

Listing E.9 `bowling.go`: Final execution

```
> go run bowling.go
Player "Mia" has 42 points!
Player "Mia" has 50 points!
```

As we've seen, the main difference is that when we pass a pointer to a function, we duplicate the pointer information (a type and an address) and not the pointed information (a list of fields), whereas when we pass a non-pointer to a function, it's copied. But let's consider a structure holding a pointer, which is often done when we want to represent an optional piece of information:

```
type Country struct {
    Name string
    NationalDay *time.Date // Not all countries have a national day
}
```

What exactly happens when we pass a country by copy? Is the `NationalDay` field (recursively) copied? We'll discuss the answer next.

E.1.3   *Shallow copies*

When we call a function and pass it a parameter by copy, it's important to remember that all of its fields will be copied. However, as we've just seen, the copy of a struct is a different struct (with memory allocated elsewhere for its fields), but the copy of a pointer is still pointing to the same address as the original. So, using the example of the `Country` shown in the code snippet in the previous section, if a function had the signature

```
func process(c Country)
```

it would receive a copy of the country we give it when we call it. However, that copy's `NationalDay` would still point to the original country's `NationalDay`, which means this function could update the initial country! This would lead to a lot of misunderstandings.

> **WARNING**   If a function's signature is to accept values by copy, the function shouldn't update values pointed by its parameters.

Copying a variable by passing it to a function or by using the = operator will only copy non-pointed values. For this reason, we call these copies *shallow* copies.

E.1.4   *Functions vs. methods*

So far, we've only used functions to understand how everything works. "But what about methods?" you might ask. Do we need another three pages to understand everything?

The good thing is that functions and methods are extremely close. In fact, every method can be rewritten as a function whose first parameter is the receiver of the method. The code in listings E.10 and E.11 have exactly the same behavior.

Listing E.10   Function vs. method when passing by value

```
// Player as parameter of the function
func showScore(p Player) {
    fmt.Printf("Player %q has %d points!\n", p.name, p.score)
```

```
}

// Player as receiver of the method
func (p Player) showScore() {
    fmt.Printf("Player %q has %d points!\n", p.name, p.score)
}
```

Listing E.11   Function vs. method when using pointers

```
// Player as parameter of the function
func addScore(p *Player, score int) {
    p.score += score
}

// Player as receiver of the method
func (p *Player) addScore(score int) {
    p.score += score
}
```

The choice of using either the first or second method is up to you, but we tend to use the method with a receiver when we want to follow the abstraction principle of object-oriented programming.

E.2   *Special types of parameters: slices, maps, and channels*

As we've seen, passing parameters by value will copy the structure that contains them (or their literal value), while passing parameters by pointer will create a pointer to the same memory address. There are, however, a few types that need to be covered because they're error prone.

When copying a `slice` or a `map`, a shallow copy will contain the very elements the original had. To obtain a real duplicate, we need to manually iterate through the `slice` or `map`, and then copy its elements to the new variable.

E.2.1   *Passing a slice as a parameter*

A `slice` is a block of memory that can grow as we need. We create `slices` with the `make` function, which allows us to specify the length (and capacity, if we really want to). Under the hood, a `slice` is a structure with the definition shown in the following listing.

Listing E.12   Definition of the built-in `slice` type (Go 1.23)

```
type slice struct {
    array unsafe.Pointer  ◄──────  The address of the slice
    len   int             ◄──────  of data in memory
    cap   int             ◄──┐
}                            │     The number of items
                             │     in the slice
                             └───  The maximum capacity of the slice
```

To understand `slices`, keep in mind two popular functions that receive `slices` as parameters: append, and `slices.Sort` of the `slices` package.

CHANGING THE NUMBER OF ELEMENTS: APPEND

Once they are created, our use of `slices` is often to aggregate a dynamic number of entities (arrays can be used when the number is static). To add elements to our `slice`, we use the built-in `append` function. Here is its signature:

```
func append(slice []Type, elems ...Type) []Type
```

The `append` function can't mutate the `slice` we pass it as a parameter. Internally, the function needs to update the `len` and `cap` fields of the `slice`, and sometimes—when we're trying to append more elements than the `slice` can accommodate—the function needs to relocate its internal array elsewhere.

But because the `slice` it works on, internally, is a mere copy of the one the user has in their scope, the clean way to share the new `slice` value is to return it. While using a pointer to a `slice` is possible, we recommend never doing it.

UPDATING THE ELEMENTS OF THE SLICE

Once data has been inserted in the `slice`, we often need to reorganize its elements, maybe because we want a random dataset or, usually, because we want a deterministic value. The `slices` package offers two functions to sort a `slice`: Sort and SortFunc. The first one requires the elements of the `slice` to be comparable with <, <=, =>, and >. The second function requires a comparison function for `slices` of structures.

The key point of these two functions is that, counterintuitively, while they both change the data that they receive, they don't return anything. This is because while they receive a copy of the `slice`, they can still move its elements around, which will be visible from the caller's scope.

E.2.2   maps, channels, and more

`maps` and channels are a lot more complex than `slices`, but they follow the same pattern: they internally use pointers to memory addresses where they store data. Just like `slices`, they sometimes need to grow based on the number of entries they contain. However, unlike `slices`, when passing a `map` or a channel to a function, it's possible, from that function, to add or remove elements from the `map` or channel, which will affect the caller's scope.

E.3   A few recommendations

We've seen some fun behaviors that are quite intricate when it's the first time you witness them. However, with a few logical steps and keeping in mind that, in Go, everything is always passed by copy (that's the bottom line), inexplicable results should become perfectly understandable. The following subsections provide our list of recommendations when it's time to write functions and methods, as well as deal with the question of adding the little asterisk.

E.3.1 *Passing by value should be the default*

Anytime you write a function or a method, the default thought process should be to start passing a copy of the input variable. There are some caveats, though. It's important to keep in mind that passing a struct by copy might not protect the original struct. Indeed, if one field is a pointer, the copy will refer to the same memory address, and the original struct might be altered by anything happening to the copy's pointer.

E.3.2 *Passing by pointer is a minor optimization*

Sometimes, if your objects are really big, copying them will take a noticeable amount of time. You can accelerate the execution by passing pointers, which are very light. However, this optimization is minor, and you'll need to do a lot of profiling to justify this extra asterisk.

E.3.3 *Passing by pointer when mutating*

If you need to alter the object in any way—increase an integer, replace the value of a field by another one, lock a mutex—you'll need to provide the shared version of the variable, which is done with a pointer to its memory address. This is the perfect use case to add an asterisk in the signature of the function.

But we also prefer to mutate an object in a received method rather than in a function that takes it as a parameter because the owner of the method has to be the owner of the struct. They will reside in the same package, and the same maintainers will know the intricacies of them both.

E.3.4 *Using slices and maps*

Because `slices` and `maps` are very light, their data is hidden behind pointers. For this reason, most of the time, passing the `slice` or the `map` by value is the best option.

When using `slices`, keep in mind the `append` and `slices.SortFunc` functions. If you need to add (or remove) elements from the `slice`, or change its length or capacity, you'll have to return the updated `slice`. If you only need to reorganize the `slice`'s elements, there's no need to return it. `maps` and channels can be passed to functions, and their contents can be updated by such calls. Passing a `slice`/`map`/channel pointer to a function should raise an alert in your code.

E.3.5 *Passing a pointer to a slice or to a map*

Most of the time, resorting to passing a pointer to a `slice` or to a `map` is the wrong approach. You're probably better off returning the updated `slice` or `map` à la `append`. However, there's one case where you want to send a function the address of a `slice`: when unmarshaling raw data into a `slice` of elements. For instance, if a string represents a JSON array, we'd unmarshal it to a `slice`, as shown in the following listing.

Listing E.13   Unmarshaling a JSON array

A string representing a
JSON array of integers

```
jsonIntegers := `[1, 2, 3, 4, 5]`    ◀

                                            A noninitialized slice
var numbers []int    ◀─────────────┘       (currently nil)

err := json.Unmarshal([]byte(jsonIntegers), &numbers)    ◀─────────┐
if err != nil {
    return fmt.Errorf("while unmarshalling %s: %w", jsonIntegers, err)
}
                                    Sending the address of numbers to
                                    Unmarshal allows it to update the fields
                                      of the slice: len, cap, and address.
```

E.3.6   *Writing your own Copy function*

If you handle structures with fields that are pointers to structures, or something tricky like that, it's quite certain that when copying—making a duplicate entity of the original one—you will end up with a pointer in the direction of the original entity's address. Sometimes, it's worth writing your own Copy function, which will ensure that the copy and the original share an absolute 0 bit of memory. This is by far the safest approach.

appendix F
Fuzzing

Testing plays a crucial role in software development. We've already explored unit tests, test-driven development, and benchmarks, so in this appendix, we'll introduce fuzz testing.

F.1 A new testing method

Fuzzing is a testing technique where smartly generated random input data is fed into the function under test. Fuzzers try to guess what input will cover new code paths. Fuzz tests complement traditional unit tests rather than replace them. They are particularly powerful for uncovering new bugs, crashes, and edge cases that might be missed otherwise. Fuzz testing was introduced in Go 1.18 as a built-in feature of the standard toolbox, simplifying our lives as developers. In real-world applications, fuzzing is instrumental in discovering critical problems such as security vulnerabilities, SQL injection flaws, and other potential breaches that could be exploited by malicious actors. By rigorously testing your code with a wide range of inputs, you ensure not only its correctness but also its resilience against real-world attacks. Fuzzing is also an amazing tool to ensure that two functions behave the same for identical inputs, which is great when we have to refactor some code and write a new version of a function.

F.2 How it works

Writing a fuzz test is straightforward: we replace *testing.T with *testing.F and then perform a few additional steps. First, our fuzz test must be in a _test.go file (it could be the same as where the unit tests are), and the function name should start with FuzzXxx instead of TestXxx. The function should take a *testing.F parameter instead of *testing.T. We'll use f.Fuzz instead of t.Run, passing in both the *testing.T (yes, T here) and the parameters to be fuzzed. An essential component of fuzzing is the *seed corpus*—a collection of initial inputs that guide the fuzzer's exploration. These inputs are provided to the fuzzer using f.Add(). It's important to note that only certain types are supported: []byte, string, int, intXx, uint, uintXx, rune, float32, and float64. The following listing is an example of a fuzz test function's structure.

Listing F.1   Structure of a fuzzing test function

```
func FuzzFoo(f *testing.F) {                          ◄─── Declares the testing
    // Adding some seed strings to test common cases        fuzzing function
        f.Add("foo")
    f.Add("bar")          Uses f.Add to provide a seed corpus

    f.Fuzz(func(t *testing.T, input string) {     ◄─── Calls the testing method
        out, err := Foo(input) {                  ◄─── Calls the target method
        if err != nil && out != "" {
            t.Errorf("%q, %v", out, err)          ◄─── Checks the error
        }
    })
}
```

In this example, we use fuzzing to test whether our Foo function returns a non-nil error and a non-empty string for some input string. We start by setting the corpus to two "interesting" values, and the fuzz tool will do the rest, generating random values from the corpus until it finds an error case.

That's it for the theory, so now let's see a concrete example to get a sense of how fuzz tests can find new bugs and help us write functions that cover more edge cases than we initially thought about.

F.3   Writing a first test

Let's explore an interesting problem: checking for palindromes. A *palindrome* is a word or phrase that reads the same forward and backward. Our task is to write a function that takes a string as input and returns true if it's a palindrome. We'll limit the scope here to strings representing numbers, just for simplicity. To get started, let's create a package named palindrome and add a file called palindrome.go. The tested function checks whether a given string represents a numeric palindrome. With fuzz testing, we'll see how we can iterate and improve our initial implementation.

F.3.1   Function under test

An initial approach is to first convert the input string into an integer using strconv.Atoi, as shown in listing F.2. If the conversion fails, we can return false directly: as it's not a number, it isn't a palindrome number. Then, the function will flip the number by extracting the last digit of the original input and storing it in a variable representing our flipped input. We then remove the last digit from the input number stored in the input variable by dividing it by `10`. At the end of the loop, we compare the original number and the flipped one and return `true` if they are the same.

Listing F.2 `IsPalindromeNumber()` **function: First version**

```
package palindrome

import (
    "strconv"
)

// IsPalindromeNumber returns whether an integer is identical when read
// both ways.
// "1221" is a palindrome
func IsPalindromeNumber(s string) bool {
    toInt, err := strconv.Atoi(s)        ◄──── Converts to a number
    if err != nil {
        return false
    }

    original := toInt // 1234               Flips the integer and
    flip := 0                               compares
    for toInt > 0 {                     ◄──
        flip = 10*flip + toInt%10 //    4 | 43 | 432 | 4321
        toInt = toInt / 10         // 123 | 12 |   1 |    0
    }

    return original == flip
}
```

While we could write basic unit tests for this function, here we'll focus on creating a fuzz test instead. Following the naming convention outlined in section F.2, we'll explore how fuzz testing can help uncover edge cases and unexpected inputs.

F.3.2 *Fuzz test*

First, we initialize the seed corpus with two basic test cases: `"1221"`, a nominal case that is a palindrome, and an empty string, which is a special edge case and technically a palindrome. We can also provide other interesting input values, such as string palindromes or strings composed of non-Latin characters. Remember, filling the input corpus helps the fuzz tool.

Next, we set up the fuzz function, which will execute the provided seed corpus and then start mutating over its contents to generate various random inputs. Our fuzz test calls `IsPalindromeNumber` with the generated input, and we'll validate the result by comparing it to a reference. We'll see in listing F.4 how we can create this reference by implementing a `reverse` function.

If the original input is detected as a palindrome number but its reverse isn't, there's an error, and the mismatch is reported. The following listing shows the full implementation of the test.

Listing F.3   Fuzz test of `IsPalindromeNumber()`

```
package palindrome

import (
    "slices"
    "testing"
)

func FuzzIsPalindromeNumber(f *testing.F) {          Seeds corpus with
    f.Add("1221") // nominal case                    some basic test cases
    f.Add("")     // empty string

    f.Fuzz(func(t *testing.T, input string) {        Calls the function
        got := IsPalindromeNumber(input)             we want to test

        reversed := reverse(input)                                A string reversed
        reverseIsPalindrome := IsPalindromeNumber(reversed)       should match the
                                                                  palindrome status.
        if got != reverseIsPalindrome {
            t.Errorf("Palindrome mismatch for input: " +
                "%s (isPalindrome: %v) and " +
                "its reverse: %s (isPalindrome: %v)",
                input, got, reversed, reverseIsPalindrome)
        }
    })
}
```

Fuzz tests are particularly valuable when comparing different implementations of a function, such as your own versus one from an external library, or your new, faster version versus some legacy code from years ago. By doing this, we can validate the correctness of our code and uncover edge cases. In this example, we use Go's `slices.Reverse` function to reverse the runes of a string. Note that reversing a string is a very complex task—think about diacritics, ligatures, and non-Latin characters. (If you want to know more about reversing a task, read the article "Counting Characters" by Egon Elbre at https://egonelbre.com/counting-characters/.)

In listing F.4, we're reversing a string made of integers, which makes the usual edge cases out of scope. By using an established, reliable function from the Go standard library, we can compare its behavior with our custom palindrome implementation and ensure both produce consistent results. Next, it's time to make a fuzz!

Listing F.4   `reverse()` helper

```
// reverse reverses a string using the built-in slices.Reverse function
func reverse(s string) string {
    reverse := []rune(s)
    slices.Reverse(reverse)
    return string(reverse)
}
```

F.4   *Running and interpreting fuzz tests*

Now that we've written our fuzz test, let's run it. Go provides the `-fuzz` flag with the `go test` command, which allows us to specify a regular expression to match the test's name. Because we only have one fuzzing test, we can run it with the following command:

```
> go test -fuzz=IsPalindromeNumber
```

When a fuzz test fails, Go provides detailed information about the input that caused the failure. Let's walk through a sample output to understand what each part means.

Here's the output that we obtained. Mind you, fuzz tests are, well, fuzzy, so there's no guarantee that you'll get exactly the same result when running it:

```
fuzz: elapsed: 0s, gathering baseline coverage: 0/2 completed
fuzz: elapsed: 0s, gathering baseline coverage: 2/2 completed,
    now fuzzing with 12 workers
fuzz: elapsed: 0s, execs: 19 (967/sec), new interesting: 0 (total: 2)
--- FAIL: FuzzIsPalindromeNumber (0.02s)
    --- FAIL: FuzzIsPalindromeNumber (0.00s)
        palindrome_test.go:20: Palindrome mismatch for input: 01
(isPalindrome: true) and its reverse: 10 (isPalindrome: false)

    Failing input written to
testdata/fuzz/FuzzIsPalindromeNumber/7f5131ea0ab9779f
    To re-run:
    go test -run=FuzzIsPalindromeNumber/7f5131ea0ab9779f
FAIL
exit status 1
FAIL    learngo-pockets/appendices/F/palindrome        0.880s
```

Before fuzzing begins, Go gathers baseline coverage by running the seed corpus (known test cases). In this case, the baseline coverage is tested against two inputs—the ones we provided by calling `f.Add()`.

After the baseline is established, the fuzzing process starts. The test is distributed across 12 workers, meaning Go runs 12 parallel goroutines calling the `IsPalindrome-Number` function with generated input.

Here, the fuzzing process executed 19 different test cases in total with a speed of 967 calls per second. In our case, the low number of 19 is due to the early discovery of a failure. Fuzz tests stop as soon as one fails, and the problem is reported.

The "new interesting" section refers to how many new, interesting inputs were found, that is, inputs that trigger different behavior in our function. Let's take a look at the failure interpretation. The test failed in 0.02 seconds and reports the exact case where it fails: the input string `"01"`. Our function `IsPalindromeNumber` returns `true` because the parsed value 1 is a palindrome, while the string `"01"`, when reversed, is `"10"`, which isn't a palindrome. So, is the string `"01"` really representing a palindrome number? If we look at it and check the specifications of our function, it doesn't match our criteria:

the string doesn't start with the same number it ends with. We need to update our implementation to handle leading zeros properly and return `false` in that case.

Go saves the exact failing input to a file in the `testdata/fuzz` directory for future reference. In our case, we can find the input in the file `7f5131ea0ab9779f` (again, your execution may produce different results). To rerun this test case, we can use the following command:

```
> go test -run=FuzzIsPalindromeNumber/7f5131ea0ab9779f
```

Now that we've detected a problem with our code, let's update our implementation to handle strings starting with zeros.

F.5 *Fixing the breach*

To handle zeros on the left of our string, we can no longer use the value returned by `strconv.Atoi`, as it will discard these unnecessary zeros. Instead of reversing the digits, we'll update our function to compare the input rune by rune from both ends. This approach will correctly return `false` for cases such as `"01"`, treating it as not a palindrome. Because we removed the conversion from `string` to `int`, guaranteeing we have a numeric input, we'll use a regular expression check. The input should be only composed of digits: `[0-9]*`.

Another problem that we encountered when writing this appendix arose when the fuzz tool generated a very long sequence of digits: `"100000000000000000001"`. The `Atoi` conversion caused an error. In this case, we'd go back to the specs to determine whether we should accept or reject such numbers. The following listing shows the new implementation of the `IsPalindromeNumber` function.

Listing F.5   `IsPalindromeNumber()` **handling padding**

```
package palindrome

import (
    "regexp"
)

// IsPalindromeNumber returns if an integer is readable in both ways.
// "1221" is a palindrome
// "01" is not a palindrome
// "004400" is a palindrome
func IsPalindromeNumber(s string) bool {          Makes sure the input
    re := regexp.MustCompile("[0-9]*")        ◄── has only digits
    if !re.MatchString(s) {
        return false
    }

    runes := []rune(s)
    for i := 0; i < len(runes)/2; i++ {           Compares first and last
        if runes[i] != runes[len(runes)-1-i] {  ◄── rune of the input
            return false
```

```
            }
        }

        return true
    }
```

As shown in listing F.6, let's add new cases to the seed corpus: one that ends with 0 and one that starts with 0. They are already present in the `testdata` folder, but in case you're not committing fuzz output files, it's best to add them to the seed corpus for future executions.

Listing F.6 Adding new test cases in the seed corpus

```
f.Add("10")    // ends with 0
f.Add("01")    // starts with 0
```

If we now run the test, we should see the following output, going on forever (it can be stopped using Ctrl-C in Windows or Cmd-C on Mac):

```
fuzz: elapsed: 0s, gathering baseline coverage: 0/12 completed
fuzz: elapsed: 0s, gathering baseline coverage: 12/12 completed,
    now fuzzing with 12 workers
fuzz: elapsed: 3s, execs: 1752621 (584082/sec), new interesting: 4
    (total: 16)
fuzz: elapsed: 6s, execs: 3502990 (583376/sec), new interesting: 4
    (total: 16)
fuzz: elapsed: 9s, execs: 5204622 (567366/sec), new interesting: 4
    (total: 16)
fuzz: elapsed: 12s, execs: 6894973 (563413/sec), new interesting: 4
    (total: 16)
fuzz: elapsed: 15s, execs: 8650840 (585323/sec), new interesting: 4
    (total: 16)
fuzz: elapsed: 18s, execs: 10361517 (570078/sec), new interesting: 4
    (total: 16)
fuzz: elapsed: 21s, execs: 12093515 (577488/sec), new interesting: 4
    (total: 16)
fuzz: elapsed: 24s, execs: 13886337 (597596/sec), new interesting: 4
    (total: 16)
fuzz: elapsed: 27s, execs: 15562255 (605306/sec), new interesting: 4
    (total: 16)
^C
PASS
ok      learngo-pockets/palindrome      27.071s
```

Go provides a `-fuzztime` flag to specify how long the fuzzing should run. Go will stop executing the test after this duration. Let's run the following and see:

```
> go test -fuzz=IsPalindromeNumber -fuzztime=15s
```

You can add a bunch of fun test cases to your seed corpus. The following listing provides a list of corner cases.

Listing F.7   Adding edge test cases in the seed corpus

```
// Fun other test cases
f.Add("\xff")                        // not a number
f.Add("+1")                          // signed +
f.Add("-1")                          // signed -
f.Add("9700000000000000079")  // very large number
f.Add("1.1")                         // float
f.Add("1 221")                       // with a space
f.Add(`{"test":1}`)                  // JSON
f.Add("1_221")                       // a valid int with "_"
f.Add("KayaK")                       // a palindrome string
```

Congratulations on uncovering all these edge cases! With our numeric palindrome checker now robustly tested through fuzzing, we have a solid implementation.

Keep in mind, however, that not having a failing test doesn't mean our code works perfectly—it only means that we haven't found any problematic scenarios. The absence of evidence of bugs doesn't imply the absence of bugs. So, keep a sharp eye on any other edge cases, even when relying on fuzz tests. To close this appendix, let's delve into best practices and common pitfalls to further enhance your fuzz testing approach.

F.6   *Best practices and common pitfalls*

When incorporating fuzz testing, it's important to follow best practices to get the most out of the process. Start with a well-designed seed corpus to help guide the fuzzing toward relevant input spaces. Ensure your checks are meaningful, validating both the correctness and safety of the code. Fuzzing should be seen as a complement to your regular testing, enhancing but not replacing traditional unit tests and other testing methods. Any code that involves parsing is a good candidate for fuzzing tests.

At the same time, be mindful of common pitfalls. Overreliance on fuzzing, without recognizing its limitations, can result in missing critical bugs. Fuzz testing relies on having a broad enough input corpus. Even though our function tests if a string represents a palindrome number, it should still be tested with characters other than numbers—words, emojis, anything that a Go string can handle—as its input. Note that for small input spaces such as uint16, it's often better to test all inputs rather than using fuzzing. Fuzzing can also be resource intensive, so it's crucial to consider performance effects, especially with long-running tests. Additionally, when fuzz testing code that interacts with external systems, it's essential to properly isolate or mock these systems to avoid unintended side effects and unreliable test results. As we've seen, Go will run as many iterations of our test as it can to find errors, so fuzz testing a function that opens a file will add a massive load on the filesystem.

appendix G
Connecting to a database

We've used in-memory databases in a few chapters, stating that nobody will ever use this kind of data storage in a real-world scenario for a few reasons: (1) when the server restarts, all data is lost, and (2) there are clever people out there dedicating time and energy to creating data storage systems and giving access to their work for free.

In this section, we'll use the example from chapter 10, our gRPC habits tracker, to show the first steps of how to connect to a database. We'll use PostgreSQL since it's a popular choice.

G.1 Setup

Before we can connect to a database, it needs to be running and listening to requests. Rather than installing a database on our local machine, we can use a containerized version via Docker.

G.1.1 Starting a PostgreSQL database locally

Make sure that `docker` is installed on your machine and that you have the proper rights to use it. Pull the latest image available for PostgresSQL:

```
> docker pull postgres
```

Then, run it with a handful of arguments.

Listing G.1   Starting a local PostgresSQL instance

```
> docker run \
      --name postgres-habits \
      -p 5455:5432 \
      -e POSTGRES_USER=user \
      -e POSTGRES_PASSWORD=*** \
      -e POSTGRES_DB=habits-tracker \
      -d \
      postgres
```

Avoids the default
port in production

Uses a safe password

Runs in the background

Using your favorite client (pgAdmin is a free UI-based tool, and `psql` is a command-line tool) or even a plugin of your IDE if it has one, connect to your new instance using this URL:

```
jdbc:postgresql://user:***@localhost:5455/habits-tracker
```

G.1.2   Seed the schema

Due to the "structured" part of Structured Query Language (SQL), we need to define a structure. This can be done with a simple script that you can run using your client, as shown in listing G.2.

Even though our service doesn't yet support users, we decided to add a table for them because it stands to reason that a habit belongs to only one person, and of course we don't want to deploy a full database per user. Segregation of data is usually done logically. Use the same caution that we used in chapter 11 regarding CSS: this isn't a book about SQL, and some of our choices could probably be improved.

Listing G.2   Seeing the database's structure

```
CREATE TABLE users
(
    id          INT GENERATED ALWAYS AS IDENTITY,
    username    VARCHAR(100)      NOT NULL,
    created_on  DATE              NOT NULL,
    PRIMARY KEY (id)
);

CREATE TABLE habits
(
    id               INT GENERATED ALWAYS AS IDENTITY,
    user_id          INT          NOT NULL,
    title            VARCHAR(255) NOT NULL,
    weekly_frequency INT          NOT NULL,
    created_on       TIMESTAMP    NOT NULL,
    PRIMARY KEY (id),
    CONSTRAINT fk_habit_user FOREIGN KEY (user_id)
        REFERENCES users (id)
);
```

Each table has a
generated ID.

Foreign keys ensure
data consistency.

```
CREATE TABLE ticks
(
    id          INT GENERATED ALWAYS AS IDENTITY,
    habit_id    INT         NOT NULL,
    created_on  TIMESTAMP NOT NULL,
    PRIMARY KEY (id),
    CONSTRAINT fk_habit_user FOREIGN KEY (habit_id)
        REFERENCES habits (id)
);
```

Each table has a generated ID.

Foreign keys ensure data consistency.

Insert one user manually (because we don't have that feature yet). You're now ready to send some structured queries using Go.

G.2   *Repository package*

As a reminder, this is the shape of our in-memory package:

```
> go doc HabitRepository
package repository // import "."

type HabitRepository struct {
    // Has unexported fields.
}
    HabitRepository holds all the current habits.

func New(lgr Logger) *HabitRepository
func (hr *HabitRepository) Add(context.Context, h habit.Habit) error
func (hr *HabitRepository) AddTick(
        _ context.Context, id habit.ID, t time.Time) error
func (hr *HabitRepository) Find(
        _ context.Context, id habit.ID) (habit.Habit, error)
func (hr *HabitRepository) FindAll(_ context.Context) ([]habit.Habit, error)
func (hr *HabitRepository) FindTicks(
        _ context.Context, id habit.ID, from, to *time.Time) ([]time.Time,
error)
```

Let's write a version with a similar interface.

G.2.1   *Injecting a connection*

Go has a basic package for SQL-based storage technologies: `database/sql`. It exposes a way to open a connection and various ways to query. As the documentation states at the start of the package, it "must be used in conjunction with a database driver," which is PostgreSQL in our case.

The type that we'll be carrying around is called DB. The documentation states that "DB is a database handle representing a pool of zero or more underlying connections." We can leave the decisions regarding the size of this pool to the library itself, or dig deeper into the documentation if need be (via the Conn object), which states the following: "Prefer running queries from DB unless there is a specific need for a continuous single database connection." At our level, we don't need that.

Let's add a pointer to this DB in our repository and require a pointer in the New()
function.

Listing G.3   Type HabitRepository

```
// HabitRepository holds all the current habits.
type HabitRepository struct {
    lgr Logger

    db *sql.DB                        Adds a pointer to
}                                     the DB connection


// New creates an empty habit repository.
func New(lgr Logger, db *sql.DB) *HabitRepository {
    return &HabitRepository{
        lgr: lgr,
        db:  db,              Uses the pointer
    }
}
```

Our main function will be responsible for creating a db object and injecting it in our
repository structure. The function that we need for this is Open. It takes the name of a
driver and a connection string, so we need to pick a driver.

The documentation for the standard SQL package points to a list of known drivers.
At the time we are writing this, PostgreSQL has three drivers: one uses cgo, which adds
a level of complexity to our project. Another, pq, is light enough but doesn't seem to be
the most maintained. We'll use the third, pgx. Registering the driver can be done with a
silent import of the package:

```
import _ "github.com/jackc/pgx/v5/stdlib"
```

Then, find a way to get the URL of the database. A const is a solution that can be used
during early development, but you'll very quickly need to find a way to inject this value
when starting the program. A command-line parameter, encrypted file, config map, or
an environment variable can do the job. For the last one, os.Getenv gives a hint. Listing G.4 opens the connection to a hardcoded database address.

Listing G.4   func main: Building a connection

```
const dbURL = "postgresql://user:***@localhost:5455/habits-tracker"
...

db, err := sql.Open("pgx", dbURL)           Opens the connection
if err != nil {
    lgr.Logf("Unable to connect to database: %v\n", err)
    os.Exit(1)
}                                       Exits with an error
defer db.Close()

                    Don't forget to close.
```

This will open the connection but doesn't check whether the database responds. A good practice is to ping the database regularly as part of a service's health check:

```
if err = db.Ping(); err != nil {...}
```

This way, we guarantee that a database is running and the service can start working. Now you can provide the repository with this db object and give it as a dependency to the server:

```
postgres := repository.New(lgr, db)
```

Replace all the methods' contents by a simple `panic("Implement me")`, and check that it's done by refreshing the index page. You can also be a little less drastic and replace the content via a log with the name of the function, but this won't prevent you from pushing code that does nothing if you're not careful.

G.2.2 *Querying the database*

We have a long list of panics, so let's fix them. Our service needs three different types of operations at the moment: select all of something, select one, and insert.

SELECT MULTIPLE HABITS

`sql.DB` has two families of methods: with context or without context. In a service such as the habits service from chapter 10, we carry a context around, so we might as well use it. For queries, the methods are `Query` and `QueryContext`. As a reminder, this is the signature of our `FindAll` function that returns all the habits:

```
FindAll(ctx context.Context) ([]habit.Habit, error)
```

In SQL, with the schema we defined previously, this translates to

```
SELECT "id", "title", "weekly_frequency"
    FROM "habits"
    ORDER BY "created_on" DESC
```

In the following listing, we first declare this statement as a string. Then, we use `Query-Context` to send it to the database, which will return a `slice` of rows.

Listing G.5 `FindAll`

```
// FindAll returns all habits sorted by creation time.
func (hr *HabitRepository) FindAll(
    ctx context.Context) ([]habit.Habit, error) {
    const findAllQuery = `SELECT ...`          ◀─────┤ Declares the query

    rows, err := hr.db.QueryContext(ctx, findAllQuery)  ◀───── Sends the query to
    if err != nil {...}                                        the database
    defer rows.Close()          ◀────┐ Don't forget to close.
```

Iterating over the `slice` lets us parse the results one by one into a Go struct. Rows hold a handy method called `Next` to tell whether there are more results and move to the next row, as shown in listing G.6. This method returns a Boolean telling when to stop.

Listing G.6   `FindAll` continued

```
h := habit.Habit{}                          ← Go struct that can hold a habit
habits := make([]habit.Habit, 0)            ← A slice for the results
for rows.Next() {
    err = rows.Scan(
        &h.ID, &h.Name, &h.WeeklyFrequency) ←
    if err != nil {...}
    habits = append(habits, h)              ← Scans the row to fill the struct
}

if err = rows.Err(); err != nil {...}       ← Checks that the iteration went through successfully

return habits, nil                          ← Returns the structured slice
```

You now have a SELECT ALL. You could nearly show the list of habits if it weren't for the number of ticks: getting that data still panics. To get all the ticks for one single habit, we need `where habit_id =` and we need to prevent SQL injection.

SELECT ONE HABIT: WHERE

SQL injection is very easy to do when developers forget to protect their system from the user's input. Here, the query we want to send to our database looks like this for a habit with ID 5C9, in the shape of a string:

```
SELECT "title", "weekly_frequency" FROM "habits" where "id" = "5C9"
```

We could simply use `fmt.Sprintf` and roll the following:

```
stmt := fmt.Sprintf(`SELECT ... "id" = %q`, habitID)
```

But what happens if a hacker gives this input?

```
"; DROP table habits; SELECT "
```

We're closing the first query, asking to drop everything, and opening an innocent query to get rid of the extra quote—well, goodbye database. This is why we always need to protect user input, and the SQL package can, mercifully, take care of that for you.

Let's see how we can get one habit from the database using `QueryContext` again. Replace all the user's inputs with numbered variables identified by a $ sign. The third parameter of `QueryContext` is a variadic list of arguments that will replace all these variables. There's just one variable in our current situation.

Listing G.7　Selecting where

```
func (hr *HabitRepository) Find(
    ctx context.Context, id habit.ID) (habit.Habit, error) {
    const findQuery = `SELECT "title", "weekly_frequency"                The ID is $1.
FROM "habits" WHERE "id" = $1`
    row, err := hr.db.QueryContext(ctx, findQuery, id)                   The first argument
    defer rows.Close()                                                   is the ID.
    if err != nil {...}

    h := habit.Habit{}
    err = rows.Scan(&h.Name, &h.WeeklyFrequency)                         The rest is similar.

    return h, err
}
```

Note that this function isn't used in the project. When we had in-memory storage, we needed to make sure that a tick corresponded to an existing habit. Now, we can rely on foreign keys to prevent us from inserting inconsistent data.

SAVE A TICK: INSERT

Last, let's look at the `Exec` and `ExecContext` methods. They don't return rows; they only execute a statement. The first returned value is a `Result`, which can give some information on the affected rows and tables. The second, as usual, can be an error.

Here's an example of a statement for inserting a tick. Habit IDs are integers, and the other column is a time:

```
INSERT INTO "ticks"("habit_id", "created_on") VALUES(2645, NOW())
```

Using the same logic as used previously to replace input values, this fits into a handful of lines.

Listing G.8　Inserting a tick

```
// AddTick inserts a new event for a habit in memory.
func (hr *HabitRepository) AddTick(
    ctx context.Context, id habit.ID, t time.Time) error {
    const insertHabitStmt:= `INSERT INTO "ticks"("habit_id", "created_on")
    VALUES($1, $2)`                                                      Replaces input values
    _, err := hr.db.ExecContext(
        ctx, insertHabitStmt, id, t)                                     Provides the replacements
    return err
}
```

Depending on your configuration, you might need to format the time to make it PostgreSQL compatible. Now that you have the basics, it's time to play with the rest of the package.

G.3   *Libraries*

Writing statements by hand is fun when you have a few tables with a few columns each, and your statements are pretty simple. It can get trickier when you start playing around with the full potential of your database.

That's why some people are writing object-relational mapping libraries and all kinds of helpers to make sure that, for example, renaming a column can be done safely. Have a look at the most popular libraries for SQL:

- https://gorm.io—A complete object-relational model (ORM)
- https://github.com/VinGarcia/ksql—Keep it simple SQL
- https://github.com/Masterminds/squirrel—SQL generation

index